PRAISE FOR
LONG GOODBYE

*"A righteous . . . riveting, and often moving legal tale.
Bill Colby takes you on a wiiiiild journey."*

— **James Ellroy,** author of the *New York Times* bestseller
L.A. Confidential

"Bill Colby's **Long Goodbye** *is a gripping legal, medical, and
personal thriller that confronts painful life-and-death questions and
illuminates the political and legal maneuverings that shape
society's answers to these questions."*

— **Robert Hellenga,** author of the *New York Times* bestseller
The Sixteen Pleasures

*"**Long Goodbye** is a stunning book. I couldn't stop reading, and didn't
want to. It reads very much like a novel, but retains the unmistakable
gravity of and texture of reality. The book packs a very powerful emotional
punch. Nobody who reads this book will ever forget Joe Cruzan."*

— **Douglas L. Wilson,** author of *Honor's Voice*

*"Few people are more central to changing the shape of how we die in
America than Bill Colby, the attorney who brought the case of Nancy
Cruzan to national attention. This book is a must-read, for the Cruzans'
story could happen to any of us.* **Long Goodbye** *kept me
turning pages until the wee hours of the morning!"*

— **Marilyn Webb,** author of *The Good Death*

LONG
GOODBYE

LONG GOODBYE

The Deaths of Nancy Cruzan

William H. Colby

Hay House, Inc.
Carlsbad, California • Sydney, Australia
Canada • Hong Kong • United Kingdom

Published and distributed in the United States by: Hay House, Inc., P.O. Box 5100, Carlsbad, CA 92018-5100 • *Phone:* (760) 431-7695 or (800) 654-5126 • *Fax:* (760) 431-6948 or (800) 650-5115 • www.hayhouse.com • **Published and distributed in Australia by:** Hay House Australia Ltd., 18/36 Ralph St., Alexandria NSW 2015 • *Phone:* 612-9669-4299 • *Fax:* 612-9669-4144 • *e-mail:* info@hayhouse.com.au • **Distributed in Canada by:** Raincoast • 9050 Shaughnessy St., Vancouver, B.C. V6P 6E5 • *Phone:* (604) 323-7100 • *Fax:* (604) 323-2600

Editorial supervision: Jill Kramer • *Design:* Jenny Richards
Interior photos (except where noted): Terry Weckbaugh
Cruzan family photos courtesy of Chris Cruzan White

Library of Congress Cataloging-in-Publication Data

Colby, William H.
Long goodbye : the deaths of Nancy Cruzan / William H. Colby.
  p. cm.
ISBN 1-4019-0011-9 (hardcover)
    1. Cruzan, Joe–Trials, litigation, etc. 2. Cruzan, Nancy–Trials, litigation, etc. 3. Right to die—Law and legislation—Missouri. 4. Right to die—Law and legislation—United States. I. Title.
KF228.C78 C65 2002
344.73'04197—dc21

                    2002002993

ISBN 1-4019-0011-9

06 05 04 03   5 4 3 2
1st printing, October 2002
2nd printing, March 2003

For my clients and friends—Joe and Joyce Cruzan,
Mel and Chris Cruzan White,
Angie, and Miranda

Contents

Preface xi

PART I: 1983–1986

Chapter 1:   Krummel Nursery Road.......................................3
Chapter 2:   Phone Calls 11
Chapter 3:   Simple Surgery...17
Chapter 4:   Feeding Nancy...23
Chapter 5:   Chigger Hill..31
Chapter 6:   Christmas 1984 37
Chapter 7:   Going Public 45

PART II: 1987–1988

Chapter 8:   Pro Bono Case 53
Chapter 9:   Lunch with the Judge...................................61
Chapter 10:   Friendly Suit 67
Chapter 11:   501 Main Street 75
Chapter 12:   Seeing Nancy 83
Chapter 13:   Motion to Dismiss 89
Chapter 14:   Expert Witness..99
Chapter 15:   Under Oath 103
Chapter 16:   The State Expert 111
Chapter 17:   Trial Begins 117
Chapter 18:   Brain Scans 129
Chapter 19:   A Valentine's Card 155
Chapter 20:   Family Matters...167
Chapter 21:   The Cruzans on *Nightline* 181
Chapter 22:   The State's Case 187
Chapter 23:   Hostile Witness 197
Chapter 24:   Throwing Mud 209

PART III: 1988–1989

Chapter 25: Joe's Mailbox 221
Chapter 26: The Decision 231
Chapter 27: Electrocerebral Silence 235
Chapter 28: Front-Row Seats..243
Chapter 29: False Alarm 255
Chapter 30: Writing Governor Ashcroft 263
Chapter 31: June Opinions 271
Chapter 32: Friends and Foes 277
Chapter 33: Solicitor General Starr 291
Chapter 34: The Supreme Court of the United States 299

PART IV: 1990

Chapter 35: Eight Words...317
Chapter 36: New Witnesses...329
Chapter 37: A New Trial 341
Chapter 38: December Decision 357
Chapter 39: Operation Rescue..367
Chapter 40: Saying Goodbye 379
Chapter 41: Nancy's Christmas Gift 385

Epilogue 391
Acknowledgments..415
About the Author..416

PREFACE

Joe Cruzan and I first talked in the spring of 1987. He was a high school-educated sheet-metal worker whose adult daughter Nancy had been in a horrible car accident, and I was a fairly new lawyer. Not long after that call, I met Joe; his wife, Joyce; and their oldest daughter, Chris. Together we went to the state hospital in Mt. Vernon, Missouri, so I could see Nancy in her hospital bed, where she lay in a permanent coma.

None of us had any real idea then about the long, often overgrown path we would walk together through the legal world, or how dramatically the lawsuit seeking permission to remove Nancy's feeding tube would affect our lives. Joe would have laughed at the idea that one day he would travel to Washington D.C., and stand before a sea of microphones, telling the world about his daughter's right to die.

My aim with this book has been to preserve the Cruzans' story in one place, on the printed page, as best I could. The sorting task alone has been daunting. My office is filled with tens of thousands of pages from the files that the Cruzans and I (along with many others) kept on the case—transcripts of legal proceedings, correspondence, memos, calendars, legal briefs, personal notes and journal entries, boxes of newspaper clippings, medical records, photos, police reports, phone records, billing logs, backs of envelopes and other random scraps of paper, and more.

In addition, I tried to cull through two tall bookshelves stacked with videotape from television news coverage, along with interviews given by the parties in the case, internal preparation sessions, and home movies. Included among the videotapes is a critically important history: three separate documentaries produced for PBS by Elizabeth Arledge. I also have shoe boxes full of audiotapes from Joe Cruzan—including a personal audio journal, conversations he'd recorded, radio programs, even his answering-machine tapes. And I went back and talked with dozens of participants in the story, some many times, to update the account.

Despite that mountain of material, in the end, the story is a simple one. *Long Goodbye* is the tale of a family with an unwavering belief that their daughter/sister should be allowed to die. It's my hope that when readers finish the book, they will understand at least this: The questions the Cruzans faced are questions that in time, one way or another, will visit us all.

Bill Colby, Prairie Village, Kansas
July 2002

CARTERVILLE, MISSOURI:
AUGUST 17, 1996, 3:00 A.M.

The heat in the southwestern corner of Missouri, near Oklahoma, seldom relents in August, even in the middle of the night. On August 17, 1996, likely just before three in the morning, 62-year-old Joe Cruzan rose from the twin bed he slept in alone, wedged against the wall in a tiny, narrow bedroom he'd made for himself in the back corner of his house.

He looked like the empty shell of the sheet-metal worker he'd once been—his square shoulders now stooped as if the muscles were missing, and his skin just hung on his collarbones. Black circles ringed his blood-shot eyes, and the thick, gray calluses that used to be on each hand were gone, replaced by soft pink buttons, smaller than a dime. By the summer of 1996, on the rare occasion when Joe Cruzan ventured out of his house and ran into someone he knew, that person would need to look twice to make sure it was really Joe.

Once out of his bed, Joe made his way to the kitchen, and in an unsteady hand, he began this note to his wife:

> *Joyce,*
> *1. I love you. 2. I love Chris & Donna and especilly Angie*
> *& Miranda. 3. Call police before going on carport.*

Joe finished his numbered instructions and left the note on the kitchen table in a conspicuous spot. Then he headed out the side door of his house into the humid August night.

❦❦❦

PART I

1983–1986

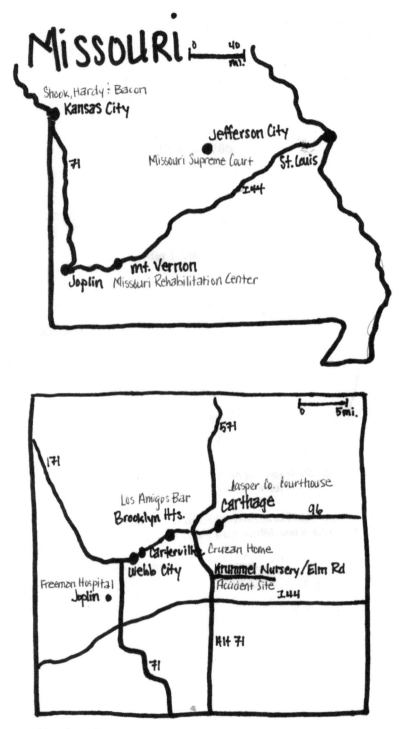

Maps drawn by Nancy Cruzan's niece, Miranda

CHAPTER 1

KRUMMEL NURSERY ROAD

Elm Road—Krummel Nursery Road to locals—is a narrow two-lane blacktop with no shoulders and few streetlights. It turns off old U.S. Hwy 71 on the south side of Carthage, Missouri, at the corner where Krummel Nursery used to sit, and heads out into the country. In many places, deep ditches come right up to the faded white-paint line that poorly marks the edge of the county road. The road is filled with twists and curves—it isn't a place for speeding or driving while drowsy, or even for missing the mark just a bit. More cows than houses populate the three-mile stretch between the point where Krummel Nursery Road turns off the main highway and the house where Nancy Cruzan (then Nancy Davis) lived in the winter of 1983.

Nancy was only 25 years old in January of that year, but she had already lived through a fair slice of adult life. In the fall of her senior year at Webb City High School, Nancy thought she was pregnant. On November 21, 1974, she married her high school boyfriend, Danny Hayes, and moved in with him and his parents. It turned out later that she'd been wrong about being pregnant, but that didn't matter. Shortly after Nancy graduated the next spring, Danny joined the Navy, and the two young people headed out of Carterville, Missouri, to see the world, eventually winding up at a base in Jacksonville, Florida. But the marriage didn't take, and in the fall of 1977, Nancy left Florida—and Danny—and moved back in with her parents.

Joe and Joyce Cruzan raised all three of their girls—Chris, Nancy, and Donna—in the same white wood-frame house at 501 Main Street in Carterville, a blue-collar town of about 2,000 people, nestled in the southwestern corner of Missouri with other small blue-collar towns: Carthage, Webb City, and the largest, Joplin. Joe and Joyce had grown up in (or near) Carterville as well, and had married in the spring after Joyce graduated from Carterville High School. Joe thought about college, but instead became an apprentice in the sheet-metal trade and joined the union. Joyce stayed at home until the girls were all in school, and then she went back to work. In the early 1970s, she landed a job as a secretary at the central office of the Webb City School District.

During the summers, the Cruzans spent most weekends at a small cabin near the edge of Sugar Creek, about 60 miles south of Carterville. On many weekend nights, the beds in the cabin were filled with adults, and cousins of all ages covered the floor—Joe had two younger brothers, while Joyce had four older siblings. Whoever used the cabin helped pay the annual rental cost, $75 for the cabin and beach. Four other cabins stood near the one Joe and Joyce rented, and those were often filled with Cruzan relatives, too. Joe's younger brother, Jim, called Joe "The Wagonmaster," because Joe was always in charge. Old home movies show Joe standing waist deep in the clear water, tanned and muscular, smiling as his girls and their cousins splashed around him, while Joyce watched from the beach.

Nancy's return home in 1977 shattered Joe and Joyce's thoughts about settling into a quiet life after the children left the nest. Not only had their wild 20-year-old come back to Carterville newly divorced and ready to party, but their youngest daughter, Donna, was suddenly acting grown up, at age 14. Their oldest daughter Chris, 22, lived nearby and often brought her two toddlers, Angie and Miranda, over for Joe and Joyce to watch. People were coming and going from the Cruzan house at all hours.

Nancy found a job at the Big Smith overall factory in Carthage, and as soon as she could afford it, she moved out of her parents' house again. In 1980, she met Paul Davis, and they began dating; soon they were living together in a small trailer outside of town. They married in the spring of 1982, shortly after they'd moved out to the two-bedroom house on Krummel Nursery Road. Joe couldn't worry too much about Nancy those last few years, he said, because Donna was keeping him busy.

Still, somehow the Cruzan family worked. They gathered together on many Sundays for dinner. Each Fourth of July, they sat in green folding chairs on the lawn at Joe's parents' house with Grandma Jack and Grandpa Les, eating watermelon and talking about their lives, laughing as Grandpa Les filled his homemade cannon with black powder, and yelling the countdown out in unison after he lit the fuse.

Nancy and Chris, best friends growing up, grew even closer as young adults. Nancy became a second mother to Angie and Miranda, dressing up as a witch to take them out on Halloween each year, and always attending their gymnastics programs, ballet recitals, and school events as they grew older. In the fall of 1982, Chris also divorced, and Nancy spent even more time with the girls. Angie and Miranda worshiped their aunt.

By 1983, Nancy thought her life was pretty good. She had landed a good-paying job on the production line at Schreiber's Cheese Factory in nearby Carthage, and she worked the graveyard shift, from eleven at night to seven in the morning. That schedule left her free to lie in the sun during the day, to sit and have coffee and cigarettes with her mom or Chris, or to do whatever she wanted. She was married to a man she had fun with, and when she walked into a bar with her trim figure and attractive face with its high cheekbones and olive skin, the guys sucked in their stomachs and stood up a little straighter. Like most families, the Cruzans quilted their lives together with a series of moments, and made it through as best they could, bonded by the good and the bad.

Saturday, January 8, 1983

Nancy woke up with a horrible hangover. She had stayed out late the night before at Los Amigos, a small roadside bar where she and Paul often partied with friends. On a normal Saturday, Nancy would sleep until she felt like getting up, but she'd promised her mother that she would help paint her parents' house. So she dragged her thick head and dry mouth out of bed and headed to town up Krummel Nursery Road, her main route into the city. Nancy drove her beat-up, two-toned 1962 Rambler, arriving at her parents' place at about ten that morning.

Nancy always drove too fast, even when making the two sharp left turns on the way to her mom and dad's house—first the left off Carterville's Main Street onto the side street, and then the immediate left onto the driveway. She especially liked to screech to a stop when she saw her dad working in the carport. He would pretend to be scared, and Nancy would bound out of her car and up the steps into the house, sometimes making a face at her dad, other times flashing him a smile as she passed.

Joe had given Nancy the Rambler in the fall of 1982. Actually, he let her pay him a little money each week for a month to help her feel like she was buying it. Joe had bought the car from a guy who was going to junk it. The car was dilapidated—torn upholstery, missing trim, no seat belts—but Joe worked on it during the summer of 1982 and was able to get the engine running again.

He had first given the Rambler to his mom, but Grandma Jack didn't really want to drive anymore. The car just sat in front of her house, four blocks from Joe and Joyce's home. Nancy told her dad that if he gave her the Rambler, then she could sell her white 1974 GMC van, which the judge had awarded to her in the divorce from Danny Hayes. She said she needed the money, so Joe gave her the Rambler. Joe said he hated Nancy's van anyway, with its loud pipes and chrome wheels. He also thought the van was dangerous, its small windows making it hard for the driver to see. He told Nancy he'd be glad if she sold it.

On January 8, Nancy spent all day and most of the evening with her mom, sister, and nieces, painting the ceiling and walls of Joe and Joyce's house. Joe had commandeered some scaffolding from work and spent the evening before setting it up. The kitchen and living room looked like a mini-construction site. Chris and Nancy were up on the scaffolding much of the day—two trim, brown-eyed, beautiful sisters in their mid-20s. They all laughed at Nancy as she danced and sang along with Abba's "Dancing Queen" and "The Winner Takes It All," which blared from a small cassette player. Nancy pretended she was high above the world, using her wet paintbrush as a microphone.

Joyce painted and helped by watching Angie and Miranda, who were now six and seven. Nancy teased Chris by inviting the girls up to paint. Chris kept warning, "Girls, stay off the scaffolding." Just after noon, Nancy said, "Chris, why don't you go to the Dairy Creme and get lunch for us all?" When Chris walked back in the door, greasy sacks in hand, she saw the girls up on the scaffold in their matching pink sweat suits, holding paintbrushes. Nancy stood next to the girls, white paint all over her blue jeans and gray flannel shirt, looking down and laughing as Chris scolded her. Eventually, Chris started laughing, too.

Chris knew that Nancy would never let any harm come to Angie and Miranda. In fact, she once told Nancy, "If anything ever happens to me, I want you to take the girls. You love them as much as I do."

Miranda, who had big brown eyes and an infectious smile, just like her aunt, said to Nancy as they painted together on the scaffolding, "You're the greatest aunt in the world. You're even better than God and Jesus!" Chris and Nancy looked at each other and laughed.

Joe wasn't much for painting. "I work construction all week. I'm sure as hell not going to do it on Saturday, too," he said. He spent most of the day out in the carport, tinkering around in his toolshed, working on the camper and the cars. His absence didn't matter. The five Cruzan women—three generations spanning ages 6 to 47—ate the Dairy Creme carryout, laughed, sang, painted, danced, and talked for most of the day. At the end of that long, good day, Chris headed home with her girls; Nancy headed out for Saturday night.

Tuesday, January 11, 1983, around 12:30 A.M.

Dale Lappin lived on Krummel Nursery Road with his mom and stepfather, their house about a mile closer to town than Nancy and Paul Davis's place. On January 10, 1983, Dale went out with some friends. He came home after midnight and crawled into bed as quietly as he could. He was just starting to drift off when he heard a sound that most young people in rural areas know, the sound of "mailbox baseball."

Dale shot out of bed and ran out the front door of the house, wearing only boxer shorts, to see if he could catch a glimpse of the culprits. About 100 yards from his front door, all the way across Krummel Nursery Road, he saw dust floating in the air and a car flipped on its top in his neighbor's field. Its lights were still shining. If this was a prank, it had gone dreadfully wrong.

Dale sprinted back up the steps and into the house, yelling to his stepfather as he went, "George, there's been a wreck. Get out here!" He pulled on the jeans and shoes he had just taken off and ran shirtless back out into the January night, over his front yard, across the road, up the neighbor's gravel driveway toward the car. The car sat about 35 feet off the road, up the long driveway.

Dale covered the ground quickly. He dropped to his knees and stuck his face into the partially crushed window of an old two-toned Rambler, but he didn't see anybody. He pounded on the car door, but no response came from inside. Frantically, Dale spun around, trying to find the driver. He looked toward the dark house at the end of the driveway and thought that maybe the driver had gotten out somehow, so he ran up to the house and rapped with his fist against another door. No answer.

Unsure of what to do next, Dale scrambled back toward the car in the dark, sweating now, even in the cold. And then he saw her. Actually, he almost tripped over her, a woman facedown and motionless on the hard ground. Dale kneeled next to the body. His frantic rushing around stopped instantly—the world switched to slow motion. He didn't dare touch the body or turn it over; that might make any injuries worse.

George Eaton had been asleep for several hours when Dale's yell startled him awake. He dressed quickly and hurried outside toward the wreck. Once he saw the scene, he turned toward his wife, Donna, who stood with a coat over her pajamas on the front porch, holding the collar of their dog, Jake. George cupped his hands and yelled, "Call the patrol," then crossed the street. Dale had just found the young woman's body as George approached, and he cried out when he saw his stepfather, "Oh my God, what if there's a kid?!" When George reached the body, he saw a baseball cap on the ground nearby, maybe a child's cap.

Donna Eaton rushed back into the house to make the call. The area had no 911 then, but she knew the emergency number because George worked in maintenance at the highway patrol. She dialed the number and waited. Outside, George and Dale looked into the car again, but found nothing. They stood and began running—across their neighbors' front yard, back to the large open field next to that yard, and up and down the ditches alongside Krummel Nursery Road—looking into the dark places where the ditches were deeper, terrified that they would find a second body, this one smaller.

A siren blared in the distance, and flashing lights soon approached Krummel Nursery Road. The car turned right into the driveway and ground to a stop on the gravel near the wreck. George and Dale rushed to the highway patrolman. Sergeant Dale Penn knew George from work. The two men told the sergeant what they knew as fast as they could. Sergeant Penn hurried over and bent down next to the motionless body, touching her neck with two fingers. No pulse. He gently rolled the body over, leaned his ear next to the bloody, bruised mass of her face, and listened for sounds of life. Nothing.

"She's dead," he said. He pulled out her wallet, which fell open to reveal a photo of two young girls. The officer stood and began his reconnaissance of the field with George and Dale, all looking for the owner of the baseball cap, presumably one of the girls in the photo. After that search turned up no one, Sergeant Penn returned once more to the body and checked again for vital signs. Nothing.

Within minutes, flashing lights filled the night as an ambulance and a fire truck arrived. Men with flashlights and loud voices moved over the field, crunching the prairie grass under their boots. Across the street, Donna Eaton stood shivering, holding tight to Jake, who was barking himself hoarse. After a time, it became clear that there was no other body, and Dale and George stepped back and let the professionals do their job.

Dale stood next to his stepfather, arms crossed over his bare chest. It was a warm evening for January, the temperature hovering just under 40 degrees. Still, the air had a bite to it, and Dale shivered now that he'd stopped moving. The two men watched the scene in subdued awe as flashing lights covered the quiet farm field and cast an eerie glow on the emergency workers who surrounded the woman with her shirt torn off, her face crushed, blood everywhere. The dust had settled around the upside-down car next to that scene. For a long time, neither man moved.

As Sergeant Penn continued to search, moving through the clumps of field grass, with the paramedics on their knees behind him working feverishly to restore the accident victim's heartbeat, he could have no idea just how widely society would debate exactly the same question that he had answered so simply, perhaps prophetically—whether this accident victim was dead. Nor could he know that the accident would indeed claim other victims. But none lay at the scene that night.

❧❀❧

CHAPTER 2

PHONE CALLS

January 11, 1983, before 3:00 A.M.

The ringing of the phone yanked 48-year-old Joe Cruzan upright in bed. Welcome news never comes at three in the morning—something had happened to one of his daughters. A frightened voice blurted words into Joe's ear: "Dad, it's Chris. Paul called and said Nancy's been in a bad car accident. They're taking her from McCune-Brooks to Freeman now."

When Joe didn't respond, Chris yelled, "Dad! We need to get over to Freeman as quick as we can. Paul said there's been a head injury and that the police told him she's in bad shape."

Joe collected himself and sprang into action. His family always described him as good in a crisis, and he proved it now. He and Chris quickly formed a plan and hung up. Joe called his parents and told a sleepy Jackie Cruzan that they were bringing Chris's girls over. He phoned the Freeman Hospital emergency room to find out when the ambulance was due. Then he and Joyce dressed and hurried out the side door to their Toyota Celica in their carport.

They huddled there with the motor running and waited for Chris. When Joe saw Chris's car, he motioned for her to follow and sped the four short blocks to his parents' house. Joe handed one girl to Grandma Jack, and Chris walked the older one up to Grandpa Les. They ran back to the Celica and raced to Freeman Hospital.

The Cruzans arrived at the emergency room before Nancy came in. The original emergency crew had taken her to a small local hospital, McCune-Brooks in Carthage. Doctors there decided to transfer Nancy to Freeman Hospital in Joplin, a larger facility less than ten miles away that was better equipped to deal with high-level trauma. The Cruzans rushed through the front door, and Chris saw Paul Davis standing at the counter, crying. She walked over and hugged him. Joe and Paul looked at one another and nodded. The ER was quiet in the dark, early morning hours of a weekday. The radio on the shelf behind the woman at the desk crackled.

Nancy's family stood looking at the wide ER doors, almost frozen into place. The sirens grew louder, closer, then stopped. Chris's chest knotted, yet her gaze remained on the doors. They burst open seconds later, and the ER area sprang to life. Two paramedics pushed a gurney right past the desk back toward the waiting curtain. The gurney rolled within a couple of feet of where the family stood, the paramedics oblivious to their audience.

Joe was confused. As he saw the gurney go by, he thought, *What's going on here? Where's Nancy?* The face of the injured person strapped to the stiff backboard on top of the gurney was unrecognizable, bruised to an unnatural green and black. The hair around the face was matted with dark, crusty blood that concealed its length and color. Tubes jutted from the body, and huge bruises and dried blood covered the bare chest, while fresh blood still flowed from the nose.

Chris said later, "I couldn't see her face very well, but I knew it couldn't be her, because this person on this stretcher, it was *not* Nancy. Until I saw the socks." The feet protruding from the end of the stretcher still had socks on them, and Chris caught a glimpse as the gurney passed. Joyce had just given all three of her daughters the same socks for Christmas, rust-colored with slivers of black thread woven in—just like the socks on the victim. "It's her," was all Chris could say as the gurney disappeared behind the medical curtain.

The group of four stood as if bolted to the floor. The scene had passed so quickly that it almost felt as if it hadn't happened, and no one knew quite what to do. Joe, Joyce, Chris, and Paul moved out to a waiting area, television mounted up high, upholstered wooden chairs against the wall, coffee table with the obligatory magazines. They sat down.

Over the next few hours, they alternately paced and cried and glanced vacantly toward the area where the paramedics had taken Nancy. They could hear nothing. Little conversation took place. A nurse came out briefly and had Paul Davis sign some surgery forms, but she had no real news. The family got some information about the accident, though it wasn't much—the police had found that no alcohol or drugs had been involved, and Nancy hadn't hit a cow or some other animal that they could find. All they really knew was that the car had traveled almost 300 yards after leaving the road, so Nancy had been driving fast, as usual.

Paul's mother and grandmother arrived and joined the wait. Joe's brothers, Jim and Butch, showed up, too. The group watched the night give way to day as the sun rose outside the windows down the hall and shone on a crisp, clear winter's day.

~ ~ ~

Nancy spent her first hour and 45 minutes at Freeman Hospital in the emergency room. Dr. D. O. Burke and the ER team worked to stabilize her by inserting a central line; providing blood, fluids, and antibiotics; and taking the steps most critical to her survival. At 5:30 A.M., they moved Nancy from the emergency room to the operating room, where two doctors were waiting for her.

Dr. Robert Willcoxon began the surgery in the operating room by making an upper midline incision in Nancy's abdomen. Her stomach had grown rigid to the touch, indicating internal bleeding. Dr. Willcoxon found the source, a laceration on the left lobe of her liver. He stitched that cut, then checked her spleen, gall bladder, kidneys, and other organs, which he found bruised but intact. Once satisfied that he had fixed the damage, Dr. Willcoxon closed the stomach incision and moved aside for Dr. B. E. Schaffer, the physician assisting him, to take the lead.

Lacerations of all sizes and depths covered Nancy's face and neck, massive swelling had completely blackened and shut the shattered socket of her left eye, a stream of bright red blood still flowed freely from her nose. A couple of teeth barely hung to her gums, and some were missing. Dr. Schaffer started on the eye. He began by making several incisions in Nancy's face. He removed pieces of bone from the floor of her eye socket and sewed it back together with stainless-steel wire. Then, one by one, he stitched together cuts in her left eyelid and eyebrow, her right eyebrow, her upper lip, and her lower lip extending down to her chin. He finished by repairing a long cut down the left side of Nancy's neck. Nurses packed her nose with gauze, along with all of the other cuts that were still bleeding. When Dr. Schaffer finished his work, Nancy was wheeled to the surgical intensive care unit (ICU).

Around eight that morning, after Dr. Willcoxon had fixed Nancy's internal damage, a nurse emerged from the operating room and approached the two small bands of family members. As she did so, she saw their expectant faces, each one a mask of exhaustion, apprehension, and guarded hope. A couple of hours earlier, a different nurse had come out with a progress report, but she hadn't been able to say much more than, "It's too soon to tell." This news would be better, and a slight smile turned up the corners of the nurse's mouth. "I think she's going to be all right," the nurse said.

The words buffeted Joe Cruzan like a blast of air. "I feel like I can breathe again," he said, the words catching in his throat. Joyce took him into her arms. Chris stood apart, her own arms wrapped tightly around her body, which shook anyway. Her parents left her alone, for they knew that Chris really only let Nancy comfort her. For the last several hours, Chris had tried to stay optimistic, but she could not. She'd concluded that Nancy was going to die. And she couldn't imagine anything worse.

Just after ten in the morning, the nurse told the family that they could come into the ICU and see Nancy. Nothing could have prepared them for the sight: tubes coming out of her everywhere, the whooshing breath of a respirator forcing air into the tube in her mouth, her entire face a swollen mass of black and blue, stitches and bandages everywhere, and blood still oozing through the gauze packed into her nose. Joe saw his daughter and said, "Oh, my God." Tears came instantly to Chris, then to the rest of the group. They stood above her for several minutes, looking down in disbelief, then returned to the relative calm and new-found familiarity of the waiting room.

Paul Davis and his family left soon after, and Jim and Butch Cruzan agreed to drive out to Donna's house to tell her what had happened to her sister, since Donna didn't have a phone at the time. Joe, Joyce, and Chris decided that they should go call work, check on the girls, and do what was needed to put the outside world on hold. As they drove home, they agreed to meet back at the hospital shortly to check on Nancy's progress. A man not given lightly to hope or optimism, Joe tried to focus as he replayed the nurse's words: "She's going to be all right." And he tried to chase away the picture in his mind of his battered and bloody daughter.

January 11, 1983, late morning

Dr. Hish Majzoub, a neurosurgeon, examined Nancy Cruzan in the ICU after the Cruzans had left the hospital. Dr. Burke, the ER doctor who had first worked to stabilize Nancy early that morning, had requested several consults from specialists, including a neurosurgeon. Majzoub would check for brain damage.

Dr. Majzoub found Nancy unresponsive, in a full coma. Her pupils were dilated and reacted only slightly to light, indicating potential brain damage. Nothing on the CT scan (a picture of the structure of Nancy's brain) done in the ER offered any encouragement. And the brief description of the accident in the chart suggested that the young woman might have been without oxygen for a significant period of time. Dr. Majzoub would not have positive news for the woman's family.

The Cruzans came back to the hospital around noon after arranging for others to take over their daily necessities. Joe and Joyce arrived first, and Chris drove her own car this time and showed up a few minutes later. They were all anxious to talk to a doctor. Shoulder to shoulder, the three huddled together in the ICU, eyes fixed on Nancy in the bed.

Dr. Majzoub walked up and introduced himself. He took a penlight from his front pocket and shined the light into each of Nancy's eyes as he spread her eyelids apart with his thumb and forefinger. Nancy's pupils moved only slightly, the limited response unchanged from Dr. Majzoub's examination earlier that day. There was no sense delaying, so he gave them the news.

"She came through the emergency surgery fine, you know, but I am very concerned about her anoxia," Dr. Majzoub said, looking at Nancy. "We'll need to wait and see what kind of response we get." Dr. Majzoub had graduated from medical school in his native Beirut and had come to the United States for his neurosurgical training. His voice still carried a significant accent, and the Cruzans had to listen carefully to understand him particularly when he used medical terms. The concern in these first words was clear enough, though.

Just hours earlier, the nurse had given them such hope. But Joe Cruzan could tell that this doctor in the starched white coat knew more. From the moment they had returned to the hospital and stood by Nancy's bed, Joe had stared down at her motionless body. She had not even moved when the doctor shined the flashlight right in her eye. Since Joe was a man more prone to doubt than hope, the doubt had started to break down the nurse's optimistic words even before this doctor showed up. Nancy just looked too damaged. Now this more experienced doctor had given substance to his fear and a mysterious name—*anoxia*.

"Okay, doctor," Joe mumbled.

Dr. Majzoub nodded. "I'll be in to check on her every day." In the hours after Dr. Majzoub left, the three Cruzans talked about the questions they would have asked him had they been able to think. *Exactly what is anoxia? Are there different kinds? Is one worse than another?* A nurse told them that *anoxia* meant "lack of oxygen," but said that the Cruzans would need to ask a doctor the rest of their questions. Later that afternoon, Chris headed back home to look after her girls. Joe and Joyce stayed the night and slept on the waiting-room chairs, checking on Nancy between dozing and waking.

Before Chris left, she paused for a long time by her sister's bed. This anoxia appeared serious. Joe Cruzan said later that after Dr. Majzoub left, he also wondered what the doctor meant by checking on her "every day." Exactly how many "every days" might this recovery take?

CHAPTER 3

SIMPLE SURGERY

On Tuesday, January 18, one week after the accident, Nancy's eyes opened. Joe Cruzan rushed out to the nurses' station. "Her eyes are open!" he said, and then headed straight back into the ICU. Joe, Joyce, and Chris huddled around Nancy's bed, talking excitedly, trying to get her to look at one of them. But she didn't look at them, or at anything else. Her blank, empty stare seemed to settle in the distance, not seeing anything.

When the nurse came into the ICU, she told the Cruzans that Nancy's open eyes did not necessarily mean that Nancy had come out of the coma. Later that day, Dr. Majzoub had to confirm the nurse's assessment—Nancy's eyes opening really did not mean anything. What they needed was a response from her, and then repeated responses, to show that her brain function had returned. Nancy's medical chart noted this reality: "Patient is out of coma, but has no verbal response and does not follow commands." Dr. Majzoub's bottom line didn't change—the Cruzans needed to wait and see.

The brief excitement passed quickly, and the Cruzans settled back into the routine they had started to establish in that first week. Joe and Joyce stayed at the hospital around the clock, sleeping on hard hospital couches, or dozing on and off through the night while sitting. Chris visited as much as she could, when the girls were in school, and when she could find someone to take them for a few hours afterwards. Chris, Joe, and Joyce constantly talked to Nancy, combed her hair, hugged and kissed her, told her jokes, and played "Shame on the Moon" and other favorite Bob Seger songs on a cassette recorder. The doctors and nurses told them that family played a critical role in trying to bring a loved one out of a coma, and they took this responsibility seriously, doing everything they could think of to try to get a response from Nancy.

But Nancy did not respond. By the time she was moved out of the ICU and into a private room on January 30, the brief hope resulting from her eyes opening just 12 days earlier seemed so distant that the Cruzans thought they might have imagined it. Not only had Nancy not responded, she looked terrible. The skin on her face, still bruised and marked with stitches, had turned a sickly gray color and was dotted with acne spots. She had a seizure and somehow knocked a tooth out of the front of her mouth, which the doctors decided not to fix. A tracheotomy tube jutted out of a hole in her throat, the result of surgery performed to send air more directly to her lungs. Worst of all, Nancy's arms and legs had started to stiffen and atrophy, drawing in slowly toward her trunk. The doctors and nurses called this stiffening "contractures." The work of the physical therapists to stop the contractures had little effect.

Tests done on Nancy's brain offered no encouragement either. Repeated CT scans remained normal, and strangely enough, that was very bad news. Had the CT scans shown bleeding in her brain or a fractured skull, Dr. Majzoub would have had ways to try to relieve the pressure or repair the break. The scans showing normal brain structure meant that something else was causing Nancy's prolonged lack of responsiveness, almost certainly anoxia. Dr. Majzoub had no tool to fix anoxia's damage.

The cerebral cortex—the thinking, feeling part of the brain—has a high metabolic rate, which means that it requires a constant, uninterrupted supply of blood, glucose, and oxygen to function. That makes the cerebral cortex quite fragile. If it is deprived of its blood or oxygen supply for as little as four to six minutes, extensive and irreversible damage can result. Once such deprivation takes place, that part of the brain is dead, and over time, will begin to shrivel. The CT scan will then show an abnormal brain with shrunken gray matter. Since that shriveling process happens slowly, a CT scan taken shortly after a brain has suffered significant anoxia may very well look normal. The cerebral cortex, nonetheless, is already just as dead as it will, in fact, appear in later CTs.

Other tests corroborated the CT scans. By late January, doctors had done three electroencephalograms (EEGs), placing electrodes directly on Nancy's scalp to measure the electrical activity in her brain. The first EEG, done the morning she arrived in the ER, showed significant abnormality with a "nearly flat background." The second one, on January 17, showed "some deterioration" even from the dismal first reading. The third EEG reading, on January 26, remained unchanged.

A flat EEG is a key indicator of "brain death." In most states, even as a respirator is keeping a patient's heart pumping, if the EEG reading is flat, then the patient is declared brain dead, which is the same as dead, and the respirator is turned off. Nancy Cruzan's EEGs in January of 1983 were not flat, just "nearly flat." She wasn't brain dead. But as Dr. Majzoub told the Cruzans, pointing down at the EEG printout with almost no spikes or valleys on it, he would have "liked to see more activity."

Nancy's appearance and lack of responsiveness, in fact, were just two among many indicators of the extent of her injury. The anoxia had shut her bodily functioning down so completely that it had become a massive medical effort just to keep her systems going. Nancy could not move—nurses had to turn her every couple of hours so she didn't develop bedsores. In addition, Nancy could not control her bowels or bladder—a Foley catheter drained urine, which the nurses periodically measured and discarded. Her bowel movements came only after a nurse gave her a suppository, and they spilled out onto a pad on the bed, requiring the nurses to clean Nancy and change the linen promptly.

Initially, Nancy couldn't breathe on her own. For five days after the accident, a machine breathed for her, one end of a large tube connected to a respirator, the other end threaded through her mouth down to her lungs. On January 17, the doctors performed the tracheotomy, cutting a hole in the front of her neck for direct access to her throat, and inserting the respirator tube through this hole. By late January, the medical team had Nancy breathing on her own, and they disconnected the respirator. The tracheotomy hole and the two inches of tube jutting out of her neck from that hole remained open, however, giving Nancy another opening in addition to her mouth for breathing, and allowing nurses easier access to suction out mucous and blood, which she had lost the ability to cough up.

Nancy also had no ability to take medicine, eat, or drink. The first night in the ER, the team inserted an intravenous line (IV) directly into a vein in her left arm, and a central line near her right clavicle. (A "central line" is an IV inserted into a larger vein capable of receiving volume more quickly.) A stiff, plastic nasogastric (or NG) tube snaked through her nose down into her stomach. On January 13, the doctors ordered that a third IV be placed in her right arm.

In the first days after the accident, Nancy's body received no nutrition through any of these lines. Her liver, fresh from surgery, and her bruised stomach weren't ready to work. Through the three IVs, she received medicine, blood, and large volumes of sterile water in an effort to stabilize her fluids. On January 14, she started receiving Aminosyn 3.5%, a nutritional solution high in glucose and amino acids, through her central line. On January 19, Dr. Majzoub ordered removal of the stiff NG tube from Nancy's nose, and insertion of a softer, more pliable plastic tube, for feeding, threaded through her nose down to her stomach. The intravenous Aminosyn was discontinued, and a new nutritional solution, Traumaide, was started at half-strength through the feeding tube in her nose.

The Cruzans took all of this bad news—the CTs and EEGs, Nancy's declining appearance, her failure to respond, and her complete medical dependence—and processed it through the filter of their exhaustion and their love. Listening through that filter, they clung to any words that gave them hope. On his evening visit, Dr. Majzoub might say, "I'm pessimistic about the lack of response"; "I'm not encouraged by her EEG"; and, in response to a question, "Yes, she might hear, but she does not have any way to process the words." After he left the room, the Cruzans would talk about how Nancy could hear.

And all of the doctors and nurses told them that other patients, at least some of them, had recovered from conditions like Nancy's. It just took time. Through their efforts and the sheer force of their will, the Cruzans intended that Nancy would be one of the ones who made it. Joyce described how they would stand by the bed, hold Nancy's stiffening hands, close their eyes, and "will strength to her body from ours. It just had to work, because it just couldn't be this way." The doctors' and nurses' words became the Cruzans' mantra: Nancy's recovery would just take time.

By the time she was moved into the private room on January 30, the Cruzans and Paul Davis had begun to discuss where Nancy might go when she left Freeman Hospital. On February 2, Joe and Joyce met with a social worker at Freeman to discuss options. The Cruzans' first choice was the Brady Rehabilitation building, next door to Freeman. But Dr. Majzoub had told them that Brady might not accept Nancy because she hadn't shown any response. Faced with possible rejection by Brady, the Cruzans also discussed taking Nancy to Joe and Joyce's home, having Paul take her home, or putting her in a nursing home.

The Social Services staff had to maneuver through the minefield of Joe's relationship with Nancy's husband. Nancy and Paul had a wild life—they both loved to party. Paul worked construction, but his work wasn't steady. Angie and Miranda liked their mysterious uncle, who was always teasing them from behind the black mirrors of his aviator shades. Joe thought the glasses just hid his eyes. The tension between Joe and Paul had only heightened during the stress of Nancy's hospitalization. Joe was at the hospital all of the time, day and night; Paul visited and left. Joe thought Paul should be there as much as he was. If Paul came with friends straight from Los Amigos, Joe shook his head with disgust. If the hospital tried to reach Paul and couldn't find him, Joe grew livid.

Nonetheless, the staff generally turned to Paul, as Nancy's husband, for necessary decisions. For instance, if Brady wouldn't accept her, Paul had talked about taking Nancy home or to his grandmother's house to care for her, with round-the-clock nursing support. In the February 2 meeting between Joe, Joyce, and the Freeman social worker, Joe said, "Paul is too damn irresponsible" to care for Nancy at home. But he also said, "If he wants to take her, I guess there's not a damn thing I can do about it." The social worker told Joe that was true—Nancy's husband had the legal authority to make decisions for her.

But all along, Joe had also been involved in making decisions for Nancy. Even though Paul had signed the consent forms for the initial surgery and the tracheotomy, one day when Paul wasn't available, a nurse had Joe sign the consent to perform a CT scan. So maybe Joe did play a role, after all. Either way, Joe told his wife after the February 2 meeting, his problem with Paul would have to come to a head at some point.

After Nancy had been moved into the private room, Dr. Majzoub also began to talk to the Cruzans about inserting a feeding tube directly into Nancy's stomach. One of her IV lines had become clogged, and even with the feeding tube through her nose, Nancy was not receiving sufficient nutrition or set up for the long-term care she'd need. Dr. Majzoub said that Dr. Willcoxon would perform the procedure, a surgical insertion of a tube directly into Nancy's stomach—a gastrostomy tube. With the gastrostomy tube in place, the feeding tube threaded through her nose could come out, and so could all of the IVs. One tube, hidden under her blanket, could provide for most of her needs.

Dr. Willcoxon scheduled the surgery for Monday, February 7, Nancy's 27th day at Freeman. Before he could do that surgery, he needed another written consent on Nancy's behalf. Joe was at Freeman that morning and Paul wasn't, so the nurse had Joe sign the consent form. Paul came in later that day and he signed a consent form, too. The forms that Joe and Paul signed were the same, titled "Freeman Hospital Consent to Operation, Anesthetics & Other Services." Like the consent forms in use in most hospitals in 1983, they included this language near the top:

> *The nature and purpose of the operation, possible alternative methods of treatment, the risks involved, and the possibility of complications have been fully explained to me. No guarantee or assurance has been given by anyone as to the results that may be obtained.*

To "fully explain the risks involved" to Joe Cruzan or Paul Davis that day, physical as well as emotional, the nurse would have needed wisdom and foresight that few people possess. Paul Davis did not discuss the language of the form or any risks with the nurse. Neither did Joe Cruzan. Joe didn't even read the form closely; he just signed the paper. None of what it said really mattered at the time.

As Joyce told *National Public Radio* correspondent Nina Tottenberg years later, "We didn't read anything we signed—if they said we needed to do it, we signed it. When it's just been three or four weeks after the accident, you think, you know, that there's a good chance she's going to get better."

Joe always said, "I had no idea I was signing away anybody's rights that day. I would have signed anything. We were just waiting for Nancy to wake up."

CHAPTER 4

FEEDING NANCY

Soon after the surgery to insert the feeding tube into Nancy's stomach, Joe began to grow more aggressive in trying to figure out Nancy's medical condition for himself. "Before I agree to have her moved," he said, "I want to know the bottom line."

He was particularly intrigued by the EEGs. Technicians performed the tests by hooking electrodes to several places on Nancy's skull. Those electrodes measured the electrical activity in Nancy's brain and fed that information to a machine, which printed out the results as spikes and valleys on a sheet of paper. These tests seemed more reliable to Joe than the doctors' simple bedside observations. Joe asked Dr. Majzoub if he could read the actual EEG reports himself, so the doctor had the printouts and written reports explaining their significance delivered to Joe.

Shortly after the accident, Joe had bought a silver-colored, handheld cassette recorder to record his conversations with doctors and nurses. Joe was able to spend more time than Chris and Joyce at the hospital, and he often found himself talking to the medical people alone. He'd been having trouble relating to Joyce and Chris exactly what the doctors and nurses had told him, so he asked if he could record the conversations.

On Wednesday night, February 9, Joe sat next to Nancy's bed and slowly read the dismal EEG reports into his recorder, one after the other. Joyce listened as he dictated the last report: "Flat background activity, coupled with the patient's history, is suggestive of a vegetative comatose state." Later on, Joe stopped Dr. Majzoub as the doctor made his rounds, to ask about the EEG reports. They stood on either side of Nancy's hospital bed and talked, not really worried at this point that Nancy could understand or even hear what they were saying about her.

"Are you fairly convinced of where we stand now?" Joe asked the doctor.

"I'm not too happy with the brain waves, you know. I'd like to see more activity," Dr. Majzoub replied in his clipped accent, looking down at the printout. "We should see a lot of waves like that," he said, pointing at one of the few spikes on her chart. The random spike on her EEG printout did not represent a moment of consciousness. To the contrary, it showed the doctor a picture of a brain whose electrical pathways had gone completely haywire.

"Has she progressed as far as she'll go?" Joe asked.

"It's a little premature, but I don't like the EEG."

"And you're not too confident—"

"I don't like the EEG."

The Cruzans didn't like the EEG either. Joe told his wife after that night that he had no idea what they were going to do.

February 12, 1983

On Saturday, February 12, almost one month after the accident and just five days after the surgery to insert the tube in Nancy's stomach, the Cruzans finally got some encouraging news. Great news, in fact—Brady Rehabilitation agreed to take Nancy. Dr. Saad Al-Shatir (or "Dr. Al"), the head of rehabilitation at Brady, had gone to Freeman and examined Nancy on Friday. Joe called from home and talked to a nurse at Brady that Saturday. After hanging up the phone, he dictated the substance of their conversation: "I just talked to the people at Brady, and they seem to talk like—apparently, he felt he could form, I won't say a line of communication, but that he could do something for her over there."

Joe's voice took on a strange sound, the softness of one speaking alone, into a recorder, mixed with the enthusiasm of newfound hope. "They said that in an older person, they oftentimes brought them over for just a couple days for evaluation, and if they couldn't help them, they didn't keep them. However, with a young person in an accident, they did work with them for quite a while. So I don't know, I don't want to get too high, but on the other hand, I think maybe it's a pretty encouraging sign."

The next Monday, February 14, Joe, Joyce, and Chris met at Brady with Dr. Al-Shatir himself. Dr. Al, an Iraqi native with a thick black moustache and broad smile, was in the business of hard cases. He was used to walking the fine line between hope and fantasy, and he tried to paint a realistic picture for the family.

"She could be still like this, still all her life, or she could get better," Dr. Al told them, after Joe asked about the anoxia. "The reason she's here is to stimulate her as much as possible. She is awfully young, and many young people, they get over it."

"Her EEG reports said something about 'comatose and vegetative,'" Joe began.

Joyce interrupted. "Can these get better?"

"You can have an EEG flat and recover," Dr. Al said. "Nobody tries to be a god, you know. But there are a few things we don't know about the brain. Some people in a coma for two or three months, they recover; some people never recover. There is no way to tell. The brain has to wake up by itself."

Dr. Al talked about the family role in stimulating a response, and Joyce laughed when he suggested bringing Nancy's dog to Brady. "I don't think they'll let us bring that big dog in here," she said.

Joe asked again about the anoxia, and Dr. Al said, "It's impossible to predict the outcome, let's put it that way. Time will tell."

Nancy stayed at Brady for nearly a month. Cost wasn't an issue because she had excellent insurance through Schreiber's Cheese. She received every kind of therapy the staff at Brady knew how to deliver. The Cruzans and Paul Davis worked even harder at Brady than they had at Freeman at trying to make Nancy respond—responses were what the place was all about. The family learned Nancy's physical therapy routine and spent hours trying to bend her stiff limbs in the way the therapists showed them. They played music, talked to Nancy, and touched her. They did, in fact, bring the big dog in to see her once. Chris repeatedly said to Nancy what she knew her sister would love to hear: "Nancy, I'll give you my car, I'll do anything, if you'll just come back."

March 13 was Miranda's seventh birthday, and Joe, Joyce, Chris, Angie, and Miranda brought a cake in, wheeled Nancy down to the cafeteria, sang "Happy Birthday," and opened presents. They tried to feed her bits of cake. Nancy did not react. She sat there strapped into her wheelchair, listing slightly to one side, eyes on the wall, drool trickling from the corner of her mouth. That night, back home, the seven-year-old said to her mom, "That's the worst birthday I ever had." Angie's eighth birthday, just three days after the accident, hadn't been much better. Chris cried herself to sleep on the sofa after the girls went to bed.

Joe spent more time than anyone with Nancy at Brady. Springfield Engineering, the company he'd worked for since 1972, was working on a big construction project at St. John's Hospital, just up the hill from Brady. Joe's foreman let him come to work late most days, allowing Joe to spend extra time with Nancy. Every morning, he rose early and headed down to Brady to try to feed Nancy breakfast before work. He would walk into her room and say "Good morning," then lift her stiff body into a special wheelchair (if the nurses hadn't already moved her) and take her down to the dining area. Brady had a policy that all patients had to eat in the dining room.

Joe would sit in the dining room, patients with varying degrees of brain injury all around, and try to feed Nancy. He put a bib on her, dipped a spoon into her pureed food, and waited until Nancy opened her mouth. When that moment came, Joe would thrust the spoon into the opening, and Nancy would reflexively clamp down with her teeth. He'd wait until she relaxed, withdraw the spoon, and watch as she appeared to choke down the food. He'd rub her throat to try to make her swallow—this was an idea he came up with, although he didn't know if it helped. The feedings took a long time each morning, and Nancy often gagged.

Joe always talked gently to his daughter as he went about the process. "C'mon, Nancy, you can do this. All you have to do is swallow a little banana, you love banana." Near the end of the hour, he'd clean her up, stroke her hair, and talk to her. He told her about the job, how close by he was, and what her therapy for the rest of the day would include. A couple of minutes before he had to be at work, he'd wheel Nancy back to her room and then would rush to the job site, eating a sandwich or apple for breakfast as he strode down the hospital corridor.

Despite their efforts, Joe didn't see much progress, and his voice as he talked into his Dictaphone at night grew morose. "The doctors are very pessimistic about her long-term prognosis," Joe said into the recorder. "I am, too. I think the responses are reflexive. I'd like to give up on Nancy, but it seems she tries so hard to talk. The doctors don't know either, in fairness to them."

He also fretted about where Nancy would go after Brady. One of the possibilities they were discussing was taking her to Joe and Joyce's house. "I have resentment toward Nancy, too," Joe said in his audio journal. "How long do you have to carry your kids? It's going to be hell on us. If I had to make the decision to move her to our house right now, I'd be literally scared to death. We're giving up a lot—freedom, money—I wonder why I'm doing it? I mean, is it for Nancy, or is it for me? The lady in Social Services told me that she felt like Nancy's 25, not our responsibility. She said, 'You and your wife have to figure out how much to give her.' Joyce and I have kicked that around." Joe yawned loudly as he finished his journal entry for the night.

As Nancy approached the four-week mark in Brady, Dr. Al told the Cruzans and Paul Davis that it didn't make any sense to keep Nancy in an expensive rehabilitation hospital any longer, because she was not responding. Dr. Al made this final entry in her medical chart before discharge: "She does not follow commands. She depends on oral feeding and gastrostomy feeding. No self-care skills. The patient's progress is poor."

Paul decided that he did not want Nancy to go to the Cruzans or to a nursing home. Even though Joe worried about Paul's ability to take care of Nancy, he didn't want her to go to a home, either. The Cruzans feared that Nancy wouldn't receive good care in a nursing home. Worse, they thought that a home would mean that they had given up on all hope of recovery. Paul decided to have Nancy taken to his grandmother's house, where he would stay, too. The Cruzans believed that on Paul's side of the family, his grandmother, an energetic woman in her 60s, was the best choice.

On March 18, the ambulance transported Nancy from Brady to Paul's grandmother's home in Oronogo, Missouri. All summer, the Cruzans visited Nancy there. The tiny house, with no air-conditioning and filled with people, added to the strain on everyone. The thick, musty smell of sickness, made worse by the oppressive heat, reached into every corner of the house. Joe said later, "I felt like an intruder every time I went to see my own daughter." Still, despite the uncomfortable setting, the Cruzans followed the final instructions from Dr. Al: Keep working for a response.

But Nancy did not respond. Her limbs continued to draw in. Her fingers appeared welded together, slowly bending up and backwards toward each wrist. Her feet turned in and her toes began to point down, which the doctors called "foot drop," a result of the damaged brain's inability to send signals to the nerves of the feet to tell them how to move. Her body grew spongy and heavy with the tube feedings. The skin on her puffy face lost its sheen, and her hair turned brittle. At times her eyes moved about the room randomly, and other times they appeared to fix on some space in front of her before they moved on. She often smelled foul in the summer heat.

By September 20, the burden grew too large for Paul's grandmother, and Paul decided to move Nancy to a nursing home in Joplin. Just six days after the move, Nancy spiked a fever of 107 degrees, and the nursing home rushed her to another local facility, Jane Chinn Hospital in Webb City. Joe's cousin, Sue Fry, was standing on the driveway near the carport waiting for Joe to get home from work to tell him. Joe pulled up on his motorcycle, Sue gave him the news, and Joe turned the bike around and gunned the engine toward the hospital.

Joe and Joyce stayed all night at the small hospital. Joyce kept saying to Joe, "I hope God finally takes her." Joe agreed. But Nancy made it through the night, and she ended up staying at Jane Chinn for a month. Once again, the Cruzans and Paul Davis faced the question of where to put Nancy. Nancy's main doctor at Jane Chinn had recently left the staff of a state hospital in Mt. Vernon, 45 miles away. He told the Cruzans and Paul about its high quality and aggressive care. He advised them on how to have Nancy admitted there and have the state pay for her care once her private insurance ran out. And he warned them not to let the hospital discharge Nancy, no matter what they said.

They followed the doctor's suggestions, and on October 19, 1983, an ambulance transported Nancy from Jane Chinn Hospital up Interstate 44 to the Missouri State Chest Hospital in Mt. Vernon. That day, Joe and Joyce began driving the roughly 90-mile round trip to Mt. Vernon twice a week to visit—once on the weekends and on one night a week. They joined a support group for families of patients and made trips up for those sessions as well. That stretch of interstate from

Carterville to Mt. Vernon soon became a part of their lives.

Interstate 44 did not become a big part of Paul Davis's life, however. Chris thought that after almost a year of Nancy being in a coma, it was clear to Paul that she wasn't coming back to him. Chris also said that Paul was probably sick of the stares from Joe Cruzan anytime the two met. The life Paul had started with Nancy—laughing, partying, living—was gone forever.

January 1984

People in Social Services at the state hospital told the Cruzans that Nancy needed official guardians to speak for her, and they thought Joe and Joyce were the logical choices. In January of 1984, just three months after Nancy's move to Mt. Vernon, the Cruzans went to court for the first time concerning their daughter. The hearing took place in the Jasper County courthouse in Carthage (about six miles from Carterville), before probate judge Charles E. Teel. The Cruzans hired a local lawyer named Walter Williams to represent them. Paul did not attend the hearing.

At the hearing, Judge Teel declared Joe and Joyce the official, legal, co-guardians for Nancy. Six months later, in July, the Cruzans petitioned the probate court again, this time seeking a divorce for Nancy and Paul. Paul attended this hearing, and he didn't oppose the request. After that day, the only time the Cruzans saw Paul Davis was if they bumped into one another around town, which happened very rarely.

Nancy didn't attend her own divorce hearing—she remained at Mt. Vernon, curled up and unaware. Just 27 years old, she had gone from being Nancy Cruzan to Nancy Hayes, back to Nancy Cruzan, and then to Nancy Davis. On July 16, 1984, she officially became Nancy Beth Cruzan once more, for the third and final time in her life.

CHAPTER 5

CHIGGER HILL

"Through this gate pass many people.
Going one way, they travel in a state of despondency.
Going the other way, they travel in a state of happiness and joy
as they return to their family and friends."

(Inscription on the stone archway standing in front of the
Missouri State Sanatorium in Mt. Vernon, Missouri, dated 1907.)

In the year 1900, tuberculosis (TB), "the White Plague," killed almost 150,000 people in the U.S., three times as many deaths as those from all types of cancers combined. The infection broke its victims down into coughing, bedridden, germ-spitting shells. With no effective antibiotics, doctors could offer little treatment other than fresh air, sunshine, nutrition, and bed rest. And isolation—sometimes state-ordered internment.

In 1905, the Missouri legislature authorized funding to build a sanatorium to isolate Missourians infected with TB. The legislature appointed a board to find a site within the state, and it gave the board the charge to find a site removed from society and at least 1,000 feet above sea level. The board found Chigger Hill, a single tall mound rising above a group of soft rolling hills in the southwestern corner of the state, just outside the small town of Mt. Vernon, near Springfield. From the top of that high hill, a view of lush green fields, golden prairie grass, and thick stands of elms, silver maples, pin oaks, and walnut trees spread out for miles. With that calming vista, along with the ample sun overhead, Chigger

Hill offered the best hope in Missouri for ridding a body of this terrible infection.

The construction plan called for 12 separate buildings set on the center of an expanse of 60 acres, grouped in a Maltese cross. Eight buildings were earmarked to house the isolated patients, and four were set up for the staff. The first patient moved in on August 17, 1907.

Tuberculosis patients often spent months, even years, away from home and society. Thus, in 1907, the sanatorium embarked on a mission that, over the years, would become as much a part of the place as the hill on which it sat: long-term care for the most desperately ill of society. The buildings on Chigger Hill became the place where Missouri would send the patients whom the rest of society had given up on. For more than 70 years, it took in Missourians afflicted with the White Plague. The sanatorium helped the town of Mt. Vernon prosper—not long after its founding, the state sanatorium became the largest employer in Mt. Vernon.

By the early 1950s, however, medical science had begun to make significant progress in the fight against TB. Drug therapies effectively controlled the disease, and patients often found adequate treatment right in their own towns. The patient population of the sanatorium declined. As the 1950s gave way to the 1960s, that decline continued, and many of the sanatorium buildings on Chigger Hill sat empty.

Fortunately for the economy of Mt. Vernon, as the health threat from TB faded, new diseases began their rise to prominence, particularly pulmonary problems such as bronchitis, emphysema, and lung cancer. The underutilized sanatorium provided the perfect place to care for these chronic patients. In 1971, the Missouri legislature expanded the mission of the sanatorium and changed its name to the Missouri State Chest Hospital. It also authorized the building of a six-story red brick hospital on the top of Chigger Hill. The beautiful facility brought pulmonary patients together with the remaining TB patients under one roof.

The staff changed little with the new name and the move to a new building. The core mission stood steadfast as it had since 1907: long-term care of the desperately ill. When the sanatorium changed to a chest hospital in 1971, the technology of respirators was brand new. The rapid evolution of the respirator over about a ten-year period showed just how fast the world of medicine was destined to change.

The first commonly used respirators, manufactured by Bird Products Corp., and in use in the mid- to late 1960s, looked like green lunch boxes on stands. They didn't even have automatic switches—young doctors or nurses would sit next to the machine, manually flipping a switch 12 times a minute to shoot a blast of air into the body. Patients on such primitive machines either breathed on their own within a day or two, or died.

Improvements in the technology came quickly, however, as companies added features such as automatic switches. Patients could live for a much longer time, sometimes years, hooked up to the more sophisticated machines. But these improved machines were large, complicated, and needed constant tinkering. So while the first respirator-dependent patients at the Missouri State Chest Hospital in the early 1970s stayed alive, they were destined to spend the rest of their lives in the new red brick building, tethered to a massive breathing machine.

The improvements in the technology kept coming. Soon, respirators started to shrink dramatically in size, even as more features were added. They became portable, dependable, and easier to use. The Missouri State Chest Hospital began developing a reputation throughout Missouri of taking in and then sending home patients that other facilities had branded "unweanable," patients who had lived on respirators for a long time. By the early 1980s, this very success, and the rapidly improving respirator technology, once again combined to reduce the patient population of the state facility.

In 1984, a new administrator arrived to run the Missouri State Chest Hospital. Forty-year-old Donald C. Lamkins held a master's degree in public health, and he had spent the ten years prior to his move to Mt. Vernon running two smaller hospitals in Missouri. Confident and handsome, with a wave of light brown hair combed back, Don Lamkins brought new energy to the Missouri State Chest Hospital.

Friends in the medical world had warned Lamkins against taking the job. "It's an old state hospital that's about to go under," one told him. And Missouri state senator Ed Dirck, chair of the Senate Appropriations Committee, had said that he wanted to "drive the first nail into the plywood" and close the place. Today Lamkins still remembers his first trip to Mt. Vernon. He was driving in from the north when he rounded the corner onto the grounds. Lamkins saw the red brick building with majestic white columns at the entrance, which sat upon broad, green lawns. He thought, *This can't be it. There must be a run-down place out back.* But he was in the right spot.

In 1984, the head of the Division of Health (it wasn't yet a depart-ment) at the Missouri state capital in Jefferson City, Bob Hotchkiss, gave Don Lamkins a broad charge: "Figure out something to do with that place." The only restriction was that the chest hospital could not become an acute-care facility, which would compete with local hospitals. Lamkins recognized immediately that improved technology was making long-term respirator hospitalizations obsolete, and that Medicare, Medicaid, and private insurers soon wouldn't pay for such hospitaliza-tions anyway.

Lamkins met with his staff, toured the grounds, made many trips to Jefferson City, and did extensive research. By the end of that process, he came up with a proposal—the Missouri State Chest Hospital should enter the emerging medical field of head-injury rehabilitation. Lamkins recog-nized that technology had, in essence, created a whole new class of long-term care patients—those pulled back from the brink of death, but not far back. By 1984, the number of these patients was growing steadily. Hospital and police dramas on television showed why: The invention of closed-chest massage, cardiopulmonary resuscitation (CPR), the portabil-ity of respirators, the ability to provide immediate intravenous fluids and medicines in the field, and training emergency medical technicians to provide these services had turned accident-site resuscitation into its own art form.

Once those victims were resuscitated and rushed into an ER, new technology such as CT scans, EEGs, and EKGs delivered sophisticated analytical information, and doctors and nurses specially trained in ER medicine could quickly diagnose and stabilize patients. After the ER, patients moved to even more sophisticated Intensive Care Units (ICUs), with monitors directly inserted into their brains to measure pressure, or onto their hearts to measure rhythm, and ICU-trained doctors and nurses were only footsteps away in case a monitor should signal trouble.

Many stories of rescue ended with remarkable, near-miraculous results. But some did not. While medical science had figured out how to start a heart that had stopped, it had made no similar progress with the brain. With advances coming almost daily in the ER and ICU, the number of these patients would surely grow, and the rehabilitation of a damaged brain would take a long time. These patients had to be housed somewhere—why not the State Chest Hospital? Its staff of nearly 400 people had spent many years on difficult medical cases, and they could be trained. The hospital's grounds offered the restful place needed for long-term rehabilitation of the brain. Missouri would need such a hospital as much as it had once needed the sanatorium.

Don Lamkins worked quickly. He met with Senator Dirck and soon converted him into an advocate for the plan. It turned out that the senator had a neighbor who had a brain-injured child, and the neighbor was having trouble finding appropriate rehabilitative care. In its 1985 session, the Missouri state legislature changed the name of the facility to the Missouri Rehabilitation Center, the name that Lamkins had suggested in his written proposal. And the legislature gave the facility a new mission: "To answer the needs of those who were seriously impaired through accident or injury and who had some capacity for improvement through an extensive rehabilitation program." The Missouri Rehabilitation Center began general physical rehabilitation in late 1985, and in January of 1986, it opened its head-injury program.

Lamkins had read the terrain ahead exactly right. With its name change and new focus, the Missouri Rehabilitation Center, or MRC, as most came to know it, flourished. After an initial slow period, the patient population began to grow steadily. The staff, reluctant to change at first, began to embrace the new mission. MRC had its share of problems, the kind found in any hospital—staff disputes here, a broken water pipe there. But in the big picture, those problems were insignificant. Lamkins's bold plan had saved the state hospital on Chigger Hill.

CHAPTER 6

CHRISTMAS 1984

The Cruzans could never explain later, nor did they understand at the time, how so much time passed. By Christmas of 1984, almost two years after the accident, and more than a year since they had moved Nancy to Mt. Vernon, they had come to believe that Nancy had improved about as much as she was going to. The Bob Seger music, the constant talk, and the efforts to get her eyes to follow them around the hospital room had gotten no response from Nancy. The Cruzans saw no way that the Nancy they had known could possibly emerge from the gnarled body in the state hospital bed. They did still wonder, though, if she could make it at least partway back, and if the right key might trigger some kind of a recovery.

So, in December of 1984, Nancy's family decided to bring her home for Christmas. Even more than the southern Missouri spring, tanning by the river in the summer or her outlandish Halloween costumes, Nancy had loved Christmas. All her life, Nancy looked forward to the family sitting around the tree together on Christmas morning, and she tackled the tree trimming and the competition for buying Angie and Miranda the most popular toys with fervor. Joe, Joyce, and Chris thought that there was at least a chance, even if only a glimmer, that a Christmas at home might provoke a response from Nancy, almost like shock therapy.

Nancy hadn't been to her childhood home at 501 Main in Carterville for almost two years, not since the Saturday when she had helped with the painting. Planning for her visit added significantly to the usual holiday frenzy and stress. Joe talked to the people at the state hospital about the logistics. The staff agreed to let the Cruzans borrow the feeding pump and the medical lounge chair from her hospital room for the visit. Joe and Joyce had to sign a liability release for the pump, and for Nancy—"We hereby relieve the hospital of any responsibility so long as we have her in our presence."

Around noon on the day before Christmas, Joe, Joyce, and Mike Burken, the driver for the local cerebral palsy center, wheeled Nancy in her special lounge chair out of the state hospital and onto the lift on the special transport van. Mike Burken hadn't met the Cruzans before, and they drove much of the trip back to Carterville in an uneasy silence, with Nancy securely belted in the back. Mike parked the van on the driveway in front of the Cruzans' carport, and Mike and Joe carried Nancy in her chair up the back steps and into the house. It was a beautiful, sunny day, unseasonably warm with the temperature hovering near 50, and a strong wind from the south. No chance of a white Christmas.

Joe wheeled Nancy through the kitchen in her special chair. "Recognize this old place, Nancy?" he asked. "Oh, and look in here," Joe said, as they moved from the kitchen to the front room. "It's the Christmas tree." He wheeled her right up to the tree in the far corner of the room, where its lights twinkled brightly. Nancy sat stiffly in her chair, the quilt that Joyce had made over her lap. Her head was turned to one side, eyes blinking steadily, face toward the wall. She didn't turn toward the tree or her mom and dad.

Nancy's parents sat down in chairs next to her. They sat with her by the tree most of that day, talking to her at times, and silent for long stretches. Just before 11 P.M. on that Christmas Eve, Joe rolled the recliner back to the front bedroom, where he'd set up a rental hospital bed, and lifted his daughter into the bed. A home health nurse from Upjohn Healthcare Services arrived as scheduled, and she stayed with Nancy through the night. Joe and Joyce went to bed.

Joyce woke early on Christmas morning and let the nurse go to her own home for Christmas. Then she walked quietly back into Nancy's room. Nancy's eyes were open. "Nancy, it's Christmas!" Joyce exclaimed. Nancy's eyes stayed on the wall, blinking every few seconds. Joyce pulled the covers back and gently maneuvered Nancy's body, dressing her for the day. Joyce made all of Nancy's gowns, often with the help of Angie and Miranda. Every two weeks, for the duration of Nancy's stay in Mt. Vernon, Joyce took a fresh set of homemade gowns to Nancy and brought the dirty ones home to launder them. For this Christmas, Joyce dressed Nancy in a denim gown with a red bandana sewn near the neckline.

When Joe woke, he helped Joyce lift Nancy's stiff body—arms and legs pulled in and spine rigid—off the bed. They set Nancy in her special chair and rolled her out to the tree. Minutes later, the back door burst open and in ran Angie and Miranda, ages nine and eight, shouting, "Merry Christmas, Aunt Nan!" They stopped when they got near her chair, and looked from Nancy, to their grandparents, to the tree, a little unsure of what to do.

Chris came in right behind them, carrying brightly wrapped presents, and with her was her new boyfriend, Mel White. Mel had been to Joe and Joyce's house just once before, on Thanksgiving; this was his first meeting with Nancy. Mel shook hands with Joe and looked at Nancy in the chair. Chris had warned him, but that could not soften the impact of seeing another human being so badly damaged. And they hadn't talked about the stale smell of sickness, which, although not overpowering, still took a noticeable place in the room. Nancy's face stayed turned toward the wall, and her eyes continued to move randomly, without apparent purpose.

The girls started to dig through the presents, and when they found one with their name on it, they'd head over to the chair, rip off the paper, and say, "Look, Aunt Nan!" Angie and Miranda had heard the adults talking quietly, saying, "Nancy loved those girls," and that seeing the girls celebrating the joy of Christmas morning "just might get through to her." The girls understood the stakes, and the role they were expected to play. They kept bounding over to the medical recliner with presents, saying, "Look, Aunt Nan, look!" louder than they needed to. The adults watched with smiles that they had to force as the morning progressed.

Chris sat next to Nancy that morning, drinking coffee, talking, stroking her sister's arm, periodically wiping the drool from the corner of Nancy's mouth. The white paint on the ceiling overhead still looked new. Christmas music played on the tape player, the large artificial tree stood in the corner, presents were everywhere. But the smell and the hospital recliner made it clear that this was not a regular Christmas.

Chris nervously watched Mel, thinking that she wasn't making much of an impression on him. And she watched her girls grow increasingly uncomfortable as Nancy's face remained expressionless, her eyes darting about all morning, oblivious to the girls' efforts. Just like the adults, Miranda and Angie knew that this Christmas at home wasn't going to make any difference at all. Their mom worried that she'd ruined their holiday. "It was the most ill at ease I'd ever felt in the home where I grew up," Chris said later. She left the house earlier than she ever had on a Christmas Day.

For three days, Joe and Joyce moved Nancy around the house in the lounger, sat with her quietly for long stretches, and went to bed when the nurse arrived. Nothing changed. On December 27, 1984, with Joyce holding the door, Joe and Mike Burken carried Nancy down the back steps and secured her in the cerebral palsy van. Nancy Cruzan was headed back to Mt. Vernon, this time for good.

≈   ≈   ≈

Just as they couldn't understand or explain how so much time had passed, the Cruzans could never pinpoint the moment when all hope for any kind of a recovery left them. Chris always said that on that Christmas of 1984, she lost even modest hope for any response at all, let alone some sort of recovery. Joe and Joyce weren't as sure. Their hope seeped away over time, and they couldn't pinpoint the exact moment it had disappeared completely.

Beginning shortly after Christmas, and continuing for most of 1985, the staff at Mt. Vernon tried to encourage the Cruzans to move Nancy to a nursing home. The staff said that she wasn't a candidate for rehabilitation, and they knew that her insurance would run out at the end of the year. The Cruzans steadfastly refused to even consider moving Nancy. Joe explained their reasoning in the annual report he was required to file with the probate judge, Judge Teel: "We do not feel that she will receive the care necessary to sustain her life for any length of time in another facility." Despite this language, Joe recognized later that their reluctance to transfer Nancy in 1985 and 1986 might not have represented hope—it may have been that they just weren't ready to let go of her. Or maybe it was inertia—visiting Nancy in Mt. Vernon simply became what Joe and Joyce did.

Whether it was hope or something else, Joe did understand after that Christmas that they needed new information. He began to read about brain injury and its rehabilitation. His efforts were slow and sporadic in the beginning, since he was trained to be a sheet-metal worker, not a researcher. But his skills improved as he did more research, and the more he learned, the more questions he had. At some point in late 1985 or early 1986 (he couldn't remember exactly when), Joe came across an article that described a kind of coma where the patient's eyes moved; they grunted, drooled, and sometimes even moved stiff, crooked limbs; but they never really responded in a conscious way. Joe did clearly remember calling Joyce to come look at the article. "This describes Nancy to a tee," he said. The article called the condition the "persistent vegetative state."

Armed with a specific name for Nancy's condition, Joe's search intensified. Soon, to supplement his reading, he was talking on the phone several nights each week—to doctors, medical ethicists, priests and preachers, and sometimes lawyers. The research, the phone conversations, and the incessant focus on Nancy all worked to direct Joe's thinking. The more he learned, the more he kept returning to a single, central question: *What would Nancy want?*

Chris and Joyce, it turned out, had been thinking about it too. When Joe finally brought "the question" out into the open one evening in the Cruzans' living room, all three felt immense relief to finally be talking about it. Chris described her version of the conclusion that it turned out each of them had reached: "There's no doubt in my mind that if we could call her up and ask, 'Nancy, what do you want?' She would say, 'Look, I realize it's hard on everyone else, but let me go. I've got other things to do, and I've got other places to go—so turn me loose.'"

August 14, 1986

Joe's research also helped him learn more about his rights as Nancy's guardian, and about Nancy's rights. On August 14, 1986, he and Joyce signed the standard Missouri Rehabilitation Center "No Cardiopulmonary Resuscitation Form," requesting that the MRC doctors and nurses not perform CPR "in the event the heart or lungs become unable to maintain life." This form commonly was called the DNR, for "do not resuscitate." A notary witnessed the signing.

Joe typed up his own form as well, which tracked the language of the DNR form provided by the state hospital, but expanded its scope. Joe's form also refused "antibiotics, medications, or medical treatments that might serve to prolong Nancy's life" in the event of illness. Both forms were made part of Nancy's medical record; that is, they were filed away in a cabinet at a nurses' station near Nancy.

Joe read about families in other states with severely injured loved ones who had gone to court seeking permission to take the next step beyond the DNR form: removal of medical treatment already in use that was keeping a family member alive. On September 24, 1986, Joe wrote nationally syndicated columnist Ellen Goodman at *The Boston Globe*, asking for addresses for the Brophys and Jobes, two of the families Ms. Goodman had written about in a newspaper article titled "There Are Times When Death Is Kinder." He also wrote a woman named Fenella Rouse, who was the executive director of a group in New York called The Society for the Right to Die.

Joe wrote in both letters: "I do not know if we could go through with removing nourishment from our daughter but I would at least like to have the option available." Within two weeks, letters arrived in Carterville, one with *The Boston Globe* return address, and one from New York City. Ellen Goodman gave Joe contact information for Mrs. Brophy's lawyer, and Fenella Rouse told Joe she could forward letters to the families for him. Joe wrote long, cautious, apologetic letters to the families:

Dear Mrs. Brophy,

We have a daughter, Nancy, who suffered acute cerebral anoxia in an automobile accident on Jan. 11, 1983. She was 25 years old at the time. Since Oct. 19, 1983, she has been a patient at the Missouri State Hospital in Mt. Vernon.

Except for a gastrostomy tube through which she receives nutrition and medication, she is on no means of life support now. Her medication is primarily anti-seizure and she is contractured very badly. [The letter describes her condition at length.] We have been told that she might live for quite a number of years in this condition. We do not feel Nancy would want this, nor do we wish to see her live like this.

We are considering court action to remove the hydration and nutrition that maintains Nancy's life. As we have followed your case in the media, we wondered if you would be willing to discuss some of your experiences with us. Some of the things we are interested in are: (1) The length of time the legal process might take. (2) The financial costs involved. Nancy was involved in an one-vehicle accident so there was no insurance settlement. Unless we receive outside help, we would have to bear the legal cost. We would not want to start something we could not afford to follow through. (3) We are concerned about the emotional consequence of such action, not only for ourselves but for our other two daughters. One is 31 and the other is 23. They both seem to be in complete accord with our anticipated action. (4) Should we expect much harassment, crank calls, and both good and bad media intervention?

As I stated earlier, we have followed your case in the media and hope that your legal problems will soon be resolved to your wishes. It must take a lot of courage to do something like you have done and I commend you for it. When medical technology has done all they can do and still leave no quality of life for a person, I believe it is absurd that society does not afford them a death with dignity without having to be involved in a lengthy court battle. . . .

Joe gave Mrs. Brophy several options for contacting him, and wrote that he was enclosing Nancy's medical records "to assure you that this is not a crank letter." He closed the letter: "If for any reason you prefer not to discuss your situation with us, we will understand. However, I would appreciate it if you would just state that desire in a note to us. Thank you for your time and patience."

Mrs. Brophy contacted Joe quickly after receiving his letter. So did the parents of Nancy Jobes. They offered information and support, and welcomed the Cruzans as new members into their tragic, tight-knit fraternity. They understood all too well that accidents just kept happening, and that soon the Cruzans would be receiving such letters of their own from other families searching for help.

CHAPTER 7

GOING PUBLIC

Sue Rowell, the head nurse on the fourth floor, had worked at MRC for more than seven years, witnessing the final days of the building as the Chest Hospital and its rebirth as a head-injury rehabilitation hospital. One evening in October of 1986, she came down the long hall and saw Joe Cruzan outside his daughter's room. The brooding, bearded, square-shouldered man she'd gotten to know over the last three years was obviously upset, with tears in his eyes. Sue stopped to comfort him. "Are you all right?" she asked, laying her hand on his shoulder.

Joe looked up at her, smiling slightly. "I'm fine," he replied, his voice uneven as he fought to stop the tears. "It's just so damn hard."

Sue Rowell nodded. "I can't put myself in your shoes, but I have an idea of what you're going through," she said.

Joe turned to her. "Why?"

Sue Rowell explained the hell of her own past year—a diagnosis of cancer for her son, then surgery, radiation, and chemotherapy. As she told her story, Joyce also came out of Nancy's room. The Cruzans liked Nurse Rowell, and they hadn't heard the sad news about her son. The three of them stood together in the semi-dark evening light of the hallway. No one else was in sight. Sue Rowell finished her story, and in that minute, Joe Cruzan decided to make a leap from private agonizing to open, public discussion.

"Sue, let me get your opinion on something," he began. Joyce felt her throat constrict, for she knew what her husband was about to do.

Years later, Joyce could still remember the exact words that came into her head at that moment: *Here we go.*

"The reason I was crying is because I just told Nancy about our decision," Joe began. "We think it's time to stop all treatment."

The words floored Sue Rowell. "What do you mean?" she asked.

"We want the feeding tube removed."

"Joe, you can't do that."

"Well, we've read and thought about it a lot, and we think this is what she would have us do," Joe replied. "I thought that you might understand, after hearing about your son."

Sue Rowell's agitated words spilled out. "It's not the same at all, Joe. You just can't do that!"

A second nurse walked up with a question for Sue, and the discussion broke up. Sue Rowell stared at Joe, then walked away.

"Well, word's out now, isn't it?" Joyce said, exasperated with her husband. Normally that kind of statement would start a fight, but for some reason, Joe kept quiet, lowered his head, and walked back into Nancy's room. Joyce followed.

Word indeed was out. That conversation with Joe Cruzan spread through MRC like tuberculosis itself, and soon the news made its way to the top. The discussion and the staff reaction came to Don Lamkins as a package: "Joe Cruzan wants to remove his daughter's feeding tube, and the staff cannot handle starving a patient to death." The moment Lamkins heard about Joe Cruzan's request, he redoubled his efforts toward what he knew was the simplest solution: Keep this issue as quiet as possible and continue to try to transfer Nancy Cruzan to another facility. Lamkins had no reason to believe that he could convince the Cruzans to transfer their daughter—he'd been trying in vain to get them to do so for almost two years now. But Nancy had long ago ceased to be a candidate for rehabilitation. A nursing home could easily provide the minimal care she required: tube feeding, turning her every two hours, bathing and changing her. And now, her parents apparently wanted her feeding tube removed, which was an even better reason to move her out of a state facility.

Yet somehow, just as he had seen the right course ahead for the chest hospital, Don Lamkins knew that he was not going to be able to move this young woman out of his hospital. The problem wasn't going away—not for this Christmas, and maybe not by the next one either.

The efforts to transfer Nancy Cruzan did fail. The Cruzans went to see Judge Teel in Carthage to complain, and the judge called his old political ally, Dick Webster, one of the most powerful men in the Missouri State Senate. Joe heard that Senator Webster phoned the Department of Health, and soon after that call, the MRC staff stopped talking to the Cruzans about a transfer to a nursing home.

On May 28, 1987, Joe Cruzan sat stiffly next to his wife and daughter Chris across the polished table from Don Lamkins in the conference room adjacent to Lamkins's office. Dr. Washburn, the Medical Director at MRC, and Imogene Cornell from Social Services, sat near Lamkins. Silence filled the room as they waited and glanced at one another. The door opened, and Lamkins's secretary walked back in with copies of the letter Joe had just handed to Lamkins. Joe had spent hours crafting the letter to read exactly the right way. Lamkins passed the copies out to each of his staff members.

Dear Mr. Lamkins,

As the parents and legal guardians of Nancy Beth Cruzan, and after long and careful consideration, we have decided the time has come to request the cooperation of the Missouri Rehabilitation Center in discontinuing the life support system that provides nutrition and hydration to our daughter. We are aware that the consequence of this action will be her death. It is not a decision we have arrived at lightly.

Nancy was an independent, vivacious person. She enjoyed being outdoors, tending her plants and her pets, and, in general, living life to its fullest. Knowing her as only parents can, and based on statements made by her to her sister at the time of their grandmother's death regarding the prolonging of life when there was no purpose left to that life, it is our belief that she would not want the life support continued in her present condition. Nancy has two sisters, both of whom are in complete agreement with our request and our feeling that this would be Nancy's request.

In September 1986, we requested a written diagnosis and prognosis of Nancy's condition from Dr. Anita Issac, Hospital Medical Director. After consulting with Nancy's physicians, her response was that Nancy has a diagnosis of Persistant [sic] Vegetative State, and that the prognosis for positive change was poor, if not absent. In nearly four and one half years since her accident, we have never been convinced that even one response by Nancy has been anything but reflexive. In short, we agree with Dr. Issac's conclusions.

We believe there is moral, ethical, and legal precedent for the Missouri Rehabilitation Center to comply with our request. In no way is this a reflection on this hospital, the medical staff, or the care that Nancy has received here, but rather a request made on our strong conviction that this would be Nancy's wish were she able to express it.

We will cooperate in every way possible with the hospital in carrying out our request. /s/ Lester L. [Joe] Cruzan, Joyce G. Cruzan, Co-Guardians of Nancy Beth Cruzan

So there it was in black and white, the rumor that had raced through the hospital the previous fall. Some of the staff understood and even supported the request, but most did not. Later in the summer, Don Lamkins would state the public position of the hospital: "We know that we can unplug a machine—that isn't nearly so hard for us to accept— but the fact that we starve someone to death, we don't do that," he said, his voice rising with emphasis. "That's beyond our ability to think, even, at this point in Missouri."

On May 28, Don Lamkins lifted his head as he finished reading the letter and found everyone in the room looking back at him. He knew this didn't need to be a long meeting. "We sympathize with your position, Joe," Lamkins began, "and you understand that I'll need to take this letter higher up."

Joe said that the family understood. In fact, when he had scheduled the meeting over the phone, he and Lamkins had discussed what would happen once Joe presented the letter. Still, even knowing the response that was coming, Joe had trouble talking about their decision without his bottom lip quivering and tears threatening. Lamkins stood and nodded politely, and the meeting ended, with Joe Cruzan crying quietly as he walked out the door.

As Don Lamkins said many times after that day, "While I didn't agree with the Cruzans' choice, I thought it was their decision to make." His personal religious beliefs simply led him to a different conclusion than the one Joe and Joyce reached. Lamkins grew up the son of a minister and a devout member of the conservative Church of Christ—"one-cuppers," he would say with a smile, referring to the practice in his church of sharing a single large cup for communion. When asked where their central church was located, church members often said "heaven." Individual congregations took their lead, not from a central church, but from the Bible directly. Lamkins applied one of the most basics tenets of the Bible for guidance with the Cruzans: "Thou shalt not kill."

Once the meeting ended that day, Lamkins sat at his desk and tried to figure out the best tack in this wind, which was gathering strength quickly. He had tried to keep the issue quiet, and he'd tried to have the Cruzans move the young woman to a nursing home. So far, his strategies hadn't worked. It struck him as inconsistent that, on the one hand, the family said they wanted Nancy to stay at MRC so she could have the best care possible, refusing to move her to a nursing home where she might contract bedsores; but on the other hand, they wanted to starve her to death. *Water under the bridge at this point,* thought Lamkins. He had not succeeded in making the issue go away; now it was time to involve people up the line.

Lamkins sent an interoffice memo that day to his direct supervisor, Lorna Wilson at the Department of Health, enclosing the Cruzans' letter and copies of legal decisions from other states that Joe Cruzan had given him. The memo made clear the gravity of the issue from Lamkins's point of view:

> I agree and understand their concerns, but legal complications, as well as possible political complications, have tremendous potential for causing problems. I feel this is something that will require a legal opinion before we allow it to happen, and possibly a political opinion.

> My guess is that you will want Dr. Harmon [Director of the Missouri Department of Health] to look at this, maybe get the Attorney General's opinion, and possibly let the Governor know.

The response from Jefferson City came back to Mt. Vernon within two weeks of Lamkins's request, in the form of an official Department of Health memorandum to Mr. Lamkins from Robert R. Northcutt, General Counsel of the Department.

Northcutt explained that the Missouri legislature had passed something called a "living will" law in 1985. The law was designed to allow Missourians to specify in advance which medical treatments they would not want should they ever fall terminally ill and become unable to express their wishes. The law stated specifically that feeding tubes were not considered medical treatment in Missouri, and that a person could *not* list a feeding tube as a treatment to forgo in a Missouri living will.

The bottom line of Northcutt's memo was hard to mistake, even before he underlined it: "<u>we will not consider such a procedure without a specific Order of the Courts of Missouri</u> in a case in which we are a party and a final decision is issued." Northcutt made clear to Lamkins just how far out of the legal mainstream he thought the Cruzans' request was:

> I have my own questions as to whether a Missouri Court, while it may be willing to remove life-support systems, will be willing to authorize the deliberate dehydration and starvation of a comatose or coma patient. Withdrawing of death-prolonging procedures is designed to allow a natural death. Dehydration and starvation are not termed as natural death and it will, in my opinion, take a very very strong argument to persuade a Missouri court to go this far.

Don Lamkins read the memo over several times—it allowed for little wiggle room. He picked up the phone and dialed Joe Cruzan.

PART II

1987–1988

CHAPTER 8

PRO BONO CASE

In the spring of 1987, Dave Waxse called me about a potential pro bono case in southwestern Missouri. Dave was a partner in Shook, Hardy & Bacon (or Shook, Hardy), the Kansas City law firm where I worked. Not only was Dave a talented lawyer, but he also worked to make a difference in the community, including volunteering as general counsel for the local chapter of the American Civil Liberties Union (ACLU).

In that job, Dave had learned of the Cruzans. He told me about this family of modest means who needed a lawyer to take on their case pro bono. *Pro bono* is shorthand for *pro bono publico*, literally translated from Latin as "for the public good"—essentially free legal work for those who can't afford a lawyer. The American Bar Association recommends that each lawyer devote 50 hours per year to pro bono work. Complex cases such as death penalty defenses consume far more than 50 hours, so small law firms or lawyers working on their own have a difficult time taking on such cases because the time demands take them too far from their paying clients.

Large firms can usually afford to let one lawyer (particularly a younger, more expendable one) devote substantial time to pro bono cases because others are there to pick up any slack. Shook, Hardy had the means and firepower to take on a big case, and it had done so in the past. However, Dave Waxse and I were not drawing up plans for a big case as we talked in the spring of 1987. As Dave said, "It may not amount to much—probably no more than a half-day trial in probate court—but the issues look interesting."

Only five years out of law school, I had no basis to judge much of anything at that point. I had graduated from law school at the University of Kansas in 1982 and worked in Washington, D.C., for three and a half years—one year as a law clerk on the federal court of appeals in D.C., and the remainder for Davis Polk & Wardwell, a large East Coast firm. In November 1985, I moved back to the Midwest and joined Shook, Hardy as an associate.

Hands-on experience for young lawyers at large law firms is hard to come by, particularly courtroom experience. Shortly after arriving at Shook, Hardy, I told Waxse that I'd help out with pro bono work in any way I could. By the time Dave called in the spring of 1987, I'd at least been around a trial and had gained some practical experience with depositions, motions, and hearings. I knew where both the federal and state courthouses were in Kansas City, which I counted as progress, and had met some of the judges. But at 31, energy was still my strong suit, not experience. As Dave described the case to me that day, I didn't really think much about meeting my *pro bono publico* duty, nor did I give much thought to the Cruzans and the tragedy of their daughter. It just struck me as an opportunity.

I'm certain that I did not think about death that day. My encounters with death up to that point had been like those of most young people: My parents were alive, and I'd attended fewer than a handful of funerals, all of people I thought of as "old." One cousin about my age died of cancer when we were teenagers, and my parents did all they could to shield my sisters and me from that tragedy. The main death I remember had come early, when I was eight (in 1963). That summer, my Uncle Bill died of a massive heart attack at the age of 51. The picture of my mother crumpling down the wall to the floor in our small kitchen as the news came to her over the phone remains in my mind today, nearly 40 years later.

The day my dad heard that news, he traded in our green Packard for a brand-new white Ford station wagon so that we had a car that would make it from Iowa to Milwaukee for the funeral, likely the most extravagant and impulsive purchase he'd made in his entire Depression-sculpted life. At the funeral, the eerie, muffled sobs of my aunt, who was hidden behind a curtain in the church's family room, filled the service. And I saw my dad cry. Even an eight-year-old could not miss the disorder of normal life on that day.

Later that fall, we rode our bikes home from school early after President Kennedy was shot. Still, these experiences with death left no obvious, lasting impressions on me; and over the years of picnics, birthday parties, and ball games, any message of mortality I might have gained in 1963 wore off. Or maybe it's just difficult for death to impress a young person unless it reaches right in and slaps them across the face. It had not done that to me yet. The big brothers of my friends who had to go to Vietnam all came back; car accidents hadn't taken anyone I knew and loved. I hadn't even encountered much illness in my life, at least nothing significant enough to leave an impression. What I mainly saw was vibrant life.

So as I hung up the phone that day after talking to Dave Waxse, I had a lot to learn—about law, medicine, the people involved, the politics—and about death itself.

On Monday, May 4, 1987, I spoke to Joe Cruzan for the first time. According to his records, we talked for 38 minutes that day—mostly he talked, and I asked open-ended questions and wrote notes on a yellow pad. He told me about Nancy's condition, the people he'd talked to before arriving at his decision, and the meetings he'd had with Judge Teel, the probate judge who oversaw Nancy's guardianship. Joe's voice struck me almost more than what he said—an interesting mix of a southern Missouri drawl combined with a cautious way of choosing his words and an unmistakable edge and insistence.

"We plan to take this as far as possible," Joe said. He told me that he had drafted a letter, a formal request, which he wanted to deliver to the state hospital. "If they say no," Joe said, "I want to say at that point that we'll pursue the legal avenue." He wanted a commitment from me: "When and how are you going to make a decision?" he asked. I explained that I needed approval from the firm's leadership and that I'd let him know as soon as I could.

That spring, Joe and I talked many times—I learned fairly quickly that patience was not a strength of his. Call by call, he taught me what he knew about the case. When I told him in late May that the firm had agreed to take the case, he was elated. We arranged for him and Joyce to come to Kansas City in July. The spring and summer of 1987 were busy times at Shook, Hardy, and therefore, busy for me. No one was pushing me to move my new pro bono case along, so initially it was the last project I turned to, and most of the work on the *Cruzan* case slid to after hours. In June of 1987, I blocked out a couple of nights for a crash course on how other courts had resolved cases like the Cruzans'.

At that time, the law library at the firm occupied half of the 19th floor. On a clear night, from the desks that lined the windows, one could almost see the glow of lights from Royals Stadium, where the Kansas City Royals played, shining on the horizon to the east. That night, as I sat down to start learning about the new pro bono case in detail, the calming pace of a summer evening at the ballpark with a beer and a hot dog felt far away. I was excited about this new case, but also a little overwhelmed. I knew that piles of unfinished work still covered my office desk five floors below, and here I was in the library, starting from scratch on some extra-credit project that nobody (except for maybe Dave Waxse) really cared much about.

Our librarian had pulled cases from around the country dealing with the right to die and had stacked the books on a cubicle with my name on top of them. The Cruzans were coming to Kansas City in a couple of weeks to talk to me, and even though it was our first meeting, I needed to know something about their case. I knew that the Karen Ann Quinlan case from New Jersey was the most famous one dealing with "pulling the plug," but my knowledge didn't extend much beyond that. I took the book that contained the New Jersey cases from the stack, opened it under the fluorescent reading light attached to the cubicle, and began to read.

Written opinions in law books are essentially snapshots. Sometimes a judge who sits through a week or two of a trial writes the opinion, but more often than not, the snapshot comes from an appeals judge who works mainly from the written transcript of the trial. Even when the written opinion is crafted with care by a talented judge, there is no way that he or she can begin to capture or know all that brought the aggrieved people to the courtroom. Still, in the words and between the lines written in the law books, a rough sketch of the families and their love and pain is visible.

That summer evening, I began to learn about the tragic cases of family after family, beginning in 1976 with the mysterious coma of

Karen Ann Quinlan. She had lapsed into the kind of open-eyed coma that Dr. Fred Plum at Cornell Medical School had named just four years earlier—the "persistent vegetative state." Her parents went to court in New Jersey seeking permission to turn off the respirator that breathed for Karen Ann. Ultimately, they won and did turn off the respirator—and she breathed on her own. For ten more years, she lay in her persistent vegetative state. Karen Ann Quinlan ultimately died of pneumonia, her tube for artificial feeding still in place.

The next case I read about also came from New Jersey. In 1983, Tom Whittemore, the nephew and only surviving relative of Claire Conroy, sought permission from the probate court to withdraw a nasogastric tube through which a nursing home artificially fed his 84-year-old aunt. Ms. Conroy, a private person, had never married and made few friends over the years. She'd been closest in life to her three sisters, all dead by then, and had lived in the same house from childhood until 1979, when she moved to a nursing home. Her nephew had known Claire for more than 50 years and had visited her dutifully for as long as anyone could remember. He testified at trial that all "Claire Conroy and her sisters wanted was to have their bills paid and die in their own house."

Now, with his aunt unable to move from a semi-fetal position; suffering from diabetes, heart disease, severe bed sores, and gangrene on her left leg; unable to speak or control her bowels or bladder, Tom Whittemore wanted all medical treatment stopped. He refused consent to amputate her gangrenous leg to save her life, claiming she would not want such surgery because he said she "feared and avoided doctors." As far as he knew, his aunt didn't visit one in her first 80 years, and then went only when forced by others. While her case made its way through the court system, Claire Conroy died, her feeding tube still in place.

Paul Brophy, a Massachusetts firefighter, deer hunter, gardener, and father of five, saved a man from a burning truck—and then threw his bravery commendation in a trash can after the man he'd saved lingered for three months in a coma before he died. Brophy said to his brother, "If I'm ever like that, just shoot me. Pull the plug." He told his daughter, "If I can't sit up to kiss one of my beautiful daughters, I may as well be six feet under." After a brain aneurysm and stroke left Brophy in a persistent vegetative state, his wife went to court. She eventually won the right to remove his feeding tube, and eight days later, he died—the official diagnosis was pneumonia.

Daniel Delio, a 33-year-old exercise physiologist from New York, had a routine surgery that went bad, leaving him forever in a persistent vegetative state. His wife, Julianne, also an exercise physiologist, concluded that they'd never exercise together nor interact again, so she sought and won court permission to remove his feeding tube.

Elizabeth Bouvia from California. Joseph Saikewicz from Massachusetts. Mildred Rasmussen from Arizona. As the evening wore on, I read more stories. In the distance, the lights at the ballpark no doubt were growing brighter against the darkening sky, and fathers and sons sat with one another and cheered. But my daydreaming had stopped. At some point that night, the seriousness of this new case started to dawn on me. I thought about what Joe Cruzan had told me over the telephone and began to feel the unfairness of the hand dealt to these people.

Questions filled my yellow pad: The right to privacy was everywhere, but should that controversial right be the foundation of our case? Some cases suggested that treating a patient against her wishes might legally be considered *battery*, defined as the touching of another person without consent or legal justification. Would a simple claim of battery under Missouri law solve the Cruzans' case?

In some cases, judges spoke of "bodily integrity," and every case referred to or relied on something called the "common law right to autonomy," which the United States Supreme Court described as far back as 1891: "No right is held more sacred, or is more carefully guarded, by the common law, than the right of every individual to the possession and control of his own person, free from all restraint or interference of others, unless by clear and unquestionable authority of law . . . 'the right . . . to be let alone.'"

This eloquent pronouncement sounded just like the kind of right the Cruzans needed. Did it matter that autonomy was a common-law right, not a constitutional one? I'd learned about the basic difference in law school, but this was no exam question. I was trying to start a lawsuit—did I need both common-law and constitutional rights? Which of these theories made the most sense in Missouri?

Figuring out the substantive law was only the tip of the iceberg. Where should we file, state or federal court? Should we try to find a way to have a jury trial? What about the probate code and Judge Teel, who had ongoing authority over Nancy's guardianship? Did we need to sue anyone, such as the state hospital or the Missouri Department of Health?

Some cases talked about the new living will laws: What exactly were they; where did they come from; and what, if anything, did Missouri's brand-new law mean to our case? Joe Cruzan had told me over the phone that the people from some organization in New York called the Society for the Right to Die had told him that the Missouri living will law was "really bad." What did that mean?

All of the cases fumbled with the troubling question of exercising these rights: If Nancy Cruzan could not speak for herself, how would her constitutional and common-law rights be exercised? Can a person in a permanent coma exercise rights at all? To exercise my right to vote, I can go to the polls and make a choice, but a person in a coma can't do that, so does she really have that right anymore?

A library is a wonderful place of solitude late at night. Although the questions swirled around in my head until it hurt and my stomach growled, I felt good. The night janitor came and went. Hours before, I'd taken off my tie and coat and thrown them over a nearby chair. The lights of the ballpark had long ago gone dark. I sat there alone in the library, with my feet on the desk, drinking a Pepsi, looking at the blackness on the horizon where the lights must have been, and thinking about this new case. I felt like a real lawyer. This was the kind of night that people wrote about in their law school applications in the "Why do you want to be a lawyer?" section.

~❧~

CHAPTER 9

LUNCH WITH THE JUDGE

Joe and Joyce Cruzan had first met Judge Charles E. Teel in January 1984, when he declared them co-guardians of Nancy. Each January since, Joe had hand-delivered the annual report required of guardians to the courthouse on the square in Carthage. If Judge Teel was in the office, he'd come out and speak to Joe. If Joe had problems at times other than the filing, he felt comfortable calling the judge, who usually had Joe come in to talk. The judge became a mentor of sorts to Joe.

On September 8, 1986, at 3:30 P.M., Joe had met with Judge Teel for one of these sessions. The judge's corner-office windows on the first floor looked out on the broad lawn of the courthouse and the town square, which Joe could see behind the judge. They ended up talking for most of the afternoon about politics, religion, paying for Nancy's care—and about taking Nancy home to remove her feeding tube. Joe told the judge he'd heard that a nurse at MRC had taken her husband home, and that he was trying to learn more. Judge Teel told Joe that he ran some real risks.

"Every rinky-dink politician is out to make a name for himself," the judge said. He went on to tell Joe that if a local prosecutor found out the Cruzans were trying to remove Nancy's feeding tube at their home, the prosecutor would "jump on it." And the judge told Joe that if he caught wind of such efforts, the law required him to intervene, and he would. "It's just like giving arsenic to your wife in small doses if she's sick," Judge Teel said. "It's still murder."

Judge Teel heard cases in the county seat of Carthage and in nearby Joplin. A probate judge in a city the size of Kansas City typically doesn't talk with lawyers on the phone. Given the number of wards (the court's name for incapacitated people) in the probate system, such an informal approach could quickly overwhelm the judge. But Carthage was a town of just over 10,000 people, so when Joe said the judge wanted-ed to talk with me, I ventured a call to his secretary to see if I might schedule a phone meeting. She put me on hold, and the next thing I knew, Judge Teel picked up the line. He told me how glad he was that Shook, Hardy was representing the Cruzans, and he asked about his University of Missouri Law School classmates who were at my firm. The judge said that he planned to be in Kansas City for a week in July, hear-ing cases in Division 11 of our county courthouse to help clear the back-log. We arranged to have lunch.

On the day of our lunch in July of 1987, the judge decided to walk over to Shook, Hardy's offices from the courthouse. As we shook hands in our reception area, I thought that Judge Teel *looked* like a judge, with his square face, gray hair, and eyes that looked thoughtful and sad, per-haps because of the broken lives they watched each day.

We made our way two blocks uphill to the Italian Gardens, a long-time downtown restaurant that the judge said was one of his favorites. We talked as we walked, beginning to sweat in the heat, and the judge's measured words crawled out in a slow drawl. I was only a few days removed from my crash course in the library, and I thought that the case might be resolved by moving Nancy to another facility, so a lawsuit wouldn't be necessary. If we did end up going to court, presumably I could file the suit in Judge Teel's court, in another state court somewhere else in Missouri, or even in federal court. The logical place, though, was Judge Teel's probate court.

Probate courts in most states are set up to govern how society takes care of those who cannot care for themselves. In Missouri, probate law is broadly divided between conservators, who handle the financial affairs of a person who can no longer do so, and guardians, who look after all other aspects of that person's life such as medical care, living arrange-ments, and so on. In certain cases, only a conservatorship is established— for example, when an elderly parent can function in her own home but needs help keeping track of financial matters. In many cases, both a guardianship and conservatorship are established.

Most times, when a young adult such as Nancy Cruzan has an accident, her loved ones talk to doctors and make medical decisions as a group. When disputes arise, they're worked out at the bedside, with no need to resort to the courts; but sometimes, they simply prove too difficult to work out this way. Some states have laws in that situation that select which loved one will make decisions for a person like Nancy who's left incapacitated. Other states, including Missouri, don't have such laws.

In Missouri, a family member faced with such a problem can file a lawsuit in probate court asking that the court declare that family member the legal guardian, the "official decision-maker" for the incapacitated person in the eyes of the law. That's the step the Cruzans took in January 1984. In such cases, the probate courts retain ongoing jurisdiction over the incapacitated person (their ward) to monitor whether the guardian is continuing to act in the best interest of that ward.

❧ ❧ ❧

The judge and I sat down at the Italian Gardens, ordered lunch, and talked about Bill Shinn and Lane Bauer, the senior partners in my firm who had been the judge's classmates in law school. He told me that he had spent his high school years in Kansas City and had played tennis on the court behind the home of another senior partner, Frank Sebree, whose grandfather had founded Shook, Hardy in the late 1800s. The judge and I also talked about the case that he was trying that day as a visiting judge, and about the formality of the "big-city courtroom" compared to his own. He only had an hour for lunch, and I wanted to know more about his "arsenic analogy," so I changed the subject.

"Judge, Joe told me over the phone about his meeting with you last fall and discussing the possibility of taking Nancy home," I began, not sure exactly how to broach this topic. "I think hearing the word *murder* scared him."

The judge looked at me. "Well, Bill, Joe told me they want to remove medical treatment to let Nancy die," he said. "I think they need a court order to do that, otherwise it is the taking of a life with premeditation. In Missouri, that's murder. That's basically what I told him."

The word *murder*, which had rolled slowly off the judge's tongue, sort of hung in the air. I was sitting in a downtown Italian restaurant, talking with this gray-haired judge about my new clients, people who now relied on me for advice. I might be the one in the dark suit and suspenders, but this country judge was clearly in charge. If it had not been apparent before, it was growing abundantly so that I had left my corporate comfort zone.

"What do you think I should do?" I asked.

"I think you need a court order if you want to fully protect your clients," the judge said. "If they don't have a court order, I'd have to intervene if I found out about it." He took a big forkful of pasta as he finished his answer, and we sat in silence for a moment.

"What kind of order should we seek?" I asked.

Judge Teel explained how he thought the case could go forward in probate court—by obtaining a declaratory judgment that sought an order declaring that the guardians had the power to act in accordance with the wishes of the ward, and in her best interests. I did not talk about a potential civil rights case that we could file in federal court or the potential of filing in an alternative state court; nor did we discuss the Missouri living will statute.

"I also believe that you need to name the state of Missouri and the state hospital as defendants so that we have all parties before the court," Judge Teel said. Dave Waxse and I had already talked about this question. It was by no means clear that we needed to name any adverse party, and generally the fewer adversaries the better. I had just about decided that we would be better off with no defendants, just a straightforward order from the court about whether Joe and Joyce's decision was in Nancy's best interest. No defendants needed, only Nancy and her coguardians.

The judge had other ideas. "I've talked with General Webster's office on another matter," he continued, "and I don't think they'll be an impediment to you in this trial." This was a bombshell—the judge and someone from the attorney general's office had already discussed the Cruzans' case, and I was still in the library reading about Karen Ann Quinlan. If I had doubts about how and where to proceed, Judge Teel did not. The more I talked with him about the Cruzans, the more I sensed that he genuinely liked the family and felt horrible about their circumstance.

He also spoke of his fondness for the attorney general, Bill Webster, whom he called by the formal title of General Webster. Webster's father, State Senator Dick Webster, was a friend of the judge, the one Judge Teel had called to stop the administration at the state hospital from trying to transfer Nancy. The judge said he'd known "Billy Webster" growing up in Carthage, long before he became the attorney general. The judge obviously had great respect for Bill Webster, and he smiled broadly as he spoke of the friendship between his family and the Websters.

Before he returned to the courthouse, I took the judge up to our offices, and we tried to find his law school classmates, but all were out to lunch. I walked him out of the building.

"Let me know if I can help," he said as he left.

CHAPTER 10

FRIENDLY SUIT

In early September, Robert R. "Rod" Northcutt, general counsel for the Missouri Department of Health, phoned to ask if we could meet for a drink when he was in Kansas City for a conference. We set the meeting for Wednesday, September 15, at 5:30 P.M. I was anxious to find out why he wanted to talk to me—maybe he had a proposed resolution for the Cruzans.

When 5:30 arrived, I made my way to the dimly lit bar of the downtown Holiday Inn. Northcutt sat alone on the terrace, relaxed in a soft chair, with a half-finished whiskey on the table in front of him. He looked to be just beyond middle-aged, with silver hair, gray plastic-framed glasses, and a red-tinged nose. I learned later that he had worked most of his life as a lawyer for one agency or another in the Missouri state government. Northcutt rose to greet me, and it quickly became apparent that he hailed from the old boy school—he wanted me to like him, and he wanted to like me. I tried not to make that difficult, because one way or another, we were going to have to deal with him.

The Cruzans had already decided that they were not going to move Nancy anywhere, not out of Missouri, and not out of the Missouri Rehabilitation Center to a nursing home. "If what we're doing is right, why do we need to move her somewhere?" Joe asked. That approach had some gut-level appeal. Other times he'd say, "We're Missourians. Why should we have to move her out of Missouri?" And in another of the unsettling paradoxes for families dealing with the persistent vegetative state, even though no family member believed that Nancy had any awareness of her world, they didn't want to disrupt it. The MRC was Nancy's home now, and that's where her treatment should be stopped.

After the small talk, Northcutt started things. "What do you plan to do with this *Cruzan* case?" he asked. A straightforward question to which I had a better answer after a few nights in the library and lunch with the judge, but I was certainly no expert.

"I don't know. I guess it depends on where the Department of Health stands," I replied. Northcutt raised an eyebrow at me while pointing to our drinks, and with my nod, he signaled the waitress for two more.

"Fair enough," he said. "Let me start by telling you what we've discussed in Jefferson City. We want this to be a friendly suit. We need clarification as much as you do on what the law is. We'll oppose you at trial, and if you win, we'll appeal, but we don't want it to be adversarial."

I hadn't been involved with a lawsuit against a Missouri state agency before, so I didn't know enough to ask Northcutt how much he would control the decisions once we filed suit and the attorney general's office entered the case to defend the state agency. I didn't try to pin him down about Nancy's condition or gain other commitments. I just liked his attitude.

"A friendly suit sounds fine," I said, "but I thought that the administrator at the state hospital told the Cruzans that the living will statute prohibits removing a gastrostomy tube." In June, Don Lamkins had sent a copy of Northcutt's memo about the living will law to Joe, who sent it to me, so I knew Northcutt's legal analysis.

"Well, it's pretty clear to me that's right," he replied. "Under that living will statute, we cannot honor the Cruzans' request."

"But how can that law apply to her if it did not even exist when she had her accident? And what about her constitutional rights—a state law can't affect her constitutional rights, can it?" I spouted with newfound authority two of the theories scribbled on my yellow pad back in the library.

"This is really about Missouri law," he said. "You're not going to make this a constitutional case, are you?" He looked surprised, though perhaps he was simply trying to steer our lawsuit in a certain direction.

"We'll see," I said. "What exactly does 'a friendly suit' mean?"

Northcutt explained that Dr. Harmon, director of the Department of Health, had agreed to cooperate with the family. He said that state health officials understood and sympathized with the Cruzans. Northcutt would accept service of papers for the state, they would produce documents voluntarily, make witnesses available for interviews or depositions, and cooperate in framing the issues for the court and any other way that made sense. They did not want this to be hard on the family.

"We just need to know what the rules are," Northcutt concluded. I believe that on September 15, 1987, that was exactly the position of the state of Missouri regarding Nancy Cruzan.

Joe Cruzan had a nearly insatiable desire to know things. He didn't just drive his truck—he could take it apart and put it back together. After a vacation trip to Florida to visit Nancy and her first husband, Joe wrote the Chamber of Commerce in Jacksonville, Florida, and asked them to send him information on how the tides worked. He wrote the Chamber in Pensacola to ask how the long bridge they'd crossed on the drive home had been built. Joe wasn't content to look and admire—he wanted to know.

Beginning with our first phone call and continuing over the summer and into the fall, Joe and I talked many times, often at length, about a potential lawsuit. Like the tides and the bridge, he wanted to learn about the law so he could understand it—just like he understood his truck. We talked about where to file the suit, what to file, and how we could win if Northcutt's memo about Missouri's living will law was right. When I tried to explain the complex relationship of state and federal laws and the Constitution, I often used abortion cases as my example. The gist of the lesson for Joe in those discussions was the basic framework I'd learned in law school.

A state legislature cannot ban abortion by state statute, even if all legislators in the state agree on that course, because our Supreme Court has ruled that the constitutional right to privacy gives a woman the right to have an abortion. Neither state legislatures nor the federal Congress may pass laws that deprive citizens of rights granted in the United States Constitution, because the Constitution is the highest law in the land.

Those state legislators can and do pass laws that regulate abortion, however, and in practice, those laws often make it more difficult for a woman to obtain one. In evaluating whether such laws are constitutional, the U.S. Supreme Court engages in a balancing process, balancing the state's right to protect potential life against the woman's right to privacy.

The hard part, of course, is deciding when the line has been crossed, when a state law infringes upon the constitutional right. Does the requirement that a teenage girl provide written permission from both parents for an abortion sufficiently infringe on the right to privacy so that a court should declare that requirement unconstitutional? May an adult woman be made to wait 24 hours after the initial consultation before her abortion, even if she can't afford a hotel in the town she's had to travel to for the procedure? Must she watch a graphic "educational" film, or meet with adoption counselors? Is a fetus considered a person that the state has a duty to protect?

In every facet of modern life, shades of constitutional gray are present. The Second Amendment may give citizens the right to bear arms as a "well regulated Militia," but can one wear a pistol to the mall? The owner of the corner store has a right to free speech, but can the zoning board limit the size of his signs to the point that he's driven out of business? I have a right to liberty, but if society finds me insane, can I be locked up in a mental institution? If my condition improves, must society let me out? If I'm locked up, can I also be shackled to my bed? Doesn't that violate my right to liberty? What if the state lacks sufficient funds for a guard to watch me if I'm not shackled?

Like many people, Joe found the law daunting. Whether Nancy, permanently unconscious and confined to a hospital bed, still had constitutional rights; how a living will law passed in 1985 could apply to a young woman injured in 1983; what exactly "the right to privacy" was—all of these difficult questions troubled Joe. I told him that he was not alone. If the books containing the laws of this country were gathered in one place, they'd fill a warehouse covering many city blocks. Where one right starts and another ends, how those rights affect the duties of others, and the proper role of the government—these are the questions and concepts that lawyers slog through, case by case, each with its own unique set of facts, twists, and turns. Lawyers confronted with these complex questions do what one might expect: They try to figure it out as best they can.

The federal right to privacy particularly intrigued Joe. Right about the time we were getting ready to file our lawsuit in September 1987, Joe (like many Americans), watched the dramatic U.S. Senate confirmation hearings of Judge Robert Bork for the open seat on the United States Supreme Court. The year I clerked in D.C. (my first year out of law school), I'd met and done some work for Judge Bork, so I had a special interest in the hearings, too.

Court watchers saw President Reagan's nomination of Judge Bork as an effort to turn the Court distinctly to the right. In his academic life, Judge Bork had long championed limiting the reach of the federal Constitution to those issues intended by the Framers. In his book *The Tempting of America,* Judge Bork said this about the 1973 abortion decision *Roe v. Wade* and the constitutional right to privacy "created" in that legal opinion:

> The discovery this late in our history that the question was not one for democratic decision but one of constitutional law was so implausible that it certainly deserved a fifty-one-page explanation. Unfortunately, in the entire opinion there is not one line of explanation, not one sentence that qualifies as legal argument.

The word *privacy* indeed does not appear in our Constitution. Judge Bork and others who profess to limit the reach of the document to the original intent of the words written in it find that fact an important underpinning to their philosophy. With his nomination of Judge Bork, President Reagan had declared war on the right to privacy, or at least that was quickly the word on the street.

Within hours of President Reagan's press conference at the other end of Constitution Avenue, Sen. Edward Kennedy spoke from the floor of the Senate: "Robert Bork's America is a land in which women would be forced into back-alley abortions, blacks would sit at segregated lunch counters, rogue police could break down citizens' doors in midnight raids." The public battle over the right to privacy had begun in earnest.

Over the course of those five days of political theater on national television, many Americans came to understand that, at the very least, privacy wasn't an ordinary constitutional right such as free speech or freedom of religion. At best, the right to privacy was a right on shaky grounds; at worst, it was viewed by some as vague or even sinister—not a great foundation for any new lawsuit.

Moreover, it wasn't a great foundation for a lawsuit in the state of Missouri. Even the most casual watcher of Judge Bork's confirmation hearings would have understood that "the right to privacy" had become code words for abortion. In the summer of 1987, strong pro-life forces were at work in Missouri, fighting to stop abortion and limit the right to privacy wherever it appeared. Many Southern Baptists, members of the Church of Christ, and other conservative religious groups populated southern Missouri from east to west. St. Louis was home to a large Catholic population, with both blue-collar and old-money factions. Missouri Governor John Ashcroft was anti-abortion without apology, and Attorney General William Webster had courted the pro-life vote from the start of his political career. In 1986, the Missouri legislature enacted a law that declared, among other things, that life began at conception. Attorney General Webster began fighting in defense of that law in the courts of Missouri in 1987.

From the original declaration of Missouri as a slave state, to the 1857 *Dred Scott* decision, up to the modern day, Missouri wasn't a place to challenge conservative dogma. But as I told Joe, virtually all of the earlier right-to-die cases, beginning with the Karen Ann Quinlan case in 1976, had discussed, or directly relied upon, the right to privacy. There was no avoiding a privacy argument of some kind in our case. And the argument *had* worked in other states.

By early October, our lawsuit was ready. I had decided to take our chances with Judge Teel. Even if he was a friend of the family of the attorney general, he also seemed to like the Cruzans and to possess a strong dose of fairness and common sense. The more I read about these cases, the more it seemed that the judge needed those two qualities as much as any others. We could also schedule the trial much more quickly in probate rather than federal court.

The friendly suit also seemed like the right course. The judge said we needed the state of Missouri in the suit, and Rod Northcutt told me that they would cooperate. Our petition would name the Department of Health and MRC as defendants, and it would contain none of the potential accusatory allegations—no alleged battery for inserting a tube and FDA-regulated nutritional supplements into this woman without consent, no claim of civil rights violations, no charge of medical malpractice, and no request for any damages (that is, compensatory money). I'd considered all of these avenues as carefully as I could, and rejected each. Instead, we would file a declaratory judgment lawsuit, a request that the judge simply "declare" what the law was. That was what both sides wanted.

Like the Cruzans, that summer I found myself joining a new group—lawyers who represented families in right-to-die cases. I talked many times with Paul Armstrong in New Jersey, who had represented the Quinlans and the Jobes families. Paul patiently educated me about his cases. I also talked with Fenella Rouse and Rose Gasner at the Society for the Right to Die. Both Armstrong and Gasner sent me copies of petitions filed in other cases to use as a model.

In the end, our petition claimed constitutional rights "generally" for Nancy and her parents, including the right to privacy. It claimed that Nancy had a common-law right to autonomy, described as the right "to be let alone." And it reasoned that Nancy's parents could speak for her since she couldn't speak for herself. The petition also tried to preempt the government response, explaining why the Missouri living will law not only did not prohibit the Cruzans' choice, but actually supported it. It was a straightforward petition, without hype or window dressing. The Cruzans just needed Judge Teel to declare what the rules were in Missouri.

Our friendly suit was ready to go, but I did not file it yet. There was one thing that I thought I should do first—go down to southern Missouri and see the young woman who would die if we won.

❧❀❧

CHAPTER II

501 MAIN STREET

On Wednesday, October 21, I rose early, put on my pinstriped and wing-tipped uniform, and headed out the door for my first road trip to Carterville. The traffic and five-lane interstates of Kansas City narrowed to three lanes in the distant suburbs, and soon I was on Highway 71 south and into the country, where pickup trucks waited patiently to cross the highway and tractors worked in the rich black fields.

Once the weather warmed up a bit, I stopped for a soda and put the top down to enjoy the perfect fall day. As I drove, I thought about the meetings ahead of me that day, and the one I'd already had with Joe and Joyce Cruzan. That first meeting, at my office in Kansas City, had started out almost comically. The Cruzans had arrived at the office with a film crew in tow (as I knew they would). I was in a makeshift space, built quickly to accommodate our rapidly growing firm. Our reception area was little more than a desk, which we had to squeeze past, and from there, our group of six waddled through a maze of narrow hallways bordered by cubicles. My small office barely had room for my desk, let alone two clients, a producer, her film crew, and their equipment.

The Cruzans had agreed that spring to allow Elizabeth "Betsey" Arledge, a producer of documentaries for PBS's *Frontline*, to film their journey through the process. Arledge had contacted the Society for the Right to Die about potential right-to-die cases, and she picked the Cruzans from a long list of families across the country, largely because of timing—the Cruzans were just about to start down the road of dealing with "the system."

Arledge phoned Joe from Boston (which impressed him) and asked if she could come to Carterville in April and spend two or three days with him and Joyce—alone, no cameras—so they could get to know one another. This flattered Joe. Once Arledge arrived in Carterville, the Cruzans took to the attractive, friendly redhead immediately. She was in her late 20s, just like Nancy. Most important to Joe, she seemed genuinely interested in his family.

Joe asked, "Are you willing to go see Nancy?"

Arledge didn't hesitate. On that April day, she walked into Nancy's room, went straight over to the bed, and said, "Hi, Nancy." Standing there, Chris tried to tell Betsey Arledge about Nancy, that "she would never want to be this way." Something about talking to this national newsperson who seemed to really *want* to know stopped Chris short, and she burst into deep belly sobs. Arledge, not sure what to do, walked over and held her for a long time. Joe and Joyce stood and watched.

When she got ready to leave Missouri after that first visit in April of 1987, Arledge said to Joe, "I want to tell your story." After she left, Joe, Joyce, and Chris talked, and a couple of days later, Joe called Betsey Arledge and said yes.

Joe told me about the filming after we'd agreed to take the case. I said, "That's a bad idea." Talking to the press (even PBS), ran counter to everything I'd learned in my early years as a defense lawyer. One of my first cases at Davis Polk & Wardwell involved a takeover attempt of Gulf Oil by oil magnate T. Boone Pickens. The lead lawyer on the case, Bob Fiske, cautioned us himself about contact with the press. Another time, when we were representing former Defense Department official Paul Thayer, we had a *Wall Street Journal* reporter camped out near the elevators. I took the stairs to avoid any chance of contact. And when I joined Shook, Hardy, our largest client was tobacco giant Philip Morris, never a press favorite.

I thought that any attention would make the *Cruzan* case harder to resolve. Joe told me that he'd made a commitment to Betsey Arledge, and as I learned as I came to know him better, Joe did not make or take his commitments lightly. In fact, under Joe Cruzan's personal code, his word was his bond, which answered the question about whether PBS would get to film without a lot of lawyer analysis.

"Besides," Joe said to me, "if we're right, why not tell our story?" That made some sense to me, too.

And, as Betsey Arledge had suggested, this was a PBS documentary, not commercial television, so it would be aimed at educating the public, and likely would not air for some time. She told Joe and later me that her crew would stay in the background, attracting little attention. That task hadn't been easy at our first meeting in July in my small office. I hoped that the meeting in the Cruzans' home would be less crowded and more relaxed. I was excited to spend the day with them.

❧   ❧   ❧

Joe had given me precise directions for the nearly three-hour trip. I left the highway at the second exit for Carthage. At the bottom of the ramp, if I turned left, I'd enter Carthage; if I turned right and traveled six miles west, I'd run into the Carterville exit. Continuing on a few miles west of Carterville, the highway led to Joplin, the biggest city in the area.

The exit off Business Highway 71 into Carterville turned immediately into the town's Main Street. From end to end, Main Street was only about a mile long, with no stoplights. Houses of all sizes, churches, and different businesses shared Main Street. Only two neon signs appeared: one centered over a large single garage door in a red brick building that said "Fire Dept," and another in the window of a convenience store advertising "Lite" beer.

Carterville had started as a mining town. Each Fourth of July, after Grandpa Les shot off his homemade cannon in the yard, Joe and Joyce would take Angie and Miranda out to the "chat piles," the gray remains of earlier lead and zinc mining, and the four of them would sit on green folding chairs and watch the fireworks explode above the Missouri Southern State College football stadium. Like many small towns, a handful of the storefronts along Main Street stood vacant. But the many well-kept homes up and down Main suggested that the town was doing fine.

One of those homes was the Cruzans', a white, one-story wood frame at 501 Main Street. As I got out of my car, I saw the broad porch and inviting front steps, which had been freshly painted and were framed by the reds and yellows of fall. I walked up the steps, and Joe opened the door with Joyce and Chris right behind him. They welcomed me into their home.

Norman Rockwell could easily have painted the three people standing in that doorway: the rough-hewn, dark-bearded father, chin out, his jeans traded for gray slacks, and cowlick slicked down for the special occasion; the stoic mother, hair tightly permed—her curls as immovable as her sense of right; and the beautiful daughter who looked up with wide brown eyes, devoted to both.

Meeting in Carterville, Joe and Joyce were indeed much more relaxed than they'd been in my office. For one thing, as Joe joked, this time they knew what to expect. When they came to my office in July, Joe said he'd expected to find some wild-eyed, long-haired "ACLU hippie," not a clean-cut young lawyer in a dark suit and polished shoes. In addition, there were no cameras for this meeting. And most important, we were in the Cruzans' home.

I met Chris (with whom I had talked on the phone) for the first time that morning. Although she and I were the same age, she was far deeper into adulthood in some critical ways—she was newly married for the second time and was responsible for two preteen girls. I, on the other hand, had been dating a woman named Kelley for a year, but I was still single and lived in an apartment with my college roommate. Then again, I was the guide through this mysterious legal process, so in that way, I was more the adult—in fact, that first morning, when Chris spoke to me, she said "Yes, sir" and "No, sir" many times.

We settled in around the Cruzans' oak dining-room table, and began the morning with my talking about the petition and the research I'd done. Again I brought up the idea of moving Nancy to Kansas or some other state, an issue I'd tried to raise with them many times. Joe clearly saw it as the wrong solution, and he told me that they simply weren't going to move Nancy. That morning, I dropped the issue for good.

We started talking about what a lawsuit in Judge Teel's court might look like. I tried to describe the three-pronged attack that most of the other cases had followed. First would be the medical part of the trial—doctors, nurses, family, and other experts would testify that Nancy was permanently unconscious, in a persistent vegetative state, and without hope of recovery. Despite all the medical jargon, this testimony to a large extent would revolve around people who would say, in one way or another, "Nancy is not inside that shell, and here's how I know."

The second part of the trial would focus on Nancy before the coma: "If she could talk, here's what she'd say, and this is why we know she'd say it." This testimony would describe how Nancy had lived her life, the kind of person she was, and her personal relationships. Any information about specific statements she'd made about death and dying or life support would be a huge bonus, but 25-year-olds typically haven't reflected to any extent on life's end.

The final piece would be medical ethics—or why doctors and medical ethicists supported the family decision. We needed to tell the best story we could on all three fronts, particularly in the face of the restrictive Missouri living will law. The filing of briefs outlining the law would take place after the trial, and the judge would then take all he'd learned, think about it, and issue his decision in writing.

That morning in Carterville, however, we mostly talked about Nancy before the coma. I toured the house (including what was once Nancy's bedroom), saw family photo albums, and heard their stories. They told me about Joe trying to get the girls ready for church—Chris and Donna cooperated, but Nancy taunted and teased him. I heard about the summers at Sugar Creek. And Joe showed me a photograph of Nancy, co-captain of the twirling team, leading the high school band down the street in a parade that he was obviously very proud of.

Joe's hard, square face spread into maybe the only true smile of his I ever saw when he talked about the summer he bought a new motorcycle and took his teenagers, Chris and Nancy, for rides. Chris, the sensible one, was cautious; Nancy, the free spirit, hopped on and clung to her dad, laughing and hooting, urging him to go faster and faster onto the highway and out of Carterville. I had the sense that before the accident, Joe's loved ones saw that smile often. But by the fall of 1987, just as Nancy was frozen stiff with contractures, Joe's mouth could no longer readily stretch to that old smile.

By flashing that smile and telling the motorcycle story, it appeared that Joe had reminded Joyce and Chris that the time when they used to see that smile was gone. To his credit, Joe tried to save the moment. "Boy, she loved speed, didn't she?" he said. The other two nodded, Chris gulping back tears. "She had this van, Bill, with glass packs on it, so you could hear her coming from three blocks away. Every time I heard that damn van, I got excited."

But the smile came to half-mast as he spoke, and then he took it down, remembering that Nancy had sold the van to a guy who lived near the Cruzans not long before her accident. "For years after the accident, I'd stop what I was doing when I heard those pipes," he said. Chris began to cry, and Joyce looked out the window, fidgeting with the pen she was holding. Joe's lip quivered, and the tears rolled down his cheeks. Instead of just sitting there, I stood up and went to the kitchen for coffee and took a couple of deep breaths. When I sat back down at the table, the emotions had ebbed.

"Tell me more about her initial rehabilitation," I said, and we headed in a new direction, from the before to the after of their lives. They again described Nancy's journey: Freeman Hospital, Brady Rehabilitation, Paul's grandmother's house, briefly to the nursing home, Jane Chinn Hospital with a 107-degree fever, Mt. Vernon, home for Christmas 1984, and Mt. Vernon.

Joyce and Chris talked about Joe staying all night many nights at Freeman Hospital in the waiting room and spending morning and night at Brady Rehab. Despite their own devastation, Joyce and Chris always said that the accident and its aftermath hit Joe the hardest. He couldn't let any little part of it go, or even ease his grip just a bit. On the recommendation of a social worker at Brady, Joyce and Joe started seeing a counselor named Barbara Carter. They saw Barbara on and off for ten years, until she moved to California.

Barbara coached Joe to try to compartmentalize his life, to put Nancy and the sadness and hopelessness in one part, and live life with his present activities and loved ones in another. The Cruzans trusted Barbara Carter, and Joe tried mightily to follow her counsel. He just didn't have those compartments. His trailer fell into disuse, he sold the motorcycle, he lost interest in the cabin on Sugar Creek, in fact, he lost interest in just about everything except trying to help his daughter. On that issue, he developed a keen, passionate, all-encompassing interest— an obsession.

As we sat around the table, we quickly moved through Nancy's chronology after the accident. The description was easy because not much had changed. I wrote notes quickly, trying to store all of the information coming at me as carefully as I could. By lunchtime, we had moved the story forward to the present. It was time to go to Mt. Vernon.

CHAPTER 12

SEEING NANCY

Chris rode with me, directing me onto the highway as we followed Joe and Joyce. I sensed the rhythm of the weekly trips of the Cruzan family up to Mt. Vernon—in the three years since Nancy's move up to the MRC, the Cruzans had made this trip nearly 200 times. The interstate peeled away, and Chris continued to talk about Nancy. The bond the two sisters shared was obvious, since they'd been together for most of their lives. The clear, excruciating pain of Chris's loss reminded me of my aunt behind the curtain at my uncle's funeral: pure, primal grief.

Chris also talked about her parents, especially Joe. "I don't want to burden you too much," she said.

"Heck, no. Go on," I said.

"I'm really worried about my mom and dad," she said. "My dad talks about Nancy all the time—he can't talk about anything else. Guys at the job site have said that they're sick of hearing him, and he and my mom are constantly fighting." I looked over at Chris and thought she might start crying again. "My mom is sick of listening to it, too."

I asked Chris about her youngest sister, Donna. I'd heard Donna mentioned on occasion, but had never talked to her myself. When Joe had shown me a picture that morning of Donna and Nancy, I'd asked, "Should I talk to Donna, too?" Joe had fidgeted and explained that while Donna supported their decision, she lived outside of town and wanted her privacy. Chris said the same thing in the car. I learned later that Donna had married a man whom Joe didn't approve of, and that they were often struggling financially. Eventually, I did meet Donna, and I found her personable and definitely in agreement with what Nancy would want, but her life wasn't intertwined with her parents' like Chris's. Barbara Carter, Joyce and Joe's counselor, said that "Nancy was the glue that held the five Cruzans together." After the accident, Donna just kind of drifted away.

I also asked Chris about Nancy's two husbands. She said that she hadn't seen Nancy's first husband, her high school sweetheart Danny Hayes, in many years. Chris doubted that he would have any information to add that might help our case; she said essentially the same thing about Paul Davis as well.

Chris and I had an enjoyable ride, talking freely for most of the 45-minute drive to Mt. Vernon. Then a funny thing happened: The first road sign announcing our destination came into view. The conversation slowed and Chris's face turned more to the fields passing by outside. I flipped on the radio. Chris was so obviously uncomfortable that I grew uneasy, too. As we exited the interstate and turned onto the two-lane highway toward Mt. Vernon, the conversation stopped altogether, and the tension in the car tightened like a vise. Discussion of the woman I was about to see stopped.

Joe and I parked our cars next to each other and walked toward the Missouri Rehabilitation Center, a stately red brick building with tall stone-colored columns atop its front steps. Once inside, Chris and Joyce led the way to the elevators, up to the fourth floor, down the long, dimly lit mustard-colored hallway. I walked next to Joe, talking to him about the Department of Health. Then I stepped through the open door, and stopped speaking mid-word. My heart leaped into my throat the moment I saw Nancy Cruzan in her hospital bed, and it stayed there for my entire ten-minute visit. I walked tentatively toward her bed and then paused, with no real idea of what I was supposed to do next. I just stood there.

Nancy's bloated face was pointed at the wall and was contorted into an unnatural grimace, its skin a chalky, sickly color, dotted with spots of red acne. Her eyes blinked every couple of seconds. Soft groans escaped from her mouth, as did a trickle of drool, which ran down her chin and onto the bedsheets. Her arms were pulled up almost like a boxer protecting his face, except, instead of fists, each of Nancy's wrists bent unnaturally back, with her fingers splayed. An embroidered pillow was wedged between her fingernails and the skin on the inside of her wrist—later I learned that the pillow stopped her nails from cutting into her skin.

Although the room looked like an average, sterile hospital room, it smelled slightly musty. The eerie quiet of a hospital floor where the patients were all vegetative was broken only by the static of a cheap radio near Nancy's head, tuned to a country station, which Nancy would have hated had she been able to hear it. I stayed glued to the floor, several feet from her bed. I did not approach the bed, and did not touch her that day.

Joe saw my uneasiness. He hung on to the railing of her bed and said, "Nancy, we brought a fella by the name of Bill Colby up here with us. He's the one who's going to represent us in this thing that we've talked about."

Nancy lay there gurgling as Joe spoke. I just continued to look at her.

"I don't think she's real impressed," Joyce said, and the Cruzans all laughed, nervously. I smiled at Joyce quickly and turned to Joe.

"Is this how she appears each time you come?" I asked, incredulous.

"Yeah, this is . . . it," Joe said. His voice came out as a sigh.

My first visit to the hospital room of Nancy Cruzan remains among the most unsettling and disquieting experiences of my life. I think maybe I expected to see Sleeping Beauty: eyes closed, skin white, serenity embodied. If the cases about other families I'd read in the law books had told me what to expect, somehow I missed it. I had no conception of the persistent vegetative state until that day. At the doorway of Nancy Cruzan's hospital room, my medical education about the brain and its potential for demise began.

I've revisited that first meeting with Nancy many times to try to better understand it. Betsey Arledge filmed the visit, and some colleagues commented after seeing the documentary months later that I seemed calm, respectful, and professional. In that video snapshot, I quietly talk with the Cruzans, I say hi to Nancy, and I ask to see her feeding tube. I'm there a few minutes, and I leave by myself.

But to me, and to those who know me well, it's apparent that I would have rather been anyplace else on Earth. In truth, I heard almost nothing that day. Although words came out of my mouth, I said little of substance. Being so close to the face of death scared the hell out of me.

I spent the ten minutes in that room stunned—for the first time, I'd seen a human being with all of her thinking brain destroyed, with only the prehistoric reflexes found in the stump of her brain remaining.

I left the room and the hospital alone, hurried outside, took a deep breath of fresh air, and headed north toward home. I'd like to say that I spent the drive time planning more strategy, and I did think about the events of the day. Mainly, though, I just wanted to escape—back to my apartment, friends, and girlfriend. Maybe even back to the insurance conglomerates, drug companies, and other clients whose work filled my days—polite businessmen in suits. Meeting with them was more predictable, less intense. As I sped off with the top down, I could not erase the picture of that poor woman from my mind. I didn't analyze the issues, didn't compare Nancy to the cases I'd read—I just wanted to get away.

October 24, 1987

A few nights later, I had a dream. In the dream, the sun came up and somehow, unnaturally, raced to its crest. Then a second bright sun sped into the sky to join the first. Together they easily burned off the morning fog. I saw that it wasn't two suns, but two eyes, radiant and black. Those eyes locked on mine, and the shutter clicked in my mind's eye as I sat up, fully awake, capturing the dream for the rest of my life. It was Nancy.

Pulling the window blinds back revealed the darkness outside just starting to give way. I walked to my closet and pulled on jeans, a Knox College basketball sweatshirt, and a baseball hat. I was ready for a Saturday of work on the Cruzans' case, but a new heaviness had settled on me. It would take some time before I understood the persistent vegetative state, before I read the various studies, had Nancy's erratic EEG readings and bleak CT scan explained to me, or reviewed in detail the years of hopelessness in her medical chart. It would take a long time—and the death of my father many years later in the fall of 1997—before I could even begin to try to put myself in the Cruzans' shoes.

By now, though, I'd reached certain preliminary conclusions about Joe, Joyce, and Chris. They reminded me of a lot of the families I had grown up with in East Moline, Illinois—moms often quiet, dads coming home tired and dirty every day from the factories at John Deere, Farmall, or Alcoa. Honest, hardworking, decent people. Over all the years we spent together, that initial assessment of the Cruzans never changed and never wavered. Life had dealt them this blow, and they really had no good options left. My personal reaction to that first encounter with a person in a persistent vegetative state, my clients' daughter, did not matter at all. I still wasn't even sure what my reaction really was—sadness, sorrow, horror? But I had figured out that this was the business of their family and no one else. I was their lawyer, and they needed my help.

An early riser heading downtown in Kansas City on a Saturday is just about alone. I flipped on NPR but didn't really listen. The weird dream I'd had stayed with me—obvious in some ways because I'd just visited Nancy for the first time. But why did the eyes in the dream stare? Today, I think back on that dream, and I like to think that maybe my subconscious mind was preparing me for the battle ahead, that the eyes were saying to me: "Get me out of here."

❦

CHAPTER 13

MOTION TO DISMISS

We filed the lawsuit in late October. Just three months earlier, Nancy Cruzan had turned 30; and Joe, Joyce, and Chris celebrated with her at MRC. It was Nancy's third birthday party there, and the fifth she'd spent with no idea that anyone was in her room, or where she was or how long she had been there. Chris kidded her younger sister about turning "the big 3-0," and the family read her cards and sang "Happy Birthday."

By this point, in some ways the family was just going through the motions. They expected no reaction from Nancy, and didn't sing "Happy Birthday" as if the song mattered. The lack of change in Nancy's condition and the years without progress had worn the Cruzans down to a nub. Joe, the perfectionist, the man who could "fix anything" with sheet metal and a pop riveter, had no tool to make his daughter better. Neither did the doctors and nurses.

In other ways, though, the Cruzans' trips to see Nancy two times a week were far from routine. The emotions of every visit remained intense. Barbara Carter, their counselor, thought she understood why. "You go through lots of different grieving processes with this situation. This isn't one where there's a beginning and an end, where the burial can be the start of stages in that grief," Carter said. "This is an ongoing process, and they go through the entire grief stage maybe once a month, depending on what's going on with Nancy. But they can never get it done—they can never go through the stages and go on with the recovery. Because Nancy's still here."

The Cruzans had been through years of grieving and waiting, and now their journey through the world of law was just beginning—a world whose slow pace often frustrates those seeking answers. Lawyers who deal with the court system every day and understand its rhythms typically view it as methodical—that's because they're usually trying to balance cases in different courts, with each case having its own set of deadlines for completing days of depositions; sorting through mounds of documents; and finding, naming, and deposing expert witnesses. Lawyers today, working in a world that moves at the pace of fax machines and e-mail, often operate in a triage mode—the same six-month period that may seem an eternity for the client can fly by in the blink of an eye for the juggling lawyer.

After filing the petition, the Cruzans and I began the work of pulling our case together. The initial assembly of a lawsuit starts with an investigation of the law and the facts. Of course, some of that investigation takes place before any petition is filed in any court. The lawyer has to know what law and facts to include in the petition and has an ethical obligation to do sufficient investigation to make sure the client has a legitimate basis for going to court.

Once the petition is filed, the client and lawyer are officially engaged in the public court system, and what lawyers call "discovery"—the formal process by which each side finds out about what the other side knows about the case—begins. The internal investigation also continues, as the lawyer assembles and sifts facts, law, and theories, trying to construct the most persuasive story to tell a judge or jury.

In a major civil action between companies, the discovery process often follows certain fairly predictable patterns. Unfortunately, a pro bono case with political overtones and a woman's life on the line fit no particular mold. In our case, it was not clear at all how much discovery would be required. Still, I knew I needed staff help. In the summer of 1987, my regular legal assistant didn't have time to take on a pro bono case, or at least that was the opinion of the partner she primarily worked for, who was also my boss.

We had a brand-new legal assistant trainee, Kim Ross, who had joined the firm straight out of college. With her curly dark hair and freckles, Kim looked young even for a recent college grad, and she'd never handled a lawsuit of her own. But she was a smart aleck (which I liked), and her cubicle was near my office, so I asked her if she wanted to work on her own case. She was enthusiastic. I walked the stack of papers, mostly copies of cases from the library and a few of Nancy's medical records, over to her desk and told her to look through them and let me know if she had any questions.

Kim had no idea when I first handed her the papers what the case was about. Years later, after we knew one another well, she told me about reading those papers that first day. As it slowly dawned on her what the issue was, she said that what came to her about her first case wasn't a question, but more of an initial reaction—*Oh my God, this lawyer wants to kill someone.*

For my part, I continued to try to figure out what to do with the Missouri living will statute. Despite the arguments made in our petition, the analysis in the memo from General Counsel Rod Northcutt to Don Lamkins worried me: "Dehydration and starvation are not termed as natural death and it will, in my opinion, take a very strong argument to persuade a Missouri court to go this far."

What if Northcutt was right? I dug for answers. Where did living wills come from, who first thought them up, how did Missouri adopt its law, and why did it look different from the laws in other states? I searched for any written legislative history, talked to Missouri senators to learn about their discussions on the law, researched the genesis of other state laws, and generally tried to dissect the statute as thoroughly as I could. I did not like what I found.

The Missouri legislature adopted the living will law in 1985, just two years before we filed the lawsuit, but two years after Nancy's accident. The legislature began with a model law drafted in the late 1970s by the National Conference of Commissioners on Uniform State Laws, a federally funded group of scholars, lawyers, and other experts, with the mission of drafting model bills for states to adopt in the hopes of making state laws more uniform. When the draft model bill reached Missouri, however, it faced major alteration.

Nationally, the Catholic Church opposed living will laws, believing that they cheapened life. The Missouri Catholic Conference was a strong force in state politics, and it lobbied the legislature aggressively, attempting to limit the applicability of the proposed living will law. In the end, their lobbying succeeded. The legislature defined "terminal illness" far more narrowly than the uniform law, limiting the people who could use the Missouri law. And it added language to emphasize its legislative desire to protect life: "This law does not condone, authorize, or approve mercy killing or euthanasia nor permit any affirmative or deliberate act or omission to shorten or end life."

Worst of all for our case, the legislature made clear that "any procedure to provide nutrition or hydration" was not considered medical treatment. Since it wasn't medical treatment, a person could not use a Missouri living will to refuse food and water provided through a tube—the exact medical treatment our lawsuit would seek to withdraw.

Joe and I talked many times about how a law that didn't even exist at the time of Nancy's accident could make our case more difficult. I explained, using Joe as the example. I told him that he could write out a living will in the fall of 1987, which met all of the requirements of the Missouri statute. It would state that in the event he fell terminally ill (defined in Missouri as a person about to die within a short time, whether or not doctors deployed life-prolonging medical treatment), he would want life-prolonging treatments, like a respirator, withdrawn. A doctor could comply with such a request by a family member brandishing that living will, and the law would protect that doctor from liability for the act of turning off the respirator.

I told Joe that he could also execute a document that stated: "In the event I lapse into a persistent vegetative state, I want my feeding tube removed." Such a document would *not* meet the requirements of the new living will law, and a doctor removing the tube in compliance with the document would not receive the protection the doctor enjoyed when honoring a statutory living will. The document itself, however, might well be valid—Joe could have a federal constitutional right to insist that doctors remove his feeding tube—or not. But the narrow Missouri living will law did not resolve that question.

What the living will law did, unfortunately for our lawsuit, was provide evidence of the public policy of Missouri as announced by the state legislature. The narrowing of the uniform bill by the Missouri legislature suggested a public policy weighted in favor of the preservation of life. In a case like Nancy's, where no written evidence of her wishes existed, a court could reasonably choose to err on the side of caution, and life, which was the course the Missouri legislature had appeared to take. No question, Northcutt had his point.

So, the living will law loomed as a roadblock, but roadblocks pop up in all lawsuits. When answers are clear, people solve their problems without lawyers. Part of any lawsuit is maximizing the good information and downplaying the bad. To do that, the lawyer simply needs to learn as much as possible about the facts and law of a case. Despite the hurdle of the living will law, we continued on.

Another issue in our case was figuring out where to begin our time line for the presentation of medical evidence to Judge Teel. The details of Nancy's accident hardly seemed important beyond the information necessary to the final diagnosis. Already more than four years after the accident, why did it matter how she came to that pass? We weren't trying to blame anyone for the accident or even tell how it happened. We needed to convince Judge Teel of three things only: that Nancy was in a persistent vegetative state without hope of recovery; that she wouldn't want medical treatment, given her condition; and that it was ethically and legally appropriate to withdraw her feeding tube.

The week after filing our petition, I received a written order from Judge Teel naming two Carthage lawyers, David Mouton and Thad McCanse, as the *guardians ad litem* for Nancy. Under most probate codes, including Missouri's, the probate judge has the power to appoint a separate advocate, typically a lawyer, to represent the interest of the incapacitated person when a disputed question is going to come up in court.

That appointment does not mean that the existing guardians (Joe and Joyce in our case) are failing to represent the interest of the ward of the court (Nancy). The *guardian ad litem,* or GAL, serves as a further protection for the ward, and as an aid to the court in the presentation of the case. The sole charge for the GAL is to protect the interests of the ward. A GAL thus often inquires into the motives of guardians making a decision—in our case, the motives of Joe and Joyce Cruzan, who were trying to stop life support for their daughter.

Mouton and McCanse were lawyers with the Carthage law firm of Flanigan, McCanse & Lasley. Their law office sat on the southeast corner of the town square. The glass front door to the office opened directly onto the sidewalk around the square, where the courthouse stood tall in the center, just across the street. Judge Teel had warned Mouton weeks before that he was considering the appointment and asked if Mouton was willing to take it on.

The judge also talked with a senior partner in Mouton's firm,

Thad McCanse, about representing Nancy. The American College of Trial Lawyers had admitted McCanse in 1977—such membership is the highest honor a trial lawyer can achieve in this country. The judge knew that the last thing McCanse needed was more work—McCanse represented St. John's Regional Medical Center, the largest hospital in the area, as well as other blue-chip corporate clients, and had long since handed court appointments like this one down to junior lawyers. But Judge Teel persuaded him to take Nancy Cruzan's case. Not only did the judge stress the importance of the case for the medical field, McCanse's area of expertise, but he also appealed to McCanse's mentoring side—he could hardly send his new associate into such a battle alone. Judge Teel enticed him with the battle itself—the attorney general of the state on one side, one of the largest and most powerful law firms in the state on the other, and all of it taking place right outside of McCanse's office door.

"A shame to miss a courtroom opportunity like that," the judge had said to McCanse one evening as the two stood outside the courthouse. In the end, Thad McCanse said yes.

After I received the judge's order, I phoned Walter Williams in Joplin and asked him what he knew about McCanse and Mouton. Williams had represented the Cruzans in Nancy's divorce and throughout the guardianship, and he had agreed to help me with this case, too. Walt told me what he knew about McCanse and Mouton, which was all positive. He added one new angle: These lawyers likely would have close personal relationships with the judge, sharing the same lunch spots, knowing each other's kids and friends—typical deep-seated small-town relationships. When Walt Williams and I finished our conversation, I phoned McCanse.

Thad McCanse was immediately likable, and we talked for a long time on that first phone call. I told him what I knew, and offered to send him whatever he needed. We also compared calendars and talked about timing. The state's answer to our petition was due just before Thanksgiving. The judge had told me that he would expedite the trial if we asked. I told McCanse that Rod Northcutt had said we could simply spend a day interviewing the doctors and nurses at MRC, and that I would make whatever time McCanse needed for talking with the Cruzans. If any party wanted experts on ethics or religion, they could figure that out soon, and each side could make them available as well.

We looked at dates in December for a one- or two-day trial.

In early November, Thad McCanse spoke for the first time to Rod Northcutt. Northcutt gave him the name of the assistant attorney general who would take the lead in the case, Bob Presson. Northcutt also told McCanse that he didn't think a December trial date was realistic. Presson had just taken on the case and had significant work to do to get up to speed; Northcutt also said that there might be some discovery to do. I phoned Bob Presson, and he confirmed that December was indeed unlikely.

In addition, the attorney general was trying to figure out how to deal with a motion filed by WGBH (the public television station in Boston sponsoring the Betsey Arledge documentary) to film the entire trial. McCanse and I had consented to the request and moved on to other issues. But the motion raised more difficult questions for the attorney general and Department of Health, and meetings and decisions from Jefferson City were still in the offing.

As November wore on, the possibility of a December trial grew more remote. Just before Thanksgiving, it disappeared. On the day after the state's answer to our petition was due, a large package arrived from the attorney general's office. Tammi Davis, my secretary, pulled it from the mail and walked into my office. I sliced open the envelope and looked with anticipation to see the state's response to our theories in their answer. I had to look no further than the title of the thick document. "Answer" did not appear at the top—"Motion to Dismiss" did. It was signed by William L. Webster, Attorney General; Robert Presson, Assistant Attorney General; and Robert Northcutt, General Counsel of the Department of Health.

I sank back in my chair, flipping through the pages and arguments, which said that there was no legal or ethical basis for this action, and that the living will law required the court to throw the case out immediately. The papers even suggested that we had improper venue, a lawyer's way of saying, "You bumblers didn't even pick the right courthouse." The attorney general said we needed to move the case to Jefferson City, the state capital of Missouri.

I took the elevator down and headed outside for a walk to try to cool down and clear my head. The perfect Indian summer day was wasted on me. *Friendly lawsuit? Just need to know what the rules are? We feel for this family?* I grabbed a soda at the convenience store right around the corner and headed back to my office. The walk only fueled my agitation. I called Thad McCanse, and he chuckled as I expressed my anger at the motion—it felt like a sort of gentle pat on the head over the telephone.

"I don't think Judge Teel will be inclined to grant a motion like this," he said. I didn't understand just yet how well McCanse knew his friend Judge Teel. At that point, I should have gone back to the preparing the case, but I didn't. I hung up the phone, dialed again, and waited on the line with a mixture of nervousness and still-bubbling anger as the secretary tried to track down Rod Northcutt to take my call.

"Hi, Bill." His tone signaled that he knew the rules had changed.

"Rod, where in the world did our 'friendly suit' go?" I asked. He tried to explain that these were just technical defenses that needed to be raised, and so on. When he finished, I used the response I had prepared in the convenience store.

"Fine," I said. "You're dismissed. I don't think we need the state for this probate trial, and if you don't want to take part, it's okay with me."

Northcutt stammered. "Bill, I'm not sure that's what we want," he said.

"When you file a motion to dismiss, isn't getting your client dismissed what you want?" I asked.

I heard Northcutt exhale. "I'm not sure what we want," he said. "I'm not completely in charge of this thing anymore."

We hung up. It was starting to look like this helping-people business wasn't going to be easy.

As December began, it grew obvious that we were not going to have a trial that month. Assistant Attorney General Bob Presson, now clearly in charge of the case for Missouri, consented to jurisdiction before Judge Teel, although he persisted with efforts to dismiss. Thad McCanse convinced me that such a motion was the last thing we needed to worry about with Judge Teel. On New Year's Eve, the judge held a status hearing over the phone. He set the trial to start on March 9, 1988, set a pretrial briefing schedule, and a schedule for discovery and depositions. Joe, Joyce, and Chris would be deposed first, on January 21. The judge talked about the issues for the trial, and the discussion from all parties suggested that it would confront a single issue head-on—the ethics and legality of removing a feeding tube from a young woman who was permanently unconscious, in a persistent vegetative state. When Bob Presson raised the question of the motion to dismiss, the judge said it was under advisement.

That day, I wrote Joe summarizing the conference with the judge, the dates for trial, depositions, and our responses to written discovery. The judge had made it clear that he would not move this trial; we would begin on March 9. I closed my final letter of 1987 to Joe with this sentence: "I truly hope this New Year will see a resolution of this matter for you." At that point, resolution of the legal battle in 1988 seemed possible. But "resolution of this matter" for Joe? That, as I would learn later, was a different matter.

CHAPTER 14

EXPERT WITNESS

Shortly after David Mouton and Thad McCanse were appointed to the case, I agreed with McCanse on a plan to divvy up the investigative work. He and Mouton would take on parts of the fact investigation—the accident; police, paramedics, and nurses; Paul Davis and his family; and Nancy's friends. I would concentrate on the doctors, medical testimony, potential expert witnesses in medicine and ethics, and the testimony of the Cruzan family. We agreed to share whatever we found.

In the cases I'd read from other states, those opposed to removing life support had nearly always disputed the medical condition of the accident victim. Rod Northcutt had said they understood that Nancy was in a vegetative state and that the trial would seek to answer the ethical question of removing a feeding tube. Whether they agreed or not, our side carried the burden of proving Nancy's medical condition. And without that proof at the base, our entire case would fall apart.

All of the ethical guidelines for doctors that I'd found allowed removal of a feeding tube from a patient reliably diagnosed as being in a persistent vegetative state—that is, their eyes were open, but they were permanently unconscious, with no awareness of the world around them, and no hope of regaining that awareness. In the handful of lawsuits from other states, opponents had tried to describe the patient as slightly outside the definition of persistent vegetative state (PVS)—"with some awareness." The ethical guidelines did not address such situations.

This apparently slight distinction was actually huge. Doctors and families found stopping treatment for a permanently unconscious patient extremely difficult. But a patient who retained at least some consciousness opened doctors to the charges made by opposition groups: These were simply handicapped people about whom the doctor no longer cared, or what Nazi doctors called "ein lebensunwerten leben," translated as "a life not worth living." No doctor wanted their medical practice compared to Auschwitz.

Without a finding of PVS, the ethical guidelines would not support the Cruzans' decision. A review of Nancy's medical records, however, suggested that we should have little trouble proving her condition. Five doctors had diagnosed Nancy as being in a persistent vegetative state, the hundreds of pages of medical notes contained no record of any interaction with the world, and in all of these years, her family had seen no communication from Nancy. Most of what I'd read suggested that after a couple of months, the diagnosis of persistent vegetative state wasn't going to change. As of January 11, 1988, Nancy had been in a persistent vegetative state for five years.

We organized and segregated the key doctors' reports in the initial workup of the case, including that of Dr. Hish Majzoub and Dr. Saad Al-Shatir (from Nancy's first hospitalizations); Dr. George Wong, a neurologist from Springfield, Missouri, who consulted with MRC; and Dr. Davis, her main attending doctor at MRC. All except Dr. Davis had clearly stated his opinion in the medical records that Nancy's diagnosis was persistent vegetative state. Although Dr. Davis hadn't made a conclusive diagnosis, his boss, Dr. Anita Isaac (medical director for MRC), *had*, in a letter to the Cruzans in September of 1986. That testimony looked solid.

Still, there were some loose ends. A medical record of a recent EEG done on Nancy stated: "This tracing shows the present [*sic*] of cerebral activity, and is probably within normal limits." How could that be after all of the abnormal EEGs, and what did it mean? Was Nancy's brain getting better? I needed to learn more. The only other tests we had were old—for instance, Nancy hadn't had a CT scan done for a couple of years. We needed current data.

In addition, I wanted to find an expert witness—ideally, one who would testify for free. Shook, Hardy had agreed to donate my time and part of the out-of-pocket expenses for the case. Pat McLarney, the managing partner at Shook made it clear that I should do whatever it took to handle the case properly. Still, I didn't want to be seen as a wild spender on a pro bono case, hiring expensive (and perhaps unnecessary) experts. The ACLU of Kansas City and Western Missouri and three groups based in New York—the national ACLU, the Society for the Right to Die, and Concern for Dying—had all agreed to help pay expenses. Yet these were not-for-profit organizations, which by definition meant that they were always out in the marketplace raising money. I didn't want to spend any of their funds without clear need, either.

Fenella Rouse, the executive director of the Society for the Right to Die, and I talked just before Christmas of 1987. She told me about the doctors who had testified in earlier trials in other states. Each of the doctors we discussed came from the East Coast. Regardless of their credentials, I had reservations about bringing a New Yorker in to lecture a judge in southern Missouri. The famous *New Yorker* magazine cover picturing the distorted map of the United States cut both ways; the opinions of experts who lived on the East Coast might carry less weight with a judge who had lived his whole life in the Midwestern "wasteland" pictured on that cover.

Then Rouse started telling me about a doctor from Minnesota. The more she talked, the better the guy sounded: military background, which Judge Teel would appreciate; trained in Illinois, which at least was next to Missouri; chairman of the ethics committee of the American Academy of Neurology; a consultant to President Reagan's commission on issues of medical ethics; one of the early writers on the specific topics of diagnosis of PVS and the ethical implications of removing medical treatment from such patients; and articulate, according to Rouse.

"Sounds perfect," I said. "Will he do this for free?"

Rouse laughed. She said she didn't know, but had found him approachable in the past. I now had five or six potential experts and their phone numbers on my yellow pad, and I wrote the number she gave me for the doctor from Minnesota at the top of the list.

I called Dr. Ronald Cranford that day. After about three "Dr. Cranford"s, he said, "Call me Ron." That was encouraging. As I laid out the facts, he began to tell me about the history of the persistent vegetative state. Before we went down that road, I figured I needed to tell him directly about his prospects. "You should know that there really isn't any money to hire an expert. I'm donating my time, and I need to be scouting around for a doctor who can possibly do the same," I said, and held my breath.

Dr. Cranford didn't hesitate. "Bill, I'm happy to do it, as long as I can get my basic out-of-pocket expenses paid," he said. Dr. Cranford went on to explain the apparently inconsistent EEG report, told me of his work on the President's Commission and with the American Academy of Neurology, confirmed the need for a current CT scan, talked about other cases, told me how the diagnosis of PVS is made clinically, and described cases found in the literature of apparent recovery that weren't really recoveries at all. I couldn't write fast enough to capture the full lesson I was receiving.

We also talked at length about the ethics of removing Nancy's feeding tube, as well as the positions of various medical groups on the issue. His enthusiasm buoyed me; on that first call, we talked for almost an hour. We ended the conversation with commitments to FedEx key information to each other: the medical records from my side; qualifications, articles, medical society position papers, and previous deposition transcripts from him. We agreed to talk again soon. A smile spread across my face as I hung up the phone. Often in litigation, a lawyer struggles to find any expert at all to take his case. It looked to me like the home team had just hit the ball out of the park.

CHAPTER 15

UNDER OATH

The glass door emblazoned with "Flanigan, McCanse & Lasley" opened directly from the sidewalk into a large room where a couple of secretaries did double duty as receptionists. At the back of this work area was a long hallway, lined on both sides by lawyers' offices. The hallway led into the firm's library, which also served as its conference room. The library was a massive, magnificent old room. The ceiling was almost 15 feet high, and the room smelled faintly of old books. Its walls were covered with antique barrister bookcases (the ones with the individual glass fronts for each shelf), which stretched ten feet tall all around. Each case was filled with law books. At the center of the room, on top of a red Oriental rug, sat a beautiful old oak conference table.

I arrived early on January 21,1988, the day that the state would take the Cruzans' depositions. Although we'd talked often by phone, I met Thad McCanse for the first time that morning. With his unruly, bushy white eyebrows and twinkling smile, he was as likable in person as he'd seemed over the phone. We sat in his office and talked while we waited for the others. As ten o'clock approached, the office started to fill up. Betsey Arledge and her film crew (Bill McMillan and Jim Astrausky) came in, and I introduced them around.

Chris, Joe, and Joyce arrived, along with Mel White, Chris's husband, who had taken time off from work that morning so that he could support his wife. Walt Williams, my co-counsel from Joplin, also came in about then. The sheer number of people turned the normal routine of the small law office on its head—the scene had started to resemble a crowded movie set.

The day before, the Cruzans and I had prepared for the depositions sitting around their dining-room table. Prior to that session, Joe and I had talked about his deposition many times on the phone—still, he felt unprepared. He'd recently watched a television program about tobacco litigation. Although he couldn't remember what the program was, he clearly remembered the image they showed of a deposition—a grueling examination by several lawyers that stretched over days until the witness, no matter how well prepared, faltered.

The fear of a slipup in his own deposition hadn't left him since. I tried over the phone, and again across his dining-room table, to dispel that image of a deposition. Despite my initial unhappiness with the motion to dismiss, my dealings with assistant attorney general Bob Presson to date had led me to believe that he would treat the Cruzans in a professional manner.

As we sat around the Cruzans' table, I began by again explaining the basics of the process. The deposition starts with an oath, and the court reporter takes down every word anybody in the room utters. Dress nicely, be courteous, show no anger, keep answers short, tell the truth—routine stuff for lawyers who spend much of their time in depositions, but a whole new world of stress for the witness being deposed for the first time. The Cruzans and I talked about our themes and the chance of making a good impression on these state officials—after all, the family was really only telling the story of their life, something they knew better than anyone. It would be almost impossible to "make a mistake" here.

But Joe wanted to anticipate as many potential questions as he could, and to try to memorize the answers. I told him that such an approach was exactly the wrong way to practice for his deposition, and I tried to get him to focus on the broad themes of the case. We did do some mock question-and-answers around the table, and Joe wrote his answers down despite my counsel. It was clear to me after a couple of hours that no three people in the world could convey love, love lost, and human pain more convincingly than the father, mother, and sister of

Nancy Cruzan. I told them so, urged them to sleep well, and headed to my motel.

No Cruzan slept much that night. Chris sat up all night in the rocking chair in her living room; Joe rose just after one in the morning and filled several more pages of his yellow pad with questions and potential answers; and Joyce lay in bed worrying about them both. So much for my advice.

❧   ❧   ❧

On January 21, the Cruzans entered the front door of Thad's office. Joyce and Chris each wore blue dresses; Joe wore a tan sports jacket, brown slacks, and tie; dark circles ringed his eyes. The family nearly marched toward me.

"I've got some more questions," Joe said, holding his pad. He looked terrified. Thad let Walt Williams and me use his office, and we spent about ten minutes squeezed in there. I mostly tried to convince Joe that he did know all of the answers, and I attempted to ease his tension. I could tell that that was not going to happen, so it was better to just start.

I stood and said, "You guys are ready to go. Let's do it," and walked toward the library. Mel put his arm around Chris's shoulder as they accompanied me.

Bob Presson and Rod Northcutt had entered the library while we were in Thad's office, and we fumbled through an awkward scene where a large group of people tries to meet and shake hands with one another all at once and then find seats. The PBS cameraman backed out of the room and shot a picture of the door closing on him—the attorney general's office had refused to allow PBS to film the depositions. I settled into my seat next to Chris and nodded to Don Holliday, the court reporter.

Holliday smiled, raised his right hand, and asked Chris, "Do you swear that the testimony you are about to give in this matter is the truth, the whole truth, and nothing but the truth, so help you God?"

Chris's body looked like a fine, taut thread about to snap, and her hand shook as she held it in the air. I thought she could burst into tears at any moment. Her husband moved his chair close to hers, and the words "I do" squeaked from her lips.

Across the table, Bob Presson smiled at Chris. This was the first meeting between the Cruzans and Presson and Northcutt. I hadn't met Presson before, either. He had strands of black hair, a small dark moustache, and he wore glasses. He wore conservative business attire—navy sports jacket, blue-and-white striped button-down shirt, solid navy tie, and gray slacks. Presson appeared to understand the tension, so he began with background questions for Chris, such as her name, age, address, and so on. The morning started to ease into a rhythm. Depositions typically begin this way, although there's no such requirement.

For years, Shook, Hardy had represented the pharmaceutical manufacturer Eli Lilly. When I arrived at the firm, I had the chance to work on cases for Lilly involving the infant vaccine DPT. Several of those cases were in Denver, and we'd gone to Wyoming to take some depositions. During a break, one of the attorneys there told a story about Gerry Spence—the well-known trial lawyer who represented people such as Karen Silkwood—now a television commentator and author. According to this attorney, Spence had started off the deposition of a doctor in a medical malpractice case by staring down at the physician over the top of his half-glasses, his accusatory drawl coming as an attack: "Doctor, what is your defense for killing my client?" A lot of lawyer objections ensued, and the deposition ultimately continued, but Spence had thrown the doctor off his stride for the day, and possibly for the foreseeable future.

No such dramatics took place in the Cruzan depositions. Still, Bob Presson was only about ten minutes into the questioning before all of the stress came bubbling to the surface. Tears filled Chris's eyes as she tried to tell Presson about her family's decision to stop all medical treatment for her sister, and we took a short break. When we started again, most of Presson's examination focused on conversations Chris had had with Nancy about the deaths of relatives. After Presson finished, Thad McCanse questioned Chris about Nancy's medical condition and about growing up together. Then Presson reexamined Chris. The entire process, including the break, only took about 45 minutes. The short deposition ended with a discussion of how Chris might react if they won the lawsuit.

"What about you, personally?" Presson asked. "How do you think you would react if the petition was granted?"

"With very mixed emotions. I love her, and no matter—," Chris stopped, then tried again. "At some point in time, she will die, as we all will, and it will be sad, but it will be somewhat tempered by the fact that she doesn't have to go through this anymore. But I have, within myself, memories to draw upon, those things."

"You say you have mixed emotions. To a certain extent, would you be sad if it were granted?"

"I would be sad when she died," Chris answered, and the tears came again.

We took our second break of the morning. Presson was finished with Chris; Joe was next. Chris walked Mel outside so he could go to work. Even today she remembers the feeling of life as she opened the front door of Flanigan, McCanse & Lasley and stepped out into the unseasonably mild, bright January day. She took a long, deep breath of fresh air, felt the brilliant sunshine, and said a silent prayer that she would never, ever, have to be deposed again.

We reassembled in the library, fortified with fresh coffee. The air had taken on a different feel. Joe Cruzan sat, hands clasped tightly, gazing directly at Bob Presson. The night with little sleep, coupled with his obsession over anticipating all of the questions and memorizing the best answers, hadn't exactly left Joe in the well-rested, relaxed state a lawyer wants for his witness.

What's more, Joe was meeting these state officials for the first time. Layered on top of his fatigue and obsession was the anger that percolated inside him because he had to go to court at all. Joe had been the mayor of Carterville at about the time that Attorney General Bill Webster was attending nearby Carthage High. "What does a young man like Bill Webster know about the decisions I have to make?" Joe would ask rhetorically.

Moreover, it incensed Joe that Webster wasn't there asking the questions himself. He felt slighted that he had to deal with an assistant. Joe said more than once that "these people" had no business interfering with his family, taking him off work for a day, asking questions about the daughter he'd raised—a woman Webster, Presson, or Northcutt had never even met. I read much of this message in the posture Joe struck—chin out, glaring across the table at Presson and Northcutt. This deposition would take longer.

Within the first minute, Bob Presson started into the same substantive issue with which he began Chris's deposition. "I'd like to go back to before the time the suit was filed and go through the process of how it was arrived at to file this suit," Presson began. "I assume there were discussions with various people. Can you tell me who you might have discussed the matter with, before the decision was reached?"

Joe could have answered this question in a lot of different ways: He could have talked about family meetings, Barbara Carter, Fenella Rouse from the Society for the Right to Die, or others. Instead, he began by telling Presson of his phone call to Dr. Anne Bannon in St. Louis, the head of Doctors for Life. (After reading a *Time* magazine article on the right to die, Joe had tracked down some of the people quoted in the article.) I kept my attention on my yellow pad as Joe spoke, thinking, *Remember, short answers, don't argue.* One minute into the deposition, and he wanted to tell the state about taking on the right-to-lifers.

From the very start, Joe couldn't understand why the right-to-life movement had any interest in his case. He often said, "I just see no parallels with abortion." To Joe, abortion took a potential life with a full future ahead of it and, undoubtedly, if the fetus had the capacity to choose, it would choose to continue. Joe saw Nancy's case as just the opposite. All he knew about how she lived suggested that she would want medical treatment stopped once the hope of recovery was gone. In her case, such hope was long gone.

And, contrary to a fetus, Nancy's life had no potential in Joe's mind. She was down to two narrow options, both bad. She could spend the rest of her days in a sterile hospital room, tended by strangers, hooked up to a feeding machine—unaware, unconscious, stiff, bloated, drooling, and curled in a fetal position (some doctors estimated she could live 30 years or more with aggressive care). Or her family could remove the feeding tube and she would die. Grim choices. The anoxia had taken the part of Nancy's brain that could *live.* Joe saw no comparison with a fetus that held the potential for life. He explained his theory to right-to-life advocates anytime he had the chance.

So, in answer to Bob Presson's question about the advice he'd sought to make the decision, Joe talked about a conversation with the president of Doctors for Life. According to Joe, Dr. Bannon's basic point in the article was that families of people in comas or PVS just wanted to be rid of the expense and trauma after a while. They couldn't take it anymore, so they sought to stop treatment. Joe said that he and Dr. Bannon had talked for 27 minutes, and by the end of the conversation, while Dr. Bannon said she still opposed the Cruzans' request for professional reasons, she admitted to Joe that she "would not want to live in a situation" like Nancy's. Joe counted that a victory.

My initial apprehension at hearing Dr. Bannon's name began to subside the more Joe talked. In fact, as the deposition continued, it grew clear that he was following the rules—his answers came out short and to the point, often "Yes" and "No." He kept his anger bottled up. The deposition was going fine. Presson spent much of the time trying to determine exactly how the family came to the decision to stop Nancy's medical treatment. Joe described literature he'd read, phone calls he'd made, and doctors and counselors he'd consulted. Although he believed that his family alone should make the decision about Nancy, he wanted to learn as much as possible to help in the decision-making process. The variety of his contacts was fascinating.

In addition to Dr. Bannon, the Lairds, Mrs. Brophy, and the Quinlans, Joe told of phone calls he'd made around the country. For example, he'd talked to Father Kevin O'Rourke at St. Louis University on the topic of medical ethics. Father O'Rourke had told Joe that if the hospital wouldn't do as the family requested, they should simply sue for malpractice (another possible strategy). Joe talked to the Missouri Head Injury Association; to Robert Veatch at Georgetown University; to Barbara Carter; to Fenella Rouse; to the family support group at MRC; and to countless doctors. As the list grew, it became clear that Joe Cruzan and his family had agonized over this decision.

Presson asked Joe to talk about Nancy. Joe had answered all of Bob Presson's questions about the Cruzans' research and their decision-making process in a straightforward, almost businesslike way. But as they talked more about Nancy, Joe's eyes misted over as he fought for control of his emotions. The lawyers for the other side watched him closely. "I hope you can appreciate how difficult it is to put into words what Nancy was," Joe said. "She was—and Christy might not like this—but Nancy was mainly my favorite." Chris's eyes glistened, and Joe turned his face to the ceiling.

Near the end of the deposition, Presson asked Joe, as he had Chris, how Joe might react if they won the lawsuit. Joe told Presson that Nancy had died the night of the accident: "I don't know that *died* is the right word, but she's been gone since the night of the accident." The tears came then, and Joe's deposition finished not long after that point.

Joyce, quiet by nature and smart about people, took the coaching to heart and volunteered nothing; consequently, her deposition started and ended very quickly. I packed up my large black briefcase, and the Cruzans and I left the building as quickly as we could. I sensed that they needed escape, and so did I. Outside in the bright sunshine, I shook Joe's viselike hand, and gave a quick hug to Joyce and Chris.

"You guys did a great job," I said. All three gave me the "I'm-really-glad-that's-over" smile, and we said goodbye. I had to hurry back to Kansas City for a case involving the crash of a small airplane, set for trial the week of February 21, a month away. I grabbed dinner at the McDonald's drive-through in Carthage and headed north on Highway 71. I thought our day had gone well—good answers, no major problems. I moved on to thinking about the plane-crash case.

Bob Presson filmed an interview with Betsey Arledge at the end of that long day. In the interview, he stated the position of the state of Missouri: "The bottom line is, she is certainly alive now. We have a legal definition of death in the state of Missouri, and she does not meet any of those. On the other hand, the relief they have asked for in their petition would certainly lead to her death, and I think that in the simplest terms are the two major factors in the case. She is alive now, and what they are asking for would lead to her death." Presson looked at the camera and stopped. There was nothing more to say.

CHAPTER 16

THE STATE EXPERT

On Saturday, February 27, I woke early and headed to the office. The previous afternoon, at the end of the airplane-crash trial, I sat and listened to the jury foreman first read the verdict against my client for actual damages, then the second verdict for punitive damages. We'd managed to keep the damages low and had a shot at having the punitive-damage verdict tossed out in post-trial motions. Still, nothing felt good about that verdict—we'd lost.

I arrived around 7 A.M. Shook, Hardy had moved into eight floors of new office space the weekend before, and despite the new marble and dark wood, the offices still looked a mess, with the hallways and reception areas filled with boxes. My own office, following a week of inattention, was a shambles, too. My desk had one high stack of paper for the Eli Lilly cases, one stack of junk mail, one stack for all other cases, and one stack for *Cruzan*. Remnants of the trial just finished were strewn everywhere. I grabbed a mug of coffee and came back to my office, surveying the mountains of paper on my desk and the files stacked on the floor, tables, and shelves.

Since the first of the year, I'd lost about ten pounds off a 6'1" frame that didn't need to lose any weight. I was beat already, and now I had less than two weeks to prepare for the *Cruzan* trial. Self-pity may have breathed into the room, but it didn't linger. My visits with the Cruzans had already given me a great gift—the understanding that I had no right, ever, to feel sorry for myself. I got to work, and, one by one, shrank the stacks.

Friday, March 4, 1987

Six days later, I headed east across I-70 to the University of Missouri Medical Center in Columbia for the deposition of Dr. James Dexter, the expert witness the state had recently named. The state's written disclosure stated that the doctor would testify about PVS, its treatment, and the ethics of removal of medical treatment for a PVS patient. Rod Northcutt told me on the phone that Dexter would testify that it's never ethically appropriate to remove food and water from a patient, however it's supplied.

The drive to Columbia from Kansas City is about two hours, and in my mind, I tried to play out all of the different ethical scenarios I might talk about with Dr. Dexter, as well as the different turns his deposition might take. Once I found the doctor's office, a secretary led me to a conference room. Dr. Dexter, Rod Northcutt, Bob Presson, and the court reporter were already there, talking. Thad McCanse had decided not to travel to this deposition and asked that we just send him the transcript.

Typically, a lawyer goes into a deposition with an outline of some sort, copies of documents, and a strategy—or at least a couple of key points to establish. The amount and detail of preparation usually follows "the Shuttle Rule." As a new lawyer in the early '80s, I traveled between the Davis Polk offices in New York and Washington on the Eastern Airlines hourly shuttle. "The Shuttle Rule" came from one of the flight attendants on that route, describing how she categorized the business travelers on the shuttle: A young lawyer typically struggled onboard carrying a couple of heavy litigation bags; a corporate middle manager might tote a three-inch briefcase; those who mattered—and won the attention of the flight attendants—carried only a folder. The most powerful might just carry a used envelope on which to make notes with an expensive pen. That was "the Shuttle Rule"—the more important you were, the less you needed to carry onboard.

New lawyers in their first depositions usually bring detailed outlines—the full bags of "the Shuttle Rule." Although I had by no means progressed to the slim-folder stage, by the time Dr. Dexter and I met, my deposition outlines no longer contained questions written out in full, such as, "You understand the oath you just swore to tell the whole truth is the same as if a judge had sworn you in a courtroom, don't you, sir?"

With Dr. Dexter, I basically wanted to learn about his ethical opinions and how he supported them. Fairly straightforward. The doctor had blocked out two hours that morning, and he was expensive ($200 an hour), so I wanted to finish my business quickly and turn off his meter.

Dr. Dexter was an affable man—short, with sandy brown hair flecked with gray, and a round face and nose. He wore a white doctor's coat. We began the standard way—no Gerry Spence surprises here. Dr. Dexter's work in neurology had focused on headache and sleep disorders. He'd decided not to take the test to achieve board certification in neurology, a chink in his armor and another advantage for us. He hadn't written on end-of-life, PVS, or ethical issues. He came to the case as a general neurologist, with credentials as the chair of the Department of Neurology at the University of Missouri, and that would count for something in a Carthage courthouse.

Northcutt's prediction of the testimony held true. Dr. Dexter testified that he had read "a whole stack of medical records" on Nancy, and in his medical opinion, this case involved a young woman in a PVS for five years, who was "unresponsive to her environment, with no evidence of cognitive capability." Dr. Dexter testified that anyone in a PVS for so long a period has essentially "no chance" of "ever having cognitive function." He said he hadn't talked with the nurses and had no intention of doing so.

"Do you plan to examine Nancy Cruzan prior to the trial?" I asked. "Do you feel you have a need to do that?"

"No, I don't think that I have a need to do that. I think that the question is not whether or not she is in a chronic vegetative state," Dexter said.

"What do you think the question is?"

"The question is whether or not anyone has the right to withhold her hydration or nutrition."

"And do you have an opinion on that?" I asked.

"Yes, I do."

"What is that opinion?"

"I do not think under the present law in the state of Missouri that we have the right to make the decision of withdrawing hydration and nutrition from this lady." Interestingly, Dr. Dexter began with the law, but not the living will law; rather, he mentioned his duty to report abuse and neglect to the Division of Family Services. He told me that removing Nancy's tube would be an incident of neglect, and that if he didn't report that neglect, he'd be committing a felony. I asked him if the law was the only basis for his belief that Nancy's artificial feeding could not be stopped. "I don't know of one that is any better, because I don't know about the rest of you guys," the doctor answered, "but I don't have any great desire to go to jail, nor do I have any great desire to become involved in a malpractice based upon neglect."

"I understand that, but is that the only basis, or do you have some ethical basis, medical ethical basis, under which you think it is inappropriate?"

"Do you want the hour lecture, the two-hour lecture, or the five-hour lecture?"

"Whatever you think is appropriate, Doctor." *So much for a quick deposition,* I thought. Dr. Dexter spent the next several minutes describing medical ethics, which he defined as the decision-making process between a doctor and his patient. Nancy's case, to him, had moved far outside the realm of medical ethics to some kind of societal ethic. Society had overrun the medical ethic of doctor-patient here—many ethics were now involved. Dr. Dexter named nursing ethics, hospital-administrator ethics, legal ethics, social-worker ethics, and family ethics.

This approach to medical ethics was new to me, and the doctor soon explained why: We were working from his own theory. He said, "So when you talk about medical ethics—and I tend to be an outsider on this one—I think that medical ethics, as we normally think of it, is dead, kaput, because medicine now has progressed to the point that it involves a whole lot more than just my ethic."

I told Dr. Dexter to assume for the purpose of my question that the law wouldn't cause him a problem—would his own personal ethic allow him to remove Nancy's feeding tube?

"Since I am over the age of 50, I would ask them to get another physician," he answered. "I don't go around playing God. I don't think that that is my personal right." Dr. Dexter's opinion was that if another doctor would be comfortable with the decision, then it would be up to him.

We ended the deposition discussing the guidelines from the American Medical Association (AMA). The Council on Ethical and Judicial Affairs of the AMA publishes a booklet titled *Current Opinions.*

First compiled in 1958, the *Opinions* are updated regularly. The AMA intends the *Opinions* to serve "as guides to responsible professional behavior, but they are not presented as the sole or only route to medical morality." Dr. Dexter took the admonition of this clause to heart—he did not necessarily put a lot of stock in the opinions of the AMA.

Section Two of the *Opinions* covers a wide range of complex issues under the prosaic title "Opinions on Social Policy Issues." The title is the only part of the section that isn't dramatic. Section 2.01 covers abortion; 2.02, the abuse of children, elderly persons, and others at risk; 2.03, the allocation of health resources; 2.04, artificial insemination; 2.05, artificial insemination by donor; 2.06, capital punishment. It goes on, covering such topics as fetal research, genetic counseling, genetic engineering, in-vitro fertilization, and organ donation.

By alphabetical quirk, the two sections that applied to Nancy's case came near the end of Section Two: 2.16, "Quality of Life"; and 2.18, "Withholding or Withdrawing Life-Prolonging Medical Treatment." Reading Section Two from start to finish made it obvious that doctors face a lot of difficult issues in their practice. What treatment to give or not give a patient forever banished to the persistent vegetative state was but one among many thorny questions.

Section 2.16, "Quality of Life," basically said that life must be cherished, and that decisions about treatment for a patient like Nancy must consider her best interest—not avoidance of burden for the family or society.

Section 2.18, "On Withholding and Withdrawing Treatment," was critically important to our case. Although it was lengthy, it boiled down to this key language: "Even if death is not imminent, but a patient's coma is beyond a doubt irreversible and there are adequate safeguards to confirm the accuracy of the diagnosis and with the concurrence of those who have responsibility for the care of the patient, it is not unethical to discontinue all means of life-prolonging medical treatment. Life-prolonging medical treatment includes medication and artificially or technologically supplied respiration, nutrition, or hydration."

Dr. Dexter and I went around and around on these sections without resolution. We ended the deposition with a hypothetical question: Assume a woman has been in a persistent vegetative state for more than five years and is being kept alive by means of a gastrostomy tube surgically implanted in her stomach. The evidence is clear that she wouldn't want the treatment continued. As the doctor, you have no legal liability whatsoever and can refer the case to no other doctor. Would you remove the tube at the family's request?

He answered that since he did not know if the patient could experience pain or not, he didn't believe starvation was the best way to go. Instead, he said, "It would be completely justified for me to use a bit of morphine, but under those circumstances only."

I stopped and took inventory. He agreed that Nancy was in a PVS, didn't plan to examine her, agreed that artificial feeding was medical treatment, didn't know whether or not PVS patients could feel pain, and had personal hesitation about withdrawing treatment because of the fear of pain. But if given a legal waiver with clear knowledge of the patient's wishes, he'd feel justified in taking the step of physician-assisted suicide. We didn't need him to go that far, so I called it a day and headed back to Kansas City.

CHAPTER 17

TRIAL BEGINS

Wednesday, March 9, was a brisk, sunny day that promised warmer days ahead. Attorney General Bill Webster moved from the morning sunshine and through the front door of the Jasper County courthouse. Handsome, with a fresh-scrubbed, boyish face, neatly combed black hair, and a belted trench coat, Webster looked at ease as he walked into the glow of the local television camera lights in the lobby. Joe Cruzan stood off by himself near a wall and watched General Webster approach.

Webster politely asked, "How are you?"

Joe glared back at him, not returning the greeting. Startled, Webster nodded and quickly moved past, pausing to shake hands with the two uniformed guards standing a few feet away. Webster's aide steered him to the stairs for the climb to the third floor, avoiding the awkward wait at the antique elevator with Joe Cruzan staring at him.

Webster appeared uncharacteristically flustered by the rude greeting on his entrance to the Carthage courthouse. Later he remarked about the irony that this emotionally charged trial, which could have landed in any of the 114 county courthouses in Missouri, had landed in his hometown—blocks from his alma mater, Carthage High, the paramedic a high school classmate, the judge a family friend. Bill Webster was coming home, and not for a holiday. Still five minutes before nine, Webster opened the doors on a full courtroom. As he walked to the front of the room, he greeted people with a handshake or a smile or by name.

Bob Presson and Rod Northcutt stood and welcomed him; then he made his way over to our table.

I hadn't slept much, waking around 5 A.M. to practice my opening statement in front of the mirror, trying to see if I could deliver it without looking at my notes, and pretending I was making eye contact with the judge. Kim Ross, my legal assistant, and I had arrived at the courthouse too early, and when we made it up to the third-floor courtroom, each pulling a stainless steel luggage cart loaded with full boxes of documents, we found the courtroom door still locked.

Now, hours later, here was the day's first big event: meeting the attorney general. Webster had not taken part in any of the pre-trial discovery or earlier hearings. Although we'd talked once on the phone, this was our first face-to-face meeting. Until he walked into the room, I hadn't really thought about him attending the trial; typically the assistant attorney general runs the trial and reports back to the capital only as necessary. Webster's presence suggested that he found our case important. We talked about my firm a bit, he asked about the Cruzans, said "Good luck," and walked back to the other side.

                           ❧   ❧   ❧

The Cruzans started their day early, with Betsey Arledge and the PBS film crew at the house to capture the nervous anticipation. Judge Teel had denied a motion by the lawyers for PBS to allow filming of the trial, so Arledge was going to film the before and after. By 7:30 A.M., Joyce and Chris were already standing in the kitchen in church clothes. Chris was next to the sink trying to stir her coffee. "Why am I shaking?" she asked. "I don't know why." Joyce moved to her daughter and hugged her gently from behind.

"I just hope we can get our point across, that we care enough," Chris said, looking out the window above the sink at the fresh dusting of late-season snow that would disappear quickly as the day warmed, her hands leaving the coffee and folding over her mother's hands on her waist.

Joyce backed away, and tried to calm her daughter. "We will," Joyce said. "We'll have today to just kind of sit back and watch."

Chris nodded, and stood quietly for a moment. Then she smiled. "She'd be armed and ready today," Chris said, talking about Nancy.

Joyce smiled, too. "I can just see her," she said, and let out a long sigh as the picture of a healthy Nancy seemed to play in her mind. "Walking in there like she owned the courtroom, just daring anybody to look cross-eyed at her." The image gave Chris a tiny laugh. Then mother and daughter stood quietly, drinking their coffee, still more than an hour to go before they had to leave for court.

By the time they reached the lobby of the courthouse, the Cruzans' anxiety had built to near fever pitch. Chris could not stop shaking, and the three stood huddled together in the lobby. Joe put his arm around Chris and asked, "What's the matter, babe?" The tension made his voice higher than normal.

Joyce patted her daughter's shoulder and said, "You'll be all right." Joyce unsnapped her purse and looked at Joe. "I tried to give her a Valium or some Xanax," she said. "I don't think a half a Xanax would hurt her. I've got Valium, too." The PBS camera turned away as Joyce peered into her purse, perhaps feeling that this exchange was too personal, and that filming any more might go a bit beyond what was necessary.

❧   ❧   ❧

The three Cruzans entered the courtroom a few minutes before nine and huddled up together near the front of the room. Earlier I'd gone downstairs to talk to them and answer any last-minute questions they might have while Joyce had a final cigarette. Now I just guided them to the bench immediately behind the bar that separated the gallery from the lawyers' tables. I took my seat next to Walt Williams and stared at the empty judge's bench, waiting.

We're in pretty good shape, I thought. Day One would start with opening statements, move to the witnesses of the accident, then jump right into the medical testimony, with Dr. Majzoub testifying briefly and Dr. Cranford likely taking up most of the afternoon. Day Two would be for family and friends. This first day in court would give the Cruzans a chance to see how the trial worked, and perhaps they would be able to relax a bit. We were ready, and had a good first day ahead. I looked behind me around the courtroom, filled with reporters, sketch artists, family, friends, and protestors. *We'd better be ready,* I thought.

A door in the front corner of the courtroom opened, and Judge Teel walked in. The bailiff stood, and the sound of nearly 100 people shuffling quickly to their feet filled the room. The judge said good morning and smiled down at Attorney General Webster, obviously pleased by his attendance. After a short conference at the bench to clear up preliminary issues, we returned to our places. The judge turned to me and said, "Mr. Colby."

I stood up and walked to the podium, carrying a yellow pad. Although my heart was racing with nervousness, I was excited and ready to go. I set the pad down, smiled up at the judge, and began. "Your Honor, we are going to try, over the next three days, to present this case to you—describe what happened in a straightforward, businesslike way in as much as we possibly can. But I need to tell you up front, we are dealing with something that is very emotional, and there are going to be some emotional times over the next three days. If Nancy Cruzan could come back today and help you decide this—she can't—if she could tell you one thing, she would say, 'Judge, stop this from happening to me.' The second thing she would tell you would be, 'Judge, stop this from happening to my family.'

"Once a week, sometimes twice a week, week after week, 52 weeks a year for the last five years, Joe Cruzan and Joyce Cruzan, their daughter Christy . . . have made the trek from Carterville up to the Missouri Rehabilitation Center in Mount Vernon to visit their sister and daughter, Nancy. As they get closer, the conversation in the car dies. They go into the hospital, up the elevator, up to the fourth floor, into Nancy's room, and in there, they find the shell of what was once their daughter and sister. They are helpless to do anything to help her without your help. They have no control. The people who love her most have absolutely no control over her life."

Five minutes into the case and already, in essence, I was throwing the Cruzans on the mercy of the court. Well, that was where we needed to be. I described Nancy's medical condition for the judge and summarized the medical, family, and ethics testimony to come. And I ventured into the law. Typically, opening statements lay out the facts a party will present at the trial. But sometimes in a bench trial (that is, a trial to a judge without a jury), the openings cover law, too. And in this corner of southwestern Missouri, an informal approach worked as long as it made sense to the judge. I wanted every opportunity to explain why the Missouri living will law didn't apply here. Neither McCanse nor Presson objected, so I went on.

I concluded by talking about Nancy's death, should Judge Teel rule in our favor: "The testimony you will hear about her death will be that it is a peaceful one, that a person in a persistent vegetative state by definition is incapable of experiencing pain, incapable of experiencing thirst, incapable of experiencing hunger. That's what happens to a person in a vegetative state. There is nothing left in their brain to experience these things. All they have is brain stem function, which controls their reflexes. That's all that's alive. Through these three days, the thing that we most hope we can show the court is that if Nancy could come back and talk to you, she would say, 'Your Honor, stop this from happening to me and my family.' It is not a step the court should take lightly. Certainly not a step that the family has taken lightly. They've thought long and hard. It's a difficult position for them to be in, but with the equitable powers of this court, it is the proper step to take. Thank you." I took a deep breath and went back to my seat.

Thad McCanse spoke next, as Nancy's *guardian ad litem* (GAL). He described the extensive fact investigation that he and David Mouton had undertaken, and what he saw as their role—not as an advocate necessarily in support of either party, but to protect Nancy's best interests. Much of what he said paralleled my opening, except in one troubling respect. McCanse suggested that those seeking to stop treatment should be required to meet a higher standard of proof—something called the "clear and convincing evidence standard."

Over the phone, I'd tried (unsuccessfully, it now turned out) to dissuade McCanse from taking this position. I thought our evidence was convincing and certainly clear. The clear and convincing evidence standard, however, is a specific term in the law—shelves of books are dedicated to defining it exactly. For the Cruzans, it meant that if Judge Teel followed this recommendation from McCanse, we'd have a much harder time winning the case. I didn't think the standard made sense for our case, so I intended to argue against it vigorously when the chance came.

When McCanse finished, the judge turned to the attorney general and said, "On behalf of respondent?" He looked from Webster to Bob Presson. Presson nodded, and the judge called him to the podium. So it looked as if we weren't going to have to try the case against the attorney general himself. That was good news.

Presson, understandably, began by trying to downplay the emotions involved in the case. He declared that the state would also offer evidence "regarding what her present condition is." MRC staff and Dr. Dexter would testify "regarding her reactions, her eyes, reflex reaction to pain, moans, facial expressions." Presson explained the state's version of the living will law as directly barring the request.

He concluded by asking Judge Teel how far he was willing to go. "I think this case will demonstrate and bring us face-to-face with our limitations of our knowledge in society and the limitations of our wisdom. If we are going to err, it should be on the error of caution in favor of life . . . I think we will all agree that if the Court grants the petition, Nancy Cruzan will die. And I think the question we have to ask and the Court will have to ask itself is: 'Are we going, as a society, to cause the death of an individual, not because of what they did, perhaps as in the case of a convicted murderer, but simply because of what they are?' Do we as a society want to begin making those judgments?"

Phrased differently, did Judge Teel truly want to be the one to start Missouri down the slippery slope of deciding that brain-damaged lives were not worth living? With that question hanging in the air, Bob Presson sat down.

In the months leading up to trial, I'd come to rely more and more on Thad McCanse's opinion. Between McCanse and my co-counsel, Walt Williams, I had two experienced, local views on the case. More important, it became clear to me that McCanse's position as the independent lawyer in the case would carry weight, and that the judge had great respect for him. We needed him to side with the Cruzans. And on the practical side, he was a seasoned trial lawyer, so to the extent he brought his skills to bear on our side, it had to help our case. Partly for that reason, we'd agreed that McCanse would open the trial, examining the witnesses with whom he and Dave Mouton had talked, the public officials at the accident scene. I thought that it would be good to start out with the judge seeing the proof put on by the Cruzan family and the GAL together, and told McCanse to take as much time as he needed.

McCanse called Robert L. Williams, the first paramedic on the accident scene (and the high school classmate of Attorney General Webster). McCanse walked Williams through the accident report and asked him to explain this entry at the bottom of the report: "MVA Code Blue, clinical save." Williams told McCanse that when he arrived at the accident scene that night, he hurried up to the state trooper, who told him that Nancy was dead. Williams explained how he and his colleagues went to work anyway, changing that diagnosis and saving Nancy—by inserting a tube down her windpipe, providing respiration through an Ambu bag, starting an IV line to transmit sodium bicarbonate directly to her heart muscle, performing chest compressions, hooking up the heart monitor, and suctioning to get the blood and mucus out of her lungs.

Williams also offered some bonus testimony for us. He'd known Nancy's husband, Paul Davis, and had seen Nancy several times over the years. He testified that she never showed any sign of responsiveness and that she didn't change from a visit shortly after the accident in 1983 to his last visit to MRC in 1987. This was yet another independent medical voice in support of the PVS diagnosis.

Bob Presson rose and spoke in a respectful voice to the paramedic. He questioned Williams generally about doing CPR, and tried to establish that Nancy's CPR went well, that in fact she'd started to breathe on her own in only one minute. The paramedic looked again at the report and explained that it had really taken three minutes. Still, Presson asked, wasn't such a quick recovery "unusual"?

"Well, it was—I don't want to use the term 'exciting,'" Williams said, "but it was very pleasurable to see such a spontaneous respiratory action within a short period of time of doing cardiopulmonary resuscitation, and it made us feel—my analysis of that time period says that we were being successful with this client—patient."

Next came Rick Maynard, the other paramedic in the ambulance with Williams. Maynard explained how they filled out the times on the reports. Records of calls to the dispatcher are exactly recorded by the dispatcher's clock; times in the field are estimates made by the paramedics when they sit down after all of the commotion is over and the patient is safely in the ER. On cross-examination, Presson asked only six questions, all geared to show that Maynard filled out a lot of reports and always did the best he could to be as accurate as possible.

To round out the preliminary testimony, McCanse had lined up all three Carthage firemen who were present at the accident scene. They waited in the hallway and came in one by one, in full dress uniform. Judge Teel had worked as a volunteer himself, and often had lunch at the fire station—he loved firefighters. The judge greeted each of the men warmly that morning, and at one point, he exchanged a smile with fireman Mike Lee, who told McCanse that he "was riding tailboard" that night.

McCanse asked for an explanation. "What do you mean by that? I'm not familiar with the term exactly." Then, smiling, he added, "I'm sure the judge is."

By the end of the testimony, we confirmed that Nancy had been in a horrible accident, and her car had traveled nearly the length of two football fields after it left the road. Nancy had been thrown 35 feet from the car before it flipped to a stop, upside down. And we knew that the times were not exact. The police report stated that the accident happened at 12:50 A.M., but that was an estimate. Fire Lieutenant Ed Nuse testified that when the firefighters had arrived at the scene, 1:12 A.M., according to their report, the paramedics at that point were still in the examination stage. Nancy was still "code blue." So Nancy may have gone without oxygen from 12:50 to 1:12 A.M.—22 minutes. If the accident happened earlier than the highway patrolman estimated, those 22 minutes could easily turn into 30 minutes without oxygen. Or more. What caused the accident—whether Nancy fell asleep, an animal crossed her path, or something else altogether—we would never learn.

❧   ❧   ❧

After a short recess, we reassembled, and it was my turn to question a witness. We'd spent the bulk of the morning establishing that Nancy had gone for some significant time without oxygen. Now it was time to find out exactly what that meant. Judge Teel nodded as he took his seat on the bench. "Mr. Colby, then," he said. I stood and called Dr. Hish Majzoub.

Dr. Majzoub hadn't treated Nancy for many years, but we'd decided to put him on first. Dr. Majzoub would offer the first medical opinion, in chronological sequence, about PVS. Walt Williams and Thad McCanse both felt that there was value in leading off with the testimony of a prominent local doctor, the first neurologist who treated Nancy, and someone who had no ties to either side.

Dr. Majzoub defined PVS and talked about its diagnosis and his significant experience with the condition. He said that he'd treated Nancy every day for six weeks after the accident and never again after that. I asked him what his prognosis for recovery from the vegetative state had been at that point, in the winter of 1983. He turned slightly to the judge and said, "I would say nil, sir."

Dr. Majzoub also explained to the judge what would happen with Nancy when a doctor removed the tube. "She will become what we call dehydrated, doesn't have enough liquids in her," he began, "her pressure would go down gradually, her kidneys would stop working, and then eventually her heart would stop."

"And what would she experience?"

"Being in a vegetative state, you know, she would not experience any pain, be no perception of pain in that case, no pain."

"Can she experience thirst?" I asked.

"No, because, you know, thirst is a higher mechanism of the brain," Dr. Majzoub said. "You have to have a functioning brain to be able to experience thirst." Dr. Majzoub explained that the same was true of dehydration or any other experience one might associate with pain. "In a vegetative state, the brain doesn't feel pain because you need the higher functions to interpret pain."

Bob Presson stood and moved to the podium. He began his cross-examination with the definition of death under Missouri law, pressing the doctor to admit that Nancy was not "dead," which Dr. Majzoub did readily. It appeared that at every turn, Presson planned to remind Judge Teel exactly what would happen to Nancy if the judge ruled in our favor. Presson moved to an area that I had struggled to understand—oral feeding versus tube feeding.

On various occasions, Dr. Cranford and I had gone around on this topic without any real resolution. We'd last talked about it the night before, over late cheeseburgers at the Holiday Inn in Joplin. Dr. Cranford explained to me that swallowing was an act that required consciousness and thought, abilities a vegetative patient had lost forever. Many vegetative patients did retain a primitive swallowing reflex, so food placed carefully on the tongue near the back of the throat could cause the patient to "swallow," forcing the food down the esophagus to the stomach. An extremely careful and patient nurse could possibly force enough into a PVS patient to sustain the patient for a short time. But the staff at a nursing home could never spend the two to three hours per meal on such primitive reflex feedings. Besides, Cranford reasoned, it could be dangerous because of the risk of aspiration.

I had asked Dr. Cranford if medical ethics dictated that the staff or family attempt such spoon feedings after a gastrostomy tube was removed. His response was clear: "At that point, the patient has lost any ability to eat or swallow voluntarily, and has lost all higher brain function," he said. "The tube was intended as a bridge to recovery, and that recovery did not happen. Forced feeding for an extra week makes no ethical or medical sense whatsoever."

On the stand, however, Dr. Majzoub gave Bob Presson a slightly different analysis, testifying that some of his PVS patients could swallow to some extent, and that some "could receive most, if not all, of their nutrition orally."

"As a matter of fact, for a time Nancy was fed orally, wasn't she?" Presson asked.

"Yes, sir."

"And she was taking soft food and pureed food?"

"Yes, sir."

"Drinking liquids like juices and water?"

"Yes, sir."

"Do you know why that was discontinued?"

"Because I think she wasn't taking enough, you know, so I think there was a question about her aspirating, so it was felt to be safe to put the tube down and feed her so she wouldn't regurgitate and aspirate."

"Would you explain what aspiration is?"

"Aspiration is when you regurgitate food from the stomach into the esophagus, back into the windpipe, and you get pneumonia from the food being in your windpipe," Dr. Majzoub explained.

"In other words, there is a health risk associated with feeding orally to someone in this state?" Presson asked.

"Yes, sir."

"And you felt it was safer to feed her through the tube?"

"That's correct."

On redirect exam, I questioned Dr. Majzoub about the American Medical Association's position that a feeding tube is medical treatment and that it is ethical for a doctor to withdraw such treatment from an irreversibly comatose patient. He explained that whether a respirator or feeding tube is involved, the effect on the patient is the same: On withdrawal, the patient could not feel pain.

On re-cross, Presson began to reveal the shape of his case—that no unanimity existed in the medical profession on withdrawal of feeding tubes despite the AMA statement, and that we shouldn't forget other equally important AMA ethics pronouncements: "Life should be cherished despite disabilities and handicaps, except when the prolongation would be inhumane and unconscionable." Presson closed where he'd begun. "Let me ask you this: Is an individual in a persistent vegetative state still a person in your mind?"

Dr. Majzoub looked quizzically at Presson. "Yes, he is still a human being," the doctor replied.

"Still a human being?"

"Yes, sir."

"I have no further questions."

The judge smiled down at Attorney General Webster and the rest of us. "Be an appropriate time to recess for the noon hour, gentlemen?" He stood, and the room of people stood with him. Down on the first floor, the local news camera crews came to life, ready to film the exits of the family and the attorney general. Their newsrooms would paste this video together with a three-minute description of the case and first day of trial. The Joplin and Springfield evening news would lead off with Webster smiling respectfully, followed by video of the bewildered Cruzans seeking to escape into the fresh air after they had to revisit the horror of January 11, 1983, on their first day in court. It hadn't been all bad though—all three family members at least felt some relief to see how the trial would work and were glad to finally be under way.

The various groups from the gallery fanned out to restaurants on the square and fast-food places a few blocks away. I stayed in the courtroom preparing for the afternoon, hoping that Dr. Cranford would take up most of it. We had Dr. Al-Shatir set to come in late in the day, and that would finish our first day. Kim Ross ran across the street for sandwiches while Dr. Cranford and I sat at the counsel table, recapping the morning and preparing for the afternoon.

Attorney General Webster didn't return to the courtroom after the lunch break. His appearance that morning had paid his necessary respect to the judge. Inside the courtroom, Webster's absence really didn't matter much; we had a lot to do. My examination of Dr. Majzoub had been choppy. I'd been nervous and never really helped him to relax.

When I sat down, Walt Williams leaned over and whispered to me, "We need to do more with Cranford."

"I know," I shot back, irritated with myself. I had to do better with Dr. Cranford. He was the key expert witness in the trial.

CHAPTER 18

BRAIN SCANS

Handsome and balding Dr. Ronald Cranford leaned forward in the brown leather witness chair, eager to talk. He looked directly at Judge Teel as the judge administered the oath. We had a long afternoon in front of us, which needed to move smoothly and stay as interesting as possible for the judge. As Cranford detailed his training and credentials, I kept one eye on Judge Teel.

Dr. Cranford had an impressive list of credentials—a tour of duty in Southeast Asia in the late 1960s; and he was a practicing neurologist, the chair of his hospital's CPR Committee and Biomedical Ethics Committee, a teacher of medical ethics to medical students since the 1970s, chairman of the state medical association committee on death and dying, and the national chair of the ethics committee for the American Academy of Neurology. In addition, Cranford was advisor to the National Conference of Commissioners on Uniform State Laws in their attempts to define death by statute and to develop a uniform living will law, a consultant to the President's Commission for the Study of Ethical Problems in Medicine, and was extensively published and widely respected. Clearly, the Cruzans had a true expert.

Dr. Cranford began by explaining to Judge Teel how a doctor makes the diagnosis of persistent vegetative state—they basically observe the patient over time. The doctor discovers the cause of the vegetative state, the duration in the state, what reactions others have seen, and does his own physical exam. Confirmatory studies (such as a CT scan)

can further support the diagnosis, but for the most part, the diagnosis depends on clinical observation at the patient's bedside over time.

Cranford described the persistent vegetative state as "a relatively new syndrome"—it was defined in 1972 by Drs. Plum and Jennett in the medical journal *The Lancet*. Cases existed before 1972, but doctors began seeing a marked increase around that time, and Nancy's case illustrated the reason for that increase—portable respirators, effective CPR, and other innovations in both basic and advanced life support.

Cranford told the judge that the brain stem (the primitive part of the brain) is far more durable than the neocortex (the upper, thinking part of the brain). The stem can survive significantly longer without oxygen and remain intact, but after just four to six minutes without oxygen, the neocortex will suffer severe damage. The brain stem can go half an hour or more and still retain primitive reflex functions.

Cranford explained that given this time disparity, as accident site "saves" increased, so did the occurrence of the vegetative state. With the brain stem basically intact, the PVS patient "has normal arousal, the patient is awake, there are sleep-wake cycles, eyes open, but the patient has no interaction with the environment, has no cognitive function, no thinking, no feeling, and no ability to experience pain and suffering, which is felt at the neocortical level." Dr. Cranford set the bar for this medical diagnosis incredibly high: "If there is any small amount of thinking or feeling or awareness or consciousness, then the patient is not in a persistent vegetative state," he said. "This is a complete lack of consciousness."

Still, Cranford had no doubt that Nancy's condition passed over this high bar. He'd reviewed the reports from other doctors—along with key medical records, nursing notes, CT scans, and EEG reports; talked with the family; and watched a videotape of Nancy. He'd visited MRC, talked with medical personnel about Nancy's course during her three and a half years there. He talked with MRC's medical director, Dr. Anita Isaac, who told him that she'd found no "consistent repeatable interaction with the environment" for Nancy.

෩ ෩ ෩

Dr. Cranford had spent about 45 minutes with Nancy at MRC the day before, performing his own medical exam to confirm everything he'd read, seen, and been told. In court, we walked through that exam in some detail—testing visual pursuit, sound reflex, contractures, cranial nerves, corneal response, pain response, and so on. The point here wasn't to know these details, but to show the judge how thorough Cranford had been. We accomplished that. Dr. Cranford's fairly sterile, clinical description did not necessarily capture the exam as I'd seen it, however.

Nancy's room had been filled with lawyers for both sides, the PBS crew, her family and friends, and doctors from MRC. Joe watched from one side of her bed, and Dr. Cranford moved to the other side. Cranford removed the stitched heart pillow Joyce had made, pulled Nancy's covers back and bent down, holding the bed railing with both hands. He talked loudly.

"Nancy? Nancy. Hear me? Look at me, Nancy." He waited for a response, but Nancy did not move. "Nancy. Nancy!" His hands let loose of the railing and reached out to clap loudly next to one ear, causing Nancy to blink. He reached across her face and clapped by her other ear, nearer to Joe, and her eyes blinked again. "Got a flashlight, anybody got a flashlight around?" Cranford asked, looking at the other doctors. One appeared, and Cranford took it and shined the beam into Nancy's eyes. No reaction.

Cranford next grabbed hold of Nancy's stiff right leg and tried to bend it straight. She grimaced. Then he reached for the soft skin on the inside of the upper part of her right arm, pinched her, and held the pinch. Slowly, as if she were a robot, Nancy's head lifted off the bed and turned. Her face locked on her father's for about ten seconds, before she lowered just as slowly to the pillow.

"That's what really concerns you, when she looks like she looks?" Cranford said to Joe, as he held the pinch. "That's all involuntary, even though it looks like she's looking right at you, doesn't it, huh?" Cranford asked, talking fast as he typically did.

"Right," Joe said, not sounding too sure.

"But you know she's not?"

"Right." Watching that scene, I thought, *How could any layperson believe at that moment that Nancy Cruzan was doing anything besides looking at her father?* That deception is part of the extreme cruelty of the persistent vegetative state for loved ones left behind. For doctors who deal with PVS, though, the grimacing and movement is simply another part of the diagnosis—primitive reflex reactions from a brain stem still intact, but not any indication of higher brain function.

For families, watching these simple reflexive movements often remains emotionally devastating to witness, and Cranford's exam appeared extremely difficult for Joe Cruzan, even though Nancy had been in this state for so many years. As the PBS camera turned off at the end of the exam, tears came to Joe's eyes and fell onto his cheeks. It seemed that he'd been trying to avoid crying with the camera directly on him.

⁓ ⁓ ⁓

Back in the courtroom, Dr. Cranford dispassionately explained the exam of the day before to Judge Teel. To Cranford, the medical reality was clear: A grimace is a reflex, which in healthy people we automatically associate with pain. Nancy's grimaces could never have connection to pain as we understand it, because the part of her brain that could perceive, understand, and feel pain was simply gone. His conclusion was that Nancy was in a classic persistent vegetative state.

I moved to corroborating evidence. I walked over toward the jury area (which was filled with sketch artists and reporters) and moved a lighted, portable x-ray reading box toward the judge. Cranford joined me and stood next to the box. I turned it on, and at first glance the two x-rays exhibited side-by-side looked the same, like two views of a tic-tac-toe board—nine heads filling each frame on the oversized x-rays. The two exhibits were CT scans of a brain. The first showed the brain of a perfectly normal 25-year-old from the radiology department at Dr. Cranford's hospital; the second was the CT scan of Nancy taken in January. Dr. Cranford told the judge that based on his clinical observation and record review, before even looking at the CT scans, he felt "beyond any doubt" that Nancy was in a PVS with "no recovery." The CT scans simply confirmed what he already knew.

Nonetheless, the judge and many others in the courtroom leaned closer as the doctor talked—the pictures were compelling. Using an old wooden pointer, Dr. Cranford showed the judge the key components of a healthy brain's CT scan, where the gray matter shows up white. With the pointer's tip, he touched the places where the skull, eyes, nose, and cerebrospinal fluid appeared on the scan of the normal brain. Then he turned to Nancy's scan, pointing to huge black spaces where the normal tissue should have been. It was right there in black and white: Nancy's brain was gone.

Dr. Cranford moved back to the witness chair, and I left the CT scan on in the background. Cranford told the judge that Nancy could live for years in a persistent vegetative state if the tube stayed in place. He explained why a PVS patient is incapable of experiencing pain and why he considered even spoon-feeding to be a medical treatment for a PVS patient: Placing food carefully in the back of the mouth to activate a brain stem-mediated swallowing reflex is not eating, and Cranford said it was "very unlikely" that Nancy could receive sufficient nutrition through such methods. He explained that she would die "quietly and peacefully" in one to two weeks once the tube was removed. The cause of death would be dehydration, not starvation. But Nancy would feel nothing.

We closed with medical ethics. Many authorities supported our position: the President's Commission; new guidelines from a medical-ethics think tank in New York called the Hastings Center; AMA guidelines recently adopted (in 1986); the American Academy of Neurology; and various state medical groups. Cranford and I talked about the medical ethics of removing a feeding tube from a patient who had been in the vegetative state for some time. I asked him if any group had an official position that opposed the Cruzans' request on ethical grounds.

"Not any medical organization or any interdisciplinary group that I'm aware of," Cranford said, "has taken any position contrary to that at all. And in fact, those groups I've mentioned have taken a very emphatic position on this issue because it is one of the more problematic areas."

Judge Teel called a ten-minute recess, and the shuffle began again. Walt leaned over and said, "That was great." I felt good about it, too. Dr. Cranford had presented our medical and ethical case persuasively. He came down from the witness chair and walked over to the railing and the Cruzans.

"How are you guys holding up?" Cranford asked. Joe said, "Fine," but his forced smile suggested that it was difficult for them to hear their story described in such an objective way in a courtroom—the CT scans that fascinated the rest of us filled the Cruzans with horror. Whenever I looked at Joe, he seemed uncomfortable—squirming on the wooden bench and constantly adjusting his shirt collar and tie.

When court resumed, Thad McCanse stood and approached Dr. Cranford. Now we would see just how closely our cases were really aligned. If McCanse adopted our expert in front of Judge Teel, it would be a huge coup.

McCanse, experienced with medical testimony, went quickly to the issue of Nancy's brain function. The CT scans done on the day of her accident and one week after showed a normal brain, but the EEG done on the day of the accident showed nearly flat background activity, almost no electrical activity in the brain—near dead. McCanse asked Cranford if this data was consistent with "oxygen starvation or anoxia."

"The brain is different than any other organ," Cranford replied. "It has no way of supplying, no way of maintaining or storing nutrients, so it requires a constant supply of blood. And within the blood you have to have a constant supply of oxygen and glucose, and the area of the brain that metabolizes most rapidly is the neocortex, the higher centers. The brain stem is resistant, and the spinal cord is even more resistant than the brain stem, so in the hierarchy of sensitivity to lack of oxygen, the neocortex suffers the most."

McCanse walked toward the doctor and pointed to the lighted portable x-ray box. "I think you said that these dark areas, those are the ventricles?"

"Ventricles, right."

"And a ventricle is what again?"

"Ventricles are spaces inside the brain; they're hollow cavities which have cerebrospinal fluid in them," Cranford answered.

"Normally, they should be quite small, and these have become increasingly enlarged?"

"These are about as large as you can get. They can't be more abnormal than that," Cranford said.

McCanse wanted to know how far the damage could progress. Cranford explained that Nancy had lost all gray matter, and now the surrounding white matter continued to deteriorate, but with "no bearing on her condition because the cortex has been gone already." He said that the brain stem, however, would remain intact.

McCanse switched to ethics, and he and Dr. Cranford talked about the decision to insert the tube 24 days after the accident with such a poor prognosis, what to do with patients caught in the limbo between life and death, and the feelings of the MRC staff. Cranford told McCanse that he could understand the concern at MRC, but that, ethically, it would be inhumane to the family to try to transfer Nancy now, and that MRC should do what's right.

"The other loaded question is, have you given thought or discussions as to how much of our resources should be devoted to this?" McCanse asked.

After some discussion, Cranford reached his bottom line: "Given the fact there is no benefit to continued treatment, no value to anyone, if we can't find a reasonable way of allocating resources for these patients, then this country is in serious trouble, which I think it is." Satisfied, McCanse sat down. I was elated. No question now, the *guardian ad litem* had taken our side.

Bob Presson saw that development, too. He rose and approached the doctor. "Dr. Cranford, do you want to expand the definition of 'death' to include persistent vegetative state?" he asked, attempting to focus the judge on the gray area once again. Presson and Cranford began to move together across the murky ethical landscape of removing a medical device from a hopeless patient, or starving a handicapped person to death, depending on the point of view. Cranford tried to be balanced in his answers, while not conceding any point to the state opponents of the family. Presson methodically prodded at Cranford's testimony for much of the afternoon.

Eventually they reached the topic of spoon-feeding. Dr. Cranford explained that while he'd never actually stopped spoon-feeding a patient, many times he hadn't begun such feeding after removing a gastrostomy tube from a PVS patient like Nancy. He told Presson that "literally hundreds of times a day," doctors took exactly that step.

This response appeared to stop Presson short. He moved away from his workmanlike approach, and disbelief filled his voice. "Do you believe it would be ethical to not attempt—even make the attempt now—to supply the nutrition and hydration orally?" The incredulity appeared genuine, as if Presson simply could not believe what he was hearing.

But Presson's reaction didn't really faze Cranford. He dealt with these issues and patients all the time, where it mattered, at the bedside.

And he'd spent a lifetime preparing to answer exactly the questions that Presson was posing. "Absolutely," Cranford answered, looking directly at Presson. "It would not make any moral sense whatsoever." Cranford explained why, just as he had to me at the Holiday Inn the night before.

Presson was well prepared. He told me later that he'd been contacted by James Bopp, a nationally known right-to-life lawyer, and his staff prior to trial. Bopp served as counsel for the National Right to Life Committee, and also ran the National Legal Center for the Medically Dependent and Disabled, which was based in Indianapolis. Their group monitored cases from around the country, and checked advocates like Dr. Cranford. They'd supplied Bob Presson with information most troubling to Cranford.

"As a doctor, have you ever been wrong in a diagnosis and prognosis?" Presson asked.

"Yes, I have been notably wrong in one case which attracted national attention," Cranford answered, and went on to explain. In December of 1979, Sergeant David Mack, a Minneapolis police officer, was shot while executing a search warrant. After ten months, he left the hospital with a diagnosis of PVS. The case raised this interesting side question: If doctors stopped all treatment, was the assailant responsible for murder, or did the doctor's action cause the death? Sergeant Mack made that a moot question, for 20 months out of the hospital, he began reacting. Eventually he regained some thinking function, yet he remained severely paralyzed. He lived five more years and died with his feeding tube still in place.

Presson pulled out an old *New York Times Magazine*. Cranford had told me about Mack, but I didn't know that the story had made it to the *New York Times*. I listened closely. Presson, holding the magazine article in his hand and appearing to read, asked Cranford whether he had said that the Mack recovery "introduces an element of uncertainty in a situation that was difficult to begin with"? Cranford explained that even today he didn't understand the mechanism of how Mack recovered, nor did any other neurologist.

He reminded Presson that Mack had happened in 1979, before powerful MRI and CT scans could show the intact structures of the brain, raising necessary questions about the clinical diagnosis. But in the end he agreed with Presson that "unknowns" remained regarding the vegetative state, and those unknowns were "very disconcerting."

I jumped back up for redirect, anxious to move back to positive ground. Cranford and I talked about the ethical obligation of MRC to remove the tube, about the hospice area, and about fiduciary duties of doctors to their patients. But we had to go back to Sergeant Mack.

Dr. Cranford explained how the Mack case had helped the work of the President's Commission, which was adopting its guidelines at about that time. He explained that no case existed in the literature of any type of recovery for a PVS caused by anoxia after five years like Nancy. And he repeated how physically debilitated and almost completely paralyzed Mack had been, even with recovery. In the interest of not protesting too much, I left Sergeant Mack.

Bob Presson approached Dr. Cranford for some final cross-examination. *More Mack,* I thought. Instead, Presson asked Dr. Cranford about doctor-assisted suicide. Wasn't it true that giving Nancy an overdose of morphine and removing her tube were the same thing, since either would cause her death?

Cranford answered that intending to kill someone with an overdose and stopping a medical treatment that hasn't worked were as different as night and day.

"Well, one final question," Presson said. "Withdrawal of the feeding tube will cause her death?"

Cranford grew even more animated (which I didn't think was possible), his hands moving fast as he talked. "No, it will not cause her death," he replied. "No more than a respirator withdrawn from a respirator-dependent patient will cause a death, no more than antibiotics that are not given to a patient who has pneumonia will cause the death." Cranford went on with his answer for some time, emphasizing repeatedly what he called the "profound moral distinction between the two."

"I guess it all depends on how you define things, Doctor," Presson countered. "If you define medical care to include nutrition and hydration, you—"

Agitated, Cranford interrupted the question. "I don't know of any group that hasn't defined it that way—any commission, any interdisciplinary organization, medical organization, or appellate court decision. None of them have defined it any other way than 'medical treatment.'"

Presson looked at Judge Teel. "Maybe you should also add the state of Missouri. We will find out. Thank you, Doctor." It was not exactly clear to me what Presson meant, but something about the way he said it, looking right at the judge, felt ominous.

Sitting at counsel table, I glanced through the tall window, out of the courtroom. Lengthening shadows slanted soft light onto the wood floor. How had so much time passed? It was just a minute ago that General Webster was walking across the aisle to shake hands. Now our first day was about done. Keeping up with Dr. Cranford had taken all of my energy. I looked at McCanse and the judge, and over at Presson and Northcutt. Everyone looked like I felt—spent. One last witness and we could regroup.

Dr. Saad Al-Shatir came out of the gallery and took a seat in the witness box. Dr. Al smiled as he sat down. As he walked us through Nancy's weeks at Brady Rehabilitation, it seemed as if Dr. Al found our entire courtroom debate almost a little silly. He shook his head when I asked whether his ethics would allow him to remove her tube if her parents came to him.

"There is no hope for her to get better. What do you expect? Five years." He lifted his palms as he spoke, not sure why everyone else could not see the hopelessness that was so obvious to him. All the lawyers talked to him about his rehabilitation efforts and his treatment of Nancy, but his bottom line was unmistakable—Nancy was in a PVS with no hope of recovery.

At 5:25 P.M., we called it a day.

❧

Joe Cruzan with baby Nancy (Chris is in the foreground), late 1957.

Joe and Nancy down at Sugar Creek.

Chris, Donna, and Nancy, Christmas 1967.

The Cruzan family, circa 1968, standing in front of the carport.

Joyce Cruzan in Joe's pickup truck, circa 1968. The only known photo of the Rambler involved in the crash is in the background.

Nancy leading the high school band during the Christmas parade, December 1973.

Nancy with one-year-old Angie at the beach in Jacksonville, 1976.

*Joe and Nancy with Angie and Miranda, unloading for a
Cruzan family reunion at Carthage Park in 1981.*

Donna, Miranda, Nancy, Angie, and Chris in September 1982, at Chris's 27th birthday party at Grandma Jack's house.

Joe and Angie in 1982.

Nancy at Los Amigos in 1982.

Nancy with the girls, January 8, 1983.

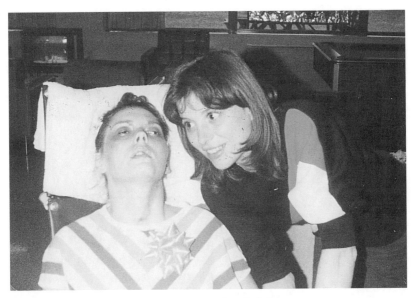

*Chris with Nancy at Brady Rehabilitation, on
Miranda's seventh birthday, March 13, 1983.*

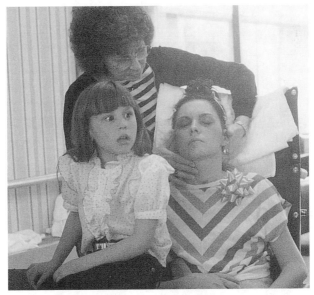

Miranda, Joyce, and Nancy at Brady Rehab.

The Missouri Rehabilitation Center (MRC), where Nancy was moved on October 19, 1983. (Fred Taggart/Courtesy Lawrence County Record)

Joe and Chris in the summer of 1984, sitting on the side steps outside 501 Main.

Gov. John Ashcroft (center), together with Don Lamkins (second from right), signing legislation to change the name of the Missouri State Chest Hospital to the Missouri Rehabilitation Center in August 1985. Also, left to right, state senator Emory Melton; representative Bob Jackson; and Lorna Wilson.
(Courtesy Lawrence County Record)

Lester and Jackie Cruzan with their three sons, Jim, Butch, and Joe, in 1986.

The Frontline *team—Jim Astrausky, Betsey Arledge, Mike Kirk, and Bill McMillan—July 1987.*

General Counsel of the Missouri Department of Health,
Robert "Rod" Northcutt. (Courtesy Missouri State Archives)

Court-appointed lawyer Thad McCanse. (Mike Gullet)

*Missouri Assistant Attorney General
Bob Presson.* (Courtesy Missouri
Attorney General's Office)

*Attorney General Bill Webster (left) and Bill Colby at a Shook,
Hardy & Bacon event hosting Webster, July 29, 1988.*

Dr. Ronald Cranford.

Dr. James Davis, Nancy's main doctor at MRC.

The Jasper County Courthouse in Carthage, Missouri.
(Ron Graber/Courtesy Carthage Press)

Trial judge Charles Teel.

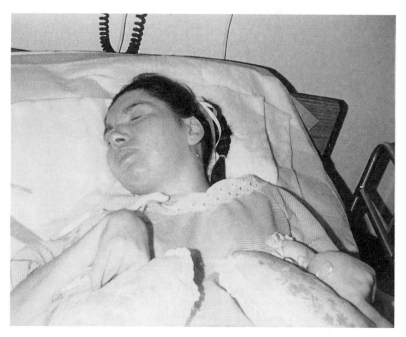

Nancy at MRC, Christmas 1986.

CHAPTER 19

A VALENTINE'S CARD

We had 11 witnesses scheduled for Thursday, March 10; and Joe, Chris, and Dr. Cranford had agreed to appear live on *Nightline* with Ted Koppel that evening. A big day ahead. I watched the three Cruzans come into the courtroom shortly before nine. If they felt more comfortable now that they had one day of the trial under their belt, it wasn't obvious. It didn't help that as they walked up the aisle to their seats, they felt the eyes of the gallery, watching them like a family at a funeral.

The judge settled in and began the day by telling the audience that he'd had a new amplifier installed the night before so that everyone could more easily hear the witnesses. Then he turned to Bob Presson, and said, "It's my understanding you had an announcement?" My pulse quickened—I didn't know anything about an announcement.

The lawyers walked up to the judge's bench, and Presson leaned in and spoke to Judge Teel in quiet tones. As he spoke, it slowly dawned on me what he was saying—family members and friends shouldn't be allowed to testify about informal statements made in conversations with Nancy, or about her views and values, when the living will statute required a formal written declaration. This was more like an atomic bomb than an "announcement."

"The problem is, essentially, we feel the living will statute will not allow an informal declaration," Presson began. "It is not competent evidence to try to offer something of less formality, less sure, to accomplish the same end. I think the evidence wouldn't be relevant, admissible, or competent, and ask that it be excluded." If the judge granted this motion, it would certainly make for a shorter day, since most of our 11 witnesses wouldn't be able to testify.

Thad McCanse spoke before I could. "Maybe I didn't hear all of that," he said.

Judge Teel joined in, saying, "I guess maybe I'm not quite understanding specifically what it is you're asking to be excluded—that's part of my problem."

As Presson made his argument again, I felt like that kid in class who's bursting with the right answer, his hand waving so high that one cheek is off the chair. Finally, I broke in.

"We're talking about a person's constitutional rights, not some narrow medical statute under which they can attempt to exercise their will ahead of time," I said. "That's not what's at issue here. We're talking about an individual's rights, and an objection on the existing statute is completely ill founded and without basis."

The judge told us he'd take the motion under advisement and suggested that the parties could file briefs on it after trial. As we walked back to the tables, I felt relief, and anger—how in the world did the state have the right to try to exclude testimony from Nancy's family and friends? No question, our "friendly suit" was dead.

I picked up Exhibit 14, a recent medical report from Dr. George Wong, who was a consulting neurologist for the MRC. The report, just a couple of months old, concluded that Nancy had been in a persistent vegetative state for at least four years and that she had no hope of recovery. Dr. Wong couldn't attend the trial, so I decided to read his report aloud to the judge. As I read, I glanced out into the courtroom and saw the newspaper reporters' heads bent over their pads, busy scribbling this conclusion from the state's own doctor.

I also wanted to continue to water the seed we'd tried to plant in the judge's head—that supplying an FDA-regulated nutrient compound through an FDA-regulated medical pumping device bore little relation to feeding someone. So, after Dr. Wong's report, I read aloud from Nancy's medical record of February 7, 1983, the description of what doctors had to do to place Nancy's feeding tube:

Pre-operative diagnosis, head injury. Malnutrition. Post-operative Diagnosis, Same. Name of Operation, Insertion of a #20 T-tube feeding gastrostomy. Operative Procedure: The abdominal area was prepped and draped. A previous upper midline incision was anesthetized with 1 percent plain Xylocaine anesthesia, IV sedation, Pryor group. The incision was opened. Bleeders were electrocoagulated. The peritoneal cavity was entered. The stomach was delivered and in the dependent portion, a 3-0 purse-string was inserted. A #20 short-arm T-tube was inserted and the purse-string tied. The stomach was secured to the under side of the peritoneum with interrupted 4-0 silk. The fascia and peritoneum were closed with interrupted 0 Ethibond. Skin and subcutaneous tissue were closed with skin clips. The patient was taken to the recovery room in a stable condition. Dictated: 2-7-83. Transcribed: 2-7-83. Signed: R.L. Willcoxon, M.D.

That sounded like medical treatment to me. I called the first witness of the day, Dr. James Davis, Nancy's primary doctor at MRC. Dr. Davis slowly made his way to the witness stand. He was a kind country doctor, a small, roundish man whose soft voice came out almost as an apology. I'd never met him before, although I'd seen him interviewed when the PBS show had aired just over a week earlier. And Dave Mouton had talked with Dr. Davis in Mt. Vernon. Thad McCanse had told me that, based on Mouton's interview, they weren't sure what Dr. Davis would say about the persistent vegetative state, but the doctor didn't believe that there was any hope for Nancy's improvement.

Dr. Davis saw Nancy Cruzan every day, and had done so since he took over her care a year before the trial. We briefly reviewed his credentials, then moved to Nancy's medical condition. Dr. Davis didn't hesitate—he said that she was in a persistent vegetative state without hope of recovery, and she only had reflex reactions, such as jumping at loud noises or grimacing when pinched. He said he'd tried to have Nancy's eyes follow things, without success. He didn't know if she could feel pain when pinched; he said he'd defer to the neurologists on that question. Davis's testimony was a bonus—I hadn't counted on such clear support from Nancy's primary doctor at MRC.

We went on to discuss the factors considered in making medical decisions for incapacitated patients—the patient's diagnosis, prognosis, chance for improvement, and the family's wishes—and the doctor's personal feelings. Dr. Davis said that he didn't personally know whether he could withdraw feeding and hydration, knowing that the patient wouldn't survive.

"Let us take it back one step, then," I said. "What if they are coming to you, and Nancy is in this condition, and you have to make the decision of whether or not to initially insert the feeding tube. Is that an easier choice for you?"

"That's a much easier choice," Dr. Davis responded.

"What would you do in that situation, sir?"

"If they requested that it not be done, I would not do it."

"And that's personally easier?" I asked.

"That, personally, is much easier." Dr. Davis and I had come to one of the great fallacies of modern medical ethics. Leading journals and medical association position papers all took the same position: No moral distinction exists between initially withholding or later withdrawing a medical treatment. Doctors should feel free to try a treatment for a period of time to see if it aided recovery and if it could serve as a bridge from injury or illness back to good health. The moral question of withdrawing that treatment should be the same moral question as whether to start the treatment in the first place.

In fact, morally, the question of withdrawal should be an easier one. Wasn't the best moral (and medical) course to at least try a treatment, even if it held only a small hope of recovery, to see if that small hope could be realized—as opposed to hesitating to start such treatment for fear it might be difficult to stop once started?

As in many cases, however, theory and practice didn't fit neatly together. The dilemma Dr. Davis posed wasn't his alone—in fact, doctors faced it all the time. "Pulling the plug" was far harder for doctors to do than simply not starting the treatment in the first place. If Joe and Joyce Cruzan had asked the doctor three weeks after the accident if Nancy was going to come out of the coma, the doctor likely would have responded, "Probably not." And if Joe and Joyce had then said, "No more surgeries, no more tubes, we're taking her home," heads would have bowed all around the room, nodding in agreement. But by trying for that slim chance at recovery, the Cruzans had lost all control.

Either way, Dr. Davis saw no good outcome for the family. "Mentally, the Cruzans are going to have problems somewhere down the line with the fact that they brought about the death of their daughter, the final demise of the body, if you will. If they don't do it, they have the same problem, 'Am I responsible for her continued suffering?' Either way, they are going to have problems."

Bob Presson had only two questions: Was Davis fully convinced in his own mind how much awareness Nancy has? And when Davis said that guidelines from the court would be helpful to him, that meant guidelines that directed him either way, right? Hearing the two affirmative answers he wanted, Presson sat down.

Moving on, I called Don Lamkins. Even though he'd made clear to the Cruzans privately and in public statements that he didn't agree with their decision, he always dealt with Joe and Joyce in a professional manner. I had only one purpose for calling him: to try to have him commit to allowing the removal of the feeding tube at MRC if we won, rather than have Nancy transferred.

Lamkins nodded politely as he strode to the witness stand in a dark suit and crisp white shirt. I handed him a copy of Petitioner's Exhibit 4, which was the memo sent by Rod Northcutt to Lamkins the previous summer. In addition to explaining why MRC must refuse the Cruzans' request, the memo also suggested that, with a court order, the tube could be removed in the hospice section of MRC. I asked Lamkins if that conclusion was correct: Was hospice the appropriate place to comply with a possible court order?

"I'm not sure that it would make any difference where in the hospital, because even in the Hospice Unit, we don't take away nutrition, hydration from a patient," Lamkins answered.

"And why is that? Is that a legal question?"

"Well, it is partly legal, but awful lot of moral issues, too."

"If the legal part is removed, this court says, 'I've addressed this issue, legally. I think it is appropriate to remove this tube,' would that be appropriate then, with that removed, in your Hospice Unit to withdraw the tube?" I asked.

"Yes, it could be done there. If you are talking about the mechanical part of doing it, it could be done."

I tried to have him commit to such a course if we won, but he'd gone as far as he was going to go on this issue. On my yellow pad, at the bottom of the outline for Lamkins, was the single word *COST*, with a question mark after it. At some level, a group of decision makers in society needed to debate and decide how to best spend limited public dollars available for health care. For example, every dollar spent in Missouri on treating a PVS patient was a dollar not available for other needs, such as childhood vaccine programs. Kids would die without those vaccines. To me personally, the decision was obvious. Why spend hundreds of thousands of public dollars on a permanently unconscious woman, against her family's wishes, while others died who might have been saved? Who could advocate such a public-health policy? Thad McCanse felt the same way, and also thought the issue belonged before Judge Teel so that he could factor it into his decision.

But we weren't engaged in a public-policy argument—we were talking about one person's life. Public policy brought to that microlevel sounded dangerously like saying a life wasn't worthy of living, that it wasn't worth the money. This is exactly the charge levied by the organized right-to-life opposition groups against families like the Cruzans. I could at least give the judge the facts, and let him do his own ruminating on public policy. Even that much made me uneasy.

I asked Lamkins about the annual cost of Nancy's care, and he told me it was about $120,000. After a couple of follow-up questions, I sat down.

Thad McCanse stood and asked Lamkins about the purpose of rehabilitation medicine. "Since the purpose of the Rehabilitation Hospital is to make people function again to some extent as well as you can, you can't do that for Nancy, am I correct in that?"

"I think the thinking is that she is probably functioning as well as she's going to," Lamkins responded.

Thad's voice grew quieter. "And how is she functioning at all?"

"She lives."

"She breathes and her heart beats?"

"Yes."

"Otherwise, she is totally dependent on others for her care?"

"Yes," Lamkins admitted. "She can't take care of herself alone."

"She can't do anything actually, can she, except her heart beats, breathe, and open her eyes?" McCanse asked.

"As far as I know, that's about the extent of her ability."

Lamkins responded enthusiastically to brief questions from Bob

where doctors told her family that Natalie wouldn't live through the night, and that if she did, she would be "a vegetable." Natalie died that night.

Athena appeared to forget that she was testifying as she recalled Nancy and that half hour of conversation. The memory came rushing out: "Nancy said that she had lost a grandparent, but she hadn't lost anyone like a mother, you know, or a sister, and that she was from a close family like I was, and that she just didn't know how she could take that—that it was hard enough to lose a grandparent.

"And I was telling her, you know, it was hard, but the only way I did feel easier about my sister was because they said if she had lived, she would have been in a vegetative state for the rest of her life, and Natalie would not have wanted to live that way. And Nancy said that she would never want to live that way either. Because if she couldn't be normal, or even, you know, like halfway, and do things for yourself—because Nancy always did—that she didn't want to live. And I said I wouldn't either, and we talked about it a lot."

Judge Teel appeared to listen attentively to Athena Comer. So did Thad McCanse, who rose and walked to Athena at the end of the direct exam. Athena brushed away tears with the back of her hand and smiled at McCanse.

"Mrs. Comer, you lived together for three months?" McCanse began.
"Yes."

"And why was it that you stopped living together?"

"Because her and her boyfriend were getting back together, and he was going to move back in."

McCanse switched to Natalie's death, asking her if they told her at the hospital "that death was a blessing, is that it?"

"Well no, what it was—they come right out to us and said that Natalie had less than one in a thousand chance to make it really through the night, but if she did, that she would definitely be in a vegetative state the rest of her life."

"Did they use the term 'vegetative state'?" McCanse asked.

"I really believe it was the term 'vegetable,' but—"

"Vegetable?"

"Yes."

"Do you know . . . in this case that vegetative state is describing a particular situation?"

"I think it sounds better than—"

"Than vegetable?" McCanse prompted.

"Right."

McCanse tried to pin down what Nancy said that night in 1981, just one year before her accident. "Can you remember the exact words she said?" he asked.

"I wouldn't say exactly, but I know that we both were talking about it and discussing it, and she said that she wouldn't want to live unless she could be at least halfway normal. I do know she said that."

"And you said, 'I would never want to go on as a vegetable,' is that true?"

"I would never want to live—I could take, like, losing some limbs or having to be in a wheelchair, but if I couldn't care for myself and be at least halfway normal, or somebody had to take care of me all the time, I couldn't, would not want to live that way."

"And Nancy agreed with you?"

"Yes. But she also discussed how she wouldn't want to live that way because if she was going to live, she wanted to be able to live, not just lay in a bed and not be able to move because you can't do anything for yourself or go enjoy your life or do what you want to do."

Athena Comer had sat next to the Cruzan family watching the trial all morning, so she knew who was on which side. As Bob Presson came toward her in the witness chair, she looked like she feared he might bite her. She needn't have worried—all Presson wanted to do was establish that Nancy and Athena didn't discuss food and water, a respirator, or really any medical treatment. That accomplished, he concluded by asking about conversations Athena had had since the one with Nancy.

"Has anyone ever said they want to be in a vegetative state?" Presson asked.

"No, everyone I know would not want to be that way because you can't—you don't have a life. You just lay there."

Judge Teel announced the lunch break, and Athena, now crying, stood and made her way back to the Cruzans. Chris put her arms around Athena, and Joe and Joyce stood next to the two young women. Walt Williams and I grabbed our notes—we had six witnesses left before we rested our case. Our group headed out of the courthouse and walked across the town square to The Deli for lunch.

The Deli had fed the lunch crowd on the square in Carthage since 1965. Many of the locals, both businesspeople and blue-collar workers, had been regulars since. Those regulars now eyed our group, talking quietly among themselves about the big trial going on. We pushed a couple of tables together and sat down, taking a collective deep breath after the morning. We were the biggest group in the place, with nine of us gathered—Joe, Joyce, Chris, Athena, Rose Gasner (a lawyer from the Society for the Right to Die who was attending the trial), Dr. Cranford, Kim (my legal assistant), Walt Williams, and me.

Joe knew he was going to be on the stand next, so he was too nervous to eat. Joyce ordered for both of them—she was oblivious to the attention, but Joe knew exactly what was happening. He watched the regulars and said that the union workers probably wondered who had to carry his load while he "took off for a week to sit in a courtroom and prance in front of television cameras."

We talked about the morning we'd just spent—specifically about the Valentine's story that Lisa Perrin had told. The Cruzans had never heard that before. "I think that other nurse is just making it up," Chris said, angry. Her parents nodded. Dr. Cranford said a similar thing had happened in the *Brophy* trial and others. He said that it might not be made up with bad intent, though, because nurses around hopeless patients every day had to find some way to have hope themselves. So they saw things in a PVS patient that no one else saw—and that just were not there.

The lunch recess passed quickly. I watched Joe walk back toward the courthouse ahead of me, the gray JCPenney sports jacket stretched tight across his shoulders. Over the last two weeks, we had talked about his trial testimony many times. He did not want to "screw it up." Those conversations always came down to the same question: "What if I forget something?" Joe and I had more than covered that ground. I pulled up next to him and tried to reassure him that he knew Nancy better than anyone and would do a great job. The worry etched on his face told me that he remained unconvinced.

The massive Jasper County courthouse rose before us. Built in the 1890s from Carthage marble quarried north of the city—with turrets above the two entrances, a tower on each corner, and a massive clock tower topped by a cupola rising from its top—the courthouse looked as if it sat on top of a mountain. Joe looked insignificant by comparison. He would have rather been just about anyplace in the world at that moment, wearing anything but those uncomfortable clothes. But he had no option, Nancy needed his help.

Up the courthouse steps he went.

CHAPTER 20

FAMILY MATTERS

On Thursday, March 10, Joe Cruzan sat uneasily in the leather witness chair and looked out on the courtroom full of friends, onlookers, family members, reporters, and courtroom sketch artists. A lump came to his throat as Judge Teel swore in Lester Lee Cruzan, Jr.

We'd decided that Walt Williams would put on the family witnesses. Joe and Walt eased into their conversation as Joe began to talk about his life. Lester Cruzan had been called "Joe" since he was two years old, and most people had known him as that ever since. He'd lived in the same house in Carterville since 1964, where he'd raised all three of his girls, and he'd had the same wife since 1954. He'd been a sheet-metal worker since 1953 and had been with the same company, Springfield Engineering, since 1972.

As Joe talked about his family, his fear of forgetting something seemed to disappear. He told Judge Teel how his middle daughter, Nancy, grew up in the white house at 501 Main in Carterville, and how she had been a contestant in a beauty pageant in grade school. Just before the end of high school, Nancy married Danny Hayes. When he joined the Navy, she set out to see the world with him—in just 18 months, they'd lived in Boston, Florida, and California. Nancy and Danny divorced after about two years, and at age 20, Nancy returned to spend her last five years in the Carterville area, except for a one-month stint in Oklahoma.

For a while after she moved back to town, Nancy lived at home—

Joe told Judge Teel about father and daughter butting heads over many issues, including the need to go to work on time. Joe remembered specifically telling Nancy one morning, "Nancy, you have got to get up and go to work—people expect you to be there, and you have got to be there or you're going to lose your job." One night she came home and just could not understand why she'd been fired. As Joe told Judge Teel about that night, his face lit up as if he were remembering opening a Christmas present—such a specific memory brought Nancy back to him for a moment. "I said, you know, 'You have got to assume responsibilities in your life, you have got to grow up.' And she said, 'I don't want to grow up . . . I want to have fun.' You know, she was that type of person."

Nancy liked her last job the best. She worked the graveyard shift at Schreiber's Cheese on the production line, packaging cheese from eleven at night until seven in the morning. The schedule allowed her to sleep, garden, go to town, hang out with her mom and sister, sit in the sun, or do what she wanted during the day.

After Nancy returned to Carterville, Nancy dated a couple of guys before she met Paul Davis. She and Paul dated for a while, and moved into a trailer east of Carterville. Later, they moved to another trailer out around Duenweg, but most of the time, Joe could remember that they were in that two-bedroom house out on Krummel Nursery Road.

Joe drew picture after picture of Nancy: The independent daughter, mad at Joe and Joyce and stomping down to the Dairy Creme; Nancy the camper—the girls grew up spending summers down at their cabin on Sugar Creek, with Nancy always in the water; Nancy the outgoing girl who made friends easily. And Joe described their last weekend together, painting on the scaffolding.

Joe and Walt moved to the night of the accident—the blood, the ER nurse saying she would "be all right"—all the way through the chronology to the present. Walt asked Joe about Nancy's condition.

"We've tried everything we could to get a response out of her," Joe said. "I can swear to God that I have never seen anything that I thought was a thought-produced response from Nancy."

In the hour and a half of talking about Nancy, Joe seemed to age right in front of us. Walt changed topics, asking Joe about what might happen next. Joe bit his lip hard and looked at the high ceiling. The hundred-plus people in the courtroom sat still. "I've told her not to be afraid, that we will be with her all the time," Joe said.

"When you say, 'be with her all the time,' what plans did you make in that connection?" Walt asked.

"Well, it depends when it comes about," Joe said. "We've got a travel trailer. Like I said, I'm in construction work, so I have to work out of town, that's my home away from home. If it's in the summertime and the hospital would be generous enough to let me park it on the lot, we would probably stay in the trailer, spend most of the time with Nancy. This is what we did at Freeman Hospital when Joyce's mother was there. We kept the trailer on the lot and we stayed in the hospital most of the time, but if someone wanted to go out and take a nap or lay down a while or fix a sandwich, the trailer was there for them. In the wintertime, I would consider possibly the dormitories on the facilities. I don't know if they would allow that or not. If not, we would stay in a motel, we would stay—," Joe looked past the people in the courtroom as he talked, as if he was conjuring up the vision. Walt interrupted and brought him back—Joe had missed the point of the question.

"Regardless, Joe, of where you actually stay, would it be your intent to be there with Nancy when she dies?"

"Yes."

"And is that preferable to you?"

"Definitely," Joe said. "I only wish I could have been with her the night of the accident." The images of his travel trailer parked at MRC and of Krummel Nursery Road five years earlier, along with the weight of the afternoon's testimony, all converged on Joe. His head dropped, and his shoulders started to shake with sobs. Walt's own eyes reddened, and he sat down. The judge looked down at the witness stand and asked, "Recess, Joe?"

Joe Cruzan lifted his head and met the judge's gaze. "No, sir," he said.

The judge nonetheless paused for a couple of beats, and then looked back at the lawyers. "All right. Mr. McCanse?" he said. Joe looked back up at Judge Teel, able to talk again.

"I wonder if I could get a glass of water?" he asked.

The judge smiled. "Surely," he said. He poured a glass from his own pitcher and handed it across the high bench to Joe, who took a drink.

"Thank you," he said. "I might add to that, if I could, that I've often—I know in Nancy's condition that she could die any time," Joe had turned and was talking to Judge Teel. "I would just hope that we would have time to get there." Joe appeared ready to cry again.

"Do you want to go, or do you—," Judge Teel said.

"I'm ready," Joe said.

Thad McCanse had stood quietly, listening to this exchange between Joe and the judge. He began his questioning by asking about Joe's role as Nancy's guardian. "Could you tell the court why you feel it is in Nancy's best interest that the feeding tube be discontinued?"

"Primarily it's because we believe it is what Nancy's wish would be," Joe said. "Secondarily, we see no purpose in Nancy being forced to merely exist. Who knows? A year, four years, six years, ten years, twenty years, thirty years, no one can say for sure, and I can see no purpose in that, in forcing her to endure the indignities that she's going through now. Nancy is totally helpless. When she has a bowel movement, they have to change her diaper." Again, Joe seemed to speak as if he was far away from the courtroom. "Nancy drools, and there have been many times that they try to keep pads under her neck, but probably, in maybe movements or whatever happens, the padding gets pulled away, her hair will be wet, her gown will be wet, the sheet will be wet. I just feel it is beneath her dignity to continue in this condition. Some people may find that hard to understand. I don't."

"Joe, I don't question that thought at all," McCanse said. He asked about Nancy's conversations. "Did Nancy ever mention to you the conversation she had with Athena before the accident occurred?"

"I know what Athena said about her intentions, and Nancy may have spoken the same intentions, but I also know when you're 25 years old, you don't think about dying. Five and a half years ago, I didn't think I would be in this courtroom. I didn't think I would have a daughter in a vegetative state. I knew that accidents happened, but they happened in other families."

McCanse moved in close to Joe, talking in a calm voice. He asked about the effect on their family if Nancy died. The question somehow took Joe back to Nancy's van. Joe told McCanse about the van with the loud pipes and the guy from Carterville who bought it from her when she got the Rambler, the same story he'd told me in his living room months earlier. Joe told McCanse how hearing the van upset him for years, but as time went on, it affected him less. For the Cruzans, *their* Nancy was already gone—she was there in spirit, but gone in person.

Joe's head dropped again as he talked about the sound of the white van, and abruptly, in the middle of his questioning, Thad McCanse appeared to make the decision that this man had been through enough. He nodded at Judge Teel and sat down.

Bob Presson didn't spend a lot of time with Joe. He established that Joe and Nancy never discussed withdrawing medical care, and he asked whether Nancy had ever expressed an opinion on something like euthanasia.

"I understand she wrote a paper on euthanasia when she was in the seventh grade, but we couldn't find that," Joe answered. "I believe Christy said she wrote one in the eighth grade, which—Nancy probably copied Christy's." At that, laughter rippled through the courtroom, and even Joe cracked a slight smile. It did not last.

Presson asked Joe to assume that Nancy could experience pain, and whether that fact would change their decision. "I think it would make me all the more determined to stop this," Joe said.

"Mr. McCanse mentioned the stress and everything you've gone through. That's not the reason why you are asking for this, are you?"

"If I thought I could bring Nancy back, I would go through this the rest of my life," Joe answered.

Joe went on to tell Presson that Nancy was a spiritual person and member of the Methodist Church, but she didn't attend church regularly. He said religion played no role in the family decision.

Presson asked Joe what he would do if he lost the lawsuit. He asked the question several different ways, and Joe tried to answer, but he couldn't really conceive of such a result. "We will cross that bridge when we come to it," Joe said.

Presson sat down, and Judge Teel excused Joe from the witness stand and called a ten-minute recess. Joe walked back toward our table. I could see by his face that he'd moved past the emotion and on to critiquing himself.

To break up the emotional family testimony, we had a couple of witnesses scheduled to testify between Joe and Joyce. I called Pat Brophy to the stand, and Bob Presson moved to Judge Teel's bench to object to her testimony.

Presson spoke in quiet, direct tones. "Judge, I object to this witness testifying," he began. "Mr. Colby told me that she will offer an opinion that her husband went through a similar process to what Nancy Cruzan will go through, and I think that is a medical judgment she is not qualified to give."

"Mrs. Brophy will offer firsthand testimony of what she saw at her husband's bedside, a lay perspective only," I replied. I leaned in toward the judge as Presson had. "Her husband's condition and Nancy's are essentially the same."

"I don't think this witness can offer any relevant comparison between her husband's situation and Nancy's," Presson said.

"It could even become repetitive," Rod Northcutt added. "Dr. Cranford has already gone through the entire situation."

"Dr. Cranford is here, and will be here the rest of the day," I said. "He's done a full neurological workup on both Nancy Cruzan and Paul Brophy. If it will help the court, we can put him back on the stand after this testimony."

The debate had picked up speed as the lawyers talked, and Judge Teel leaned back and thought a moment. "Pretty hard to Monday-morning quarterback something when you don't have a real concept of what's coming," he finally said. "It may be that petitioners can establish similar circumstances—then maybe some testimony concerning what she observed would be appropriate."

Thad McCanse offered support. "I would like to present everything that we can to the court that bears on this issue, just to make your job a lot easier," he told the judge. "I personally would welcome this type of evidence because it is coming, not from an expert's point of view, but someone who has been there."

Pat Brophy sat impassively through this whole exchange—unlike the Cruzans, she'd been through it all before. The courtrooms, the protestors, the media, and finally, her husband's death had all given her the bearing of someone with the calm and sadness that came with that experience. I had talked with her on the phone only twice, and had never laid eyes on her until that day.

On March 1, she'd watched the *Frontline* show on the Cruzans. That evening, she thought, *That's the guy from Missouri who called me last year,* and decided to offer to help. The next day she called Joe, and nine days later she was on a plane from Boston to Joplin, Missouri. Kim Ross had picked her up at the Joplin Airport and brought her straight to the courthouse.

Now on the stand, Mrs. Brophy told the judge about her job as a nurse at a state institute for the mentally retarded, about her husband's brain aneurysm and his descent into the persistent vegetative state, and their trial in Massachusetts. She said she called the Cruzans to offer support in any way she could, and to give them encouragement because she felt they were doing a "very, very tough thing."

I asked Mrs. Brophy to talk about the physical appearance of her husband as he died, in an effort to disarm the claims that the right-to-life advocates often made about death after removal of a feeding tube, conjuring up the image of a parched, dying person crawling across the desert. Such an image would no doubt come before the judge in the form of post-trial briefs from interest groups (called *amicus briefs).*

Brophy told the judge that her husband's lips were not cracked, his tongue was not swollen, and he didn't have dry heaves. "It is not that we put him in a corner to die," she said. "We cared for him, did all the personal hygiene. He didn't dry out."

Then she began to describe her husband's last day. The room went silent—even some of the sketch artists set down their pencils and listened. Pat Brophy's clear voice filled the courtroom. "I stayed with him 24 hours a day for the eight days that it took for him to die. He didn't look any different from the three and a half years that he had been in his persistent vegetative state. The whole family was there. The grandchildren came—they played on his bed, they were unafraid. They kissed him goodbye because he was going to heaven."

Mrs. Brophy held her head up as she described the end. "I was sitting on one side of the bed holding his hand, and my son was on the other side of the bed. In the ten minutes before he died, he kind of made a funny noise and vomited, and then his respirations just petered out and he died very peacefully."

"Was it a calm death?" I asked.

"Yes, I think one that I would like to—the way I would like to die, just stopped breathing."

Bob Presson made sure that Judge Teel knew that Paul Brophy, unlike Nancy Cruzan, had talked to his wife many times over a seven-year period about life support. His job as an EMT firefighter brought him face-to-face with the limits of medical technology all the time. Paul Brophy had left no doubt whatsoever about his wishes. Pressons's questions of Mrs. Brophy made the implicit argument that the Brophys' case was easier than the one before the court now.

Judge Teel excused Pat Brophy. She stepped down from the stand and walked to the Cruzans. No one else there—not the doctors, not the judge, and certainly not me or any of the lawyers—could understand the Cruzans' pain in any real way. But Pat Brophy could. She nodded at Joyce and Joe as she passed, and they all knew that she understood.

I called Dr. Cranford back to the stand. He had examined Paul Brophy before that trial, during the eight days after his feeding tube was removed, before his death. Cranford's bottom line was that Paul Brophy suffered from the same condition as Nancy, and she would likely follow a highly similar course with removal of the tube.

Before we ended our day with Joyce and Chris, we had one more witness, Barbara Carter, the counselor the Cruzans had begun to visit weekly not long after the accident. The attractive, silver-haired woman touched Joe on the shoulder as she walked by him on the way to the stand.

When Carter first met Joe, Joyce, and Chris, they were having trouble sleeping and eating, often sick to their stomachs, and in a constant state of sadness. She told Judge Teel that the sessions with Joe and Joyce were far more exhausting for her than those with her other patients. "Being in the presence of that amount of pain, if you are trained to be empathetic, you can protect yourself to a certain degree from that, but you know, that pain was overwhelming, and that pain was all over the place, and it was very exhausting at times." Joe and Joyce were always her last appointment of the day—she had no steam left after the Cruzans.

As it grew more apparent that Nancy was not going to recover, Barbara Carter had suggested to the family that they needed to "compartmentalize," or put Nancy in a separate place in their minds and find some relief for themselves. She steered them toward various support groups, including the Head Injury group in town. But in some ways, that group ended up compounding the Cruzans' isolation, because others in the group got to see improvements in their loved ones. No one wanted to discuss what to do with Nancy, the woman who wasn't coming out of her coma. And although Joe tried, he just couldn't find different compartments for the parts of his life.

When the family began to think about removing treatment for Nancy, the Cruzans came to Barbara as a group—even Donna came to town for one session. The discussion always centered on what Nancy would want and what would be best for her. Carter testified that the Cruzans were unanimous in their belief that Nancy would want treatment stopped.

She also told the judge about the effect Nancy's situation had on the family: Basically, Joe and Joyce had stopped the majority of their social activities over this five-year period. They used to be active outdoors people, and she pushed them to continue going away for weekends. They tried. They would take the trailer and go somewhere, but then they'd end up just sitting there looking out the window or crying. So they finally just gave up doing those things. And their different coping styles had made it very difficult for them to be there for each other. Joyce was private and took her grief and pain inside, while Joe needed to do things, fix things, be active and speak to people. Joe would want to talk, and Joyce would say she didn't want to talk anymore, which left Joe very frustrated.

"You know, they can't always have the energy to give to the other person, and the understanding to give to the other person, because they are just trying to cope," Carter said.

Thad McCanse had no questions for Barbara Carter, and the judge turned to the state's table. Bob Presson leaned over and conferred quickly with Rod Northcutt, then looked back to the judge. No questions. The judge excused Barbara Carter, and through her tears she smiled at the Cruzans as she walked past.

The lengthening shadows came through the tall windows of the courtroom again, telling us that another day had somehow almost gone by. We were near the end, ready to finish our direct testimony with Nancy's mother and sister. I didn't see how, based upon the last two days, any judge could rule against this family. But if any doubt lingered, Joyce and Chris should chase it away. Walt stood and called Joyce Cruzan to the stand.

Joyce knew what she had to do and she wanted it over with. Through the years of the Cruzan family's public battle, reporters invariably described Joyce as "quiet" or "private" or "keeping her emotions inside." All true, but these descriptions did not capture her strength. Joyce provided the counterweight to Joe's emotion and the decisiveness to overcome his indecision. In public, she appeared quiet and reserved, but Joyce guided the family and often made their decisions.

On the witness stand, Joyce sat perfectly upright, hands folded on her lap, her face framed by her brown permed hair. With little sign of nervousness, and without emotion, she described Nancy's current condition and the decision to stop medical treatment. The only time Joyce's mask slipped was when she talked about the Nancy before the accident.

Nancy was always in the most trouble, and she was the only one of the three Cruzan girls whom Joyce's mom had ever spanked—after Nancy screamed that Grandma was an old witch. Grandpa had fared no better: When she was three years old, Nancy got mad at him when he teased her and she stomped on his ingrown toenail, sending him to the bathroom howling in pain.

Nancy spent days laying out by the river when she was older, so she was always tan. She was the first one to wear the new fashions, an outlandish dresser. One by one, Joyce described the memories in Exhibits 22–28, which were all photographs: Nancy the twirler, with her sister Donna; Nancy in the PTA program; Nancy on her bicycle; Nancy shortly before the accident, reading to her two nieces. Upon seeing Exhibit 27, the photo that Joyce had taken of Nancy up on the scaffolding with Angie and Miranda, Joyce smiled. "We couldn't have planned a better day if we tried," she said.

As Walt and Joyce moved into the time after the painting photo, Joyce's smile faded, her posture stiffened, and her stoic face returned. She described Nancy's lack of response over the past five years, even though they'd tried everything to stimulate her. Joyce also discussed how unhealthy Nancy looked—she'd ballooned up to 139 pounds from her natural 115. And when asked about her plans for Nancy's final days if Judge Teel granted their request, Joyce didn't have a long and involved answer like Joe.

"I would just be there," she said, her hollow voice and impassive face making her look as if she was dried out, as if she'd used up all of her tears in the first months after the accident, when she'd really lost her daughter. "That's all I can do now, just be there," Joyce repeated.

Bob Presson had few questions. He mainly established that Joyce and Nancy had never had a specific conversation about death and vegetative states. He had nothing to gain from any cross-examination of Nancy's mother.

Chris Cruzan White had little of her mother's calm as she took the witness chair. Her hands shook so much that she gripped them tightly in her lap. Yet, with her set jaw, wide brown eyes, and flowing brunette hair, it was obvious that Nancy's sister sat before the court. Her answers were polite "Yes, sir"s and "No, sir"s—her desire to please had always been the counterweight to Nancy's impudence and mischief-making.

Chris told the court that she and Nancy had been close growing up. They were less than two years apart in age and were together all of the time in their small town. Their bond grew even stronger as adults, with Nancy like a second mother to Chris's girls—present at their births and a huge part of their lives from then on, taking them to gymnastics, recitals, and trick-or-treating. Chris described her independent, head-strong sister, the one who had lots of friends and was proud of her body, and said, "Nancy would be horrified at the state she is in now."

Walt asked, "Any time since Nancy's accident, have you seen any response from her to suggest Nancy is aware of herself or others or her environment?"

"No, sir."

"Have you looked for those kinds of responses in her?"

"Sir, we have begged for those kind of responses from her."

"Christy, had your sister Nancy ever said anything to you that would indicate what preference she would have in this situation?" Walt and Chris had reached a critical part of Chris's testimony. Unfortunately, it was not much. In the fall of 1981, just a little over two years before the accident, their sister Donna, who was only 18 at the time, had given birth to a stillborn baby. Nancy took the death particularly hard, and a day or two later, while sitting at Chris's kitchen table over coffee, Nancy had concluded that this baby's death was maybe part of a greater plan. But Chris could not remember Nancy's exact words, and she did not think that the topic of machines and life support had come up.

A month after this conversation between Chris and Nancy, their grandmother was admitted to Freeman Hospital for surgery to receive a pacemaker. She'd been in and out of the hospital, and she'd nearly lost her eyesight and was in constant pain. Shortly after the pacemaker operation, she died at home. Again over coffee, Nancy suggested to Chris that death was sometimes not the worst situation one could be in. Going in and out of the hospital, with no real hope of ever really getting better, was worse. Still, there was no discussion of machines, and Chris had no memory of the exact conversation so long ago.

"Even though there wasn't any discussion about respirators or other machines, do you think that Nancy would have wanted to be kept alive by some type of machine or artificial life support?" Walt asked.

"I would object to that," Bob Presson said, rising. "It is asking the witness to speculate now, not on the basis of anything that Nancy said."

"Be overruled," Judge Teel said.

Chris continued. "It wasn't just those two instances that I knew, it was through a lifetime of experience and in that, Nancy being kept alive within me, within my heart, within those of us who love her." Chris's voice rose as her hands gripped the arms of the witness chair. "Her body is being maintained, and Nancy would want to live where she could live to the fullest. Where she lives to the fullest is within us. It is not within that body that's being maintained at Mt. Vernon."

It appeared that the weight of the day's emotion would overtake Chris, and when Walt asked her about the effect of Nancy's accident and the court battle on her parents, the tears began to flow down her cheeks as she talked about their lives drawing in, and her belief that Nancy would want to spare her parents any further pain.

Walt's voice cracked, and tears came to his eyes as well. Enough. He nodded at the judge and sat down. Thad McCanse and Bob Presson talked to Chris briefly, but there wasn't much more to say.

It was almost six o'clock, and when the judge asked for our next witness, I told him we were finished. "Would you all come up just a minute, please, and visit about our future tomorrow?" he asked.

Thad McCanse smiled at the judge. "I'm getting in a persistent—"

Judge Teel interrupted McCanse, kidding him: "You came that way." The judge asked if we would finish tomorrow or go over into Saturday. He moved the start up to 8:30 A.M. the next day, and made his preference clear that he did not want to go over into Saturday. We all agreed and headed back to gather papers.

"Bill, can we talk to you guys for a second?" Rod Northcutt asked. Walt and I walked over to the state's table.

"We've decided to have Dr. Dexter examine Nancy. He's doing that tonight, and you're entitled to attend," Bob Presson said. Dexter was the state's expert witness.

"You can't do that, Bob. Dexter testified a week ago that he didn't plan to examine Nancy," I said. "I need to prepare for your other witnesses tonight. I'm not driving clear up to Mt. Vernon."

"We felt that after the nurse's testimony, we needed to have him examine her."

"This is bullshit, guys. You knew about that testimony before today. I'm not going up there."

"Fine, we just wanted to let you know," said Presson, and we returned to our tables.

Walt, Dr. Cranford, and I huddled with the family in the front of the courtroom, recapping the day and looking ahead. That night the Cruzans were going live on *Nightline* with Ted Koppel. And now I had a new project for the night—Dr. Dexter's deposition. We made our plans at the table and headed down to meet the television cameras in the lobby.

CHAPTER 21

THE CRUZANS ON *NIGHTLINE*

Joe Cruzan had never before begun his day dressed up at 8:00 A.M., only to find himself putting on a fresh suit 13 hours later. Exhausted after the last two days and fighting a nasty cold, Joe now faced the biggest public moment of his life.

Sitting shoulder-to-shoulder with Chris in the small local studio of a private religious broadcaster, Joe watched the television monitor. Local reporter Jennifer Andrews was telling the story of the day's events at the trial: "Joe Cruzan caused the courtroom to fall silent as he described, following deeply emotional pauses, how his family had lost hope."

The local news finished, the commercials came on, and then the unmistakable voice of Ted Koppel filled the studio. "Nancy Cruzan is in a condition that is known medically as a 'persistent vegetative state.' She doesn't need a respirator to breathe, but she must be fed through a tube implanted in her stomach. After five years, her parents now feel that this has gone on long enough—but removing Nancy's life support literally means starving her to death. Good evening, I'm Ted Koppel, and this is *Nightline*. Nancy Cruzan's parents are now pressing her case in court."

Joe's face and voice suddenly filled the screen, taken from the PBS documentary broadcast nine days earlier. He was saying something he said often: "If the decision's wrong, if we're playing God, then I'll have to live with that, and I'm willing to." Just as quickly, Ted Koppel was back on the screen, saying, "Our guests include Nancy Cruzan's father and her sister." The familiar *Nightline* music faded in.

Joe and Chris huddled closer together in the small studio. The music ended, and the camera came back to Ted Koppel, who said, "This is, at one and the same time, one of the simplest and one of the most complicated stories with which we have ever dealt." A still photo of Joe touching Nancy's forehead appeared in the upper right-hand corner of the screen: The graphic "Right to Die" labeled the photo.

Koppel continued. "Simple because for five years a woman has been in what has been called a 'persistent vegetative state.' Unable to function in any manner on her own, with two very crucial exceptions: Her heart continues to pump blood through her body, and she is breathing on her own. She could live, if that is the appropriate term, for many, many more years. Her family doesn't think she should. And so, they have petitioned a court—and here is where the case becomes so painfully complicated—to authorize the removal of a feeding tube from the woman's stomach. Without nourishment, of course, she will eventually die."

Joe watched as his face again filled the monitor in front of him, starting an eight-minute segment clipped from the PBS documentary the Cruzans had watched for the first time just days earlier. The voices of Joyce, Joe, and Chris; Nancy's doctors; and Assistant Attorney General Bob Presson told the Cruzans' story in minutes. And pictures of Nancy filled the screen—including one of her stiff body being raised by a small, silver medical crane from her bed to a chair for a few minutes.

Then the short documentary was over, and Chris and Joe were back in the present. Koppel told his audience that Joe and Chris would join them later in the show, live. Joe fidgeted in his chair as the commercials played on the monitor in front of him, while Chris sat still and stared stone-faced at the television.

Before he talked to the Cruzans, however, Ted Koppel wanted to further set the stage. After the commercial break, he interviewed Dr. Cranford, who was at a different studio in Joplin, and Dr. Mark Siegler, a well-known and respected doctor and ethicist from the University of Chicago, who was appearing from a station in Toronto. Dr. Cranford explained the difference between a vegetative state and a coma, and Nancy's clear diagnosis. Koppel and Cranford went on to discuss the "horrifying" reality of PVS—the patient is just as unconscious as a brain-dead one, but their eyes are open and move about.

Koppel asked, "How do we know? I mean, I realize that's a terrible question to ask you, but there's that even more terrifying question: What if? What if, despite the incapacity to say anything or communicate anything, there is some cognitive power still in that head?"

"It's a good question," Cranford responded. "We know that those thinking parts are gone because we have accumulated a great deal of experience in the last five to ten years with this condition. We can recognize the findings on examination. We know that Nancy suffered from anoxia, or lack of oxygen to the brain. We have CT scans and other specialized x-ray studies to determine that those parts of the brain that have to do with thinking and feeling, the neocortex, are destroyed. And, like in Nancy's case, we know with a high degree of certainty, based on our clinical experience—just like other diagnoses we make all of the time. So with her we know. But it's still horrifying, and your question is very legitimate and your concern is legitimate."

Koppel turned to Dr. Siegler, whom Koppel had introduced at the beginning of the segment as an ethicist and doctor who generally opposes legally sanctioning the removal of life support. "Dr. Siegler, on the points that we have made so far, and that Dr. Cranford has made so far, no disagreement, right?"

"No disagreement," Siegler said, "except that the questions you ask, Ted, are so important, because they're very confusing for families—and often for doctors and hospital staff, too. It's important to get that clarification."

"All right," Koppel said. "I mean, the only reason I asked those questions first is I wanted to make sure there wasn't any clinical disagreement. We are engaged here—and I was going to say 'simply,' but nothing could be more complicated—but we are engaged in what is basically an ethical debate? Right?"

"It is," Siegler replied. "The real question, despite what Dr. Cranford has said, is whether people like Nancy Cruzan should be treated as if they were dead. You heard the assistant attorney general of the state of Missouri say that she didn't meet the brain-death standards or the cardiac and respiratory standards to declare death in that state. And the question is whether the state of persistent vegetative state is so debilitating that one ought to deal with her as if she were a dead person and withdraw simple intervention such as feeding and fluid delivered through a tube."

Joe and Chris sat transfixed as this debate played out before them. Under the surface, Joe seethed. His daughter was being debated like a textbook, and his own name was being pronounced in three different ways: "kroo-zan" (which is correct), " kroo-zahn," (like "Autobahn"), and "cruisin'."

Ted Koppel brought the ethical debate between the doctors to an end as they sparred over the question of whether allowing the Cruzans to remove Nancy's feeding tube would lead to sanctioning of active euthanasia. This was hardly an issue that Joe or Chris cared at all about. As Koppel cut away to a commercial, the camera panned to Joe and Chris, side-by-side in the small studio. Joe sat upright, his jaw set with energy, strength, and the firm resolve to protect his kin—both the daughter next to him and the one in the hospital bed.

After the commercial, Ted Koppel gave the audience a little background about the accident and explained that Joe and Chris had testified earlier that day. Then he turned to Joe with the first question—and the topic that had piqued his interest from the interview of the two doctors: Why did Joe make the decision to allow PBS and Elizabeth Arledge to film his family's anguish?

Joe had been sitting silent and still for a long time, and his voice cracked as he began to speak. He told Koppel that his family had decided that the public had to know how far medical technology had outpaced society's ability to deal with it. What started as a miracle had turned into a nightmare.

Koppel started to ask, "When did—"

Joe cut him off. "Secondly, secondly," he started in, trying to deal with the slight delay from his earpiece as Koppel's voice sped across the country to Joplin, Missouri. "Secondly," Joe said a third time, "we thought that was where we could get a fair telling of our story."

In later years, Joe substituted a new answer to that question: If some good was to come out of Nancy's tragedy, then her family wanted to achieve that good. Chris often said that she thought they'd made the decision just so someone would talk to them about Nancy, rather than turn away with eyes averted anytime the topic came up.

"Let me ask you, Ms. White," Koppel said to Chris. "You probably heard Dr. Cranford a minute ago say, and I didn't want to interrupt him, that you all know this is what Nancy would want. How? How do you know this is what she would want?"

"Yes, sir, we know that because of the way she lived her life. She was a very active, vivacious, so independent—," Chris's words trailed off. She sounded tired at the end of this long day, and tired of trying to answer this specific question.

The question is perhaps a key one, but hard to put the answer into words. A sister or a parent just *knows* about their loved one, but that isn't really much of an answer. And even though she was on national television, Chris was near the end of her rope. Still, fatigue cannot mask unconditional love, which filled the screen as she talked.

"How can you know that that is what she would want? I mean we're talking here about a very slow, lingering form of death, starvation, quite literally," Koppel said. "I hate to put it that brutally, but that's what it is." That question jolted Chris back to attention, and she sat up in her chair, her voice now forceful and filled with conviction.

"Well, I don't think that her death is—my sister died five years ago, actually. The things that we knew about her, the way that she was, the way that she participated in life, those things all ended five years ago. So yes, her body may cease to exist, but Nancy won't. Nancy lives within us, and she has for the past five years."

The question also sat Joe upright. He squirmed in his chair, waiting for his chance to speak. Although phrased diplomatically, Koppel's next question to Joe boiled down to this: Dr. Siegler had essentially said the Cruzans had made a mistake by making this issue public—they should have quietly and privately had Nancy's tube removed. A slight smile came to Joe's face, and he said, "Let the doctor rest assured that if we could have done that, we would. We faced criminal charges if we took that step. It was no option." Ted Koppel nodded, seeming to appreciate the answer.

Before the next commercial break, Koppel asked Joe the question Bob Presson had asked earlier in the day: "If you lose, will you abide by the decision?" Joe gave the same answer he gave Presson—that the question was premature, and they'd have to see what the court decided. But he went one step further, telling Koppel that they might have other options, such as moving her to another state.

As I watched on my hotel bed, I cringed. Several months earlier, I had a new associate at Shook, Hardy do the legal research on Nancy's constitutional right to travel. There wasn't much law on the topic, and the issue made me a little nervous. I did not want word out that we were considering moving Nancy out of Missouri. We did the research under a code name for the file, and I met with the associate behind closed doors to stress that he could speak to no one, not even his peers, about the project. I apparently didn't need to worry about secrecy on that issue any longer.

After the break, the screen came up with all four guests pictured together, outlined in boxes. Ted Koppel asked a final question of Dr. Siegler, and then turned to Dr. Cranford, saying, "If you had to summarize, and you do have to summarize in a very short period of time, I'm afraid, the argument is what?" Koppel had no idea what a challenge he had set before the loquacious doctor, who could easily talk for five minutes ordering breakfast. Nonetheless, Dr. Cranford delivered a clear and succinct summary of the *Cruzan* case, focused on the "medical reality . . . and the hopeless existence" of Nancy.

Koppel began his usual ending to his show. "All right. I'm very grateful to all of you. Dr. Siegler, Dr. Cranford—"

Joe Cruzan cut in, his voice agitated, "Could I make one point here?"

"Yes, please, go ahead," Koppel said, the tape delay again altering their communication.

"I don't like this word *starvation*. Dr. Cranford testified, and we feel that there is—that Nancy will feel no pain at all. It's, it's, a procedure that will just simply allow her to die peacefully."

"I thank you, Mr. Cruzan," Koppel said. "This must have been a very painful interview for you to do, but you have suffered a lot of pain over the last few years, and we all empathize with you—and with you, Ms. White. Thank you all very much for being with us. My apologies to our affiliates—we ran over a few seconds, but I think you will agree that we had to hear what Mr. Cruzan had to say. That's our report for tonight. I'm Ted Koppel in Washington, for all of us here at ABC News, good night."

CHAPTER 22

THE STATE'S CASE

While Joe and Chris were talking to Ted Koppel, I was in my hotel room reading through the transcript from Dr. Dexter's deposition and going through stacks of Nancy's medical records.

Kim Ross had taken Dr. Cranford to the studio for *Nightline*. When she returned, she took the nurses' notes from me and continued the project she'd begun the night before, combing through the notes one final time for any reference to Nancy crying, laughing, or interacting with the environment. At two in the morning, we met and set the files out on the table in my room. Kim's verdict: If some nurse had seen some reaction from Nancy over the last four years, he or she hadn't found it important enough to write down. Page after page of the notes contained the same statements, either "no response" or "persistent vegetative state."

But we had a problem. The records we had for Nancy only covered the time period from her admittance to MRC, in the fall of 1983, until Halloween 1987. I didn't have any records for this past Valentine's Day. I chided myself for not updating the document production from the state just prior to trial, but that did little good now. Plus, it didn't really matter. For the state to try to suggest that after all these years they'd suddenly found that Nancy was conscious—rather than the "no response" and "persistent vegetative state" patient described in a thousand pages of their own medical records—would sound highly suspect.

Dr. Dexter was another matter. I didn't think the judge would exclude his testimony, any more than he'd considered sending Mrs.

Brophy out of his courtroom earlier that day, even though I intended to argue as persuasively as I could that he should. So I prepared to talk to the doctor about his statements to me at the deposition, just seven days earlier, when he'd raised his hand and swore an oath to tell the whole truth. I planned to talk to him for a long time.

I fell asleep around three and had breakfast at seven with Kim and Dr. Cranford to talk about the nurses' notes. A front had come in during the night, and Thursday's promise of spring had changed into an ominous threat of storms by Friday. When we headed out of the Holiday Inn, the warm, gusty wind that blew in our faces, completely out of place for an early March morning, seemed like a not-so-subtle omen.

❧   ❧   ❧

When they arrived in the courtroom on the last day of the trial, Joe, Joyce, and Chris were more relaxed. With their own testimony and *Nightline* behind them, the worst was over for them. I kidded Joe about making every affiliate in the country go off schedule when he interrupted Ted Koppel at the end of the show, and he chuckled. He liked the idea of that kind of power and control in the hands of a sheet-metal worker from Carterville, Missouri.

Judge Teel entered the courtroom and said good morning. All that was left in our case was the routine work of entering documents and depositions into evidence. When that was done, I tried to look the judge directly in the eye and said, "Your Honor, at this time, petitioner rests." The judge asked the other two parties for motions. Thad McCanse made none, and Bob Presson raised again his pending motion to dismiss.

"All right, sir. It will continue under advisement," Judge Teel said, just as McCanse had told me many months before that he would. With that, the judge turned and nodded to Thad McCanse, who only had three more witnesses to put on the stand. I planned to say little to them and hoped to sit quietly for a while and wait for Dr. Dexter later in the day.

McCanse's first two witnesses, Diane Logan and Geraldine Reed, had worked at Schreiber's Cheese with Nancy. They each added a voice to the theme of Nancy's independence, and testified about an important area, but one on which our side couldn't dwell—that Nancy loved her family and would never want to put them through this ordeal. I asked no questions of either witness, and their testimony passed quickly.

The final witness for the *guardian ad litem* was Alice Johnson, the nurse's aide who said she saw a reaction from Nancy after the Valentine's card.

Alice Johnson, a small, roundish woman with glasses, walked to the stand. She'd worked at MRC for ten years, since it was the State Chest Hospital. She told McCanse that Nancy Cruzan had been her patient for nine months, and that every day she'd given Nancy a bath, changed her gowns, done range-of-motion exercises, and performed the tube feeding. You could tell that she cared about Nancy.

McCanse wanted to know her assessment of any reactions from Nancy. He asked, "What about her eyes? Are they opened?"

"Yes, sir."

"And do they focus on anything as far as you can tell?"

"I wouldn't swear to that, but she hears your voice, she looks that way," Johnson answered. "I don't know whether she is hearing it or seeing it."

"She has responded to sound, though, your voice?"

"Definitely."

"How often does that take place?"

"Oh, I would say 75 percent of the time, but to some people—not to all people—but to some people, yes, there is a reaction," Johnson replied.

"And what other reactions have you noticed?"

"I've seen her cry."

"You've seen what?" McCanse asked, surprised.

"I've seen her cry."

"When did you see her cry?"

"Her nieces sent her a Valentine's card, and we read it to her—and I never thought much about it, but I turned around and went back, and she was crying."

"Did she have tears in her eyes?"

"She was crying—"

"Did she make noises or sob?" McCanse interrupted.

"No, she didn't sob, she just cried."

I turned slightly in my chair and looked at the Cruzans sitting in the front row of the seats, just behind the wooden railing separating the two sections of the courtroom. A perturbed look covered Chris's face. Joyce shook her head in disgust. And Joe's face looked like a champagne cork ready to pop. It appeared he wanted to jump up and shout, "Judge, for God's sake, stop this testimony!" He no doubt wanted me to do that, too.

Mrs. Johnson told Thad McCanse about Nancy grimacing in reaction to pain, and how Nancy had pulled on her hand during physical therapy. McCanse asked if she'd ever seen Nancy smile, and she replied that she had, one night while telling Nancy a story. "I accidentally told her one time, about my smallest . . . and a skunk, and definitely she smiled. Most definitely. All over."

"Has that happened more than once?" Thad asked.

"I had not ever got that reaction," she replied. "Honest to God, I thought she was going to laugh."

McCanse may have swung toward our position, but he was still trying to give Judge Teel a full view. I obviously would never have let this woman near the courtroom. Yet it struck me that I would gain almost no mileage out of trying to aggressively cross-examine her about what she saw—what basis did I have to dispute her, other than to call her a liar, without direct proof?

In briefs filed after the trial, we could outline the implausibility and the insignificance of her testimony. One or two random reactions over a five-year period, with no further evidence since? Even if it was something other than wishful thinking, it was hardly evidence of Nancy's emergence from the vegetative state. The doctors had already told us as much. I didn't believe that Judge Teel would want me to browbeat a nurse's aide in his courtroom—better to be nice and send her off the stand quickly.

On cross-examination, I established that Mrs. Johnson hadn't seen a pattern of these reactions from all of her daily visits, only the smile story and the valentine, and that she didn't have the training to explain, for example, why Nancy appeared to startle when the television came on.

"Would you have to defer to a neurologist to determine where . . . that reaction is coming from in her brain? Whether it is a reflex reaction or whether she's really having some thought?" I asked.

"I would have to—they are more—they have the teaching," she said.

I sat down.

In his examination, Bob Presson drew out Mrs. Johnson's opinion of the Cruzans' request. "I cannot hurt an animal as far as starving them to death," she responded. "I can't see this, no."

As Alice Johnson left the courtroom that day, Joe Cruzan watched each step she took—these two people would never again chat together over Nancy's bed.

Thad McCanse had told Bob Presson that he wouldn't take up a lot of their day on Friday, and true to his word, when he rested his case, we hadn't even reached the morning break yet.

Judge Teel smiled down at Bob Presson, and asked, "Are you ready to proceed, sir?" Presson called Sue Rowell as his first witness.

Rowell was the nurse who Joe had first told, a year and a half earlier, about the family's decision to remove Nancy's feeding tube. Joe liked the forthright way she stood up and spoke her mind, even when she disagreed with him. She reminded him of himself.

Presson and Nurse Rowell eased into their conversation as the state's case began. They discussed the nurse's background and how long she'd cared for Nancy. Her description of Nancy's condition fit with the testimony from the family the day before, and she agreed with Presson that Nancy only received the most basic of nursing care, which could certainly be given in a nursing home.

Next, Presson asked, "Now, Miss Rowell, do you have an opinion upon the family's request to withdraw nutrition and hydration?"

Sue Rowell paused, her face wrinkled in consternation, and she looked at Joe. She appeared torn. "I empathize with the family," she said. "I feel morally I cannot participate in the withdrawal of feeding and hydration."

"Have you talked with other members of the nursing staff about this?"

"Well, I haven't sought out a conversation, but I'm basically the charge nurse over the 24-hour period; it has been brought up through all three shifts," she replied. "I have not heard one person that has said they would participate in it. They would prefer to see Nancy be either taken home or in a private type of situation rather than get involved."

Nurse Rowell's direct testimony closed with a discussion about the Cruzan family, which she described as "very private." She said, "It is very difficult on the family, and I think the nursing staff realizes that."

"Did Mr. Cruzan ever make a statement to you that he believed that Nancy had died the night of the accident?" Presson asked.

"I believe what he said was that he felt that Nancy had died, but he had never been allowed to bury her," Rowell replied.

Presson was finished, and the entire exam had taken less than 15 minutes.

Thad McCanse approached Sue Rowell—again, I sat hoping that he would actively take up the Cruzans' side. McCanse established that any responses, such as Nancy's eyes opening when her name was called, were inconsistent and that her condition was dire. "You are a rehabilitation center. Is there any evidence that she's shown that rehabilitation efforts have improved her condition?" he asked.

"When Nancy was admitted, we were not a rehabilitation center. The fourth floor is not considered part of the rehab programs that are offered at this facility. We are more of a chronic care-type floor."

"So what is happening now is that she is just being maintained in her present condition?"

"She is being given supportive care," Rowell answered.

"That is not curative care, that—," McCanse interrupted.

"No, it is just supportive care."

"And in that sense, she is being maintained in the state she is in and that's—," Thad McCanse seemed to struggle to find a descriptive word.

"That's right," Sue Rowell broke in.

The state's first witness had been actually helpful to the Cruzans. She spoke well of them, her observations supported the diagnosis of persistent vegetative state, and she offered no hope for improvement. On my yellow pad were three phrases: "her son," "take her home," and "purpose of health care." I walked, with that pad in hand, toward Sue Rowell. "Ms. Rowell, I understand this is a difficult situation and your testimony has been very fair," I began. "You have a son—what condition does he have?"

"He has Hodgkin's disease."

"And you have discussed his situation with Joe Cruzan and the family before?"

Rowell nodded and recounted the night that she'd found Joe crying in the hallway.

"Do you think the Cruzan family is sensitive to the needs of Nancy?" I asked.

"Oh, yeah, I think they're very sensitive to her needs, and I think the nursing staff realizes that this is something that they feel they have to do," Rowell answered. "There is no animosity between the nursing staff and the Cruzans whatsoever. I think it is difficult for us as health-care professionals to—when you've spent, like myself for 22 years basically, in trying to provide good patient care—to ask us to do just the opposite of what we've always done."

"Do you think there is any chance in your mind, as a nurse, and a health-care professional, that Nancy will ever get better or improve in any way?" I asked.

"No, sir, I don't," she said.

We talked for the next several minutes about why the Cruzans couldn't take Nancy home quietly, the mission of medicine, the role of treatments like a gastrostomy tube as a bridge to recovery, and the red tags above all 13 patients on the fourth floor that signaled "No CPR, Do Not Resuscitate." Most of the discussion was aimed at Judge Teel—I wasn't really cross-examining Nurse Rowell. She provided a very commonsense and unbiased look at the ethical issues that the judge would ultimately have to decide.

Nurse Rowell went on to describe a specific incident where a respirator was removed from a patient at MRC whose heart was still beating and his lungs still breathed with the machine, but he had two flat EEG readings, or no brain activity. In other words, he was brain dead.

I asked what seemed like a logical follow-up question to learn the effect on the patient after removal of the respirator: "Did the patient die?"

"Yes, within just a short period of time," she answered.

Actually, though, the question is not logical at all. If someone is brain dead, he's dead, even though his heart is breathing and his lungs are pumping. Stopping those artificial functions does not kill the patient— he cannot die, because he is already dead. (Unless he's in New Jersey, in which case he may be alive, because New Jersey law defines death differently.) The line between life and death, amazingly, is not a clear one. I complimented Sue Rowell on MRC's nursing care and sat down.

Bob Presson had no further questions, but Thad McCanse stood up, his face pinched with curiosity. He asked Nurse Rowell about the brain-dead patient. "So a respirator can keep the heart beating and a person breathing even after death?" he asked.

"Yes, they can keep—yes," she answered.

Thad shook his head quizzically and sat down.

Judge Teel recessed court for the morning break. Everyone shuffled to attention as he walked out, and then they collectively exhaled. The state had only three witnesses left: Janie Bowker, a nurse at MRC; Dr. Anita Isaac, the MRC medical director; and their expert, Dr. Dexter.

During the break, I talked to Joe and Chris outside the courtroom while Joyce ran out for some fresh air and a cigarette. The family looked tired—the relaxed state in which they'd begun the morning was long gone. Joe couldn't believe that MRC had sprung the valentine story on the family at trial, rather than telling them at the hospital if it was so important. When I explained to Joe why I'd spent so little time with Alice Johnson, he nodded his head, but the look on his face seemed to say that he didn't understand lawyers and didn't want to. But both Joe and Chris perked up when I discussed the possibility that the trial might not take the rest of the day, with only one nurse and two doctors left.

❧   ❧   ❧

Nurse Janie Bowker took the stand after the break. Her testimony was brief, but it set the tone for the remainder of the day. She told Presson on direct examination that she graduated from nursing school in 1981 and had worked at MRC ever since. Prior to nursing school, she worked at the psychiatric center in the city of Nevada, Missouri, for 25 years—so she'd spent most of her life around hard cases. Bowker had been a registered nurse on Nancy's floor at MRC for a little over a year, and her testimony mirrored the nurse's aide from her floor. She testified that Nancy responded when she talked to her, and that she had seen Nancy cry maybe five or six times over the last six months. She told Presson that she couldn't give him the exact dates because she hadn't recorded the crying in Nancy's medical records. She agreed with Sue Rowell and Lisa Perrin about the family's request.

"I feel quite consistent emotions about—," she began, then started again. "It must be very difficult to see a child that you love in this condition. But I was trained to maintain life and give them as good a life as possible—regardless what that level might be—not take it from them. So I cannot, cannot participate." She told Presson that the nursing staff was united in their reaction: "We cannot stand by and do nothing and watch her dehydrate and starve to death."

Presson sat down and McCanse approached the nurse. "You have mentioned that you've seen expressions of pain and moaning and tears?" he began.

"Yes."

"Otherwise, is her expression, call it neutral, placid?"

"It is very flat."

"Have you ever seen her give an expression of happiness?" McCanse asked.

"There have been a few times in which you swear she's going to really smile and laugh out loud, and some of my staff have told me, yes, they have seen her smile."

"How many times has that reaction been reported to you?"

"It has been three times that I can recall. One has not been too awfully long ago."

"Was that last Valentine's Day?"

"No, it has been in the last two weeks." Bowker said that they had an assistant who liked to take on extra duties. One day, she came over from her wing and asked if she could give Nancy a bath. She did that, and also trimmed Nancy's nails and did her hair. When the two nursing assistants assigned to Nancy came into the room, the assistant who had given her the bath said to them, "Doesn't she look squeaky clean?" According to Bowker, the nursing assistants "heard a 'huhmph' behind them, and they turned and looked and Nancy had snickered, and she had a smile on her face that was very obvious."

It appeared that this testimony was too much for even mild-mannered Thad McCanse. He remained polite, but asked, "Is it true, Mrs. Bowker, that sometimes the people taking care of a patient such as Nancy become somewhat emotionally attached?"

"I'm afraid we do."

"Including you?"

"Including myself."

McCanse sat down.

Walt Williams cross-examined Nurse Bowker for our side. He established that she had no formal training in ethics, hadn't read the American Medical Association guidelines, and didn't know Nancy's personal wishes or factor them into her opinion. Both Walt Williams and Nurse Bowker spoke in angry tones, and the cross-examination was the most combative exchange in three days. At one point, Judge Teel even cautioned Walt about arguing with Nurse Bowker. I thought Walt had done it just right.

It wasn't even lunchtime, and we were almost through—just two doctors to go.

CHAPTER 23

HOSTILE WITNESS

Bob Presson called out the name of Dr. Anita Isaac, and a gray-haired woman with glasses stood and walked from the gallery to the witness stand. Dr. Isaac spoke in a clear, confident voice as Presson began his questioning. Her confidence had a solid foundation: She'd graduated from medical school in 1949 and had been practicing rehabilitation medicine since 1953. Don Lamkins had hired her two years earlier to come in and lead the new head-injury and rehabilitation program at MRC. Even if she didn't talk about it in a courtroom every day, the doctor knew the subject on which she was about to testify.

Dr. Isaac told Presson about the number of head-injury clinics that had opened all over the country in the last ten years, and she suggested that new data in rehabilitation journals was on the way. PVS patients who began rehabilitation in the first year could improve—not enough to be able to care for themselves, but they could improve.

My alarm bells went off, not unusual when a witness for the other side starts to talk about potentially damaging information that the lawyer has never heard of before. I objected that the witness hadn't been identified as an expert to testify about the persistent vegetative state, and the studies she was talking about apparently did not even exist yet.

Judge Teel overruled the objection, but testimony about these forthcoming journals stopped there, and the doctor turned to the head-injury victim who had not started rehabilitation in the first year after her accident—or the second, third, or fourth, either—Nancy Cruzan.

Dr. Isaac explained that, while not directly involved in Nancy's care, she'd talked to the family several times, and had been on call on the fourth floor on occasion. Presson asked if she'd formed an opinion about Nancy's condition. This doctor had never examined Nancy—she'd only been on Nancy's floor on occasion, and she'd already hand-delivered to the Cruzans her written medical opinion that Nancy was in a persistent vegetative state. Presumably, that was the opinion she was about to deliver to the court.

"Well, I think she's been, what we could call a very low-level head-injury patient that has been isolated for a long time and has developed contractures so that she has really no function, has been maintained in a nursing home-type section, really, in custodial care."

"We mentioned earlier the term *persistent vegetative state*—how do you think that applies to Nancy, or does it?" Presson asked.

"Well, I think she is certainly somewhere in between that, but in most of these patients, there are some holes in their ability," Dr. Isaac said. "It seems to be, from what I've seen and heard of Nancy, that she can hear . . . so she does perceive what's going on from the environment."

"Do you believe it is possible to know how much Nancy is aware of or experiencing at the present time?"

"No, I don't. I think there are some areas where she seems to perceive what's going on, but we can't prove it, you know—it is somewhat inconsistent except for the auditory function, I think that's fairly consistent," she said. "She does seem to communicate for longer periods with some of her environment, and it's been kind of a gradual improvement, even though she has been very isolated and there has been kind of a determined effort to keep her in a coma for a long time."

"When you say 'determined effort,' by whom?"

"Well, I haven't really been asked to be involved in her rehabilitation efforts."

"Have you been asked of anything with regard to Nancy?" Presson inquired.

"Well, I have been asked to help remove the hydration and nutrition."

"And that's the only request?"

"That's the only request I've ever had."

I sat scribbling as fast as I could on my yellow pad. *The only request, yes, except for a request for a written diagnosis, for God's sake. No one asked her to help? Is that a new standard for medical care?* My pad was filling fast.

The doctor went on. She said that neurologists weren't as good as therapists at recognizing responses because not many neurologists would take the time to sit there and wait for one. Dr. Isaac mentioned another patient on Nancy's floor, named Youngblood, who had emerged from a PVS after more than a year, due to rehabilitation efforts.

"Do you think it can be said with any degree of certainty that certain improvements couldn't be made in Nancy's case?" Presson asked.

"I can't say for sure, no," Dr. Isaac replied.

Presson established that Dr. Isaac believed that, based on the reports of the nurses, Nancy could perceive pain, and that her care currently was only custodial, which could be done in a nursing home. And he had the doctor explain the typical phases a family goes through in dealing with a severely disabled loved one: denying it happened; admitting it happened but taking blame ("If only I'd taught her to wear a seatbelt"); asking the doctor to prolong treatment and insisting on improvement; and finally, when the patient plateaus, sometimes there are negative reactions ("I can't visit every day anymore. I need to get on with my life").

"Are these phases that you've described fairly well documented and recognized?" Presson asked.

"Yes, this is in almost all the social and psychological literature in rehabilitation care."

"Have you had any dealings with Nancy's family?"

"Yes."

"Would you describe what those dealings were?"

"Well, I met—shortly after I got to the Center, with Mr. Lamkins, the administrator, and the family, on I think, on their request—was to try to clarify what it was that the family wanted the hospital to do," the doctor began. "That would have been back in 1986. Then again, the family came to me, or just two of the members . . . Mr. Cruzan and Joyce—and again, tried to persuade me to change my mind."

"Was there anything about those meetings that struck you as unusual or out of the ordinary?" Presson asked.

"Yeah. One of the things—of course, you know, and I had been worried about—is that Mr. Cruzan is very insistent about what he wants and getting his way, and he tends to become somewhat intimidating."

"Did that happen on this occasion?"

"Yes, it did," Dr. Isaac said. She glanced from Presson to Joe Cruzan, who was sitting in the front row of the courtroom, as she talked.

"What do you mean, 'intimidating'? Would you describe that?"

"Well, you know, it has been a while, I really don't remember the details of it, but I can remember saying to him, you know, 'You are beginning to threaten me,' and he did pull back some."

"How do you think that fits in with your general understanding of reaction of families who have patients in an unresponsive state?"

"Well, you know, in all the years and all the patients I have had that have been in this kind of situation, I've never had anybody ask me to remove a tube before," the doctor answered. "I always wondered what I would do if this would occur, but it has never happened to me until this time. I have had all the other things happen to me. I had divorces, and the other traumas that the physicians have, to try to work through during this period of time. But this is kind of the ultimate in rejection as far as I'm concerned—asking me to participate in it."

Dr. Isaac told Presson that the Cruzans' request fit the last stage of the process, rejection, and that removing the tube wasn't appropriate.

"Could you explain why you don't think it is appropriate?" Presson asked.

"Well, it is basic human care."

"Do you consider—," Presson began.

"To feed somebody," Dr. Isaac interrupted.

"Do you consider it medical care in any sense?"

"No."

The testimony went on. According to Dr. Isaac, Nancy would feel pain if the tube was removed, not to mention that such an act was against the law of Missouri and unethical, too. I sort of shut down, and stopped writing on the yellow pad. The unfairness of this testimony was beyond comprehension to me, and I had a new goal: I wanted to have Dr. Isaac see a new "ultimate in rejection"—her cross-examination at this trial.

As Thad McCanse started to question Dr. Isaac, he appeared irritated as well. He established that her story of the rehabilitation of a PVS patient in the first year was really irrelevant to Nancy's situation after five years. He then tried to clarify her diagnosis. "Earlier, I think you said that you thought Nancy was between a persistent vegetative state—"

"There is no in between, they tell me now," Dr. Isaac interrupted. "The neurologists tell me now there is no in between, so I would have to really answer that as no, she probably isn't in PVS at this time."

"She is?" McCanse asked, confused.

"No, she isn't, because there is some evidence that something is going through her or may have gone through before," Dr. Isaac said.

"Well, that's what I—I didn't know in between what, so I asked the question," McCanse said. "But she is not in a PVS at this time?"

"Not at least as we understand PVS."

"And what is your understanding of what a true PVS is?" McCanse asked.

"True PVS is an individual who has really no way of responding to the environment."

"And you feel from what you've related—"

"There is some responses," Dr. Isaac broke in.

"There have been some responses?"

"Small responses."

McCanse discussed the extent of atrophy of Nancy's brain, the significance of her contractures, and moved to his final topic—feeding. "Do you think that she would have the ability to swallow either fluid or foods at this time?" he asked.

"As far as I know, it hasn't been tried for a long time. It would be risky."

"Would that be because of the danger of aspiration?" McCanse asked.

"Yes."

"And that means getting the fluid or food into her lungs and developing pneumonia?"

"That's aspirational pneumonia," Isaac confirmed.

"That's a very critical situation, is it not?"

"Yes."

"And life threatening?"

"Yes."

Thad McCanse nodded that he was finished. The judge looked down at the rest of the lawyers. "You all want to come to the bench?" he asked. We came forward, and he said to me, "The miracle of finishing your examination in the next several minutes appears rather remote to the court." He was smiling, but the last hour and a half had snuffed out my sense of humor completely.

"Nonexistent, Your Honor," I replied.

"Nonexistent?"

"Don't beat around the bush, Bill," McCanse said. The judge gave me the pat-on-the-head smile he no doubt kept for agitated young lawyers. He turned to Bob Presson.

"How many more witnesses, Bob?" The judge looked pleased to learn we only had Dr. Dexter left to go. He told us to come back at 1:15 P.M., and said he'd hear closing arguments after Dr. Dexter.

I stayed in the courtroom over lunch, preparing for the afternoon. Joyce Cruzan was as angry as I had ever seen her. She and Joe went over their notes together: Their first meeting had been with Dr. Washburn, not Dr. Isaac; Joyce had never disagreed with Joe about removing the tube; Dr. Isaac had never asked about their motivations; Dr. Isaac could be just as intimidating as Joe. After a few minutes, I had their thoughts, and they walked across the street to The Deli.

That afternoon, Dr. Isaac and I started on the point that seemed most incredible to me—that state hospital officials hadn't told the family that Nancy had improved, and instead decided to deliver that news to them in a public courtroom. "Had the hospital told them that before today?" I asked the doctor. "Have they sent a letter to the family?"

"I have no idea," she answered.

"Well, you are the medical director."

"I was."

"Have the doctors tried to tell them that? When you treat patients at your hospital, if there is some improvement, isn't that the kind of thing you like to convey to their loved ones, that you normally convey to them?" I asked, speaking quickly. "I mean, when you saw some improvement in Nancy—"

The doctor interrupted me. It seemed I had missed her point. "I doubt there has been an improvement in the last several years as far as Nancy is concerned," she said. "I expect what we're observing now has been pretty much there all along. If, you know, somebody gets interested enough to check."

"Well, I guess I need to get my first question clear," I said. "Are you telling this family that there's any hope for the recovery of their daughter?"

"No, we're not telling them that."

"Are we telling them that there has been any improvement in her condition?" I asked.

"No, we're not."

"What is it that you've seen that is different than these other doctors?"

"Well, I think the question has come up because of this hearing, that there needs to be some definition of what's 'living' and what's not, and I think the issue has to be addressed now a bit," she said. "It's not all that simple, it's not a black-and-white issue."

We discussed what the nurses had said about Nancy's reactions, and what that information meant. "Now, do you know if her neurologist, neurologists that have examined her have—"

Dr. Isaac cut me off again. "A neurologist really is there for a very short period, just to make a quick assessment," she said. "The nurses that are with her 24 hours a day are more likely able to observe than—"

"Your examination of Nancy was longer than the neurologists who have been there?" I asked.

"I did not examine Nancy, but I take care of a lot of patients like Nancy."

We continued to go around like this—you haven't discussed your findings with any neurologist, Nancy has no chance of improvement, you're not an expert in the vegetative state, your opinion is different from that of Dr. Davis who sees her every day and different from Dr. Wong, and so on. But Dr. Isaac had made her point: The nurses are with this woman every day, while doctors come in for only a few minutes— who is better able to see a little response?

Defiant, Dr. Isaac batted each of my questions back for well over an hour, not interested in giving an inch to some young lawyer, particularly one who represented Joe Cruzan. And her basic argument was believable. She wasn't saying that Nancy was a candidate for therapy, that she could improve, or that she could do much of anything. All she was saying was that the nurses had seen something that wasn't the vegetative state.

I needed to change course. We talked about the American Academy of Neurology's definition of PVS and their research. Repeatedly, I tried to emphasize that Dr. Isaac's opinion was contrary to every other doctor (from MRC and elsewhere), and that she'd never actually examined

Nancy. Ultimately we came to the question of stopping treatment.

"Doctor, tell us what's going to happen when this feeding tube is removed," I asked, "to Nancy."

"Well, I think it will be painful for everybody—," she began.

"How about for Nancy?"

"She'll show her discomfort in ways that we expect her to, as she does now, when she has a bladder infection or when we stretch her too hard, when we make her uncomfortable."

"Have you read anything on this topic, what happens to a patient when nutrition and hydration are—"

"No, and I really—," she jumped in.

"Have you talked to any doctors that have done it?" I asked.

"No, I did hear a little about it since the other day."

"And that's—"

"That's not a procedure that I have ever contemplated."

"You are basing your opinion on, 'I heard a little bit about this procedure since the other day.' Is that your scientific background for your conclusion?" I asked.

"Yes," answered Dr. Isaac. Her tone suggested that she'd had about enough, that she was tired of playing lawyer word games.

"Now, Doctor, you told us the only request made to you with regard to Nancy Cruzan was that the tube be withdrawn?"

"Yes."

"Did they ever request of you information about Nancy's condition, some definitive statement from the hospital?"

"No—"

"Are you aware of any request like that?"

"I don't remember it, and I was not aware that that was ever a serious request."

I walked quickly back to the counsel table, and Kim Ross handed me Exhibit 15, which was the letter written just a year and a half earlier from Dr. Isaac to the Cruzans, concluding that Nancy Cruzan was in a persistent vegetative state. I walked back toward the doctor, handed her a copy, and asked her to identify it. How she could have forgotten this letter was beyond me.

"It is a 'To-whom-it-may-concern letter' concerning Nancy," the doctor said, looking up after reading it.

"Prepared by—"

"Me," Dr. Isaac said. "That, 'I reviewed Nancy's records and talked to her physicians and agree that Nancy has a diagnosis of persistent vegetative state following a motor vehicle accident in January of 1983. This is a term interchangeable with *coma*'—which it was in my experience at that time. 'The prognosis for positive change is poor, if not absent, after the more than three and a half years of this condition.'" Dr. Isaac finished reading the letter, and I moved that the court accept it as evidence.

"Now, you don't remember writing this letter to the Cruzans?" I asked.

"No, I don't."

"September 26, 1986?" I raised my palms, suggesting it had only been 18 months earlier. "Has Nancy's prognosis changed since that time, improved?"

"I would assume. I changed my mind, because I just said so," she answered, angry.

"I realize you are saying she is not in a vegetative state—," I began.

"Her prognosis is still poor," she interrupted.

"If not absent?"

"Poor."

"So you have changed your prognosis because—"

Dr. Isaac cut me off again: "I said it was poor."

"Well, this last sentence of the letter you wrote in September of 1986, and tell me—"

"'If not absent' is what I said."

"So, what's her prognosis now—only poor, or poor if not absent?" I asked.

"I would say if not absent," she answered. We moved on.

"You have talked a little bit, Doctor, about this second meeting that you had with the parents to discuss withdrawal. Do you remember that well?"

"Not too well, but I do remember it."

"Do you remember telling the parents that you couldn't do this because the hospital didn't need the publicity?" I asked.

"Yeah, I sure do, at the time. That was one of the reasons I gave—"

"*Did* the hospital need the publicity?" I jumped in.

"No, they didn't, and they don't need it now, either."

"Then you are in trouble?"

"Right, you haven't helped us any." Dr. Isaac and I shared a brief moment of humor—just a moment.

"You told them that you didn't think that it was ethically right?" I asked. "I mean, this is a serious decision to them. What did you consult to come to that opinion? Did you talk to other doctors?"

"I made the decision with them, I suppose, on the spur of the moment. I didn't feel it necessary to defend a position of that nature."

"Did you review the position of the AMA?"

"I know the standard the state took as far as my license was concerned, and that is reason enough not to do something—"

"I'm not talking about legal questions, Doctor," I interrupted, "I'm talking about—"

"You asked me, sir, you asked me what were the reasons at the time that I answered the question, and that's the way I'm answering it, sir." I had gotten too close to the doctor, and I stopped and backed away. This wasn't the first time the judge had peered over his glasses at me.

"What about the ethical question?" I asked.

"The ethical question makes it even easier," she said, still angry. "I feel this is—was a man who was asking me to kill a patient." I asked her about the AMA ethics position, the President's Commission, and articles throughout the medical literature to the contrary. "Did you review *anything* that they said before you talked to the Cruzans about this?"

"No, I did not."

"Did you review any articles on the propriety of doing this? Did you talk to any ethicists, did you talk to any religious people, did you speak to anyone before giving the Cruzans this advice?"

"I didn't have to." The doctor and I were near the end.

"Now, you have testified this morning that you thought the Cruzans were motivated by a desire to move on with their lives?" I asked.

"Yes."

"When is the last time you talked to them about their motivations?"

"I never did talk to them about their motivations, except to try to answer the question of whether I would remove support."

"Before you give an opinion to a court in such a serious matter, don't you think it would have helped to talk to them to find out if that was true? What their motivations were?"

"Well, sir, I spent several hours with the Cruzans," she began. Again the accusatory question appeared to anger Dr. Isaac. She explained her different meetings with the Cruzans, their presence at group sessions, her conferences with the social worker. Back and forth we argued with no resolution, and we came back to where we'd started hours earlier, with Joe Cruzan. I asked her how the family's thinking had changed over the last few years.

"I think Mr. Cruzan has become more and more determined to get his way—that's exactly what I think," she said, and she met Joe's angry gaze as she spoke.

"And why is that?" I asked.

"I don't know. Isn't that strange?"

"Do you think they are motivated at all by concern for their daughter and the fact that she wouldn't want to exist like this?"

"I don't know that either. I can't say. I'm not sure." I stood looking at Dr. Isaac for an extra second, turned to Judge Teel, neither able to nor interested in masking my anger. Dr. Isaac obviously felt the same way about me. I shook my head and sat down. After a couple of minutes of redirect from Bob Presson and a brief cross-exam from Thad McCanse, the judge excused Dr. Isaac. Joe Cruzan watched every step the doctor took as she walked past him.

CHAPTER 24

THROWING MUD

One witness left, and then closing arguments. The atmosphere in the courtroom had grown tense, and I guessed that Dr. Dexter, who sat through Dr. Isaac's testimony out in the gallery, would not be the same jovial academic doctor I had deposed just a week before.

But he was. As Bob Presson started down his credentials and experience, Dr. Dexter spoke in a friendly manner. He was at ease in the courtroom, particularly a courtroom that wasn't in the city. Lawyer and doctor moved seamlessly over the material, into PVS and other diagnoses of unconsciousness, through his full review of Nancy's medical record. Then the hammer dropped.

"Have you also examined Nancy?" Presson asked.

"Yes, I have."

"And when did that take place?"

"Last night."

While Ted Koppel was telling the nation that no dispute existed regarding Nancy's condition, that the case presented a purely ethical debate over proper treatment for a patient in a PVS, Dr. Dexter was in Mt. Vernon examining Nancy. Dr. Cranford had been right after all: Even with Dr. Dexter's deposition testimony, the state was going to say that Nancy had improved, just like state officials had in the other right-to-die cases. I objected, and moved to the judge's bench.

Speaking quickly, I told the judge about the deposition, about the doctor's testimony under oath that he didn't plan to examine Nancy, that he knew she was in a persistent vegetative state, and that his sole purpose for coming to Carthage for this trial was to talk about ethics. I moved that he not be allowed to testify. Rod Northcutt jumped in.

"Your Honor, Mr. Colby was notified that Dr. Dexter would be going to the hospital yesterday evening, would be examining—"

"Also had the opportunity to be there," Bob Presson broke in.

"Offered the opportunity to be there," Northcutt finished. The state lawyers needn't have worried; it wasn't Judge Teel's style to toss a doctor out of his courtroom without testifying. The judge could sort through and decide what testimony to credit or not. He said that he'd hear the testimony, and we could make our objections later.

Dr. Dexter's testimony over the next hour bore little resemblance to his deposition. He told Judge Teel that during his exam the previous evening, Nancy had fixed her eyes on his face, which he found significant. She oriented toward sound, also significant. She frowned in response to the wooden tip of a cotton applicator stuck in her face, which was a pain reaction higher than reflex. Most of the questions Bob Presson asked prompted long, involved, homespun responses from the doctor.

"Have you changed your opinion in any way about Nancy's condition?" Presson asked.

"No, not really, because I believe the nurses," the doctor began. "I will tell you what this court is hung up on—it's really sad, you are hung up on words. You are hung up on definitions of what kind of state this patient is in. Right now, we have all kinds of confusion in front of this court coming from the President's Commission, when it says 'unconsciousness'—*unconsciousness* means 'coma' . . . no response whatsoever, no sleep-wake cycles, means unconsciousness. We are drifting back from definitions. It is again the proverbial case in which the law and the medical definition need to get together and define some of the things that they are talking about because what's happening is plain and simple. Families like Nancy's family are getting caught up into this whole thing, making some judgments on the basis of words, and this is not fair."

"What do you consider not fair, Doctor?" Presson asked.

"Well, they have asked that in Nancy's case that she be denied, or the nutrition and hydration be removed from her, on the basis she is in a persistent vegetative state, okay? They are taking that in good faith. The nurses, on the other hand, are responding to a person who is doing more than being in the persistent vegetative state, and the question is—is she truly in a persistent vegetative state or not? When somebody is in there for 30 minutes, if they don't have some considerable training, they don't know how to test for this, okay? The nurses are seeing her 24 hours a day. Of course, there's not a nurse in there all the time, but there are nurses around, and they are experiencing—in other words, everybody is seeing Nancy from two different standpoints, including the neurologist and—if I could go ahead, Judge, or do I have to wait for a question?"

"Well, do—," Judge Teel began.

"Would you like to turn this on," Dr. Dexter interrupted, pointing toward the box with the CT scans, and continuing to speak as Presson turned on the box's light. "Folks, CT scan, and I'm one of the masters—that's anatomy. That doesn't tell you anything at all about what the physiology of that brain is. Sorry. That's not the way it works. I can show you children who had arrested hydrocephalus who are up walking around and bowling, appropriately bowling, because they got heads this big, and they have a brain that looks just like that, and they are in school. That's anatomy. We have had introduced also at this same thing, we have had the process of the PET scan. The PET scan is a totally experimental tool. Anybody who is extrapolating anything on a clinical basis by an experimental tool is, in fact, unjustified, and neurologists tend to do this all the time because in fact there is a large number of people who would like to eliminate the Nancy Cruzans from this world. They feel that they are a burden. That's anatomy, that's not physiology, and those of us who teach neurology spend a great deal of time straightening out with our students and residents that you cannot extrapolate one from the other—"

"If the court pleases," Thad McCanse stood and interrupted the doctor, "in the interest of orderliness, I really didn't sign up to hear a lecture—although I appreciate the answer—and I think it will be far better to respond to specific questions."

Judge Teel smiled. "Are you ready to return to that mode, are you, Mr. McCanse?"

"I sure am."

"That will be sustained. Mr. Presson," the judge said.

"Sorry about that," Dr. Dexter said to the judge.

"All right, sir."

"Is it a fair conclusion from what you've seen that Nancy does receive some sensory input?" Bob Presson continued.

"Absolutely."

I stood. "Objection—leading. And I might point out, your Honor, we have had wide latitude here over the three days when we put on one expert witness, just as the state is putting on, but we didn't lead him through his testimony. Let him testify from his knowledge," I said.

"That's open to some interpretation, Mr. Colby," Presson said.

"Well, you gentlemen better start addressing your remarks to the court or there will be some problems," Judge Teel said.

"Sorry, Your Honor," Presson said.

I offered nothing more, and the judge sustained the objection. The tension in the courtroom had built slowly for three days—we were all on edge.

Presson asked Dr. Dexter whether he believed Nancy was in a vegetative state, and Dexter said he didn't.

Presson continued. "How would you characterize her condition?"

"I think Dr. Isaac stated it very well: She is a very low functional person, but not in a persistent vegetative state."

Presson and the doctor next discussed the definition of death, feeding tubes, and medical ethics as the direct exam drew to a close.

"Doctor, let me ask you—do you have an opinion if the food and water were to be withdrawn from patients, such as in Nancy's case, do you have an opinion upon whether there would be any adverse consequences in general on society from taking that step?

"I think that's a marvelous step," Dexter said, "which allows us to withhold it on a large number of people in which we do not have adequate data about their outcomes."

"Do you think that would be a dangerous step to take?"

"I think it would be a very dangerous step to take because it is a short distance between that and euthanasia."

Bob Presson sat down, and I stood up immediately and walked directly toward the doctor. I'd read about what to do when a witness changes his testimony from deposition to trial; I'd seen it done by others in the courtroom. Now it was my turn to try. I didn't believe the doctor had lied the week before—instead, it seemed to me that the strategy had changed at the last minute (maybe at some level of the government above Assistant Attorney General Presson), and they were following orders as best they could. (Bob Presson told me later that no such directive existed. He had made the decision at the last minute so that their expert would be on the same footing as our expert.) Still, what this doctor was doing to the Cruzans was wrong, and he deserved my best shot.

"Dr. Dexter, you and I have met before, haven't we?" I began.

"Yes, we have," he replied.

"When was that, sir?"

"Last Friday."

"Where were we?"

"In my office."

"What was the purpose?"

"A deposition."

"What's a deposition?"

"A deposition is where a couple of lawyers and a court reporter get around to question someone, just like being in a court of law."

"What does the court reporter do before you start the deposition?" I inquired.

"Swears me in," Dexter answered.

"What's that mean?"

"I swear to tell the truth, the whole truth, and nothing but the truth."

"Did you do that last Friday?"

"You bet your life." Dr. Dexter spoke with defiance at the edge of his voice. He hadn't done anything wrong. I wanted the judge to see it a different way.

"Doctor, you are a national expert in headache and sleep disorders, is that correct?"

"That's correct."

"All of your research is done in those two areas?"

"No, it isn't."

"Most of your research is done in those two areas?"

"No."

"Could you tell us what most of—"

"Most of my research has probably been on drunk pigs, or the development of an alcohol model in miniature swine." The doctor laughed as he gave this answer, an effort to break the tension. I turned around to look at Joe, and saw the intimidating eyes that Dr. Isaac had described.

I took a couple steps toward the family as I asked the next question.

"You find research in drunk pigs helpful to the court in deciding the questions we have here today?" I asked.

"I practice neurology, too," Dexter said, now frowning. I asked him to tell us about the articles he'd written on medical ethics. "I haven't written any medical articles on medical ethics. I have given quite a few lectures on medical ethics, and I'm in the process of writing an article on medical ethics at the present time."

"You are starting your first article now?" I asked.

"That's exactly right. I have a minor degree in philosophy and religion—," he began.

"Is that your undergraduate degree?"

"That's my undergraduate degree."

"That was your minor, undergraduate—"

"I have taught in the Missouri School of Religion with regard to this, and I am not without an understanding of what ethics are," he said.

"I didn't say that, Doctor." We switched topics. "Describe for us the articles you have written on either coma—unconsciousness if you would like to call it that—brain death?"

"I don't have to," he said. "I haven't written anything on brain death and coma, but I do have 100 publications in literature, and I know enough. Just because you've written some silly article doesn't make you an authority in anything."

"That's true, Doctor."

"Okay."

"Describe for us the articles you have written on PVS?"

"Never written one."

I walked back to the counsel table and picked up the transcript of the doctor's deposition, which was more than 100 typed pages bound together. Page by page, the doctor and I reviewed the discrepancies between his testimony under oath from one Friday to the next.

I read to the doctor: "Page 11, beginning at Line 22: 'Question: Do you have an opinion, Doctor, as to Nancy Cruzan's prognosis? Answer: Yes. Question: What is that opinion? Answer: Well, the opinion that I have is that she has a minuscule probability of ever having any cognitive function, that we can define, return. Question: And what is the basis for that opinion? Answer: The basis is based on the medical literature that anyone who has been in a chronic vegetative state for this long would have almost no chance.' Doctor, were those questions asked and answered at your deposition last Friday?"

"That's correct," Dr. Dexter responded.

"You were under oath at the time?"

"That's correct."

I walked Dexter through several of the inconsistencies in his testimony and glanced up at Judge Teel, who nodded. He'd taken the point and wanted me to move on. Topics filled the yellow pad on the lectern in front of me. The doctor and I talked about many of them, including his belief that it was important to talk to the family, which he hadn't done in this case. We also discussed his belief that the Missouri law prohibiting neglect of patients covered this case; we debated feeding tubes. Regardless of the topic, we could reach no agreement.

By the time we turned to the subject of medical ethics, we had been arguing for over an hour. Like Dr. Isaac before him, Dr. Dexter appeared intent on not giving an inch. We talked about the American Medical Association and the President's Commission guidelines on withdrawing treatment. He explained several places where he didn't necessarily agree with either set of guidelines, but said in the end that those disagreements didn't matter because Nancy didn't fit the guidelines: "Nancy is aware of her environment; she fulfills a criteria of being alive."

Blood pounded into my temples. "She wasn't aware of her environment as of last Friday when we talked, was she, Doctor?" I asked.

The doctor's face flushed a blotchy red and white. "I had different data when you talked to me on last Friday and incidentally, I thought it was very nice," he said, his voice growing loud, too. "I think I had two days before the deposition, so let's don't throw mud around. Now, one of the things—"

"Doctor, if we are talking about throwing mud around—," I moved toward him.

"Just a moment—," Dexter started.

"Your Honor—," Bob Presson began an objection.

"Doctor—," Judge Teel said at the same time.

"I have—," the doctor tried to speak again, leaning forward toward me.

Judge Teel took control. "Just respond—now Doctor, you listen to me for a moment," he said. "Just respond to the questions that are pro-pounded to you, the questions of the lawyers."

The courtroom stopped for a second, and I backed away from the witness. The doctor and I talked for a few more minutes, but our encounter had ended. I sat down.

In a short time, Thad McCanse established several key points. Dexter agreed that the CT scan was a tool to back up the clinical exam, not a picture from which a doctor made a diagnosis, and that Nancy's scan showed severe brain damage. He also agreed that after five years, Nancy wasn't a candidate for rehabilitation, that her physical damage was permanent, and her prognosis was poor.

"So really, Doctor, it's not very important what we call this, is it?" Thad pointed out. "I think you said that, 'Let's don't get hung up on definitions.' Let's talk about her condition. What is her prognosis for any kind of a cognitive ability in your opinion?"

"Very, very minute," Dexter admitted. McCanse nodded, asked a couple more questions, and sat down.

On redirect exam, Bob Presson asked Dr. Dexter what Nancy's death would be like if her feeding tube was removed.

The doctor said that it would be an inhumane way to die. "If a judge told me that I would have no liability and that I wouldn't be wiped out of what little bit of financial security I have for my old age, and it was in keeping with the family to go ahead and let her die, I think it would be much more humane to give her a little bit of morphine, a lit-tle bit too much, because I think that that's the more dignified way to go, okay? That's me."

I walked back toward the state's expert witness for my final cross-examination. We were about done. I quickly brought him to euthanasia and asked him what he'd do if a judge told him it was legal to remove the feeding tube.

"I just explained it to him," the doctor began, pointing toward Bob Presson. "I would still refuse to take this out because I do think it's inhu-mane. What I would do, if they told me it was legal to kill her, to ter-minate her life, then in fact, Jim Dexter—not representing the medical profession or anything else—I would in fact feel that it would be per-fectly all right for me to terminate her life with a batch of morphine."

"Doctor, from your medical point of view, there is no difference from active euthanasia—injecting somebody with morphine—and removing medical treatment for a hopeless patient?" I asked.

"When it is absolutely predictable, there is no difference because the outcomes are both guaranteed without exception: death."

"Doctor, can you cite one piece of literature, one body, one inter-disciplinary body, one religious group, one ethical group, one medical group, any writing by anybody in the world who adopts that position—that active euthanasia is the same as removing medical treatment? Anybody?"

Again, Dr. Dexter grew agitated, and spoke fast. "What you tried to do—what you are trying to do is, you are trying to—I told you what I would do as Jim Dexter, okay?"

"I agree with you, but can you tell me of anybody else in the world—," I began again, but the doctor interrupted.

"And given it was legal. Oh, I think I can get you, anytime you want, 150 physicians and fill this courtroom, give me three weeks and I will fill the courtroom with physicians who don't know the difference, that—who are willing to say that there is no difference between starving a patient to death and injecting them with morphine, and that injecting them with morphine would be in fact more humane."

I looked at Judge Teel, who looked like he'd had enough for the week. "Nothing further, Your Honor," I said, and sat down.

McCanse and Presson had no additional questions for Dr. Dexter. The state rested, and neither McCanse nor I had any rebuttal witnesses. Just like that, our three marathon days were over. Judge Teel called a recess and asked us to report to his chambers. The advancing darkness outside of the courtroom demonstrated that we'd failed miserably in our attempt to finish early. In chambers, the judge decided he had indeed heard enough for one day, and he asked the parties to include any closing arguments in their post-trial briefs.

Back in the courtroom, Judge Teel spoke to the entire room of people, all waiting and wondering what would happen next. "We have had another one of those secret meetings that everybody complains about between lawyers and judges," he began, smiling out at the crowd. "I'm about to take the secrecy from it and explain to you what we have done." He told the press that each of the parties would file written briefs with him (essentially their analysis of the trial just completed and suggested outcome), on April 8, 1988. He'd then allow some time for reply briefs and issue his opinion after that date. He encouraged all interest groups so inclined to file a brief with him as well. He closed by thanking Thad McCanse and David Mouton for their service as court-appointed attorneys and adjourned court at 5:03 P.M.

As the people left, Joe sat in the first row as he had throughout the trial, but now his head was down. Joyce had her arm loosely over his shoulder. So far from the comfortable familiarity of a job site. Such a strange week. The afternoon, with Dr. Isaac followed by Dr. Dexter, had been a difficult ending to an emotional three days.

We made our way down to the lobby of the courthouse, and the lights from the local television cameras came on, catching Joe, Joyce, and Chris as a bewildered trio. I talked briefly to reporters—with my shiny forehead and messy hair I looked a little like a mad professor. I choked up as I tried to explain how Nancy would die if we won—I ended up walking away midsentence, waving off the camera. The Cruzans stood to the side and watched.

All week it had seemed to them that the witnesses discussing the gnarled, stiff body in the bed in Mt. Vernon were talking about somebody besides the Nancy they had loved. Their Nancy was gone. Maybe normal life was gone, too.

❧

PART III

1988–1989

CHAPTER 25

JOE'S MAILBOX

Letters started to come to the Cruzans' mailbox in a steady stream. The documentary that PBS aired on March 1, 1988, the *Nightline* appearance on March 10, and the Associated Press's reporting of the trial on the national news wire introduced Nancy Cruzan to the national stage. The letters came from Haverhill, Massachusetts; Doylestown, Ohio; Santa Maria, California; and other places across the country— some were handwritten, some came off word processors, and some were typed on old manual typewriters. Many were crazy, some were negative, and others were supportive. And some were heartbreaking, as they told the tale of another family's ordeal. Nearly all offered advice, like this:

> *Dear Mr. Cruzan: It's my opinion that you're overlooking the one most important fact—Nancy Cruzan was dead. The paramedics worked 47 minutes to restore a pulse. Paramedics should not have the power to restore a pulse and make "vegetables" out of people and cause all this anguish and heartache.*

Perhaps for those observing paramedics in other locales, the line between miraculous saves and heartache was clearer. In Carterville, Missouri, such letters did little more than make Joe Cruzan angry. He couldn't believe that from watching him on TV, people thought he was so stupid that they needed to write him letters about things he already knew better than they did.

The mailbox quickly became a focal point for Joe Cruzan. During the week, if he was on the road, he'd phone home to ask about word from the lawyers or the court, media inquiries, and the day's mail. If Joyce and Chris were sitting in the kitchen having coffee, as they often did, the ringing phone signaled the end of the work day as reliably as a factory whistle. If Joe was working in town, he'd head home and, after greeting his granddaughters (who often stayed with Joe and Joyce after school), he'd go down to the basement with the stack of mail Joyce always left on the kitchen counter.

On the weekends, Joe watched for the mailman—he'd keep an eye out for the blue uniform and would walk around to the front of the house to check the box several times. When the mail finally came, he'd grab the stack and retreat with it to the carport, scanning for news. It was hard to say which was worse—the cliché of the slow wheels of justice, or the all-too-frequent letters from strangers about his daughter.

Joe read each letter over and over and wrote replies to some of them, but when a family wrote about an injured loved one, he and Joyce always responded. They received many such letters. The Cruzans remembered their own trepidation when they first wrote the parents of Nancy Jobes and the wife of Paul Brophy a year and a half earlier, families that they had learned about in the news, so Joe and Joyce understood how important a response from them could be to a family in a similar situation. On many weekends and evenings, responding to letters was all Joe did.

Joe and I talked often about the mail his family received. That spring, one letter particularly troubled him. It came initially to Shook, Hardy (as many letters for the Cruzans did), and we sent it on to Joe. The letter was from the parents of a woman named Donna Rae, who apparently was in a persistent vegetative state. I say "apparently," because neither Joe nor I could fully decipher the full-page, single-spaced, italicized ramblings. Here it is verbatim:

AN OPEN LETTER TO THE JURY IN THE NANCY CRUZON CASE: (Joplin, Missouri), March 15, 1988. It has been more than 12 years since that third day in December 1975 which witnessed and laid quasi-tombstone-testament of the 'functional-demise' of a happy, healthy, motivated, full-time student/part-time-tuition-paying-wage-earner, self-directed, self-actualizing lovely young 22-year-old woman; with her eyes and heart set soundly-and-profoundly on the future. The future of the GREAT historic and reliable PROMISE of the American Dream!!!—held so dearly, and so preciously, by her forefathers and by her parents as well. All this deeply set within her Soul, the very fiber of her Soul; within her American heritage, as in the GENERATIONS of Americans before her who believed in, strived for, and usually achieved a better tomorrow! She was PROFOUNDLY family-loving AND family-loved! Her name was Donna Rae.

The letter went on in this fashion for paragraph after paragraph. Joe studied the strange words and bizarre punctuation. He believed Donna Rae's parents were in extreme pain, but he couldn't figure out what they wanted from him, or even what they were saying, exactly. He said he thought that "maybe they'd gone crazy."

Joe called Shook, Hardy on our toll-free line often, sometimes twice a day. He wanted to know when the judge would decide, how the Cruzans would be notified, why it took so long, what he could do to help, if he could call the judge, if Thad or Walt had heard anything, which way I thought the judge was leaning, and so on. If he couldn't get me on the phone, he'd talk to Kim Ross or my secretary. He was desperate for any information. By the time Joe finished with the mail and phone calls, he'd often revved himself up so high that he could not fall asleep until late into the night.

In late March, I sent Joe a copy of a four-page memo we'd received from Thad McCanse regarding a bizarre encounter between a woman named Jacqueline Hodge and Nancy. This woman and her husband had contacted Judge Teel, and based on that call, he asked McCanse to meet with them. The memo reported on the investigation that McCanse and David Mouton had made, and it made Joe as angry as I'd ever seen him.

The Hodges lived on Krummel Nursery Road, and Mrs. Hodge had treated Nancy as a massage therapist and faith healer for about a month before Nancy was moved to Mt. Vernon. Mrs. Hodge told the judge that she'd been able to get Nancy to talk, and that she had an audiotape reflecting this progress.

So the judge sent his two *guardian ad litem* lawyers to investigate. It turned out that the tape did not, in fact, have Nancy talking, but instead had Mrs. Hodge reflecting in a soft voice on the power of faith healing. She went on to tell McCanse and Mouton that she believed her experience with Nancy was her "opening" into the world of faith healing. Mrs. Hodge's therapy consisted of gentle massage, praying, talking to Nancy, and focusing certain kinds of energy and light on her. And although she hadn't "treated" Nancy since 1983, she apparently went to visit her at the state hospital in Mt. Vernon once.

The *guardians ad litem* concluded their memo to Judge Teel on the assignment he'd given them with tongues firmly in cheek: "Judge Teel will be gratified and relieved to know that Jacqueline Hodge states that whatever decision is made in this case, she is sure will be the right decision. Jacqueline did not have any strong feelings one way or another as to the propriety of the family's request, but she does have some extrasensory perceptions about the matter."

Joe saw no humor in the Hodges or the memo. He asked me why the judge would delay ruling—and spend time interviewing crackpots—and how in the world this woman gained access to see Nancy at MRC. My response—that maybe the judge was just trying to be careful, and that the woman probably told the MRC staff she was a family friend—didn't really give him much satisfaction. In fact, the majority of our conversations, with my trying to explain how so many strangers had made their way into his life, never ended in much resolution for him.

Judge Teel had set April 8 as the deadline for the post-trial briefs from the parties. I mailed Joe a copy of the state's brief, which was 67 pages long. He called me at my apartment the night he read it, and we talked for nearly 45 minutes. More than once he said, "This is a goddamned lie!" For instance, on the very first page, the state's brief said that at Brady Rehabilitation Center, Nancy was "fed orally and the rehabilitation records indicate she was making improvements in that regard."

Joe said, "*I* was the one feeding her; she didn't make any goddamned improvements!" He marched through most of the 67 pages that way, and I just listened.

The April 8 deadline also brought Joe's mailbox some good news—spectacular news, in fact. The brief came in from Thad McCanse and David Mouton, the lawyers officially charged by Missouri law and Judge Teel to discover and protect the best interests of Nancy Cruzan, the lawyers whose office looked out on the courthouse of Judge Teel, and who sometimes had lunch with the judge. Finally, firmly and unequivocally, this brief took the Cruzans' side. Our side had won over the lawyers from Carthage. That left us with just the judge.

ↄ҉   ↄ҉   ↄ҉

Even though he was an old Army man, Judge Teel had always been pulled to the water like a sailor. He and his wife, Jean, had been coming to the same spot on Table Rock Lake for more than 20 years. They didn't have a cabin—the judge and his wife would put their 21-foot inboard/outboard onto the lake and sleep under the stars. Judge Teel's boat, and the lake, had given him solace and refuge for about as long as he could remember.

A probate judge sees a sad side of the world each day—broken families, only there because some official or piece of paper told them they had to be. Judge Teel had looked out across the lake on many weekends, trying to sort out the cases he'd seen: divorces, wife beatings, child abuse, and families trying to lock up their own relatives in mental institutions. Always before, this lake had helped the judge sort through tough cases, but he'd never judged a case like Nancy Cruzan's.

The politically expedient course was obvious to anyone with even a rudimentary understanding of politics. The judge had been involved in Republican politics in southwestern Missouri for many years. As a young man, he earned his stripes driving local bigwigs around to make speeches and worked his way up. Attorney General Webster and his father, the senator, were good Republican friends of the judge.

Obviously, the powerful attorney general opposed the Cruzans—his lawyers had worked for three days in Teel's courtroom to make that crystal clear. So did Governor Ashcroft's Department of Health. The governor himself hadn't taken a public position on the case, but the judge had heard he was following it. Judge Teel had thought from time to time that he'd like to finish his career on the appellate bench. If politics were driving his decision, the course was clear.

But judging and politics are not the same thing. Judge Teel said a judge owed the public what he called "a fresh mind," which brought clarity, common sense, and a sense of fairness to a problem. Some days he would leave his courtroom to take a walk, trying to clear his head and see the issues reasonably. As the judge sat in judgment over people from his high wooden bench, politics played no role—fairness meant everything to him. Yet as he surveyed the water around his boat in the spring of 1988, the frequent churning in his stomach told Judge Teel that fairness and politics were going to collide in Nancy Cruzan's case, with, as he said, "Chuck Teel caught right in the middle."

The judge later spoke about the anguish he felt as he tried to decide the Cruzans' case. As spring gave way to summer, the judge found that scribbling covered the yellow pad sitting on his lap—he was making no real progress toward his final opinion. From the day that Joe Cruzan had first come to him two and a half years earlier, Judge Teel believed that the Missouri living will law would prevent the Cruzans from removing Nancy's feeding tube. Now, after three days of trial, he wasn't so sure, and he did not know which way to turn.

The handful of cases decided by judges in other states regarding the removal of life support typically relied upon the constitutional right to privacy. The judge respected United States Supreme Court Justice Harry Blackmun, calling him "a kind and learned man," but he did not have much use for the right to privacy that Justice Blackmun had recognized in *Roe v. Wade*. Teel knew that he did not want the abortion controversy tied up in his *Cruzan* opinion. He didn't think the issues were related, for much the same reason that Joe Cruzan always used when discussing abortion—the potential life had a world of possibilities ahead, while Nancy only had permanent unconsciousness. The cases from other states relying on the right to privacy didn't help the judge's analysis much.

The bench seat at the back of the boat held Judge Teel's notes from the trial, the Constitution of Missouri, and the Constitution of the United States; on the deck sat the voluminous official record of the trial. He sat in the back of the boat, bright sun overhead, and read and reread the constitutions and wrote and rewrote sections of his opinion. The more he wrote, the less persuaded he was by his own opinion. After several weekends on the boat, he wasn't sure of much anymore, except that fate had given this family a raw deal, and it was up to him to figure a way out of it.

Judge Teel set May 20 as the deadline to file any reply briefs, which were the written responses to what others had said in the initial briefs filed on April 8. By early June, still no word had come from the judge. Even Thad McCanse began trying to read tea leaves. The judge had asked McCanse a couple of times to find out how much money the lawyers had put into the case. What did that question mean? Did the judge intend to write about spending money unnecessarily on lawyers, or on the need to keep cases like Nancy's out of the court system?

In mid-June, I received a thin envelope from the Jasper County Probate Court. My secretary plucked it out of the mail and immediately walked it straight to my office. The look on her face told me to drop what I was doing. I tore open the envelope and pulled out a single page. It was not the decision in our case, just a letter from the judge.

Judge Teel's letter said that he'd received a phone call the day before from the National Legal Center for the Medically Dependent and Disabled, a national right-to-life group. The judge had told them that he would allow an amicus brief supporting the state, if they filed it quickly. The letter said: "This group has views apparently similar to the Right to Life Society, which chooses to ignore this court. New decision date feasibly can be around July 15." I handed the letter back to my secretary and asked her to send it to Joe. I didn't have the heart to call him—better to give him another couple of days before he found out that the right-to-lifers were going to intrude on his family's lives again.

The brief from the National Legal Center came in the mail on July 11. It was apparently filed by a subsidiary, a group called the Nursing Home Action Group, which was a not-for-profit organization composed of members with physical and mental disabilities. Both groups were based in Indiana and, as I would learn later, an important part of the national right-to-life network.

When Joe received the brief, he and I had another long talk. He was furious. The brief, almost 60 pages long, had kept him up late the night before. It made him especially angry that lawyers for disabled people thought Nancy belonged in their group.

"She's not disabled, for Christ's sake," Joe said. "What do they think, with some wheelchair access ramps she'll be back in the marching band?"

The brief reviewed testimony about Nancy from the trial and tried to put a new spin on it. The group felt that the independent spirit Nancy expressed—talking back to her father, for example—might just as easily suggest a strong will to live, not a strong will to die, as the family believed.

"What in the world do they mean? They say she can swallow, she can eat on her own. What the hell is this?" Joe asked.

I didn't want to try to explain the right-to-life brief to him. The brief was actually well written and made a strong case for caution on the judge's part. It reminded him, repeatedly, of the irretrievable nature of a decision in favor of the Cruzans. I feared that if the judge was on the fence, these arguments could affect him.

Four days later, on July 15, the Missouri Citizens for Life brief came in. This brief was much worse for Joe, perhaps because it came from his own state and he knew the local spokesperson, Dee Conroy. Conroy had begun to appear on local television in southwestern Missouri in opposition to the Cruzans early on. Joe had written her for the first time on December 3, 1987, months before trial, and their relationship hadn't exactly started on a respectful note: "Seldom do our lives cross with one of your obvious intelligence who has the ability to so profoundly express her opinion on a situation she knows absolutely nothing about."

The Missouri right-to-life brief also revisited in detail the testimony from Dr. Isaac, that had started Joe shaking with anger. The brief quoted a passage where the doctor had talked about him: "The ethical question makes it even easier. I feel that this is—was a man who was asking me to kill a patient." And the brief accused the Cruzans of violating Missouri laws regarding abuse and neglect of children. Joe thought about that at home, on the job, and in his truck. He wanted to talk man-to-man with the lawyer who wrote these words, who thought he was neglecting his daughter. Joe told me that he wanted to convince this lawyer of how absurd that claim was and then punch him in the nose. And he wanted to know how Judge Teel could possibly "fall for any of this crap."

Shortly after receiving these final briefs, Judge Teel made up his mind. Later he described the moment: Around 2:30 A.M. one mid-July day, after a long night of writing, the judge came in from his desk and woke up his wife. "Let's go for a walk," he said.

The Teels pulled on their clothes and boat shoes and headed out the front door. Indiana Street stretched before them in both directions, and they walked along the shoulder of the road in perfect quiet—even the cicadas had stopped chirping for the night. The judge strolled next to his wife and took her hand in his, already warm in the muggy July night. After about a block, he broke the silence. "I think I just maybe made a decision that has ended my career as a judge," he said.

CHAPTER 26

THE DECISION

On Wednesday, July 27, the loud ring of the doorbell startled Joe Cruzan. Even though the judge had promised to have the opinion hand-delivered to the Cruzans' house at nine, and even though he'd been waiting for this moment since before the sun rose, the ring still startled Joe. He'd taken another personal day from work to be home, and he, Joyce, Chris, Angie, and Miranda had milled around the living room all morning, walking around one another and the PBS crew setting up in the living room. Although he knew that the film crew would be there that morning, Joe hadn't really cleaned up—his disheveled hair and drawn face showed the wear of the last several days, ever since he'd learned that the opinion would actually be coming on July 27.

When the doorbell rang, Joe held the door open, and Joyce took the envelope from Caryl Lewis, the head of Judge Teel's staff. Joyce opened the manila envelope and handed the pages inside to Joe, who nearly marched through the living room toward the dark oak dining-room table.

As he sat, he asked Betsey Arledge, "You want me to read all of it or—"

"No, just read the part that tells what it is first," Joyce broke in, scanning the document herself over Joe's shoulder. Angie, Chris, and Miranda stood behind Joe, too. Chris was shaking, with tears in her eyes even before Joe began. She leaned on 12-year-old Miranda for support.

Joe read down the first of several pages, stroking his beard as he read. "Let's see, there's . . . do you want me to find just—"

Again, Joyce spoke. "Just find where it says . . . I thought it'd be at the front." They both continued to read. After another minute, Joyce leaned in closer still over her husband's shoulder and said, "Well, I still haven't found it." A wife reading over the shoulder of her husband conjures up the stereotype of an irritated husband, and in normal times, with his newspaper for example, Joe would fit that stereotype well. Now, as he focused on the document in front of him, he wanted Joyce's help.

Joe continued to turn the pages and scan them as quickly as he could—and then he stopped. Chris leaned on the table and pointed at the paper. Joyce did the same, saying, "We found it."

Joe cleared his throat and began to read:

> There is a fundamental right expressed in our Constitution as the right to liberty which permits an individual to refuse or direct the withholding or withdrawal of artificial death prolonging procedures when the person has no more cognitive brain function than our Ward and all the physicians agree there is no hope of further recovery while the deterioration of the brain continues with further overall worsening physical contractures.
>
> The Respondents, employees of the state of Missouri, are directed to cause the request of the Co-guardians to withdraw nutrition or hydration to be carried out. Such a request having Court approval, shall be taken the same as a request for discontinuance of any other form of artificial life support systems. Under those circumstances, further feeding could raise the spectre of civil liability and recovery of damages from the provider. The care and compassion the Respondents and their associates have already shown our Ward and her guardians, incomparable by any standards, are in keeping with the overwhelming tragedy that has been visited on us all.

Joe stumbled on some words as he neared the end, and Joyce rubbed his shoulder with her hand. Joe was not used to reading a legal opinion out loud, certainly not at the same time that he was trying to figure out what it said. He paused after he finished, and stretched his first finger up alongside his eye, in thought. "So, what does it say?" he said, with little gaps between each word.

"It says that she doesn't—," Joyce interrupted again, but this time Joe continued.

"It says they are directed to cause the request of the co-guardians to withdraw nutrition and hydration to be carried out," Joe said, still reading. Joyce ran her fingers back and forth across the top of the empty envelope she was still holding, and nodded in agreement. Chris stood still, her arm around Miranda; Angie looked from person to person.

Joe's thick, no-nonsense voice filled the room: "So, if that's winning, we won." Then nothing could fill the air, and after a long, uncomfortable minute, Joe stepped past the camera, walked out to the kitchen, and began to punch buttons on the phone.

✒ ✒ ✒

I was in Houston for a deposition, so I did not have the chance to read the opinion until later in the day. Although we'd won, parts of the decision troubled me. In particular, the judge had not ruled, as I had requested, that Nancy was in a persistent vegetative state. He described Nancy's condition as "unresponsive and hopeless" with "no cognitive purpose for her except sound and perhaps pain." If, in fact, she could experience pain (a possibility left open by the language of his opinion), then by definition she wasn't in a vegetative state. The medical position papers we relied on dealt only with PVS. Once outside that diagnosis, Nancy began to fit the description of a severely disabled person, which all of the right-to-life briefs had discussed. I worried that our entire case could unravel on appeal.

But we would cross that bridge later—for now, and for the Cruzans, the decision was great news, direct affirmation that their position was the right one. Joe's reaction appeared on the front page of *The Joplin Globe* the next day. "It was a bittersweet victory for us," he said, "but a great victory for Nancy and the people of Missouri. It will give them some control over the kind of treatment they may or may not want." The article noted that Joe and Joyce had spent the afternoon in Mt. Vernon with Nancy, delivering the news of what they had "won" on her behalf.

Those on the other side appeared to agree with my assessment. Attorney General Webster called Judge Teel's opinion "wide-ranging" and "extremely troubling"; Don Lamkins said he expected "very strong objections" among the staff at MRC that he would "need to deal with"; and Dee Conroy expressed shock and concern for vulnerable people, saying, "If somebody deems their quality of life is not sufficient, they could be starved to death."

And in Mt. Vernon, Dr. Isaac told a reporter: "It's like the concentration camps in Nazi Germany. The guy up above made the decision to murder people, but the guy down below had to carry it out."

CHAPTER 27

ELECTROCEREBRAL SILENCE

Near the end of the workday on July 22, 1988, five days before he planned to issue his *Cruzan* opinion, Judge Teel had walked across the courthouse lawn to find Thad McCanse. As the two men stood on the sidewalk outside McCanse's office, the judge made an unusual request—he wanted McCanse to appeal the judge's decision in *Cruzan*, regardless of the outcome, on the day it came out. And Judge Teel wanted the case appealed directly to the Missouri Supreme Court, bypassing the Missouri Court of Appeals.

McCanse agreed, and on July 27, he appealed the decision hours after the judge issued it. McCanse explained to reporters (confused by his appealing a case in which the side he'd taken had won) that to protect Nancy's best interests, as the *guardian ad litem* was charged to do under the law, he thought he should seek a decision from the highest court in the state.

Less than a week later, the Missouri Supreme Court announced that it would hear *Cruzan* on September 29, the last day of its September session. When a reporter phoned me with the news, I was completely flabbergasted. And elated. Just days before, my conversations with the clerk's office at the Missouri Supreme Court had led me to believe that we were already too late even for the January 1989 session, so our appeal wouldn't happen until the following spring, nearly a year later. The imminent September session was not even a remote possibility when I had called.

As I learned later, in mid-July Judge Teel had received a phone call from one of his law-school classmates—William H. Billings, Chief Justice of the Missouri Supreme Court. Billings had called with an extremely unusual request: He wanted to know if Teel could have the *Cruzan* opinion finished by the end of the month and if he could arrange for its direct and immediate appeal to the Missouri Supreme Court. Teel wrote Billings on July 22, confirming that the decision would come down on July 27, and that an appeal would be taken the same day. Then he set off to find Thad McCanse.

So the Missouri Supreme Court (or at least its Chief Justice) knew about the case and wanted it on their docket—apparently right away. But why? The August 3 order contained, perhaps, a clue—on September 29, the court would also hear arguments in the case of Phillip Rader. Apparently, Chief Justice Billings was attempting to arrange a day of appellate argument like no court had ever seen.

❧   ❧   ❧

In the late 1970s, many state legislatures grappled with the question of how to define "death" in the new world of medical technology. Missouri passed a new definition of the death law in 1982. This new law allowed a doctor to declare a person dead in Missouri using one of two definitions. One was the traditional notion of death—that is, the heart and lungs stopped working. Historically, when a person's heart stopped, all other organs including the brain would stop shortly thereafter, and death would then arrive. Modern medicine altered that process and created the need for a second definition of death: so-called brain death. Emergency-resuscitation techniques and follow-up supportive procedures enabled medical teams to keep the heart and lungs of a patient functioning, mechanically, even after the brain had completely ceased functioning. The Missouri Supreme Court would confront that medical question in the case of Phillip Rader.

In 1987, on the Tuesday before Thanksgiving, 17-year-old Phillip Rader entered a south Kansas City hospital for the third and final corrective surgery to repair his cleft palate. The family expected that the hospital would discharge him that weekend, and that he'd be back in school the following week, driving his mint-condition 1979 Trans Am, with his face already healing and the final vestiges of his cleft palate gone.

According to Philllip's doctors, his surgery went well, but his recovery was difficult. Pain and nausea kept him awake much of Tuesday night. At some point early Wednesday morning, he stopped breathing. A respiratory technician found him and called a "Code Blue" (the call over the hospital intercom that a patient has stopped breathing). Doctors rushed in, and Phillip was resuscitated. The length of time that he'd gone without oxygen, however, was unknown. An EEG taken immediately after the incident, though abnormal, showed signs of electrical life in the brain. Five hours later, Phillip's heart stopped again—this time the EEG taken after the event found no electrical activity—described in Phillip's medical chart as *electrocerebral silence.*

The next day (Thanksgiving), doctors told Phillip's family that he was brain dead, or legally dead.

"They were very emphatic that Phillip was dead and there was no hope for recovery," Phillip's father, John, said.

Phillip's family discussed organ donation and an autopsy. The problem was that Phillip was still breathing and his heart was still beating—with the assistance of a respirator, feeding tube, medicine, and monitors. His parents believed their son was alive and refused permission to withdraw the machines.

"We look at him and we still see Phillip," John Rader said. "There might be something that they've overlooked."

The hospital complied, and with aggressive nursing care and careful monitoring, Phillip's body persisted. By June 1988—more than six months and no resolution later—the frustrated medical team had had enough. They brought the issue to court, and Kansas City judge Tom Clark held an emergency trial. Seven doctors, including two brought in by the parents, told the judge that Phillip met the Missouri definition of brain death.

His mother still wouldn't believe it—she testified that Phillip's face flushed and his blood pressure rose 95 percent of the time when she entered the room. "I *know* he knows we're there," she told Judge Clark.

"It is a matter of time before he will awake and rise," Phillip's father testified. "We believe that Phillip can hear us. Parents can perceive these things where medical authority can't."

On July 7, Judge Clark issued an opinion that began, "With sadness and regret," ruling in favor of the hospital and concluding that it could turn off the respirator. He gave the family ten days to appeal—they filed on July 13 in the court of appeals. On July 18, that court sent a request to the Missouri Supreme Court, asking that, based on the importance of the case, the high court take the case directly and skip over the court of appeals. Shortly after that date, Chief Justice Billings phoned Judge Teel; within days, the Missouri Supreme Court had a September date set to hear both the *Cruzan* and *Rader* cases, one after the other.

The irony that the court would face in the two cases was amazing. Phillip Rader's doctors said he was dead, but his mother told the judge, "I *know* he knows we are there," and asked him to leave the respirator and feeding tube in place. And Nancy Cruzan's doctors (and state officials) said she was alive, but her father told the judge, "My daughter died the night of the accident," and asked the judge to authorize removal of her feeding tube. Chief Justice Billings had certainly arranged an interesting morning for his brethren.

⁓ ⁓ ⁓

As a lawsuit moves from the trial stage to an appeal, there's far less involvement from the parties whose lives are at stake. No one takes the witness stand—the appeal involves lawyers talking to judges, and much of the process takes place on paper, with lawyers from each side filing lengthy briefs. The painful testimony and tears of the trial are reduced to a black-and-white transcript that appellate judges read.

The actual interaction between the lawyers and judges, the oral argument, is extremely brief and highly structured, typically lasting an hour at most. Lawyers for each side wrangle with appellate judges over often arcane legal points and their nuances, trying to fit the facts of their case into the law—often akin to pounding round pegs into square holes. The family is left to sit and watch from the gallery, and that watching is typically done in a location far from their homes and local courthouse.

Joe Cruzan felt this shift in attention acutely in the summer of 1988. For example, it bothered him that reporters had started discussing the ramifications of the *Cruzan* case rather than talking about the Cruzan family. Joe and I talked about his feelings of being left out of the process, and I tried to include him as much as possible, sending him drafts of our briefs to comment on and copies of briefs from the other side. But I really couldn't worry about him that much; I was preparing for the first appellate argument of my life, in a highly public case.

The blue-covered briefs from Presson and McCanse arrived in early September—the arguments hadn't changed significantly from the post-trial briefs filed with Judge Teel the previous spring. The language about Nancy's feeding at the Brady Rehabilitation Center, however, had become more specific. On the first page, the state's brief talked about Nancy drinking juice and eating "mashed potatoes and bananas to poached eggs to link sausage" after the accident. Joe seethed, telling me yet again over the phone of *his* basically futile efforts for hours to force this pureed food into Nancy.

Two briefs also arrived with green covers, which indicated that they were *amicus*, or friend-of-the-court, briefs—filed by groups with an interest in the case. The two briefs supporting the state came from the same two right-to-life groups that had filed late briefs with Judge Teel: the Missouri Citizens for Life and the Nursing Home Action Group from Indianapolis. This time, joining the Indianapolis brief was the Association for Retarded Citizens of the United States, an organization with more than 160,000 members throughout the country.

These briefs argued extensively and passionately about the slippery slope our case had set before the court. The Missouri right-to-life brief laid out in detail a history of devaluing handicapped lives, both in the United States and in prewar Germany—essentially accusing the Cruzans and their supporters of following Nazi thinking. The brief quoted at length from the chief war crimes investigator's 1949 report: "Whatever proportions these crimes finally assumed, it became evident to all who investigated them that they had started from small beginnings. The beginnings at first were merely a subtle shift in emphasis in the basic attitude of the physicians. It started with the acceptance of the attitude, basic in the euthanasia movement, that there is such a thing as a life not worthy to be lived."

The brief also described as "shocking" my questions at trial of Don Lamkins, about the cost of Nancy's care: "To question Nancy's worth by measuring how much she costs society, as Colby's questioning implied, is to suggest that human beings should be done away with as soon as the ledger sheet on their economic contributions starts to dip into the red."

Our reply brief was due September 19. I had excellent help from one of my mentors, Elwood Thomas, and from a young partner who had clerked on the Missouri Supreme Court, Laura Stith. (Both of these lawyers would later leave Shook, Hardy and take seats of their own on the Missouri Supreme Court.) Our brief spent significant effort arguing that Judge Teel's opinion had in essence meant persistent vegetative state, even if it hadn't actually stated the words. My initial concern on reading Judge Teel's opinion in late July had only grown—I'd built and staked our entire case on the position that it was medically and ethically appropriate to remove a feeding tube from a patient in a PVS.

Our side did win the battle of green *amicus* briefs, with five coming in supporting the Cruzans, compared to the state's two. The two groups from New York, Society for the Right to Die and Concern for Dying, filed on our behalf, as did the American Academy of Neurology and American Medical Association. Important in-state support came from St. Louis, in a joint brief filed on behalf of the Sisters of St. Mary Health Care System (the largest provider of health care in Missouri), and the Center for Health Care Ethics at St. Louis University Medical Center— formal Catholic support for the Cruzans.

The right-to-die issue posed difficult questions for the Catholic Church. On the one hand, the church advocated respecting life, and it fought any expansion of the constitutional right to privacy—the basis for the abortion right—that found its way into the courts. On the other hand, many Catholic theologians, especially those involved in health care, campaigned for a sane church policy on end-of-life decision making, knowing that the great growing fear of most Americans, Catholic or not, was living out the end of their days in a sterile hospital room, hooked up to unwanted machines and tended by strangers.

The St. Louis brief drew an unusual response—a letter from Lou DeFeo, the lawyer for the Catholic Bishops of Missouri and the Missouri Catholic Conference, which suggested that the St. Louis brief supporting the Cruzans did not represent the official church position:

> In the Catholic Church, the official teaching authority (Magisterium) at the local level is vested in the Bishops (not in individual theologians or theological scholars). Neither the Bishops of Missouri nor of the United States have issued an authoritative statement on the application of Catholic ethical and theological principles

to the question of withdrawal of sustenance from persons in situations similar to Nancy Beth Cruzan. The issue is now pending under study before a Committee of the Catholic Bishops of the United States, headed by Joseph Cardinal Bernardin of Chicago, and also before a congregation (department) of the Vatican at Rome.

If an authoritative statement is made by either the committee of U.S. Bishops or the Vatican while the instant legal case is pending, we shall share that document with this honorable Court.

It boggled my mind that people in the Vatican were thinking about our case. I guessed that if Cardinal Bernardin or the Pope filed an amicus brief, it probably would get read pretty quickly.

~~ ~~ ~~

During the briefing period, the *Rader* case took some strange twists. By August 3—the day the court announced that it would hear arguments in *Cruzan* and *Rader* on the same morning—Phillip Rader had been brain dead for more than eight months, and still his heart pumped on. The *Kansas City Times* reported that the longest previous case of someone being sustained after brain death was four and a half months. One doctor told me that parts of Phillip's body had actually started to decompose, even though his heart somehow continued. No one knew how much longer he could go.

Things grew stranger. On August 16, John Rader came into his son's hospital room and found that Phillip's life-support systems had been sabotaged. Someone had pulled out his feeding tube and thrown it in a trash can, and Phillip's neck was marked with bruises where someone apparently tried to jerk out his breathing tube. Police were called, and they discovered that a mentally disturbed patient from another floor had ventured into Phillip's room. The detective told Phillip's mother that the police couldn't do anything about the woman, however, because under Missouri law, Phillip was already considered dead. But doctors reinserted the feeding tube.

Two weeks later, on August 31, Phillip's heart stopped again. This time efforts to revive him failed, and Phillip was dead under any definition. His death left Nancy Cruzan's family and lawyers on their own to tell the Missouri Supreme Court about the illusive line between life and death, to try to explain a world where a newspaper could run a headline like this on the day Phillip's heart stopped: "Brain-Dead Youth Dies."

And so, it turned out that the court was not going to have its day of death on September 29—only the Cruzans. That was a big enough day all by itself, from our point of view.

CHAPTER 28

FRONT-ROW SEATS

On September 28, the glass elevator at the Capitol Plaza Hotel in Jefferson City headed up toward the ninth floor, the highest of the building. Twelve-year-old Miranda stood close to her grandfather as the interior courtyard, with its fountain and tables, grew smaller below them. This was Miranda's first ride in a glass elevator, her first trip above the fourth floor of any building, and she and Joe had been riding in it for almost half an hour.

When others entered, the two grew quiet, pretending they were just waiting to reach their floor, although Miranda had the giggles. As soon as the intruders left, Miranda would press "9" if they were headed up, or "Lobby" if they were going down. Neither granddaughter nor grandfather could sleep—she'd been excited about staying in the big hotel, while he'd been dreading the day to come. Why not have some fun? Joe looked down at the shining, giggling face of the granddaughter he loved, the girl who looked like Nancy, and he laughed aloud.

In Chris's hotel room, however, no one was laughing. She and Betsey Arledge from PBS were crying. The relationship between these two women had started to grow from the moment Betsey first visited Nancy, when Chris had sobbed in Betsey's arms. For more than a year, Betsey had been in Carterville for the important moments in Chris's life. Now the tears came again, but for once the reason was a happy one— Betsey had just told Chris that she thought she was pregnant.

Meanwhile, in my room, outlines of topics the court might cover the next day blanketed the bed. I practiced the opening of my argument before the mirror over and over. On September 20, I'd taken the train to Jefferson City, where I'd watched a morning of arguments from the gallery. I then spent the rest of the day in the court's law library until it was time to take the train home. On September 22, I'd done a practice argument in a conference room at Shook, Hardy with some Kansas City lawyers who had clerked at the Missouri Supreme Court after law school.

Shortly after I'd arrived in Jefferson City on September 28, I did another round of questioning in a meeting room at the hotel, with Walt Williams, Dave Waxse, Rose Gasner from the Society for the Right to Die, and Mark Haddad, a lawyer from a large firm, Sidley & Austin, which was representing the American Medical Association.

Thankfully, having just turned 33 that summer, I didn't have the inclination to step back and think about exactly how little experience I had to argue any appeal, let alone a highly controversial and public one. I put my energy into the preparation. All of the hundreds of pages of legal briefs and published cases, the trial transcript and trial exhibits, medical journal articles, position papers—everything I wanted to remember—was condensed into several small blocks on a couple of crowded pages on a yellow pad:

Gastrostomy tube feeding is medical treatment
- surgery required
- FDA-regulated device and nutrients
- the purpose of the tube was to serve as a bridge to recovery

Persistent vegetative state
- definition
- six doctors made the diagnosis, including three employed by MRC
- the only suggestion to the contrary came after filing the lawsuit

"But Mr. Colby, you're not telling us that the trial judge found she was in a persistent vegetative state, are you?" I could hear the question, and I did not have a great answer. I intended to argue, as I had in the brief, that the judge's findings were certainly consistent with PVS, even though the opinion didn't name Nancy's condition, and hope for the best.

I read and reread the yellow pad: why the living will law didn't apply to our case; why the common-law right to autonomy and the federal rights to liberty and privacy supported the family; how the family could exercise these rights on Nancy's behalf; why this case bore no resemblance to abortion cases; what courts in other states had done.

Books about appellate advocacy instruct that by the night before an oral argument, the lawyer should set aside his papers, have a nice dinner, and relax. It's probably good advice, but not for me, not that night. I paced the room, answering questions out loud with my arms waving. If a maid had walked in right then, she might have thought I was crazy.

I had gone about as far as I could in studying my yellow pad, and it wasn't even ten o'clock yet. I had to escape from that room and do something, so I pulled on my still-damp running shoes, a fresh T-shirt and a reflective vest, and I headed out of the hotel for my second run of the day. At the top of the hill, I looked at the lighted dome of the capitol to my left, and the red façade of the Supreme Court building to my right. Then I cut across the lawn of the capitol, already starting to sweat, and in a few blocks, the cold stone walls of the Missouri State Penitentiary came into view. I passed by with the answers on the yellow pad methodically cycling through my mind.

❧   ❧   ❧

As I was running off my nervous energy, a drama was unfolding on the fourth floor at MRC, which I wouldn't learn about until days later: Lodema Sue Luce, whose room was down the hall from Nancy's, was dying. Doctors stood by as Lodema suffered a heart attack and fluid filled her lungs. They took the steps necessary to make her comfortable, but they made no effort to save her.

Both Lodema and Nancy were PVS patients, kept alive by high-quality nursing and medical care, and a single life-support system that artificially supplied food and water. Lodema's parents had appeared on *Frontline* on March 1, and they'd told Betsey Arledge that while they empathized, they couldn't do what the Cruzans were doing. But was their course really much different?

Had I learned immediately about this death, and known then what I came to know later, I could have started my argument in court dramatically—"At 1:30 this morning, on the fourth floor of the state hospital, congestive heart failure slowly ended the life of a patient in a persistent vegetative state. She's dead now. Doctors stood by and did nothing, at the parents' request. Neither the attorney general's office nor the Department of Health made an appearance. Why does Nancy Cruzan need the state to protect her from her parents, but Lodema Luce does not? Why didn't the medical director confront Lodema's parents and charge them with the 'ultimate in rejection' for failing to intervene? These medical decisions are hard enough for loving families to make without inappropriate, unnecessary interference by outsiders."

Or something like that. But I didn't know about Lodema yet.

❧ ❧ ❧

The marshal called the Supreme Court of Missouri to order, as a door on the far right side of the courtroom opened, and the seven black-robed judges entered single file. Joe and Joyce sat directly behind me in the front row of seats, with Chris and the girls next to them. This was the girls' first trip to a court. Angie sat still—she said later that she was worried about how she was supposed to appear and whether people would watch her; Miranda's eyes darted around.

Bob Presson carried the burden to prove to this court that it should overturn the lower court's decision, so he would speak first. McCanse would be second, and I'd go last. Presson stood and moved to the podium, which had three small lights on top—green to go, yellow for two minutes left, and red to signal time's up. As Presson stood at the podium, it struck me how close he was to the seven judges, almost as if they were having a conversation in a living room—one with seven guests sitting in high chairs, looking down.

Presson began to talk about the facts of Nancy's accident, picking up on the themes in his last brief to Judge Teel and those filed with the Missouri Supreme Court. He argued that Nancy's feeding tube was inserted for convenience and safety, and that during rehabilitation she'd received pureed foods. This case was about stopping feeding for another human being. Presson moved to the living will law—saying that whether it existed at the time of Nancy's accident was immaterial. The clear public policy of the state was that patients must be fed, by tube or otherwise.

The court, needing to warm up like everyone else, listened to his argument on behalf of the state for some time before interjecting. Judge Charles Blackmar, who had a football player's large, square head (now bald), finally waded in. "Suppose this problem is presented, and the physicians say the only way to keep this person alive is a surgical operation to insert a tube in her stomach," Blackmar began, "and the guardians say we just don't choose to do that. And let's assume the record shows that the patient is otherwise stable, like Nancy."

"Well—"

"Where does the physician get the authority to say she has to go through that procedure?"

Presson answered that a guardian's power comes from state statutes, which require basic, minimal care. A guardian failing to consent to feeding would arguably be guilty of abuse. A good answer.

Judge Andrew Jackson Higgins, a World War II veteran and member of the Disciples of Christ Church (as was Judge Blackmar), entered the fray. "I believe the trial judge viewed the tube as medication, which is also excepted under the statute. What do you have to say about that?"

Presson told Judge Higgins that it didn't matter. The living will law said that a procedure to provide food and water was carved out as an exception under the statute.

"Mr. Presson, is there anything in the record as to how long treatments of this kind have been available?" Judge Blackmar asked.

"Not directly that I recall, Your Honor. I think there is some general testimony indicating that certainly this was not possible, maybe 15 years ago. There are new intubation techniques that certainly, if not totally new, have certainly rendered it more feasible to do this."

"Isn't it true that over the centuries, people who were in this situation were simply not provided with food and water by artificial means, and death followed?"

"That's probably true, Your Honor, but that's probably true of a great many forms of care for a great many forms of people," Presson answered. "I'm not sure that the historical record, even if it supports that view, necessarily justifies saying that that's what we do here today."

"We could make the same argument about penicillin, couldn't we?" Judge Edward "Chip" Robertson asked. Often in appellate arguments, the questions from the judges are intended for their colleagues on the bench as much as for the lawyer at the podium. This question appeared to fall in that category. Judge Robertson likely chose such moments carefully. Governor Ashcroft had appointed Robertson, who had been Chief of Staff, to the court just three years earlier, when Robertson was only 33 years old. His fresh-scrubbed face and full head of blond hair made him look even younger. The next youngest member of the court was born in 1924.

Presson appreciated the penicillin question from Judge Robertson. "Any new medical technology," Presson agreed. "You know, we could even go back and adopt a very Spartan attitude that for all deformed children, we take them out on the hillside, and it's their own inability to walk or otherwise provide for themselves that results in their death. I don't think we can take that sort of laissez-faire attitude here." Bob Presson made a couple of additional points, then reserved his remaining time for rebuttal.

The Cruzans sat in the front row, straining to hear and to understand the questions. The *Associated Press* report described the Cruzans as sitting "stoically in the front row of the crowded courtroom." Joyce laughed later that they were hardly stoic, just confused.

Next, Thad McCanse came to the podium. He also began with the living will statute, then described a different kind of public policy behind the statute, claiming that it supported removal of virtually all manner of medical treatment because the legislature had made clear that stopping of medical treatment wasn't mercy killing. McCanse's role as Nancy's *guardian ad litem* repeatedly brought him back to the question of her condition and what she would want could she speak.

"How significant is the evidence that she might react when somebody comes in the room, or it made a difference that somebody talked to her before they touched her?" one of the judges asked.

"Whether she feels pain or maybe has some slight recognition, maybe makes her situation even worse," McCanse answered. "She experiences nothing. She's someplace between life and death. The legislature defines death, and I assume that if you're not dead, you're alive. But she's mindless, as far as the situation is concerned." McCanse searched for words. "She's a helpless—I don't know how to describe it—a helpless mass of humanity in a sense, who has no mind, who can do nothing on her own. Her present condition is just as far removed as you can possibly get from the type of person she was."

McCanse stopped his description, and the courtroom remained silent as the judges, lawyers, and gallery considered what he had just said. The topic switched back to a legal one: constitutional rights of liberty and privacy. "The question is an individual's rights against the state interest," McCanse told the court. "And the right to liberty I think necessarily means that you cannot invade a person's body without their consent. I think if liberty means anything, it at least includes that." He was coming near the end of his argument, and I took a drink of water to try to chase the cobwebs out of my throat.

Thad McCanse moved his notebook, and we passed each other as I replaced him at the podium. The green light came on. I took a deep breath, half-exhilarated and half-petrified, and I began to tell the court how we knew that Nancy wouldn't want the treatment, and about all of the groups that supported the Cruzans' request as medically and ethically appropriate.

By now, the court was fully warmed up, and Judge Blackmar started the questioning, which did not stop for most of my allotted 30 minutes. "I'm much more interested in what the family thinks than any medical organization," Blackmar said, which was another statement perhaps aimed more at his colleagues than at the lawyer at the podium.

I agreed. "The *guardian ad litem*—who had the duty to be an independent fact finder—in his post-trial brief found by clear and convincing evidence that the family was motivated by a desire to do what their daughter would want, and that Nancy—an independent, outgoing person—would not want this treatment continued."

"What guidelines do you find in the trial court order to allow the tube to be withdrawn, as far as this case, or future cases?" Judge Rendlen growled. Rendlen was also a veteran of WWII and later a Coast Guard commander, and he appeared to want order in the law, and answers—quickly—from the "soldiers" reporting to him.

"Specific guidelines may not be spelled out in the opinion, but the requirements are there," I argued. "Irreversibility of her brain damage must be proved—there is no dispute on this evidence, or suggestion she will recover. Second, the motivation of the family must be proper, again not disputed. The third point is to look at what this patient would have wanted. If this patient has rights, there is no dispute that Nancy can't come here today and tell you what she wanted—"

Judge Billings interrupted me. "Isn't that just speculation?"

"She cannot speak."

"I'm talking about speculation about what she would want if she could speak."

"We do not know what she would say," I agreed, "but that's no reason to ignore her rights. Other states addressing these cases have tried to find the best way possible to make a decision that best reflects what this person would want. One way the trial court here did that was to examine prior statements of Nancy of what she would have—"

"Do you think that's an essential part of a case of this kind?" Blackmar jumped in.

I explained that such information could be helpful to families, and described in detail Nancy's discussions with her sister and Athena Comer, which had been part of the trial evidence.

Judge Blackmar wanted to know about cases where no evidence existed. I answered that such situations might present harder cases, but that either way, decisions had to be made. Judge Rendlen returned to the guidelines, asking whether the legislature was the better place for enacting them. I stated that the court couldn't defer to the legislature in this case, because Nancy Cruzan was before them now, with "an inalienable constitutional right to liberty to be free from this medical treatment."

Judge Robertson broke in. "Now is that the strongest legal basis for your argument, for withdrawing the tube at this moment? What is the— so far your argument, to me, is just not giving any legal basis for what you want to do," he said, his voice rising to emphasize what he appeared to see as a flaw in the argument. "So far it's been—and I understand why—a very emotional sort of an argument. But what's the legal basis?"

I had practiced the answer to this question, in a way to avoid discussing the right to privacy, which we'd started calling "the P word" around my office. I started a history, as I understood it, on the constitutional right to liberty. "The legal basis, Your Honor, is about as strong a legal basis as you could find in any case in any court in the country. When the Framers adopted our Constitution, when the writers wrote our Declaration of Independence, there was a body of natural law that they drew from to guarantee individual freedoms to people in this country. Most important to those people—and the historical writings we cite in the brief discuss this—was the right of individuals to be free from intrusion by the state. To make decisions about their own bodies that they wanted to make. The—"

"Aren't we beyond that in this case, Mr. Colby?" Judge Robertson interjected. "This woman can't make the decision. I want you to give me some legal basis that would allow me to consider the judge's order as being legal. So far, you've said an individual has the right to make a decision about their body. That may or may not be the case, but assuming it is for the moment, how can this person make a decision?" Judge Robertson had gone straight to the fundamental issue in our case, and all cases like it: How can a patient in a hospital bed, with no ability to think or speak, exercise rights at all?

"If we assume she has that right," I said, "admittedly she cannot tell us now how she would exercise that right. But this is the unfortunate circumstance that we're caught in. If she has any rights at all based on her prior expressions, then she has a right to have a decision made that reflects her interest."

"How do we have any certainty to know what that is at this moment?" Robertson asked.

"If we are talking about equal protection of people," I answered, "competents and incompetents, the alternatives you have are to try the best way possible to discern what this person would want, based on prior statements—based on loving family members who best understand this person. Or to simply ignore any rights simply because she's incompetent, and treat medically in whatever way is possible simply because it is technologically possible. It's not a perfect world, but the first solution—to honor those rights—is certainly a better solution, alternative, to trying to find no way at all to honor those rights, and simply pass by the wayside because she can't tell us."

I stammered a little, struggling to make this crucial point as clearly as possible. "It's, it's—in the state's brief they discuss, for example, the right to marry or the right to vote, and how an incompetent person loses that. And Nancy can't vote, we understand that, and she can't go out and marry. But, a state-run hospital isn't forcing her every day to marry someone she'd find abhorrent. But it *is* forcing her to accept medical treatment that prior evidence suggests she would not want. It's a unique situation, and we submit that the better choice is to find the best way to exercise these rights. She can't tell us, but there is information that can tell us what she would want, and she has a right to a decision made that reflects her interests."

Judge Robertson swiveled slightly in his leather chair and leaned back as I talked, looking out the tall windows. Judge Billings didn't look happy either. Judge Blackmar stepped into the brief silence at the end of the long exchange with Judge Robertson. We discussed the state paying for Nancy's care, how the living will act supported the family, taking Nancy home, and expert testimony about the gastrostomy tube. I tried to paint a picture of Nancy as I held my arms above the lectern and bent my hands and fingers in—I told the court about the small pillows that Joyce had made to wedge in that space so that Nancy's fingernails wouldn't cut into her wrists. My yellow light came on.

"I'm prepared to sum up if there are no further questions," I said. None came, so I continued on. "The family came to the trial court after long and careful deliberation. Either way this court decides, the Cruzan family does not win. The trial court found that it was Nancy's wish, clear wish, to be free from this unwanted medical treatment, and we would request that this court affirm that decision."

My voice started to crack, so I sat down. Bob Presson came back to the podium for rebuttal and answered a few further questions, and we were done. Everyone in the courtroom stood as the judges filed out.

Joe came up and shook my hand. "How'd we do?" I asked him with a smile.

Joe appeared as though he might cry. His emotions had been bottled up all morning. All he said was, "Good, good," nodding at me with a tight smile.

The Cruzans and I made our way through the crowd in the hallway outside the courtroom and down to the front steps of the building. The reporters who had gathered there mainly had legal questions, so I did most of the talking. One reporter from Springfield asked Joe, who stood on the steps behind me, what the family hoped would come from the hearing. I moved so that he could speak into the microphones.

"I hope they rule in Nancy's favor because that's what this is all about," he said, and his eyes quickly grew moist. "We're here for Nancy, not for us."

Joe answered a few more questions, but then the reporters returned to the argument, so he stepped back and stood by his wife, daughter, and granddaughters. A woman approached Joe from the sidewalk and walked straight at him. She reached out and squeezed his arm, said "God bless you," and quickly walked away. Joe didn't know if she was for or against him, and he looked at her like she was some kind of alien. The questions ended, I picked up my briefcase from the sidewalk, and we all walked back down the hill to the hotel to say our goodbyes.

~&   ~&   ~&

Reporters and others often said to me, "This case must be hard on you." Mostly, it was not. I was having an experience that young lawyers dream about. As I stood in that gray day, with reporters surrounding us and firing questions at me while television cameras rolled, I thought that this was about as meaningful a morning as a lawyer could have. My voice had cracked at the end of the oral argument as I told the court that either way it decided, this family would not win. But it just cracked for a second, and I may well have been emotional because I'd made it through my first appellate argument and felt pretty good about it.

The Cruzans, by contrast, had deep reservoirs of tears, which constantly opened. During the first eight weeks of the Cruzans' ordeal, while Nancy was at Freeman and Brady, Joyce would often find herself alone in the shower crying, wailing at the top of her lungs—unedited belly sobs would shake her frame as the hot water fell on her. Chris and Joe described similar experiences, speculating that perhaps the hot water somehow triggered their tears.

Of course I cared about the Cruzans, and growing closer to them and their enormous pain had an effect on me. I liked them as people, I felt horrible for them, and I wanted to win the case for them. In fact, I wanted to win very badly. And ultimately, the case had a significant effect on my life, probably in ways I still today can't understand. But it was *never* "hard on me." My family and my life were intact, happy, and healthy.

The Cruzans drove home to Carterville after the argument, and that night they sat together silently and watched as the local newscasters talked about them. I drove down to the Lake of the Ozarks for Shook, Hardy's annual two-day retreat, and listened with a smile as my three friends (who had attended the argument) recapped the highlights. The next day, Joe and Joyce headed up to Mt. Vernon to tell Nancy—as if they really understood the legal wrangling or that visiting and talking to Nancy made any difference to her. I played tennis.

CHAPTER 29

FALSE ALARM

Joe Cruzan sat at his kitchen table watching the phone on the wall. Earlier in the fall, the Missouri Supreme Court had announced three dates for handing down decisions: October 13, November 15, and December 13. At 1:00 P.M. on each of those days, the clerk's office would set copies of the opinion at the reception desk for lawyers, reporters, and anyone else who was interested. Copies would then go by mail to the parties in the cases.

Tom Vetter, a lawyer in Jefferson City, had agreed to walk over to the courthouse to help me learn the news quickly. We hadn't expected a decision on October 13, and Tom called shortly after one o'clock that day to confirm: no decision.

November 15 was different. In the days prior, several reporters had called requesting interviews, saying that they'd heard from reliable sources that the decision was definitely coming down on the 15th. So many reporters called that I sent out a press release explaining our plans in the event of a decision. Chris and Mel both took November 15 off work, and Chris let the girls stay home from school. The four of them went up to Joe and Joyce's for lunch. Joe and Joyce had taken off work as well. After lunch, the group milled around the kitchen and waited, talking quietly, like parishioners waiting for church to start.

Joe and I had talked about possible responses to the press, depending on the outcome, and how we'd approach the people at MRC if we won. We were optimistic, because in the few other states where the supreme courts had heard a case like the Cruzans, the families had won. All morning Chris thought about Nancy and whether this was the day she would start to die. The thought of losing her sister terrified Chris—the thought of losing the case did, too.

I thought the case was just about over, but Tom Vetter called me just after one o'clock, and I called the Cruzans and told them that there had been no decision that day.

Joe let out a loud, theatrical sigh. "I guess the press don't know everything, do they?" he said.

The family and I marked December 13 on our calendars and agreed to talk after Thanksgiving. Chris and Mel left and took the girls to school for the afternoon. Joe and Joyce sat and thought about the day that might have been. A sense of relief took the edge off their disappointment—they wouldn't have to say goodbye to Nancy just yet.

❧ ❧ ❧

The next day, Chris left work and stopped to see her insurance agent, Don Gould, as she'd planned. While she was there, Don's phone rang and he handed the receiver across his desk to Chris. It was Mel, calling from work, which he seldom did. He was obviously upset, telling Chris that she had to go home right away.

"What's wrong?" Chris asked, panic creeping into her voice.

"The girls are fine, but you need to go home," he said again.

"Mel?"

"Just go home, okay?"

Chris handed the phone back to Don and left his office. She sped from Joplin to Carterville, her mind turning over the possibilities, which she narrowed down to three: Grandpa Les had died, Grandma Jack had died, or Nancy had died. Her car ground to a stop on the gravel driveway, and she ran up the wide steps of her back porch. Inside, Joyce stood with her arm around Angie, and Miranda was close by. Chris stopped in the doorway.

"What's wrong?" she shrieked. Her body shook. "What's wrong!"

Joyce watched Chris's anguish, unable to protect her eldest daughter. "Bill called and said they released the decision a day late," Joyce said. "It's against us."

Chris fell through the doorway toward her family, and the four of them—Joyce, Chris, Angie, and Miranda—stood and sobbed in an awkward circle of intertwined arms.

The deep drawl of transplanted Tennesseean Carl Manning, the Associated Press reporter in Jefferson City, had brought me the news that afternoon. I called Tom Vetter, and he hustled over to the courthouse, grabbed a copy of the opinion, gave me its bottom line over the phone, and faxed me all 82 pages.

By the fall of 1988, Shook, Hardy had a staff that basically shuttled faxes all day long from machines to lawyers. One of the guys brought me the fax in 20-page chunks, and I hurried through the pages, trying to quickly understand the bottom line. I was shocked. I spent the afternoon on the phone—with Joe, Ron Cranford, Thad McCanse, Walt Williams, reporters, and others. Joe and I finalized the press release. The family planned to say nothing to the press. At 4:30 P.M., I held a news conference in the large conference room on Shook, Hardy's top floor.

The decision led off the television news around the state that evening, and the following morning the case played out in newspaper headlines. The articles typically followed the same pattern—basic facts of the decision, followed by comments from parties and interest groups. The ruling was a 4–3 decision, authored by Judge Robertson. Joining Judge Robertson in the majority were Judge Billings, who had phoned Judge Teel the previous July; Judge Rendlen; and Missouri Court of Appeals Judge James Reinhard, who had sat at the argument in place of Judge Donnelly, who was retiring later in the year.

Robertson wrote that Missouri law provided no basis for Nancy's parents, as guardians, to choose her death. It relied on the public policy found in the living will law: "In the face of this State's strongly stated policy in favor of life, we choose to err on the side of life, respecting the rights of incompetent persons who may wish to live despite a severely diminished quality of life."

He concluded: "It is logically inconsistent to claim that rights which are found lurking in the shadow of the Bill of Rights and which spring from concerns for personal autonomy can be exercised by another absent the most rigid of formalities."

Judge Blackmar's dissent deferred to the family: "I am not persuaded that the state is a better decision-maker than Nancy's parents." He clearly agreed with the family's decision: "If she has any awareness of her surroundings, her life must be a living hell." Judge Higgins' dissent called Judge Teel's opinion "a courageous voyage in an area not previously charted by Missouri courts." Judge Welliver's dissent argued, among other things, that since the case split 3–3 with the regular members of the court, it should be thrown out and reheard in January after Governor Ashcroft chose a new justice to replace Justice Donnelly.

The issue I had worried so much about—Judge Teel's decision not to describe Nancy as in a persistent vegetative state—had not made any difference at all. Every opinion of the court acknowledged that Nancy was in such a condition: for the majority, that simply wasn't enough.

The Cruzans' hometown paper, *The Joplin Globe,* carried the headline "Attorney General Lauds State Supreme Court's Ruling." They quoted Attorney General Webster as saying that he supported the decision and doubted that the U.S. Supreme Court would take the appeal. The attorney general also said that he had "great compassion for the family." He reminded the reporter that this accident had happened in his hometown, that he had gone to high school with one of the ambulance attendants for Nancy, and that Judge Teel was a family friend.

Thad McCanse called the opinion "nonsense. The people who knew [Nancy] best were absolutely, unequivocally of the opinion" that she would want the feeding tube removed, he told reporters. Others, predictably, praised the ruling. Samuel Lee, state legislative chairman for the Missouri Citizens for Life, said, "It's reassuring that the Missouri courts agree that handicapped patients have the same right to receive the basic care, including food and water, that is provided to the non-handicapped."

The Cruzans said little. Joyce told Jane Fullerton at *The Springfield News-Leader* that the family had been ready for the decision on Tuesday, but not Wednesday. "We were disappointed, of course, and we were surprised to have it sprung on us without any warning."

"The only comment we have right now is that it will be appealed," Joe told a couple of reporters.

On November 16, Mel came straight from work to Joe and Joyce's house and found the family in disarray. Disappointment had given way to seething anger—anger at the decision, and anger that the court had surprised them with the special release. Joe withdrew to his blue chair after watching the early evening news and rocked, his eyes fixed upon the wall.

❧   ❧   ❧

Three days after the Missouri Supreme Court decision, Joe, Joyce, and Chris came up to Kansas City and we spent that Saturday morning discussing options. Since the Cruzans' last visit, Shook, Hardy had moved their offices into a huge black glass skyscraper. In fact, the elevator ride up to my floor popped Joe's ears. Betsey Arledge wanted to film the meeting for PBS, so we met in a large, windowed conference room. Joe couldn't believe the view of the city below—he could see the downtown airport and the point where the Missouri and Kansas Rivers flowed into one another.

Kim Ross, my legal assistant, joined us, and we all assembled across a polished, cherry wood conference table, with Styrofoam coffee cups atop expensive coasters, and new, unmarked yellow pads in front of each of us. We discussed the petition for rehearing that I was going to file at the Missouri Supreme Court, the possibility of moving Nancy out of Missouri now, and the appeal to the U.S. Supreme Court.

Chris told me about a woman who had called her recently. It seemed that Nancy had briefly worked as a teacher's aide at a school for handicapped students and apparently had had a conversation about life support with one of the teachers. That teacher recognized the photo of Nancy Cruzan on television as the Nancy Hayes (Nancy's name from her first marriage) she'd known, and she called Chris. I thought this information could possibly come in handy, and I filed it away for future use.

Mostly we just spent the morning together so that the Cruzans knew that they still had an ally and a friend, and that they hadn't lost the fight. As the meeting closed, I tried to give them reassurance. "We absolutely will get this done, Nancy's not going to lie 40 years like that," I said. "That's just not possible, and it's not going to happen."

All three looked unsure. Joe looked as if he were listening to the promise of a politician.

"Trust me, I'm a lawyer," I said. Joyce and Chris laughed, but Joe did not.

We ended the day agreeing that what Joe and I had both already said publicly was true—after Missouri, the U.S. Supreme Court was the next step, despite the long odds. If that court turned down the request to hear our appeal, then we'd start looking at moving Nancy out of Missouri.

As I escorted the Cruzans out of the building that day and said goodbye, it struck me how sad and tired all three of them were.

          ❧   ❧   ❧

Chris called me a couple of weeks later to talk about Joe. She said that he'd been on "good behavior" in my office, and that they were seeing a different side of him "back home." For one thing, the mailbox was driving him nuts—the stream of letters from strangers had become a torrent after the Missouri Supreme Court decision. Words of support, words of disdain, advice for the lawsuit—one letter even had a piece of chamois cloth stapled to its corner. The writer claimed that it had come from the Shroud of Turin, and if they rubbed it on Nancy's head, she'd walk again.

Wherever Joe Cruzan went, he couldn't stop talking about the case or the "goddamned Missouri Supreme Court." In Wal-Mart, if someone wanted to talk, Joe would stop and explain at length the changes needed in the state—no matter whether the person was familiar or a stranger. He'd pull newspaper editorials out of his pocket, their newsprint smeared, for emphasis.

Joe took it as direct confirmation of his position that most papers in Missouri supported his family. *The Joplin Globe*: "Nancy has suffered enough. The family has suffered enough. The state should let it go." *The Springfield News-Leader*: "The decision ought to be between the Cruzans and their daughter, not lawyers, doctors, and bureaucrats." *The St. Louis Post-Dispatch*: "It is too late to spare the family of Nancy Cruzan the long and painful ordeal they have suffered for the last five years. But it would be an act of compassion for other families."

As Chris and I talked that day, I had no idea what to tell her. The prospect of things getting better anytime soon seemed remote. She knew that I was with them, for what that was worth. I didn't have much else to give.

December 13, 1988

The case was briefly back in the news, as the Missouri Supreme Court issued its opinion denying the petitions for rehearing that Thad McCanse and I had each filed. Such petitions are rarely granted. The year before, the court had gone 60 for 60 in turning down rehearing requests. In our case, the petition again split the court 4–3, which was unusual. But the court hadn't granted a rehearing, so our time in the Missouri courts was over.

As Christmas approached, the Cruzans understandably struggled to find any holiday spirit. Joe did an interview with Betsey Arledge, and his anger nearly came through the television screen when it was broadcast in a second *Frontline* documentary. "The reason they stated was that we did not have the right as guardians to make that decision for Nancy," he said, talking about the Missouri Supreme Court. His voice grew agitated and loud. "And, I mean, in other words—where did they get the authority to make that decision? Because they *did* make a decision. There had to be a decision made to let her live, or let her die. We wanted to let her die. They made the decision that she should live."

Joyce was angry, too. "She wouldn't want that," Joyce began, "and yet, somebody out here says it doesn't matter what she wants, it doesn't matter what you want as her family. The state says life is precious, therefore it doesn't matter what you want. It doesn't matter at all. Nancy doesn't matter."

Joe talked about the legal process. "It's made a very pessimistic, angry person out of me, frustrated," Joe said, and he looked over at his wife to make sure he wasn't going too far in describing his true feelings. "I mean, I feel like I am in a sack, and I want to get out of it, but I don't know where to hit, I don't know which way to turn, I don't know what to do."

When I told Joe over the phone just before Christmas that, based on the date of the rehearing denial, our papers to the United States Supreme Court would be due on March 13, 1989, and that we wouldn't know anything from the court until well after that date, he had laughed—like a madman.

Joyce made a decision that Christmas to return to their smaller Christmas tree. Joe was allergic to pine, so the Cruzans had always had an artificial tree. In December of 1982, about two weeks before Nancy's accident, Joyce had gone to a sale at Wal-Mart and bought a huge artificial tree at half price. Joe was home sick from work that day. He didn't like most purchases, and characteristically, he found this tree an unnecessary extravagance. As he struggled to get the big box into the house and down the basement steps, all the while refusing Joyce's offers of help, he'd said "goddamn box" and "goddamn tree" so often that the phrases strung together like a monologue.

Then came January 11, 1983. The tree, bought just days before as a symbol of a growing family of grandchildren and the joy of Christmas, became just the opposite—it turned into an eight-foot-tall reminder of the before and after of their lives. After five years of trying in vain to make Christmas special again, Joyce decided to leave the big tree in the box in the basement. She returned to the smaller, simpler tree, which had stayed in its own box in the basement since the accident.

That Christmas, after their traditional morning with family, Joe and Joyce drove to Mt. Vernon to see Nancy, as they usually did on Christmas afternoons.

Chris said later about Christmas 1988, after the decision from the Missouri Supreme Court, that "it was worse than the Christmas when we tried to bring Nancy home."

CHAPTER 30

WRITING GOVERNOR ASHCROFT

The United States Supreme Court agrees to hear a minuscule percentage of the requests it receives for appellate review. In 1988, the year before we filed our petition, 2,147 parties filed seeking relief, and the Court agreed to take only 239 of those cases; in the almost 90 percent of the cases the Court didn't take, the refusal of the request by the Supreme Court meant that the lower court decision stood. Given the high profile of our case, I thought our chances were somewhat better, but they still weren't great. Four of the nine justices had to vote to take our case for the Court to hear it.

The legal brief seeking review is called a petition for *certiorari*, or *cert* petition. A party must file a *cert* petition within 90 days of the final disposition in the lower court. That made our deadline March 13, 1989. By January, Shook, Hardy & Bacon had 145 lawyers in two offices in Kansas City, a newly opened office in London, and widely known national expertise in handling mass product-liability disputes for a variety of companies. But we had no Supreme Court expertise, and I needed help. I called my friend Ned Kelly at Davis Polk & Wardwell's office in Washington, D.C., to see if the firm as a whole, and Ned specifically, wanted to join the case. Ned and I had started at Davis Polk at the same time, and we'd played basketball together over many lunch hours for nearly three years. He'd come to the firm directly from a clerkship with Justice William Brennan on the U.S. Supreme Court, and was one of the smartest guys I'd ever met. He also had the Davis Polk name behind him. Ned agreed to take the case.

We had other expert help—Mark Haddad from Sidley & Austin in Washington, D.C., the American Medical Association counsel, remained involved. Mark had also clerked for Justice Brennan, and the partner who ran Mark's section at the firm, Carter Phillips, was a well-known U.S. Supreme Court advocate. Other friends who had clerked at the Court agreed to help as well.

Our librarian at Shook, Hardy bought a copy of *Supreme Court Practice,* a thick, black single volume that the D.C. lawyers told me I needed. The book was filled with useful and specific instruction, found under headings like "Table of Page Limits and Cover Colors," "Preparing and Printing the Joint Appendix," and "Oral Argument." The book stayed on my desk.

In January, I began in earnest the work of capturing in 50 pages (preferably fewer), the plea of the parents of Nancy Cruzan, asking the nine justices of the United States Supreme Court to take her life into their hands. That plea had to take exactly the opposite tone of what it truly was. It had to be businesslike, not emotional, and it had to urge the court that the problem wasn't unique to Nancy—it was happening everywhere, and it was high time for the Court to wade in. I also spent significant time lobbying groups to file *amicus* briefs.

I was spending more time on a pro bono case than anyone ever had at Shook, Hardy. While some questioned the expenditure of time and other resources, the firm leadership continued to support an all-out effort. Happily, on January 1, 1989, I became a partner, which took some pressure off and allowed me to focus on *Cruzan* as much as I wanted.

❧   ❧   ❧

The coming of the New Year in 1989 may not have returned hope or faith in the system to Joe, but it did seem to revive his stubborn streak, and he began to write letters. Lots of them. Even before the accident and the subsequent chain of events, Joe Cruzan had called himself the "lightning rod"—the guy who stirred things up. He had never been one to sit home and watch football on television. In a yellow file kept in his bedroom—and marked simply "My Letters"—years of correspondence accumulated, going as far back as the early 1970s.

In April of 1979, for example, he wrote his congressmen—Senators John Danforth and Tom Eagleton and Congressman Gene Taylor—about proposed congressional pay raises. "Dear Senator Danforth, I am mayor of Carterville for the sum of $10 per month. If you people cannot make ends meet on the paltry sum of $66,125 to $82,500 (plus perks) per year, I simply cannot find words to express my indignation . . . . It saddens me to see my country go down the chute, but I honestly feel this is happening, and largely because of leadership in the federal government that puts its own selfish interest before that of the nation. God help my children and grandchildren." As always, Joe sent copies of his letters to *The Joplin Globe.*

Senator Danforth's professional but obviously edgy two-page response to Joe concluded: "This issue is a complex one, and easily falls prey to simple rhetoric." The senator's diplomatic response only spurred Joe, never one to give up the last word on a subject, to write more. "Dear Sen. Danforth, my wife and I made a combined $25,000 in 1978, you made three times as much and need a pay increase? I stand by 'my simplistic rhetoric.' I think *The Joplin Globe* hit the nail on the head. They printed my letter under their heading 'Congress Taking Care of Number One.'"

In February 1985, a proposed Missouri seat belt law lit Joe's fuse. The local paper published six different letters from Joe: "Mandated use of a seat belt would be a very negligible price to pay if it would bring back this daughter and sister who we loved so much." Two months later, he was back at Senator Danforth, urging him to oppose taxing employee benefits. In May, he complained bitterly in a letter directly to the *Globe,* copy to Empire District Electric, about Empire awarding its construction contract to an out-of-towner. President Lamb of Empire replied to Joe and the paper that the local bids were $400,000 higher, far more than the "little bit more" Joe wrote about in his letter to the paper.

In July 1985, Joe took on MAP, Mothers Against Pornography, and their planned march on the Joplin city hall. "Some time ago I vowed no more letters to the editor," his letter began, but he couldn't help himself. "Will people never learn? You cannot legislate morals. You never could, you never will."

He wrote to *The Joplin Globe* to offer condolences and praise to a fellow Carterville city councilman; to complain to Sen. Dick Webster about raising the salaries of the Public Service Commission members; to invite people to the local head-injury association meetings the third Tuesday of each month at the Brady Building; to complain about big business bias in government, and about antiunion bias, the unemployed, and Missouri wage laws. When Joe was sitting in his basement, or at the desk in his bedroom reading the paper, his typewriter was never far away.

In January 1989, that typewriter turned to his family's case. He responded to the mail from strangers, explaining why the Cruzans hadn't just brought her home to die in peace. And he wrote to people in authority—the Missouri Supreme Court, Senator Webster, and Governor Ashcroft.

The governor had taken no public position on the case, but he did have strong pro-life values. As a politician, much of John Ashcroft's private life was written about in newspapers—he was a gospel singer, the son of a preacher, and a member of the evangelical Assemblies of God church. Rod Northcutt had said early on that the governor "supported" the Department of Health's efforts, and that was enough evidence for Joe. Joe said that the governor was "behind the harassment" of his family, and he constantly railed against Ashcroft. At a public forum at Rockhurst College in Kansas City, held two weeks after the Missouri Supreme Court decision, Joe had been asked what the worst part of the legal battle was. He responded, "To watch the governor of the state wipe his feet on the body of my daughter."

On January 6, the morning newspaper's story about the execution of George "Tiny" Mercer sent Joe straight to his typewriter. He spent much of the day composing a letter to Governor Ashcroft. Joe quoted to the governor passages from the Supreme Court's decision about Nancy: "The state's concern with the sanctity of life rests on the principle that life is precious and worthy of preservation without regard to its quality." And, "The state's interest is in life; that interest is unqualified." Joe emphasized in his letter that he did not mean to defend George Mercer or condemn capital punishment—he just wanted to illustrate the "glaring contradiction."

"[The] state does make qualitative judgements regarding life," Joe wrote. Nancy must continue to exist regardless of her medical diagnosis, while George Mercer must die irrespective of his wishes. "Is the state's interest in punishing Nancy by life as it punished George Mercer by death? I do not believe so."

He concluded by urging the governor to call for legislation to amend the living will statute to allow removal of artificial nutrition and hydration "when it serves no medical purpose except to punish a person to a mere existence." Joe wrote that most Missourians would support such legislation. The letter concluded: "Please do not confuse this issue with abortion, they are as different as night and day. I would appreciate a response to this letter."

Joe had little time off that winter, because Springfield Engineering had started a major renovation at Cottey College in the town of Nevada, Missouri, about an hour north of Carterville, which meant that Joe's regular workday now had a two-hour commute tacked on to it. So he squeezed his letter writing into his nights and weekends— long, passionate letters about the case. He wrote the AARP in Kansas City (following up on his phone call from the previous night), enclosing videotapes from *Nightline* and the PBS documentary and urging them to support the Missouri surrogate bill and file an *amicus* brief with the U.S. Supreme Court. He wrote to state representatives from across the state; to *The Joplin Globe,* requesting that his letter to Governor Ashcroft be published even though "I know it is rather long"; and to Kirk Johnson, general counsel of the AMA, to plead with him to file a brief supporting us.

He wrote to Steven Bochco of the television show *L.A. Law,* requesting that if he ever did another show on PVS he should contact a family who knows about such cases so that he could have an accurate portrayal. And he wrote to James Kilpatrick, nationally syndicated columnist at the *Richmond News Leader* (in Virginia), asking if he'd "consider a column on the plight of" Nancy. Kilpatrick wrote Joe back and also wrote about Nancy in his column on April 23, concluding, "A merciful system of justice will authorize removal, and release her for a better life to come."

It turned out though that not everyone saw the issues as clearly as Kilpatrick did.

                    ᴥ   ᴥ   ᴥ

State senators in Missouri debated a bill that winter that would have provided some potential relief to the Cruzans and others, but significant opposition scuttled the bill. Joe and I traveled to Jefferson City again, this time to testify before the Senate Committee on Aging, Mental

Health, and Elderly Affairs, in support of the bill—apparently we didn't persuade anyone.

Groups considering filing *amicus* briefs also struggled with the question of whether to publicly support the Cruzans. The board of directors of the Missouri Hospital Association discussed the case at length, and ultimately decided not to participate as an *amicus* due to "the diversity of membership in the association on the moral and legal issues raised by this case." The Sisters of St. Mary Health Care System (SSM), the largest provider of health care in Missouri, had filed the *amicus* brief supporting the family with the Missouri Supreme Court, but the SSM leadership decided to bow out at the national level.

The Missouri State Medical Association planned to debate a resolution advocating repeal of the living will law at its 131st annual convention in April. The president-elect of the association wrote Joe that the chance of passage of the resolution was "not good" and that, given the "political sensitivity of the issue," he needed to stay "behind the scenes" with his support of the family. Several groups stood firm, though, including the important backing by the American Medical Association. (Ultimately, the Missouri association joined in this national brief.)

As the winter started to give way, I continued work on the *cert* petition. The U.S. Supreme Court required parties to have briefs printed and bound, and I learned that about six blocks from our office in Kansas City was a small company that printed briefs from around the country. The company president, Wallis Gochnauer, agreed to print our brief for half of his cost. I sent drafts of the *cert* petition to Davis Polk, Sidley & Austin, and others; comments came back and the petition improved. By March 13, we had a *cert* petition that my Supreme Court experts thought had a decent chance—although each reminded me of the almost astronomical odds faced by a petitioner to actually get to the U.S. Supreme Court.

Bound together with an appendix on 6" x 9" paper stock, the *cert* petition felt and looked like a small book. The printer sent the required 40 copies to the Court by express mail. A new wait began.

❧   ❧   ❧

A two-page response from Gov. John Ashcroft to Joe's January letter arrived in the Cruzans' mailbox on March 18, four days after we filed
the *cert* petition. The governor noted the difficult time for the family
and lauded their courage and compassion. He wrote that he'd "thought
and prayed about a proper response" to Joe's letter, and he could only
conclude that the Missouri Supreme Court had reached the right result.

Governor Ashcroft wrote, "The court's decision is based on the
proposition, with which I agree, that life is precious and worthy of
preservation without regard to its quality. . . . I am not at ease with the
notion that the legislature can empower anyone, no matter how close to
the person, to decide to make that person die by withholding food and
water. We simply are not equipped to make the moral judgments about
life that are inherent in any such analysis." He concluded: "I respect you
for your views, and for your love for your daughter. May God bless you
and your family in these difficult times."

The governor's opinion obviously stayed true to his pro-life values,
but his letter was thoughtful and worked to show consideration for the
family's obvious pain. Joe was having none of it. He had little tolerance
for differing points of view—you were either for him or against him.
Across the entire front of the page of Governor Ashcroft's letter, Joe
scrawled in large yellow letters from his highlighter, "CLOSED
MIND!" With that addition made, Joe stuck the letter in the file box on
the floor next to the desk in his room.

※

CHAPTER 31

JUNE OPINIONS

The Supreme Court's annual term begins on the first Monday in October. The Court hears oral arguments in four cases that Monday, and four more each on Tuesday and Wednesday. It hears arguments in this fashion during different weeks from October until the end of April. In those six months, the justices hear arguments in roughly 150 cases, although the number can vary significantly some years—it all depends on what the justices choose to hear.

Each Wednesday, the justices leave the bench after hearing the last argument of the day and week, usually around 3:00 P.M., and meet in private conference in a room adjoining the chief justice's chambers. Here, the Court deals with the four cases that were argued the Monday before. This meeting is called "the Conference" by the justices themselves, and only the nine justices attend.

On Friday, the justices return and spend most of the day in the Conference, discussing the remaining eight cases that were argued on Tuesday and Wednesday, and handling any other Court business, such as petitions for *certiorari*. This process continues throughout the entire term.

Life in the U.S. Supreme Court building grows frenzied each spring. By June, the lights throughout the four-story, white marble building shine late into the night seven days a week, as the justices and their clerks work feverishly to bring the term to a close. The timing of the summer recess depends on the ability of the justices to finish the written opinions in all the cases argued. In recent years, that point is typically reached in late June, but in some years, the term has spilled over into July. The tag "June opinion" is used at times to suggest that the work product, produced under intense pressure at the end of a term, might at times show the rough edges inherent in the nature of such deadlines. *Cert* petitions can be caught up in this time crunch along with the other work of the Court.

❧   ❧   ❧

After our petition went to the Court on March 13, I had just a few jobs left—the first was trying to enlist *amicus* groups to file briefs in support of our petition. An article by one of the authors of *Supreme Court Practice* suggested that *amicus* briefs at the *cert* stage, which emphasized to the Court the broad importance of a case, might well be more critical than such support after the Court had accepted a case. I looked for all the voices of support I could find—I wrote more than 100 groups from inside and outside Missouri and talked on the phone to members of many. Any briefs were due on May 12, the day the state's opposition brief was due. By that date, we'd enlisted 23 groups, which joined seven separate briefs filed in support of the Cruzans' *cert* petition.

I also turned to the second job, what I assumed was the real work in the case at that point: developing a strategy for the day we might learn that the Court had rejected our petition. On March 20, I sent a confidential, sealed memo to Shook, Hardy's new managing partner, Gene Voigts, and to Dave Waxse, the lawyer who had originally called me about the case in 1987. Dave understood criminal and constitutional litigation, and both men had extensive practical experience with difficult cases. When current Senator Danforth had been attorney general, Gene had served as number two in the office. He also had criminal litigation experience and was our firm's lawyer, which meant that he knew most of Shook, Hardy's secrets—going to his office at times had the feel of going to the principal's office. My memo stated:

> I would like to set up a time when I can sit and talk to both of you about our advice to the Cruzan family in the event that the United States Supreme Court denies our petition for *certiorari*. It is currently the plan of the Cruzans to move Nancy from the state of

Missouri and have the artificial feeding terminated in another state if *cert* is denied. Two specific questions I need guidance from the two of you on are: (1) should we seek assurances from Attorney General Webster and the local prosecutor in Jasper County that they will not try to prosecute or stop the Cruzans; (2) what is the best method to contact the probate court that is in charge of Nancy's guardianship.

I would hope that we could meet the week of March 27 or the week of April 10. Please give me a call or have your secretary call me and let me know your availability. These are obviously questions I need to keep extremely confidential for the present. I will wait to hear from you.

The three of us met on March 29 in Gene's corner office on the 26th floor. The office had so much paper stacked on the desks, couch, coffee table, and floor that it looked as if no one would be able to finish the work in one lifetime. It made an interesting obstacle course for me, since I was hobbling around on crutches and dragging a plaster cast from hip to toe after snapping my Achilles tendon playing basketball.

We talked for nearly an hour. Gene was extremely concerned about potential criminal conspiracy charges, and not only against the Cruzans, but for me and Shook, Hardy. The one conclusion on which we all agreed was that caution and confidentiality were absolutely essential. Gene told me to document each step as completely as possible, and to spare no effort making certain that we reached exactly the right resolution. "Be careful," he said as I left.

The *Cruzan* case often left me with a yellow pad full of questions, and this meeting was no exception: "Murder? Possible conspiracy? Aiding and abetting? New jurisdiction statute? Order from the probate court? Constitutional right to travel? Crime in one state, not another? Seek attorney general opinion? Declaratory judgment in federal court?"

I met with the lawyer who would do the most sensitive research and gave her a one-month deadline to answer five separate subquestions that followed from the lead question of my memo to her: "What exposure might the Cruzans, and Shook, Hardy, as their lawyers, have criminally should the Supreme Court deny *certiorari* and the Cruzans decide to move Nancy to another state to terminate her treatment?"

Shook, Hardy had suffered leaks of memos to the press in controversial cases at least once before, and the possibility loomed over such sensitive research. People at the firm raised concerns about our representing the Cruzans—I was told that at least one attorney quit because of our involvement in the case. One new lawyer asked me at a luncheon, "Doesn't a part of you worry about the morality of what you're doing?" I said something about people of good will differing, and "that I couldn't imagine anything more moral than defending the Constitution."

I talked at length behind closed doors with the associate doing the research about the extent of caution that was appropriate, and my assignment memo to her reiterated my near paranoia: "<u>Absolutely no one</u> in the firm other than myself, Gene Voigts, David Waxse, you, and my secretary—should be consulted on these issues. Obviously, discuss this with no one outside the firm."

I was especially concerned about a new Missouri jurisdiction statute. In 1987, the Missouri Court of Appeals ruled that the state had no jurisdiction to bring murder charges against a man who had kidnaped a woman in St. Louis, took her to Illinois, and murdered her there—the jurisdiction belonged where the murder took place. In reaction, the legislature passed a new jurisdiction law that year, which provided Missouri with jurisdiction to try any offense as long as "conduct constituting any element of the offense" occurred in Missouri. First-degree murder in Missouri required these elements: (1) knowingly (with intent), (2) causing the death of another, (3) after deliberation. I could envision a pro-life prosecutor describing the extensive "deliberation" in which the Cruzans and I had taken part—phone records showed these deliberations happening just about every day in the spring of 1989.

Other associates were busy with research projects, too. How did the newly amended Probate Code affect our case? Could we file in federal court now? What was the best way to raise Nancy's constitutional right to travel in the event we had to move her out of Missouri? By the end of May, I thought we'd prepared for the contingencies about as well as we could.

Sandy Nelsen in the U.S. Supreme Court Clerk's Office told me that *Cruzan* was on the list for the Conference on May 25. I wrote to different people and told the Cruzans that we'd likely hear word on Tuesday, May 30, which was the first hand-down date after the May 25 Conference. On May 30, I received word that the stack of decisions for the day didn't include *Cruzan*. I called Joe.

Later in the week, I called Sandy Nelsen again. She told me that *Cruzan* was now not on the Conference list for June 8 or June 15, and that in their computer, *Cruzan* had an asterisk next to it, which meant that it had been put on hold, pending resolution of some other action by the Court. The last possible Conference date for the term was June 29, and it looked as if *Cruzan* would wait until then.

Joe and I had talked several times on the phone about when the decision would come down, and what to do if the Court denied *cert*. By now, his voice was a study in forced control—he said thank you to me often, and I believe he truly was grateful for the legal help. But I was a part of the legal process, even if I was on his side. He couldn't mask his occasional sighs and constant undercurrent of frustration with a system that couldn't see that *he* should be making choices for his daughter, not them. He thought the entire world was losing its proper focus.

Joyce told me later about a funeral for a buddy that Joe had attended that spring. He came home incredibly angry about the service. "I felt like God died," he said, "because that's all anybody talked about." He told her, "If we ever get out of this mess, Nancy's funeral is going to be about Nancy."

June 29 came and went with no word from the Court. On July 3, the justices met in the Conference for the last time in the term. The shouts of hundreds of abortion protestors assembled on the front steps of the building rose toward the inner sanctum of this secret room, for they were awaiting final word in the abortion case that bore our attorney general's name, *Webster v. Reproductive Health Services*. That day, the justices also had to dispose of a second difficult case from Missouri—the petition for *certiorari* in *Cruzan v. Director, Missouri Dep't of Health*.

Justice Thurgood Marshall's papers, made public after his death years later, revealed that the Conference had first discussed *Cruzan* in March, and only Justice Byron White and one other, unnamed in Marshall's notes, voted to hear the case. Although a majority isn't required to take a case, four of the nine justices must vote in favor—two wasn't enough. For reasons also not explained in Marshall's papers, the Court didn't deny *cert* that day, but held the case over for later consideration. And even though the clerk's office had said it was on the list for the Conference on May 25, the Court didn't resolve it that day either.

Justice Marshall's tally sheet for July 3 listed each justice's vote as the fate of Nancy Cruzan moved down the seniority line:

Chief Justice Rehnquist—denied.
Justice William Brennan—denied.
Justice Byron White—denied.

Justice White, who had initially voted in March to hear the case, had apparently changed his mind.

With only six votes left, the Cruzans had no votes in favor of taking the case.

Justice Thurgood Marshall—denied.
Justice Harry Blackmun, the author of *Roe v. Wade*—granted.
Justice John Paul Stevens—granted.
Justice Sandra Day O'Connor—denied.
Justice Antonin Scalia—granted.
Justice Anthony Kennedy—granted.

Later that morning, my phone started ringing, and it didn't stop. The United States Supreme Court had agreed to take our case. With four pen marks, we were back in the game in a big way. When the call came in, I hung up the phone and let out a yell so loud that people looked in my office door to see what was going on.

We did not need to worry about criminal charges, or choosing between Missouri state and federal court, or any of the other contingencies—we were heading to Washington. By the time I called Joe, he'd already heard. He was so overcome with emotions he likely couldn't even name—happiness, relief, anticipation, dread—that he started clearing his throat when his voice caught, about ten seconds into our conversation, and he struggled to speak again.

CHAPTER 32

FRIENDS AND FOES

Duane "Tootie" Lett had worked by Joe Cruzan's side at Springfield Engineering for 18 years, and he was the closest thing (outside of his brothers) that Joe had to a best friend. They worked together on the Cottey College project, installing new duct work in the college's theater. Some of the other guys from Springfield Engineering didn't want to take the job at the college—not only because of the long commute, but also because the work was high in the air and dangerous. Joe said he needed to keep busy and wanted the work.

Most days, Tootie and Joe spent at least two hours together in the car, commuting to the job site and back. They would typically meet at an exit off the highway near Carthage, around 6:30 A.M., and take turns driving, either in Joe's pickup or big "work Oldsmobile," or in Tootie's company truck. Often other workers traveled with them, such as Eldon Bagwell or Don Young, but it was Tootie who heard daily replays of the events in the *Cruzan* case—the unedited, sheet-metal worker version.

The morning of July 5, "the case" was the main topic on the way to the job site. All the men had seen the article in *The Joplin Globe* or the television news coverage the previous day. Joe talked about traveling to Washington later in the fall, and about how quickly his life had turned around. He said that just days before, he and Joyce had had a long talk with me about their potential criminal exposure if they tried to move Nancy without a consent order after the Supreme Court denied *cert*. He and Joyce had talked seriously about doing it anyway—they were willing to take the risk. Then, with one phone call, hope of eventual legal victory returned. As Joe told one reporter, "We're pretty elated around here. My whole family feels the same way. There was a lot of bittersweet emotion around here this morning, but we were also very happy." The guys on their way to work that morning felt the same way.

The July 3 order from the U.S. Supreme Court meant that I had about a six-month sprint in front of me. On July 6, I sent a memo to 61 people around the country, from all walks of life—lawyers, CEOs, academics, doctors, the solicitor general's office—addressed to "Friends of Nancy Cruzan." It appeared that I had some new hope as well. The memo noted that 23 different groups had supported the Cruzans' petition for *certiorari*, and urged the addressees to work on expanding that list significantly. The memo began, "The family is ecstatic, their hope rekindled," and concluded simply, "Please call or write me soon with your ideas. We are going to win this case."

That Thursday I spoke with Sandy Nelsen in the Supreme Court clerk's office and sent her a letter by overnight mail, seeking an extension of the deadline for filing our brief. On July 14, I wrote the Friends again, explaining that the Supreme Court had extended the deadline until September 1. My memo offered to coordinate the obtaining of required consents for all *amicus* briefs, asked to review drafts of all briefs to avoid inconsistent positions, and attempted to inspire the troops: "The intensity of the battle now joined will only grow over the next several months. The time to start working is now."

I had our brief to write, *amici* to recruit, press to deal with, and practice arguments to make at some point. Also, I wanted to make a trip to D.C. to watch the Supreme Court in action, something I'd never done, even though I'd clerked at the federal court of appeals for a year, which is only blocks away from the Supreme Court. And I had trial set in one of my other cases in August. At the end of each day, I'd make a horizontal line across that date in my calendar with a highlighter. The lines were coming faster than they ever had before.

❧ ❧ ❧

The solicitor general of the United States, or SG, is sometimes called the tenth justice of the Supreme Court. The SG's office represents the interests of the United States before the Court, and is involved in about two-thirds of all cases the Supreme Court chooses to hear each year, either as a party, or as an *amicus* supporting one side or the other.

The solicitor general, of course, is not the tenth justice—he has no vote on the Court—but he does wield tremendous influence. The SG has his own office in the Supreme Court building itself, in addition to the main offices in the Department of Justice building, making the solicitor general one of only two people in the United States government who has formal offices in two branches of government. (The vice president is the other.)

The great lawyer Robert Jackson, who served as SG in the years before WWII, once received a letter addressed only to "The Celestial General, Washington, D.C." Apparently, the postmaster knew where such a letter should go among all of the dozens of titled generals in D.C. Given the SG track record at the Court, maybe some higher power is at work. Petitions for *certiorari* filed by the solicitor general are granted in an average of 70 percent of cases, compared to less than 3 percent of the time for ordinary citizens. And once the Court agrees to take a case, SG support is equally critical: If the SG supports one side or the other in a case at the Court, then that party's chances improve dramatically. A citizen seeking relief from the Supreme Court wants the solicitor general on his side.

The solicitor general is a political appointee. In the spring of 1989, as the Presidency passed from Ronald Reagan to George Bush, the office was in transition. Charles Fried, a Harvard law professor, had served as Reagan's SG. Fried had returned to Harvard in January, and President Bush hadn't yet appointed his replacement. Yet even though the executive branch was in transition, the rest of the government did not stop. Business at the Supreme Court moved forward.

That spring, the SG's office and the attorney general of Missouri were working together on an important case, fighting against the right to privacy. The SG's office filed its *amicus* brief in February 1989 in *Webster v. Reproductive Health Services*. In the first paragraph, under the title that leads off every SG brief, "Interest of the United States," the brief began, "The United States continues to believe that *Roe v. Wade . . . should be overruled by this Court."

For the oral argument of the case on April 26, the solicitor general's office hired Professor Fried to return to Washington to make the government's case. He shared the podium before the justices with his ally in the cause, Missouri Attorney General William Webster. By April, General Webster was nearly a regular in the SG's office, meeting for practice, or moot, arguments, and talking strategy with Deputy Solicitor General Tom Merrill (the number-two person in the office) and his staff.

Tom Merrill decided to stay on and see who President Bush named as the new solicitor general. Merrill later couldn't remember exactly when he'd heard about the *Cruzan* case, but he remembered his reaction clearly: "Oh my God, let's steer clear of this one." Merrill did not see a strong federal interest in the case, and he'd just been through one war with Missouri—on abortion.

In May, the U.S. Senate confirmed President Bush's choice of federal appeals judge Kenneth Starr to serve as his solicitor general. By June, Starr had moved the three blocks from the U.S. courthouse, which housed the court of appeals, to the Department of Justice.

Cruzan turned out to be one of the first cases that Merrill and Starr worked on together. Starr didn't share Merrill's reluctance to get involved. "The Court needs our help on this one," Starr said. Starr went through an exhaustive fact-finding process to determine the answer to Merrill's question: What exactly was the federal interest?

On two occasions, high-ranking officials from the Veterans' Administration came to the Department of Justice building. Lawyers and secretaries looked twice as the men, decked out in dress uniforms, made their way through the halls. Merrill and Brian Martin, the junior member of the SG team for *Cruzan*, sat in the meetings. Starr probed methodically to learn about the care of veterans, and what different positions in the *Cruzan* case might mean to them. If a resolution of our case by the Supreme Court would have an effect on veterans and VA hospitals, that effect raised a specific federal interest that justified the entry of the solicitor general into our case. General Starr also made a field trip to Bethesda Naval Hospital to learn about the issues firsthand at patients' bedsides.

Starr relied on Merrill to help him sort the case out. *Cruzan* ended up being the biggest case Merrill worked on with General Starr. In a lengthy *New York Times Magazine* article profiling Starr years later (after his stint as the independent counsel investigating President Clinton), Tom Merrill talked about Starr's thoroughness and methodical nature, using the *Cruzan* case as an example. Starr would say, "Let's take a walk," and he and Merrill would take long strolls up and down the Mall in D.C., discussing *Cruzan's* legal issues, how to square the case with abortion cases, and the human tragedy of the case. Merrill found Starr deeply concerned about this family from Missouri, people he'd never even met.

The Mall is the broad grassy area that runs about two miles from the Capitol to the Lincoln Memorial, with much of the Smithsonian Museum facing it. Lining the grassy area on each side are 20-foot wide paths of crushed, orange-tan gravel, with park benches all alongside. Every day, government workers on break jog up and down the paths, weaving in and out of visitors from all over the world. In the summer of 1989, those visitors would also have had to veer around the two bespectacled, middle-aged men in suits, deep in conversation, trying to figure out what to do about Nancy Cruzan.

My first conversations with the solicitor general's office were with Brian Martin, who had graduated from law school after I had. Martin, though cordial, was extremely careful when he spoke to me and hesitant to disclose details. It seemed clear, though, that people within the SG's office were sympathetic to the plight of the Cruzans, and that the office was struggling with the case. I believed that there was a decent chance they could come in on the "top side" (our side). I discussed with Martin the narrow approach we'd likely take, one that the solicitor general could support, I argued.

Later I learned that two internal memos were circulating among the SG team that summer—one advocating coming in on the top side, the other arguing in favor of taking up the bottom side.

❧ ❧ ❧

The volume of mail coming to Carterville increased significantly after July 3. Many times the Cruzans' postman had to leave a stack of mail on the porch after he'd filled the box. Media followed the same course. Joe screamed at the television or radio as he watched or listened to right-to-life advocates distort the facts about his family. Pat Robertson, for example, told his *700 Club* audience: "Euthanasia, the right to die, or the right to kill? [Nancy Cruzan] can experience pain and joy; she expresses tears and smiles. But she was sentenced to die a horrible and painful death by starvation." Joe was livid when he told me about the show.

But Joe had ample chance to tell his side of the story through the media, too. His July calendar was filled with amazing entries for a sheet-metal worker from a small town in Missouri—Carl Manning from the Associated Press; Al Kamen from the *Washington Post;* the *Los Angeles Times;* the *American Medical Association News,* and so on. And the Cruzans agreed to make a trip to New York City in August to appear on *Good Morning America.*

Talking on the phone to a reporter while sitting in his basement in Carterville—or even appearing on *Nightline* from a Joplin studio—was one thing. Flying to New York for *Good Morning America* was a very different matter. Joe's uncle George Chenoweth, a pilot in WWII, had kept his license active and had flown Joe over the Joplin area a handful of times in a single prop two-seater—and Joe had always felt relief when his feet were back on the ground. Joyce had never set foot in a plane of any kind. In the days leading up to the New York trip, we talked constantly about what to say, what to wear, and what to do.

The Cruzans were scheduled to fly out of Tulsa on Tuesday, August 15, and Joe took Monday off work to prepare. His calendar read, "Off getting ready to go to N.Y."

We talked on the phone one last time on Monday, and Joe said, "I just hope to God New York isn't much worse than Kansas City." The drives up to see me always left him feeling as if he'd mistakenly turned onto the Indianapolis Speedway.

I laughed. "Joe, traffic in Kansas City looks like Mayberry compared to New York City."

A dumbfounded "good God" escaped from his lips, and we talked again about where they'd find the man with the sign that said "CRUZAN" at LaGuardia Airport. Despite his nervousness, Joe had a new energy in his voice when we talked now. The Supreme Court taking his case meant that he hadn't lost, that he still had a chance.

I found Joe and Joyce in the lobby of the Essex House hotel in New York on Tuesday evening. They'd made it, although they'd never forget the first limousine ride of their lives—from LaGuardia to a hotel facing Central Park.

On Wednesday morning, a car from the show picked us up early. *Good Morning America* was already very much alive when we arrived. All three of us kind of looked around in wonder—producers were talking to us, people were scurrying everywhere, and we were ushered to a special room where makeup artists sat us down and powdered our faces. Each time we looked at one another, we smiled.

After makeup, we were taken through a door into the studio. Contrary to the set's cozy appearance on TV, we found ourselves in a huge room with an enormously high ceiling, and various living-room arrangements scattered around like displays in a vast furniture warehouse. Cameramen, producers, and other workers moved rapidly, oblivious to us. Charles Gibson and Joan Lunden sat and talked on one set some distance away. Joe, Joyce, and I were moved to a second set, and the staff started hooking up microphones, asking us each to speak so they could check the sound level. During a commercial break, Charles Gibson came over and introduced himself, and said he'd be moving over to our set to do the interview. He seemed likable and genuinely sympathetic to Joe and Joyce.

On a large television screen right in front of us was the face of Missouri Sen. John Schneider, who apparently was going to give the opposing point of view that morning. The senator was in St. Louis, and the sound wasn't turned on, so we just watched him on the screen. Joe didn't like Schneider, and he didn't enjoy having to sit and look at him.

We watched the show going on as Gibson and Lunden sat next to one another on a white, plush couch, and then Joan Lunden gave the lead-in: "Coming up, the right to die." We got ready. During the commercials, Gibson moved to our set and some people helped him get situated. A producer said "Ten seconds," and then pointed to Gibson.

"The Supreme Court this fall is going to hear what is expected to be another landmark case from Missouri," Gibson began. "Like the recent abortion case, it's going to deal with a highly emotional issue. This time, it is the right to die." He talked about Nancy's several minutes without oxygen, her persistent vegetative state with no hope of recovery, and how she was fed through a tube. Then clips from the PBS documentary came on, with Chris saying that, if Nancy could talk, she'd say, "Turn me loose." Gibson next described the state's position: "State officials in Missouri say that allowing Nancy's feeding tube to be removed would be in effect a death sentence," followed by clips from the PBS interview Betsey Arledge did with Bob Presson.

"This fall, when the Supreme Court hears arguments in the *Cruzan* case, it will mark the first time that the high court has taken up the right-to-die issue," Gibson continued. "With us today are Nancy's parents, Joe and Joyce Cruzan, and their attorney, Bill Colby, is also with me here in New York. Nice to have you all with us." The camera panned to Joe and Joyce and me as Gibson made the introductions. He began with the Cruzans, asking about Nancy's condition. Joyce described her contractures, her inability to function, her complete dependence, and her wake cycles.

"When you're there to visit her, does she recognize anything—can she—does she respond to any kind of stimuli, does she—," Gibson began.

"We've never seen anything," Joe interrupted.

"And the doctors have said this is absolutely, for certain, irreversible?"

"Right," Joe and Joyce said together.

"And she can, I gather, live in this condition, with this feeding tube in her stomach, for—"

"Possibly 30, 40 years," Joyce said, and Joe nodded.

Gibson and the Cruzans talked about how and when they'd come to their decision, and what the response had been from the state hospital.

Gibson turned to me. "Bill Colby, is there a difference in the way the state responds to this because it's feeding tubes, as opposed to the cases we've heard more about, which are respirator tubes, breathing tubes?" he asked.

"Well, it's hard to say because there hasn't been either case in Missouri," I began. "What medical experts say is that, whether it's a gastrostomy tube or a respirator, the person has lost a natural ability because of this accident, and a machine has taken the place of that natural ability. Whether it pumps in air or pumps in food, Nancy can't do it on her own anymore, and a medical treatment has taken its place."

"Any estimate of how many people in the nation are in this kind of state?"

"The medical literature suggests there are 10,000 people in the persistent vegetative state, which is a very specific, clinical diagnosis of a person who has no cognitive functioning whatsoever, no perception of the world around her, and never will again. They have brain-stem functions."

"Now the state says, 'We have an interest in life,'" Gibson said. "And the state says that 'we would allow the removal of life-sustaining equipment if death were inevitable within a short time,' right? But it is not in this case—she can go on living, indefinitely?"

I grew more animated, responding that families had always made such decisions, talking about the Cruzans' initial consent, when hope remained. The camera cut away to the Cruzans as I answered. Joyce nodded in agreement, watching me. Joe sat rigid, still looking directly at Charles Gibson. As I finished the answer, Gibson turned to Senator Schneider, his white hair and tinted glasses filling the monitor. Gibson said that Schneider must be sympathetic with the Cruzans, but, "I gather that you very strongly believe that this feeding tube should not be removed."

Senator Schneider began to talk about the Missouri Supreme Court decision, his words coming fast. "What the court found, and I think clear what the issue is, that we're dealing with a case of not whether or not just to allow Nancy to die, but as the court found, whether or not we're going to cause her death by denying her food and water, whether or not we're going to cause a starvation, a dehydration of a person who is otherwise alive. And this whole case started when the nurses, frankly, objected to stopping feeding her. And what their testimony was—that Nancy does wake, she does open her eyes, she will follow voices with her eyes, she responds to pain stimuli, it does not appear that she can comprehend, I can say it does not appear. We have hundreds of people in the state of Missouri who are in this kind of a condition, and we're talking about whether or not to cause their death. Now there's a substantial difference between this and denying some extraordinary medical kind of treatment, for example—"

"But, but, Senator—," Gibson tried to break in.

"If we're talking about pulling a plug on a respirator, that's one thing—the person could still be allowed to breathe—but if we're talking about stopping their access to breath by, for example, putting a pillow over their, and suffocating them, that is similar to what we're talking about here because all we're talking is whether or not we continue to pour food and drink into a tube, which costs us $21 a day—"

"But, but the question is: What is the purpose in allowing this to go on, with somebody who all the doctors say this is—," Gibson broke through, but Schneider continued.

"The question is, as the court found, was the only purpose in denying her food and drink is to cause her death, and we're talking about hundreds of people in the state, and frankly, once we decide that we can cause the death of people, hundreds in our nursing homes, if we just raise the level a little bit and because people can't comprehend, we have lots of people who may be able to respond with, or just make noises—"

"All right—"

"Who can't comprehend, if we decide that we're going to cause their death, we're talking about a lot of people."

"Let me take that to Bill Colby, because you do start down a slippery slope—the senator makes the point that you start down a slippery slope, and there are hundreds, perhaps thousands, of people who would say, 'The quality of my life is no good, my family says I should be allowed to die, why not?'" Gibson asked, his calm voice slowing the pace of the dialogue.

"I think there are two points to make there," I said. "First, these are obviously not decisions that you want to make in a cavalier fashion, or that society wants to. But to say that we're going to make our next decision incorrectly, so let's not make this one because it's a hard one? Or, even though we might agree with the Cruzans, we're afraid what the next decision might be? That doesn't give much credit to our doctors and to our society to make proper decisions. And the second point is," I said, my voice growing louder, struggling for emphasis, "that it's not up to the state to tell families, 'Here is the medical treatment you have to give for your family member, here is the medical treatment you don't have to give.' It's a family right, it always has been a family right."

"The date with the Supreme Court is in the fall. Joe and Joyce Cruzan, our best luck to you. Bill Colby, thank you for being with us. Senator Schneider, thank you for being with us from St. Louis." Gibson shook hands with each of us, somebody unhooked the microphones, and someone else led us away.

After the commercial break, Gibson talked to Harvard Law

Professor Arthur Miller, who frequently appeared on the show. We watched from the dressing room as an attendant removed the makeup she'd applied earlier. Gibson mentioned that the Supreme Court had turned down such cases in the past, including the famous *Quinlan* case from the mid-'70s, and he wondered whether taking *Cruzan* meant something important was brewing. "Do you expect that this is going to be a major decision that will be very definitive in these right-to-die areas?" he asked.

"No, no," Miller responded in his distinctive, almost theatrical voice. "This is the first case that the Court has taken—there are all sorts of ways that the Supreme Court can back away from the issue. I think the Court took the case because it now realizes something it didn't realize at the time of the *Quinlan* case—that this is going to be a major phenomenon. We have 10,000 [people] on respirators or in a persistent vegetative state now, we will probably have 40,000 by the year 2000," Professor Miller said. "They know it is an important question, but that doesn't mean that they're going to jump in the pool, they may just stick their feet in the pool. They may decide this case on the basis of its facts. Now it's always conceivable they will make a major announcement. They could announce that there is a constitutional right embraced in the liberty clause of the Constitution, the right of privacy, that the individual does have a constitutional right to control his life—they may not."

"But that is the issue that they will consider this fall?" Gibson asked.

"Yes, absolutely."

"Arthur Miller, thank you for being with us. It's 23 after the hour—we'll be back."

The Cruzans and I gathered our belongings and headed out on to the sidewalk. Outside, it was not quite nine in the morning. New York City wasn't fully awake yet and the yellow cabs still found room to maneuver. The sun was up but hadn't burned off the muggy August haze. We walked back to the Essex House, talking about the last 24 hours, all three of us sweating slightly. Our case had taken up almost a half hour of *Good Morning America*. I thought we'd presented a compelling argument in an important public forum, that Joe and Joyce had done a terrific job, and that Senator Schneider had come off as pretty radical. I was happy with my answers, too, and excited. I wanted to go back to the hotel, change clothes, run all the way around Central Park, and think about my brief and the amazing autumn that lay ahead. Joe and Joyce could muster weak smiles of enthusiasm for only one thing—going home.

⋅❦⋅ ⋅❦⋅ ⋅❦⋅

September 1, 1989, predictably, came quickly. The task of seeking approval within various organizations to file *amicus* briefs, and then finding lawyers to write those briefs, once approved, turned out to be a formidable one in the August vacation season. Just as you don't realize how many people are pushing baby strollers at the mall until you have a baby yourself, since I was single, I had no idea that much of the working world took large parts of August for family vacations before the start of the school year. Even with that hurdle, I thought we'd cobbled together a formidable show of support by our deadline.

The American Medical Association, as it had in the Missouri courts, stood firmly by the Cruzans. Now it had company. Twenty separate briefs went to the Court in support of the Cruzans, and many of those were signed by multiple parties—when the membership was added together, the briefs represented the voices of millions of Americans. Those voices came from across the country and from all walks of life, such as the United Methodist Church, the American Geriatrics Society, and the National Hospice Organization. And many, many others.

I thought our 43-page, blue-covered brief made a compelling argument as well. The first title in the Argument section framed the approach from which the entire brief flowed: "All Persons Have a Fundamental Liberty Interest to Stop Unwarranted Bodily Intrusions by the State." The liberty argument for Nancy built brick-by-brick in three sections: incapacitated people didn't lose all constitutional rights; historically, the Court had looked to families to speak for those who no longer could; and a state had to articulate some specific interest to override a family decision—a general claim to protect life wasn't enough. The brief cited cases dealing with the physical restraint of a mentally retarded man in a state institution, the forced sterilization of inmates by the state of Oklahoma in the early part of the century, and the cases prohibiting police from pumping the stomach of a suspect searching for drugs.

In a different time, with a differently constituted Supreme Court, the lead argument title for a brief in a case like ours might well have read, *"Roe v. Wade* guarantees a right to privacy for all Americans to make decisions about medical treatment for their own bodies." But, in several decisions in the 1980s, the Supreme Court had made something abundantly clear: Privacy was a right hanging by a thread. The margin of victory in recent cases challenging abortion and the right to privacy had shrunk to 5–4. Even more important for us, the Court had rejected any attempt to expand the right to privacy into any other area. Trying to win our case using the right to privacy just didn't make sense with this Court. We stayed as far away from *Roe v. Wade* as we could.

❧   ❧   ❧

On September 2, the *St. Louis Post-Dispatch* reported what I'd just learned, too—that we'd lost the battle to have the solicitor general take up our side. The article stated that just two weeks before the September 1 deadline, "it had appeared that the department might enter the case on behalf of the Cruzans." On September 1, a spokesman for U.S. Attorney General Richard Thornburgh told the *Post-Dispatch* that the federal government would not file with the family.

Worse yet, the spokesman said that the SG "may enter" the case later in the month on behalf of Missouri instead. The paper reported that groups were claiming credit for the apparent position shift: "Leaders of anti-abortion groups said that the department shifted positions after their protests, including a letter to the department by the National Right to Life Committee."

The article also noted that while more than 100 hospitals run by Catholic groups had filed a brief in support of the Cruzans, arguing for the rights of families as the "primary decision makers," other Catholic groups were "sorting out" where they stood. According to Richard Doerflinger, spokesman for the powerful U.S. Conference of Catholic Bishops, after a meeting in August to discuss the case, the group had decided to file against the Cruzans. Their brief would urge the Court not to "constitutionalize" the right to die, as the right to abortion had been constitutionalized 16 years earlier, leaving "no room for the

Catholic point of view."

The Catholic Bishops definitely entering on the bottom side, and the solicitor general's office reportedly considering such a move—this was not good news.

CHAPTER 33

SOLICITOR GENERAL STARR

In the fall of 1989, it seemed as if much of the legal world was talking about *Cruzan*. During the first week of October, I traveled to New York for the mock arguments at the NYU law school; on October 12, I was in Columbia, Missouri, on a panel sitting next to Missouri Supreme Court Judge Robertson. The judge joked in his opening remarks that it didn't seem fair to him that he had to discuss the case with me in the particular room we were in—the Shook, Hardy & Bacon classroom.

I'd now appeared on a handful of programs with the judge, and I found myself having a surprising reaction: I liked him. Although he was three years older than I was, he looked younger, and he was obviously just trying to do a difficult job. Years later he told me that if you compare his signature on the *Cruzan* opinion (the opinion that we were now appealing) and others he signed at the time, his signature on *Cruzan* is hard to read—as he signed the opinion, his hand shook. Joe Cruzan could never understand how I could spend time with Judge Robertson. To Joe, Robertson was against his family, and that meant he was against him.

Two days after the program at the Missouri Law School, I saw Robertson again, this time at a forum in Kansas City put on by the Midwest Bioethics Center. Joe, Joyce, and Chris attended this forum, in part because Judge Robertson and Senator Schneider were scheduled to speak, as were two doctors who supported the Cruzans. I sat with the Cruzans in the front row of the audience, none of us participating in this forum. The senator delivered remarks much as he had on *Good Morning America,* and Joe bristled, shaking his head as he listened to the senator discuss his daughter. He wanted to move to the microphone and tell people the only truth in the case: his truth.

Joe was glad that the U.S. Supreme Court had decided to hear his family's case, but he felt less and less in control as the case moved onto the national scene. He resented that lack of control. The press interviews were no longer coming primarily from Missouri; now reporters from all over the world were calling. Many came in person, including Connie Chung, who sat at the dining-room table at 501 Main Street with Joe and Joyce. Chris said her dad "was starstruck by that visit." On the other hand, when Pat Robertson and other right-to-life advocates talked about his daughter like someone out of a book, or when they distorted the facts, Joe seethed. National commentators on all sides of the issue often misspoke and called Nancy "Karen," confusing her with Karen Ann Quinlan. And, just as with their initial national appearance on *Nightline,* commentators frequently mispronounced the Cruzan name.

At one point, Joe had a run-in with the lead lawyer for the state. In early October, Joe telephoned Bob Presson to tell him about what Joe thought were inaccuracies in the state's brief. In particular, the statements that Nancy had been eating "sausages" and the like after the accident, as if the feeding tube had been inserted merely for convenience, angered Joe.

Nancy had a feeding tube in place—first a temporary one, which was later replaced by a permanent one—from the time of the accident. Joe himself had been the main one trying to feed Nancy pureed food, and those efforts had taken place later, in the Brady Rehabilitation facility. Joe knew better than anyone the lack of success in those efforts. Scrawled across the cover of the state's brief, in large letters, Joe had written: "Damn lie re H & N on page 2." (H & N were hydration and nutrition.)

Bob Presson was somewhat taken aback when Joe called him, telling Joe that he could not talk with him directly—the rules of lawyer conduct required Bob to talk with me, or with Joe only when a lawyer was present. Joe hung up and wrote Presson an angry letter: "Through ignorance I obviously breached legal ethics in my phone call to you this morning. I apologize for doing so. Several times during the trial I visited informally, indeed, even shook hands with you. In phoning this morning I believed I might speak with you man-to-man. Apparently that is not so. If you wish our relationship to be adversarily *[sic]* then, by God, in the future it will certainly be so." I convinced Joe not to send the letter, that Bob Presson had done exactly what he should have.

Perhaps worst of all, Joe and Joyce's weekly visits to see Nancy had grown tense. The reporters didn't just stop in Carterville, they came to Mt. Vernon as well. Even the nurses who agreed privately with Joe and Joyce didn't appreciate the attention, and the nurses who did disagree with the Cruzans' decision were downright hostile at times, glaring at Joe and Joyce as they moved through the polished corridors. When Joe recognized a nurse who had made what he thought were inappropriate comments to the media, he glared right back.

~ ~ ~

On October 16, the state of Missouri, the solicitor general, and 19 other *amicus* groups filed their briefs in opposition to the Cruzans. After a day and a half, I still hadn't read all of the briefs. Predictably, the one from the U.S. Catholic Conference was well written, and troubling for our side. The brief emphasized that, despite efforts in my brief to narrow the issue and focus on liberty, this case sought the expansion of the right to privacy to an entirely new area. It warned the Court against the "unbalanced jurisprudence" of the abortion cases, which was certain to follow in this new area of the law if the Court sided with the Cruzans.

Even more troubling was the brief from the solicitor general. The SG's office, although it came in against us, had decided internally to take a far more moderate approach to *Cruzan* than it had in the *Webster* abortion case the previous spring. The brief made no call this time to overturn *Roe v. Wade,* nor did it attack the right to privacy. Instead, it set a clear path before the Court for resolution of the case—a path the Cruzans could not possibly like.

The SG's brief began with its argument foundation: States have a "profound interest in preserving human life." By definition, an incapacitated person such as Nancy had lost the ability to give careful thought to life-and-death decisions about medical care. Therefore, before a third party sought to speak on behalf of Nancy and make the irrevocable decision that would lead to her death, a state could require proof that the decision was one that she would want. And a state was free to protect its vulnerable citizens, as Missouri had, by requiring a higher showing of proof to support that decision—proof by clear and convincing evidence. The United States Constitution certainly did not prohibit a state from choosing to err on the side of life.

I read and reread the solicitor general's brief, as did my Supreme Court clerk friends. As a matter of constitutional analysis, for anyone who believed in states' rights and in allowing states to make their own policies, the SG's approach was persuasive. For a Court not interested in expanding privacy rights, the brief presented a clear solution—defer to the state, particularly a state that chooses to protect life.

As fall advanced, the brown-covered solicitor general's brief and my blue brief stayed together on top of my desk, growing dog-eared and stained with each new reading, as I tried to find the narrow approach that could woo five justices away from the solution the SG had offered them.

In early October, a letter had arrived from Sandy Nelsen at the Supreme Court, announcing that the Court had scheduled our argument for December 6. All planning worked back from that day. At the end of October, I spent three days in D.C. to strategize with lawyers from Sidley & Austin; Mayer, Brown & Platt; and Wilmer, Cutler & Pickering. I also spent a morning watching arguments at the Court, did research in the Court's library, and talked to Nina Tottenberg at the National Public Radio offices.

On November 15, I filed our final brief. The brief actually *was* brief (at least by legal standards)—a mere ten pages. The bulk of its argument addressed the SG's brief, and it sought to change the question—not whether a state could require clear and convincing evidence before medical treatment is stopped, but whether a state had to articulate specific reasons before interfering with a family.

෨ ෨ ෨

I had three practice arguments, or moots, set up for November 16, 27, and 30. The first one was at New York University Law School, organized by my friend Bob McKay. Bob had spent the spring of 1982 in Kansas, teaching as a visiting professor at KU during my last year in law school, and trying to recover from the devastating loss of his wife to cancer the year before. I spent many hours with Professor McKay that spring, in class and outside.

For the moot argument, I stayed with Bob at his apartment near the NYU campus. He'd recruited Burt Neuborne and Marty Guggenheim from the NYU faculty. Steve Shapiro from the ACLU was going to participate. Ned Kelly, and the general counsel of Shook, Hardy's largest client—Murray Bring from Philip Morris—also planned to take part. Bring had clerked for Chief Justice Earl Warren on the Supreme Court in the '60s, and applauded our firm's pro bono efforts on the case. His support gave me excellent cover internally from those who complained that the firm was spending too much money on the *Cruzan* case.

I began behind the lectern, pretending that the assembled lawyers were the justices. They fired questions at me, I answered, and afterwards we talked about strategy.

Burt Neuborne was enthusiastic. He said, "You're ready to go right now!" I sensed that he was trying to pump me up, like a coach sending in a skinny freshman up against a much bigger, more experienced team.

Back in July, shortly after the Court had agreed to hear our case, I'd talked with Joe Cruzan about enlisting a seasoned Supreme Court advocate to make the argument for the Cruzans. A handful of lawyers in the country made their living doing little else—some of these lawyers had even helped with the briefing, and would participate in the moots in D.C. Joe said, "We've come this far together, we should go the final mile," and decided to stay with me.

Of course, what else could he say? If I truly believed that hiring an appellate specialist was in the Cruzans' best interest, perhaps I should have presented the issue not as a question, but as a tactical step we needed to take. The Cruzans were, after all, relying on my advice. On the other hand, I knew that no other lawyer could know the trial record as I did, and no other lawyer would be as genuinely passionate as I was about this family. And maybe I'd earned the right, with the hours I'd devoted to the Cruzans' cause. As for the constitutional law and specialized advocacy part, I would learn it as best I could.

Joe told me later that he had talked with his friend Tootie about the issue soon after I'd raised it. Tootie had gotten to know the legal process along with Joe, although Tootie said he didn't understand it like Joe. He'd say, "Joe Cruzan is the best educated man in the United States on the right to die." Before the trial in March of 1988, when the first pre-trial briefs were filed, Joe brought his copies over to Springfield, Missouri, where he and Tootie were working on a job. They stayed near Springfield, and after work, Joe and Tootie would sit around in one of their travel trailers and read the briefs.

Tootie had taken off work on the afternoon of March 11 and had come over to watch the last half day of our trial before Judge Teel. At work the following Monday, Tootie and Joe talked about the cross-examinations of the two doctors that last afternoon, joking that "we got them pretty good." When the question of hiring a Supreme Court advocate came up months later, Joe told Tootie, "If he's good enough to handle it this far, he can handle it all the way." Tootie had nodded in agreement.

Back in Kansas City, as I watched the tape of the NYU moot, I felt pretty good about my performance. Some questions still presented problems, though. Repeatedly, in different ways, the assembled moot judges had asked: "Are you asking us to find that the federal Constitution prohibits a state from using a higher burden of proof in this case? Where in the world does the Constitution say that?" We talked about the best ways to maneuver around this question, posed so ably by the solicitor general's brief. No one in our assembled group in New York had a fool-proof solution.

On November 29, I was back in D.C. for one final prep session. I attended arguments at the Supreme Court, and the topic of the day was abortion and the right to privacy. The Court heard three cases, from Illinois, Minnesota, and Ohio: Two dealt with the requirement for a minor to give notice to both parents, and the third with the question of a state requiring an abortion clinic to be equipped like a hospital. The various lawyers ranged from flamboyant to somber, and all scrambled to keep up with the questioning from the justices. I left the Court thinking, *I can do that.*

I walked roughly eight blocks down Pennsylvania Avenue to meet with Solicitor General Ken Starr. I'd called General Starr to see if he wanted to meet while I was in D.C., and he'd been surprisingly receptive to the idea. A secretary retrieved me from the guard area, and Starr came out of his office to greet me when I got upstairs. His office was massive, and we sat on couches, drinking coffee from delicate china cups. I told him why the Missouri standard couldn't work in the real world, and Starr explained the interests of the VA hospitals and the narrow approach he planned for the case, one of deference to the state. The federal government also intended to avoid the right to privacy.

However, he was most interested in and concerned about the Cruzan family. We talked about the stress the family was experiencing, particularly Joe, and Starr asked if he could meet the family on December 6. I told him that I'd let him know. General Starr spent nearly an hour with me, which amazed and flattered me. I left the building thinking that I liked him.

When I called Joe, he did not share my appreciation. "What in the hell do I want to meet with him for?" he asked. "He's against us, isn't he?" I phoned Starr and explained that the Cruzans couldn't meet with him. He was disappointed, but understood.

The next day I did my third and final moot argument and flew back to Kansas City. I was down to one week.

General Starr went through two separate moots. Bob Presson traveled to D.C. to watch him, and to go through the paces of his own practice argument in the offices of the National Association of Attorneys General. I'd watched the Court in action and read everything that I thought mattered. In my own three moots, I'd answered a lot of questions, which was great practice, and had talked strategy with some of the brightest Supreme Court advocates in the country.

But no consensus emerged on how to deflect the solicitor general's brief—why it was somehow unconstitutional for a state to err on the side of life—or how to begin the oral argument at the Court with this case, a topic the Court had never before addressed. Some of the experts suggested that I should start with the family's powerful story and use it to appeal to the conscience of the Court; others thought that the Court wouldn't really care about that story, and believed I should start by describing this case as a simple bodily intrusion case, like other such cases that the Court had resolved in the past.

Many of the most astute scholars of the United States Supreme Court had given me their opinions, which were all reasonable. And I had one week left. Now it was up to me to choose the final approach.

CHAPTER 34

THE SUPREME COURT OF THE UNITED STATES

I didn't sleep much on the night of December 5. When I did doze off, I'd wake with a start, my heart racing. It didn't help that the heat in the hotel was stifling and apparently beyond all human control. My girlfriend, Kelley, was with me, and she just watched and worried. I finally got up around five, took a shower, and dressed. I wasn't tired, just on edge.

Arguing before the Supreme Court is a formal affair. At one time, Court rules required all lawyers to appear in "morning clothes"—a gray cutaway jacket and striped trousers. Today, the rules allow a conservative business suit, "preferably in a dark color, in keeping with the dignity of the Court." The formality is by no means gone, however—the rules even provide guidance to lawyers on buttoning: "If vestless, gentlemen should keep their jackets buttoned." By tradition, the solicitor general and his lawyers still appear only in formal morning clothes. When females joined the SG staff in the 1970s, they adapted, wearing a black suit with a white shirt.

I put on my best navy blue suit, white shirt, and blue-and-red striped tie. If ever a case represented the colors of our flag and the cause of liberty, this was it. That, anyway, was what I hoped to convey. Down in the hotel lobby, I bumped into Betsey Arledge, who noticed, and said, smiling, "Red, white, and blue, very patriotic." I was so uptight I didn't even respond—Betsey told me later I just glared at her as I walked by.

Around 8:30 A.M., our group—the Cruzans, the lawyers, my family, and some friends—walked together over to the Court, with PBS's cameras out in front of us. Still an hour and a half before the argument, and already hundreds of people were gathering out in front of the courthouse, protestors staking their place near the cameras, and lines of people hoping to gain admittance. We stopped and said hello to Kim Ross; my secretary, Dana; Walt William's secretary, Ann; and Ann's daughter, Gretchen, who were waiting together in line. They'd lined up at 5:30 A.M., and were wrapped in blankets and ski coats to ward off the cold. We wished them luck and headed up the long marble steps to the Court, flanked by marble candelabra with intricate carved panels at their bases—on one side the sword and scales of Justice; on the other, the Three Fates weaving the thread of life. We passed by.

The general public can see arguments at the Court in a couple of ways. For tourists just interested in catching a glimpse of the Court in action, the "short" line cycles groups in and out of the back of the courtroom every three minutes. Those wishing to sit through an entire argument have much more limited access—the marshal's office had told Kim Ross the day before that only about 20 seats out of the hundreds in the courtroom were available for the general public to hear the argument in *Cruzan,* and those seats would go on a first-come, first-served basis.

Also, arguing counsel is typically given seats for six guests, if space is available. This seating is arranged through the marshal's office. I actually was able to commandeer 12—my friend Ron Blunt, who clerked for Chief Justice Rehnquist, had seats from the Chief Justice for me as well. My parents flew up from Florida to attend, even though my dad worried about how his heart would handle the cold. He hadn't seen winter weather since his quadruple-bypass surgery five years earlier. My older sister and nephew from Dubuque, Iowa, flew in, too, and she took care of my parents. Friends from law school and colleagues from Shook, Hardy also attended.

Arguing counsel is required to meet the clerk in the lawyer's lounge to the Court, on the first floor, between 9:00 and 9:15. I arrived well before that time. Three lawyers sit at counsel table for each side: Walt Williams and Ned Kelly would sit with me on the Cruzans' side. I wanted Ned there so that the justices might see at least one familiar face on our side. Solicitor General Starr and Attorney General Webster would sit with Bob Presson across from us. Webster and Presson arrived at the lawyer's lounge, and after instructions, we all made our way into the courtroom and waited.

❧   ❧   ❧

High in the air directly above and behind the chair of the Chief Justice hangs a massive, golden clock with roman numerals—that morning, it slowly inched its way toward ten o'clock. My papers were ready, my water was ready, and I was as ready as I could be. Standing in the middle of the cavernous Supreme Court chambers, a lawyer can feel small. The lawyer stands at a podium, facing a long mahogany dais where the nine justices sit. Behind that bench, four 30-foot marble columns stand like sentinels, framed by five equally tall maroon curtains directly behind the columns. The curtains look as if they're made of soft velvet. More massive columns line each wall of the room, and etched into the marble above the columns, different carved figures of justice look down from all sides. The carved ceiling looks very far away.

As ten o'clock approached, I watched this magnificent room fill with people—friends, colleagues, reporters, and strangers, and I felt as if I'd been dropped (perhaps mistakenly) into one of those great paintings of the founding conventions of this country, with earnest men in powdered wigs, arms raised to make their point. I couldn't breathe deeply enough to chase the butterflies away. Promptly at ten, the marshal, dressed in formal morning clothes like the solicitor general, stood and cried out: "The Honorable, the Chief Justice, and the Associate Justices of the Supreme Court of the United States. Oyez! Oyez! Oyez! All persons having business before the Honorable, the Supreme Court of the United States, are admonished to draw near and give their attention, for the Court is now sitting. God save the United States and this Honorable Court." As his voice rang out and filled the room, the nine justices emerged from the curtains in three groups of three and moved to their seats.

William Rehnquist, the Chief Justice of the United States—a tall, balding man who appeared uncomfortable with a bad back even while sitting—spoke: "We'll hear argument first today in No. 88-1503, *Nancy Beth Cruzan v. The Director of the Missouri Department of Health.*

Mr. Colby."

With no more fanfare than that, it was my turn. Somehow I was at the podium and my legs bore the weight. I moved my lips, and words emerged. "Thank you, Mr. Chief Justice, and may it please the Court."

Six years earlier, I'd talked to the Chief Justice in his chambers, one on one, as I interviewed for a clerkship. We'd talked about Professor McKay and his equal protection seminar at KU. Chief Justice Rehnquist asked me something like, "Which of my equal protection decisions did you disagree with in class?" I often wondered if I had replied, "All of them," and if I could have explained my reasoning, whether he would have picked me as a clerk. Instead, I fumbled with an answer, never able to get comfortable sitting so near one of the most powerful people in the world. Now, in the intimate setting of the United States Supreme Court, I wasn't much farther away from him, and my answers had to be better.

I'd decided to start with what I knew best, and what mattered most—Nancy and her family. "Nancy Cruzan is a 32-year-old Missouri woman who is in a persistent vegetative state." After all of the hand-wringing about exactly how to begin the argument, it may not have mattered at all, because I only made it about 40 seconds in before the questions started coming, and they did not stop.

Justice Antonin Scalia—young for a justice, but quick-tongued and brilliant—started things: "Mr. Colby, apparently your opponents say that it is—it would have been more difficult, but that she could have been fed manually by, by massaging the food down her throat or something of that sort. Is that correct or not?"

"I think that is—is not correct," I said. I explained the insertion of the tube in the ICU, the diagnosis of malnutrition, the efforts in rehabilitation to feed her orally and not being able to meet her needs. In *Supreme Court Practice,* in a section titled "Nervousness," the authors note that novices and even experienced counsel are nervous, but "if counsel is adequately prepared on the facts and the law, any nervousness quickly subsides, usually within a minute or two." As the questions started coming from all sides of the bench, the book turned out to be right: I was too busy responding to be nervous. Could the family have refused this surgery? Yes, consent was required. By state law? Yes. Common law or statute? Common law. It would have been a battery to perform surgery without consent.

"Suppose the parents were Christian Scientists," Justice Scalia asked, "or for some reason did not want a relatively ordinary surgical procedure to be performed . . . would the state have to accept that determination, or would the state not be able to appoint a guardian and have the guardian make it?"

"The state would not necessarily have to accept that determination, and certainly there are instances, like the Jehovah's Witness cases, where the state will intervene and take steps to provide the medical treatment. My statement is that, in this case, where the parents would have been—," I struggled to find the right example. "Had a doctor come to them and said, 'There's virtually no chance your daughter is going to recover from this car accident. We want to do this surgery, we need your consent to do it,' and the parents said, 'I don't want to give that consent, I don't think she's going to recover,' the doctors would have honored that request. Now, if the decision is considered abusive, if it's considered one that's not among acceptable medical alternatives, then the state has an interest in intervening."

I argued that the state interest was narrow. For the state of Missouri to override the parents, who were making a decision among acceptable medical alternatives, and in accord with all evidence about Nancy's wishes, the state had to do more than just claim it had a general interest in life. "The Fourteenth Amendment and the liberty guarantee there protects individuals, conscious or unconscious, from such invasion by the state, without any particularized interest for that invasion," I said.

Justice Sandra Day O'Connor, the first woman on the Court, seated at the far right end of the bench from my point of view, jumped in. Her voice had a tiny quaver in it; when coupled with her perfect posture, she seemed regal sitting above the rest of the room as she spoke: "Mr. Colby, does a competent adult have an absolute constitutional right to refuse food and water?"

"I believe a competent adult has an extremely strong right to refuse the surgery necessary to provide a gastrostomy feeding tube when the person has lost the natural ability to swallow," I said.

"How about if no feeding tube is required?" Justice O'Connor asked.

"And what would the mechanism be?" I said.

"Can the—can the adult, the competent adult, absolutely refuse food and water in a hospital setting, and the state can't override that decision?"

"There could be situations where that decision may be considered irrational or abusive, and the state could override that—that decision, I believe," I said. "But if we're—"

"The individual isn't very competent then." Justice Byron White, who President Kennedy appointed to the Court in 1962, interrupted, entering the discussion.

"That may well be right," I said. "In the case of suicide, for example, that's a situation where we presume that the decision is irrational. And if that person is refusing to eat, the state may well have a need to override that decision."

Justice Scalia returned: "Why do you presume it's irrational? I mean, let's assume the person is in a state close to as hopeless as this individual here, and the person says, 'I want to die. I am of sound mind and it is my desire to die.'"

"It would be difficult—," I started to answer.

"Could a state overrule that?" Scalia asked.

"It would be difficult for a person to be in a state close to the vegetative state and—and be competent."

"Well—well, then change it from a vegetative state," Justice Scalia continued. "It's just a state of enormous pain, deformity, quality of life is—is—is nil, and the person says, 'I want to die.'"

"Could that patient refuse surgery to insert a gastrostomy tube?" I said. "Absolutely."

"No, I'm asking Justice O'Connor's question," Justice Scalia said. "Must—must the state allow that person—must the state allow that person to refuse food and water?"

"I believe they—they do have an obligation and that the Fourteenth Amendment protects that person's right to be free from a state intrusion," I said. "And as long as that decision is not considered irrational, then the state doesn't have a reason to intrude."

"Now, can that—," Justice O'Connor began, but Justice Scalia continued.

"Well, what—what's your—what's your standard for—for irrationality?" Scalia asked. "Do you mean it's an objective test? Someone else decides whether a person's particular decision is rational or not?"

"There no doubt is a continuum, and all kinds of decisions will be made along that continuum," I said. "There will be some situations where the state is going to have a greater need to intervene, where a decision is going to seem inappropriate."

The questions ranged from all over. Justices Scalia, O'Connor, and White articulated for their silent brethren—those on my side, presumably—the dangers of Pandora's Box. The Jehovah's Witness/suicide questions were tangling me up, and I tried to draw the discussion back to a permanently unconscious person with no hope of recovery.

My head had been nearly swiveling as I switched from Justice Scalia on the far left end of the bench to Justice O'Connor on the far right. I found myself turning slightly to address Justice O'Connor—the key vote according to Supreme Court followers.

When Justice Scalia asked why Missouri couldn't simply have a rule protecting all life, I responded that permanently unconsciousness people, such as Nancy, would lose important rights.

Justice O'Connor joined in again. "Well, Mr. Colby, in that situation, a person acknowledged to be in a persistent vegetative state, do you think that there is some kind of per se rule, or presumption, that the federal Constitution mandate be applied, that the person would prefer to die? I mean, is that your position? That the state must, because of the federal Constitution, apply some kind of presumption here?"

"There certainly is a presumption, Your Honor," I replied, "that before the state can intrude and order that person to receive medical treatment at the order of the state for the rest of their life, that the state has to show some specific reason for doing that. The state here has shown no reason specific to Nancy Cruzan that—"

The questions kept coming: Doesn't the state have an interest in making sure the patient's wishes are followed? Does the Constitution prohibit a clear and convincing evidence standard? Does the Constitution require a state to allow the nearest relative to make the decision? Isn't it enough to allow family members to testify at a hearing? Does the family have any separate rights? Amazingly, the white light appeared on the lectern, signaling five minutes left. I tried to tell the justices that Nancy Cruzan had limited options, that if she could choose between her right to life and right to liberty, she'd choose liberty, and that the state shouldn't interfere with that decision.

At the end, Justice Harry Blackmun, the author of *Roe v. Wade*, spoke up. "What if the expense was the family's, and they had several other children—would the welfare of the other children be a factor?"

I answered that the finder of fact would need to determine that the parents were acting in the best interest of the child. I sat down.

"Thank you, Mr. Colby. Mr. Presson?" The Chief Justice looked over the bench. Bob Presson received no more breathing room than I did. He opened by telling the Court that he was there defending "a vastly different opinion of the Missouri Supreme Court than has been portrayed by Mr. Colby." He explained that it was appropriate for a judicial body to be involved in making decisions for a patient such as Nancy Cruzan, and he focused on the standard of withdrawing treatment only when it was unduly burdensome, or otherwise "in the best interest of the patient to do so."

Justice Blackmun interrupted. "Or his family?"

"Pardon?" Presson said.

"Patient or the family?"

"The patient or the family what, Your Honor? To make the decision?"

"In the best interest of—you—you said it would be in the best interest of the patient, and I'm asking—"

"Oh—"

"Do you include the family also?" Blackmun asked.

"No, I do not, Your Honor," Presson answered.

"The answer is no, even though the expenses were on the family, which it is not in this case, and even though there were other siblings?" Justice Blackmun sounded as skeptical of Bob Presson's answers as Justice Scalia had been of mine.

"I believe under Missouri law, the expense would not be on the family; it would not be on the guardians. They are not—"

"But what if it were, is my question," Blackmun said.

"If it were, we would have a different case, and that might present some problems."

"Well, you're evading the answer, aren't you?" Blackmun asked.

Presson responded that in his understanding, Missouri law didn't require guardians to spend their own assets.

Justice John Paul Stevens, an appointee of President Gerald Ford, joined the argument. "Under Missouri law, could the judge ever authorize the withdrawal of the life-support procedures if there was no certain evidence with regard to the intent of the patient?" he asked.

"I believe from my reading of the Missouri Supreme Court opinion, yes, that could happen," Presson said.

"What—what kind of circumstances would justify that?" Stevens asked.

"Well, I don't know that we can be global or totally exclusive about it," Presson began. "Some factors, I think, were mentioned by the Missouri Supreme Court. They did mention the possibility of pain, the heroic or extraordinary nature of the treatment. For instance, if a patient, such as Nancy in this case, were to develop cancer, whether they would approve chemotherapy or major surgery. I think it would present an entirely different case to them."

"Well, why—why—why would that be different?" Stevens asked. "Is that just because it's a different amount of dollars and cents involved? Here it costs about $10,000 a month—supposing it costs $100,000 a month with all—"

"I don't think, based upon the Supreme Court's analysis, it's just a matter of dollars and cents," Presson said.

"So dollars would not be relevant, even?"

Presson attempted to answer. "I—I—well, they certainly didn't indicate that it would be."

"The one factor that would be relevant would be discomfort to the patient, pain?" Stevens asked.

"That's not the only—I think they—"

"Well, what else would be?"

"They indicated whether it would be ordinary or extraordinary care," Presson said. "In this instance—"

"But what's—why—why is that significant, except in a dollars-and-cents way?" Stevens asked. "What difference does it make if it's three nurses instead of one, or two tubes instead of one? Why does that matter?" Even with his bow tie and silver hair, Justice Stevens no doubt did not appear grandfatherly to Bob Presson at this moment.

"Well, it would be a more invasive-type procedure. The petitioners have—"

"But if there is no pain involved, so what?" Stevens persisted. "Why does that make a difference? I don't understand."

"Well, to me it makes a difference because we are talking about an asserted right, since we disagree whether it stems from the common law or the Constitution, but—"

"Well, it has—for your opponents to win, it has to stem from the Constitution. We can't decide this on a common-law basis." Presson batted the questions and answers back and forth with Justice Stevens. Since he had ceded ten of his allotted thirty minutes to Solicitor General Starr, Presson's time was passing quickly.

Justice Stevens focused on his perceived lack of a standard used by the Missouri Supreme Court. "The question for me is: What is the standard? And is there any possibility of withdrawing the support in the event that the patient's desires are not knowable? Because I would think that would be the typical case."

"And I respond that yes, I think that is a possibility—"

"And that would depend on proof of pain?"

"Not limited just to pain, Your Honor."

"Pain or a lot—well, a more elaborate procedure than we have here?" Stevens asked.

"An elaborate procedure, which might be, as they said in the opinion, heroically invasive," Presson said. "I would think it would also be a question of whether we are talking about some procedure where the effectiveness is only 50 percent versus something where it is virtually 99-percent effective. Whether you—"

Justice Stevens broke in. "Effective at doing what? This is 100-percent effective at sustaining life, and that's all it does."

"I think the effectiveness—"

"How can you have 50-percent effectiveness in that sense?" Justice Stevens asked. "I don't understand you."

Bob Presson responded by talking about the best interest standard. Chief Justice Rehnquist asked whether hydration and nutrition were different from other treatments, and Presson answered they were, but Justice Stevens wouldn't let up.

"I simply don't—shoot, I simply don't understand that argument," Stevens said. "If one procedure will sustain life for twenty years and another will sustain life for ten years, which one is the better? And why is one better than the other? And they're equally invasive, and the patient in each case is in a persistent vegetative state?"

"I'm not sure I understand—," Presson tried to break in.

"How can the state draw a distinction between those two?"

"Well, I'm not sure I understand the question—"

"Well, you said 50 percent would be the different case, and I'm asking you why."

Justice Stevens and Bob Presson went back and forth for several minutes. At one point, the Justice said, "And you think that a rational, competent patient might say, 'Yes, I want to remain in this state for twenty years, but if I can only stay in this state for ten years, I wouldn't do it'? That's what you're saying?"

Justice Scalia made an effort to change the topic, asking a lengthy question about the cost of Nancy's care. Justice White also followed up, with a troubling question, from my point of view. "And I suppose all you need to do to prevail is to say the state is entitled to prefer another decision maker besides the guardian?"

"I think in a nutshell that's what it does come down to, Justice White."

Justice O'Connor asked her first question of the lawyer for Missouri. "Well, Mr. Presson, do you think that the state of Missouri has articulated some clear standard here? It's the best interests of the patient?"

"I think that standard is implicit from the probate code itself, Your Honor, and I think—"

"That's not what the Court said, though."

"Pardon?"

"Is that what the Supreme Court of Missouri said?" Justice O'Connor asked.

Bob Presson spent most of his remaining time trying to explain what the Missouri Supreme Court had said, and how far a state could go. Could the state say it would never listen to evidence from family members? Could the state say it would only accept a written document? Could a state create a separate category for nutrition and hydration, and require even competent patients to receive such treatment if necessary? Even if they were in pain?

Near the end, Justice Blackmun interrupted. "Mr. Presson, before you sit down, I'd like to ask an impertinent, and perhaps an improper, question. Have you ever seen a patient in a persistent vegetative state?"

Bob Presson stopped, and if possible, the courtroom grew quieter than it had been. "I have seen Nancy Cruzan herself," he answered.

"You have seen Nancy?" Justice Blackmun said.

"Yes."

"Any others?"

"Yes."

"How come?" Justice Blackmun asked.

"I was at the hospital, at Mount Vernon Rehabilitation Center," Presson said. He stopped for a beat, and looked almost quizzically at Justice Blackmun, then turned away. "To perhaps get back to your question, Justice Kennedy, as to whether or not the—as I stated in my brief, even though it's not directly presented, it would seem to me the state in that instance might have to engage in some very delicate decision making. Is this just a desire to die, to reject one's state of life, in which case it amounts to nothing more than suicide, and does the Constitution required the state to sanction and recognize that, or is it a case—"

Chief Justice Rehnquist interrupted. "Your time has expired, Mr. Presson. Thank you," he said. "General Starr."

Solicitor General Kenneth W. Starr moved to the podium. With his striped trousers and long coat, formal manner of speech, and stature as the solicitor general of the United States, the former federal judge set a new tone that Bob Presson and I could not. This was a discussion among equals.

General Starr began by noting that "although the medical care providers sympathize deeply with the family's plight, they respectfully disagree with the decision and many will not participate in withdrawing nutrition and hydration." Justice Stevens asked three questions to clarify why the staff disagreed, and then the solicitor general spoke largely without interruption.

At the crux of his argument, just as he had in his brief, General Starr laid a path before the Court: "In this highly sensitive and deeply vexing area, the due process clause should not be interpreted to force the states or the federal government" to adopt a particular approach; it should allow flexibility. The standard should be reasonableness. And a clear and convincing standard, while not required of any state, is not unreasonable under the Constitution.

Justice Stevens asked, "Suppose the state says, 'We're never going to honor a choice by the patient or by the parents or anybody else where food and hydration is concerned'? Would the due process clause forbid that?"

General Starr smiled. "It would raise very difficult questions, and I'm not prepared—." A slight rumbling of laughter from the justices, and in the courtroom, interrupted General Starr. "I'm not prepared to answer that authoritatively, definitively," he said, smiling. "It's certainly not presented here, and this Court should not be distressed by the question because of the common law right recognized in Missouri." At the end, General Starr agreed that where clear evidence of a person's intent is present, the Constitution "clearly is implicated in terms of the significant liberty interest in being free from unwanted intrusions. I quite agree that it is implicated."

Chief Justice Rehnquist said, "Thank you, General Starr. Mr. Colby? You have one minute remaining."

I stood. "If Judge Starr is correct," I said, "I have read the opinion below too broadly and all it stands for is the proposition that this state hospital cannot be forced to remove a tube that they didn't insert—we would accept that reading of the opinion gladly, if Nancy has some place else to go in the state to have this procedure done that she doesn't want." I closed by saying, "It's important to understand what the practical effect of this decision is going to be, which is to say to families shortly after an accident, 'Your daughter's just had an accident. We think she could recover, but if she doesn't—'"

"Thank you, Mr. Colby," Chief Justice Rehnquist interrupted. "Your time has expired. The case is submitted."

Directly behind arguing counsels' two tables is a second set of tables, a bullpen for the lawyers who will argue next. The lawyers seated there now began nervously gathering their papers, and Bob Presson and I assembled ours with ease. I grabbed the quill pen left at my place, which is the Court's souvenir for counsel who argue at that podium. Quickly we were out the door and back into the grand hallway. Smiles and handshakes were everywhere. Ned Kelly, Mark Haddad, Ron Cranford, my family, the Cruzans, and everyone said, "Great job!" After months of preparation, I felt one abiding, overriding emotion—relief.

The rest of the day was easy by comparison. On the steps out front we answered questions from a crowd of reporters standing in front of a sea of microphones. Attorney General Webster took over for Bob Presson at this stage, and Presson welcomed the break from the limelight—he said he felt most comfortable doing the lawyer work. Presson stood away from the microphones, talking with Dr. Ronald Cranford, my trial expert. Down at those microphones, a reporter asked how I felt the argument had gone. I said I was ecstatic and particularly encouraged by Justice O'Connor's skepticism about the appropriate standard.

From the press conference, we moved to a second press conference, lunch, and then to the local PBS studios by limos (filled with an entourage of family and friends) for the filming of a one-hour round-table discussion moderated by well-known journalist Fred Friendly. The panel consisted of national experts such as Dr. C. Everett Koop, Dr. Fred Plum, Dr. Joanne Lynn, Professor Alex Capron, columnist Nat Hentoff, and Father Bryan Hehir—and Attorney General Webster and me. After that I headed down the hallway at the PBS studio for a live interview on the *MacNeil-Lehrer NewsHour,* had dinner with my family, and finally returned to the hotel. Early the next morning, I boarded another limo, heading to the *Today* show for an appearance with Attorney General Webster. From the studio, I rushed to the airport and just made my flight to Colorado for a vacation.

On the plane, I read through the accounts of the previous day in the *Washington Post* and the *New York Times,* and as I looked out the window, I thought about the day I'd just had and the weeks ahead. After a ski trip with my buddies, I would just have a short time back in the office before heading down for Christmas in Florida with my family, and from there farther south for a week with my girlfriend (soon to be fiancée), Kelley, and her family. I thought about Joe and how angry and distant he'd looked all day. I closed my eyes and asked that the ordeal would soon end for this family. Somewhere over the Appalachian Mountains, I fell asleep, and I didn't wake up until Denver.

❧ ❧ ❧

Joe Cruzan's day on December 6 went downhill from the time he woke up. In D.C., Joe felt like a stranger in a hostile, foreign land. At least in Mt. Vernon, Joe knew the nurses, doctors, and Don Lamkins; he knew the roads, where to park, and how people talked. In Carthage, he knew Judge Teel. At the Supreme Court, that familiarity had vanished— the Cruzans had to pass by marshals and metal detectors just to enter the chamber where nine strangers would decide the fate of their loved one.

Chris had only been through one other metal detector in her life, at the airport before boarding the flight out. She hadn't seen those detectors go off, and she became nervous as the line at the Court grew shorter. Finally, the Cruzans made it to the front of the line, and Chris stepped through the archway. The alarm sounded. Panic flooded through her. The guard walked her around and told her to step through again, and again the alarm went off. Tears came to her eyes, and red blotches rose up her neck, showing above the scoop neckline of her black knit dress. She was holding up the line, everyone was looking at her, and she feared she would not be allowed in. Finally, after removing her belt, she passed the test. Joe stood by, mortified. He had no idea what to do to help his daughter in this place.

Inside the courtroom, the marshal ushered the Cruzans to seats in the front row of the gallery, just behind the brass railing. Joe had trouble seeing over the several rows of chairs in front of the railing once they started filling with men and women in suits. Later, he was incensed to learn that these special seats went to lawyers with no stake in the case, who were just there to watch. The rules also allowed those lawyers to take notes, while he couldn't even take a notebook into the courtroom. Once the arguments started, Joe couldn't follow them, in part due to the arcane yet rapid-fire questioning, and in part due to the poor sound system in the courtroom.

Angie and Miranda could hardly see at all. Joyce, normally unflappable, was flabbergasted that the sound system in the United States Supreme Court was so poor. And she said over and over, "I cannot believe these lawyers get to sit in front of us."

Outside the courthouse, the cameramen and reporters swarmed around the family like gnats at the river. When one bumped into Miranda, she grabbed my trench coat for balance, and Joe moved menacingly toward the man and growled, "If you get into my granddaughter again, there's going to be a problem." He reached toward the cameraman who wouldn't move and said, "Get out of my way," and the man finally moved. Miranda looked at her grandfather, startled. From behind, a female reporter stuck her microphone over Joe's shoulder, and she stumbled as she tried to simultaneously keep up with him, ask questions, and keep the microphone in his face.

That afternoon, at the PBS studio in northern Virginia, Joe sat with his family in the audience and watched the new one-hour documentary on their case, together with a hundred other people. Betsey Arledge sat directly behind the Cruzans. She'd never watched the screening of one of her documentaries with the subjects—and she was anxious about the Cruzans' reaction. When the film ended, Joe leaned over and whispered something to his wife, then he turned around and looked at Arledge. "We love you," he said, crying, and he turned back around.

The moment did not last. Immediately after the documentary, the round-table discussion started, and Joe was again on the outside, watching talking heads who had "no clue who Nancy was" discuss his daughter as if they knew something important. By the time he made it back to the Capitol Hill Hotel that night, he said he just wanted to slug someone or something.

The Cruzans stayed on in D.C. to try to take advantage of being in the nation's capital. But a constant, cold drizzle dampened their tourist spirit, and they misjudged from the map how far apart attractions such as the White House and the Lincoln Memorial were. Chris later said that "walking around a block in Washington, D.C., was much longer than a block in Carterville." For two days they went through the motions, seldom smiling, a cloud hanging over their trip like the non-stop drizzle overhead.

Finally, back in Carterville, Joe went down into the basement and retrieved the box with the smaller artificial tree, and Joyce set it up in the living room. The next week, Joe's company had him back working on a project at Freeman Hospital, where he'd spent many days and nights seven years before. His seething anger wouldn't subside. He kept telling Joyce, "I'm gonna take my shotgun up there and end this thing."

She kept saying, "No, you're not."

PART IV

1990

CHAPTER 35

EIGHT WORDS

The calendar that hung next to the phone in the Cruzans' kitchen had the first three Mondays in June 1990 marked with the letter "D," indicating potential decision days from the Supreme Court. My office calendar was similarly marked. June 4, 11, 18, and 25 each bore a green "OD," for "opinion day."

The Supreme Court hears the last of its oral arguments in April, then it works to finish writing its opinions in all cases prior to the close of the term, typically in late June or early July (whenever the last opinion is finished). Opinions usually are issued on Mondays, but as the Court nears the end of its work, it can issue the opinion on any day. The Cruzans' calendar reflected that reality, as the entry for June 19th read "Day by Day." Each Monday found the Cruzans experiencing a quick buzz of anxiety around nine in the morning, as they waited to see if the phone might ring. So did I. And beginning on June 19, that buzz came every day.

We were preparing for a decision either way, but, given the analysis of Court pundits about the reluctance of this Court to recognize any new liberty or privacy interests, we weren't hopeful. In May, I sent Joe and Joyce two draft press releases. The release for a favorable decision was brief: "While the family is relieved that their struggle is near the end and that Nancy will soon find some peace, they do not believe they have won anything. They lost a long time ago—the night a tragic accident left their daughter and sister permanently unconscious and vegetative."

The release stated that the family would take steps immediately to move Nancy to the hospice area at MRC, a strategy I'd discussed with Don Lamkins.

The adverse-decision release was almost two pages—continuing to argue for family rights, citing public opinion polls that families should make medical decisions for unconscious loved ones. The release concluded that Cruzans' family plans were unclear, noting the new witnesses who had emerged as a result of the publicity, and that a new trial in Missouri was possible—although I wasn't exactly sure we could get Judge Teel to grant us one. The draft release also suggested for the first time, formally and publicly, that we might move Nancy to another state.

By June 19, reporters who followed the Court said that there were few opinions left to issue, and that the business of the term was nearly complete. Joe was working on a project in Springfield, at the Famous-Barr department store, so he'd take a break just after nine each morning and call home to check for news. Joyce and Chris sat at the kitchen table at Chris's house, drinking coffee, talking, and watching the phone—when it rang, the two women would let the machine answer.

"Joyce? It's Joe, pick—"

Joyce would reach for the phone, and she'd tell her husband, "No news." He'd grumble a response and hang up.

Each day brought a rumor from some newsperson that "tomorrow is the day," and each day brought another disappointment. Joe took June 22 off work, and after lunch, he, Joyce, and Chris drove up to Kansas City to attend the ACLU's annual dinner. The speaker was Fenella Rouse, the Executive Director of the Society for the Right to Die, the woman Joe first wrote to on September 11, 1986, looking for a lawyer. And I was receiving the 1990 Civil Libertarian of the Year Award for my work on the *Cruzan* case.

The Cruzans were standing together at the reception when Kelley and I arrived that evening. We were greeted as we always were by now—a full hug from Chris, a half hug from Joyce, and a vice-grip handshake from Joe, his eyes not fully meeting mine.

Joe said, "I can't believe I feel at home at some ACLU dinner," but he did. It amazed him that an ACLU function could be filled with normal-looking people in business attire. He almost took comfort when he spotted the occasional "long-hair" tucked in here and there in the crowd.

We talked about the coming Monday, which really did look like "Decision Day," based on my talks with the press and the clerk's office earlier that day, though, as Joe said, "We've heard that before."

The Cruzans were ready. We also talked about the coming Friday, wedding day for Kelley and me. Chris said that the girls were really looking forward to the trip, staying in a hotel in Topeka, and attending the "fancy" wedding. I was starting to worry about the increasingly real possibility that the decision and the wedding could happen on the same day.

Joe laughed when I told him about the meeting I'd had with a young, bearded, red-haired priest at the Most Pure Heart of Mary Catholic Church, Kelley's childhood church. Being a non-Catholic, I had to sit down and talk with a priest at the church (among other things) before the wedding could go forward. When the priest had asked about any objections I might have, I launched into a diatribe about the U.S. Conference of Catholic Bishops taking political positions as opposed to caring about individuals and said that the bishops had been a huge thorn in my professional side. I also told him that many individual priests, such as Father O'Rourke in St. Louis and Father McCormick at Notre Dame, had been quite helpful. We talked for almost an hour. At the end the priest smiled and said, "I think we'll let you in."

After the ACLU dinner, the Cruzans headed south for the two-and-a-half-hour drive home, and Kelley and I had a drink in the bar at the Westin. We'd been together for four years now, so the Cruzans and their case were part of her life, too. What an amazing experience this whole thing had been, nicely capped off by this wonderful evening.

My experiences that spring had not all been so pleasant. Two national lawyer magazines had reviewed the oral argument I gave to the Supreme Court—*The National Law Journal* article had described my narrow approach to the Court as a smart move, but the *American Lawyer* article (which was longer and more detailed) lambasted my argument as one of "missed opportunities." The day that magazine arrived, I shut my door and read the review with my heart in my throat, knowing that it would circulate throughout my firm and the legal community. It made me sick to my stomach for a week.

~ ~ ~

On Monday, June 25, my phone started to ring just before 9:00 A.M., and it continued all day. Five to four, the United States Supreme Court had decided against the Cruzans. It hadn't mattered that the pundits had predicted just such a result—I was sick to my stomach again. I didn't want the Cruzans to experience the same reaction, at least not at the hands of a reporter, so I quickly punched Joe and Joyce's number. I wanted to be the one to break the news. Their answering machine clicked on.

"Joe, it's Bill pick—"

"Bill," Joe said, picking up the receiver. "Jesus." His voice quivered. I had not made it in time.

"So you heard already?" I asked.

"Yeah, Betsey called."

At least they'd heard it from a friend. I didn't have much idea what to say about the emotional side of things, so I took refuge in the law. "I'm just getting the first part over the fax," I said. "Apparently it's five to four, with several dissents. I'll read it as fast as I can, and call back to tell you what it says."

"All right," he said. Then he started to cry.

I felt like a kid who'd been beaten up on the schoolyard, completely helpless. I had nothing to say to my client to ease his pain. The only thing I had left to tell him was that I wouldn't quit on him. Now that we were near the end, even that meant less. "Joe? We go from here, right?" I asked.

"Yeah." He hung up.

The hallway outside my office was chaos. Dana Peterson (my secretary) and Kim Ross were trying to keep people out of my office and trying to figure out who they should let in. They also screened the constant phone calls, but still buzzed me over the intercom—or opened my door and peeked in—when a call came that they weren't sure about. In addition, Shook, Hardy's marketing people wanted to know about press; the managing partner's secretary wanted to know when to expect television cameras in the office and on which floors. And the guys from the fax center were running in and out, bringing me chunks of the opinion as it came across.

Everyone wanted to know exactly what the opinion said. Finally the fax machine stopped, and I had well over 100 pages of paper on my desk. The opinion was already printed as it would eventually appear in the law books. I hunkered down in my office with the door shut, reading furiously and making notes.

The public assumption about a decision from the Supreme Court is that the written opinion will decide, and state clearly, that one side wins and one side loses. The reality is more complicated. The main ruling of the Court, called the "majority opinion," must have at least five justices who agree on certain basic points. That majority opinion can uphold or overrule lower court decisions, and it can do so in whole or in part.

Further complications can arise when the language in the opinion seems to undermine statements made in a lower court opinion, without directly overruling those statements. A justice who is one of those signing the main opinion can also write his or her own separate opinion, called a "concurring opinion," which sets out points that the concurring justice believes but couldn't persuade others to adopt. And justices who disagree with the main ruling in the majority opinion can write dissenting opinions as well.

In *Cruzan,* five of the nine justices wrote their own opinions—the majority opinion, two concurring opinions, and two dissents. I glanced through each to understand their gist; then I went back to the start. I began with the main opinion, written by Chief Justice Rehnquist. I read each word about the Cruzans, oblivious after a while even to the incessant ringing of the phone. I buzzed Dana and asked her to bring me fresh coffee, something I almost never did because I thought lawyers should fetch their own coffee. She found me bent so far over my desk that my nose almost touched the paper.

As I read the opinion, I thought that they should have simply pasted the words from the solicitor general's brief to the page, as it would have saved them some work—states can protect life; a clear and convincing evidence standard is reasonable way to do so; it's not unconstitutional to err on the side of life.

And then, I came to a passage near the end of Chief Justice Rehnquist's opinion that told me how wrong I was—the language most certainly had not come from the brief of the solicitor general. The passage that stopped me hadn't appeared in any brief to the Court that I remembered—it certainly hadn't come from mine.

Tucked away by the Chief Justice, the words were so inconspicuous that it felt as if I'd almost stumbled upon them. I read the language, then read it again. In fact, I sat at my desk and read the paragraph over and over and over again.

> An erroneous decision not to terminate [life support] results in a maintenance of the status quo; the possibility of subsequent developments such as advancements in medical science, the discovery of new evidence regarding the patient's intent, changes in the law, or simply the unexpected death of the patient despite the administration of life-sustaining treatment at least create the potential that a wrong decision will eventually be corrected or its impact mitigated.

Then I focused on the key phrase: "discovery of new evidence regarding the patient's intent." Eight words. After all we'd been through, the thousands of pages written, could the case really have come down to just eight words?

At my meeting with the Cruzans in November of 1988 (right after we received the Missouri Supreme Court opinion), Chris had told me about the woman who had contacted her, the one who had a conversation with Nancy when they worked together at the school for handicapped children. And in December of 1989, a man from Oklahoma had written Joe after watching coverage of U.S. Supreme Court argument, saying that Nancy had worked for him briefly, and he described a conversation they'd had about Karen Ann Quinlan.

I stood and turned away from the desk, looking out the windows at the tops of buildings and parking lots below me. We had exactly what the Supreme Court was talking about—new evidence—so maybe the Court had given us what we needed after all. It would just take a little more work. The first smile of the day came to me. I turned away from the window and called Joe.

For the past few weeks, people calling the Cruzans had been greeted by a message recorded in Joe's hard drawl: "We are not returning media calls. Don't mean to be rude and we hope you understand." Then the machine beeped. This morning, Joe had changed the message to say, "We will have no comment on the Supreme Court decision until we have had the chance to analyze it."

Joe picked up when he heard it was me, and we talked about all of the calls on his machine and dealing with the press. He sounded as down as I'd ever heard him—which was really saying something. So I tried to pick him up. "Listen to this, Joe," I said, and I read the language from the opinion of the Chief Justice.

"What's it mean?" Joe asked.

"It means that the United States Supreme Court says we get a new trial," I said.

That afternoon I held a press conference in a packed conference room at the firm. I talked about the positives: Justice O'Connor had written in a concurring opinion that artificial feeding was medical treatment; and Chief Justice Rehnquist had recognized, in the main opinion, a constitutional right to liberty for competent people to refuse medical treatment—something the Court had never done before.

Most important, in answer to the many questions about our next move, I read directly from the opinion about the discovery of new evidence, and I told reporters about the new witnesses. I said more than once what I'd decided that morning should be my main message—that the Supreme Court had ruled that we should have a new trial.

But, like the Cruzans, I was tired of this case. Although we'd perhaps found a solution, a new trial wouldn't happen for a while, and the Court certainly had not ruled directly in our favor, as it could have. On top of that, I had a cold—and my wedding was four days away. I told the assembled press that the Cruzans wouldn't comment, and I read a statement from Joe:

> The decision to stop treatment and allow a loved one to die is one of the most difficult decisions a family can face. However, because of our lifelong shared love with Nancy and our understanding of her values, we concluded that we had no choice but to try to set her free from this hopeless condition she is trapped in. Not to do so would be to disregard the very meaning of Nancy's "lived" life.
>
> Since our initial request in May, 1987, to the state hospital to discontinue treatment and allow Nancy the dignity of death, our goal has never wavered, nor does it now.

As I read Joe's statement, I had an overwhelming desire to just be done with the day.

Reaction from the opposition was muted. Attorney General Webster held press conferences describing the decision as "correct," but calling for legislation to help families caught in "medical-legal limbo." The newspapers noted that the legislature had roundly rejected such efforts the previous February.

Governor Ashcroft issued a written statement: "Our thoughts and prayers remain with the Cruzan family. I am grateful that the U.S. Supreme Court reaffirmed Missouri's objection to the removal of life-sustaining food and water from an individual who has made no clear expression of her wishes."

The decision stood life on its head at the Missouri Rehabilitation Center. Reporters roamed the hallways, and television lights glared. A news helicopter landed not far from the day-care area at MRC, and the pilot allowed the giddy toddlers to touch it. The staff on Nancy's floor tried to go about their daily business. They kept Nancy's door shut all day. One of Nancy's nurses, Marcia Hopper, said to a reporter, "If there was one thing the staff from Nancy's floor would like to get across, it is that we empathize with the Cruzans' feelings." Sue Rowell, the head nurse whom Joe first told of his plans almost three years earlier, told reporters that even nurses who disagreed with the Cruzans worked to "keep personal opinions aside from their professional life."

Don Lamkins had just returned from vacation, and he spent the day in one interview after another. He expressed sympathy for the Cruzans, but mostly, like the rest of the people at MRC, he was glad it was over. "It's a relief that we're not going to have to do anything here, and it's not going any further here."

Joe Cruzan spent the day bunkered in his house, peering out the window as reporters drove by slowly and then made a U-turn on Main Street to drive by again. He drank coffee and listened to the answering machine. Joyce did the same.

Mixed in among the phone messages were dozens upon dozens of hang-ups once the caller realized that he or she had reached the machine. The recorded voices carried a range of emotions and degrees of engagement with the Cruzans:

"Joe, this is Tom Miller at the *Kansas City Star*. Will you be home today or in Kansas City?" A friendly voice.

"Mr. Cruzan, this is Mike Shilling at KY3 in Springfield. Please call when you can." An impatient voice.

"This is Lisa Richardson at KYTV in Springfield. I want to be in line when you decide to talk." Bubbly.

"Mr. Cruzan, Dan Rather wants to talk with you if at all possible. I know this is a difficult time. Please call him at—." Urgent.

"This is Nancy Segernow at CNN in Washington, D.C." Also urgent.

"This is Rita Braver at CBS News. I am so sorry about the decision. If you do feel like talking, please call." Braver had been to the Cruzans' home, and her voice on the machine was filled with concern.

"I cannot tell you how sorry I am—," Grandma Jack, Joe's mom, started crying, unable to finish. Joe picked up.

"I'm calling from California. You don't know me. Our prayers are with you."

"This is Kent Zimmerman at the AP in Kansas City. Please call when you can." Friendly.

"I wish they'd let you bring the girl home, and you would answer to God for it. I was in a coma and came out of it." An angry, high-pitched drawl.

"Mr. Cruzan, this is the phone company, calling about your question of installing another line. If you're still interested, call me back."

"I'm calling from Portland, Maine, to tell you how your rights have been infringed upon. If you have the right lawyer, you can tear them apart for what they've done. The decision of the Supreme Court can just blankly and frankly be ignored. Their decrees just interpret statutes, they do not have the right to usurp parental authority with all of their fallacious interpretations."

"This is Cathy Bond calling from Webb City. I'm the mother of four, and I wonder if we can get up a petition and take it to the Court for you?"

"This is Rob Sacardo in New York, my heart goes out to you. I want to talk to you about something promising. I see a tremendous amount of love from the newspapers."

"I'm calling again in case the tape cut off—just ask for Rob, don't discuss any other thing with anyone. This is my family's house."

And a third message. "This is Robert Sacardo. Did you call me? Someone did, but I did not get to the phone. This has nothing to do with any of that Supreme Court stuff, I just want to help you."

"This is Jacqueline Stalls in Dallas, Texas. I have a large home, live in the nicest part of Dallas—you can stay here. I have a friend who just went through this."

"Joe, this is Bill Montgomery at the post office. I just received an express mail for you. You can pick it up before five, or we'll bring it tomorrow."

"This is the *Arkansas Gazette* calling. I just got off the phone with our attorney general. He says you can come here. Is that a possibility? Call me."

"Hi, Brother, do you have a minute to visit with your brother, and let him wish you a Happy Birthd—." Joe picked up and talked to his brother, Jim.

Joe stayed inside all day Monday, moving from the front window back to the answering machine. Monday night he watched the news; Tuesday morning the calls slowed to a trickle—by Wednesday they had stopped. The press had moved on. But the mail from strangers started up again on Tuesday, and no doubt more would come Wednesday. That delivery didn't usually happen until mid-afternoon, however. Joe was laid off for the week, so Wednesday morning he decided to go out to the carport to try to find a project.

By ten o'clock, it already felt like walking into a furnace outside. Joe stood on his carport and surveyed his options. No motorcycle to tinker with and ride—he'd sold it after the accident. No vacation planned this summer, thus no need to work on the trailer—anyway, he and Joyce had only used it twice since the accident, at the insistence of their counselor, Barbara Carter. Donna lived outside town. Chris had her own family. Nancy was gone. He went back inside—sweating, panicked, angry—and found his wife.

"Joyce, I'm going up to Mt. Vernon," Joe said. "I'm going to take a pillow and end this thing. Maybe I'll take my shotgun up and fix myself, too."

"That wouldn't help your granddaughters much," she said, employing one of the tactics she customarily used for this discussion. "Sit down and have some coffee," she ordered. Joe did.

After coffee, Joe headed to the carport and started his truck. He drove to Wal-Mart with the list Joyce had given him. She knew that he'd spend a long time in the store, slowly walking each aisle, nodding at the other shoppers, hoping someone would recognize him and start a conversation about the case. Joyce knew this because that's what he did every time he went into Wal-Mart now. It was the only project he had left.

Joyce talked to Chris, who phoned me that day to say that they weren't going to come up to the wedding on Friday after all. "We're worried about my dad, and what he might say and do," Chris said. "We don't want to ruin your wedding."

I told her that they couldn't ruin anything, but that I understood. I promised to call as soon as Kelley and I returned from our honeymoon. That Wednesday I left the office and decided to try to put the case out of my mind for a couple of weeks. Hundreds of family members and friends were descending upon Topeka to celebrate our wedding, and from there Kelley and I were heading to Stowe, Vermont, for a week of hiking and bicycling. I vowed to try not to worry about the case again until we returned home.

CHAPTER 36

NEW WITNESSES

On July 24, one month after the U.S. Supreme Court decision, I drove down to Jefferson City to meet with Attorney General Webster. Webster greeted me like we were old friends, and perhaps in some sense we were. At the very least, we'd been on television next to one another a handful of times. And while I was on the other side from him, I'd worked in public comments not to claim political motivations for Webster, as some pundits were doing. Although he hadn't formally announced it yet, speculation in the state was that Webster was going to run for governor in the 1992 election. Any move he made came under public scrutiny. I tried to keep the case on a professional level.

Webster's new chief deputy, Jim Deutsch, joined us, and we sat on couches facing one another near Webster's desk. Deutsch had worked on a proposed bill for the Missouri legislature the previous January, which the press came to call the "Nancy Cruzan bill." I'd spoken with him many times about that legislation; so had Joe. The bill had ultimately failed, scuttled by the right-to-life lobby. Through the process, however, the attorney general's office had almost looked like our friend, instead of our adversary.

At this meeting, I was curious to see how far that new attitude reached. I had one goal: I wanted the attorney general's office to dismiss the state as a party to our case once I filed for a new trial. This was in line with the legislation they'd just supported.

They did not tell me their plans, although Webster said more than once (just as he had publicly), "We need a solution for families like the Cruzans." The impression I had by the end of that meeting was that Deutsch and Webster thought the battle had been fought, and they were now looking for an appropriate way to steer clear of this new trial. Although the appellate courts hadn't taken up the Cruzans' side, public opinion polls showed overwhelming support for the family, so perhaps we'd won in that venue. But whatever the motivation was, it didn't really matter—it looked like the attorney general might not fight us in the next trial.

✥ ✥ ✥

In August, I faxed Thad McCanse (Nancy's *guardian ad litem*) and Jim Deutsch my draft petition, and I asked each of them to send me potential trial dates. On August 30, I filed the petition for a new trial in Judge Teel's court. Part of the reason I waited a couple of months was so the attention on the case would die down a little. The new petition did bring the case back to the front pages, but the highly charged emotional edge of late June had, in fact, worn off.

The local Joplin and Carthage newspaper reporters talked to Joe and Joyce at length about the new trial. The Cruzans discussed the eight words (the language from Chief Justice Rehnquist's opinion that opened the way for the new trial), the new witnesses who had known Nancy only as "Nancy Hayes" and "Nancy Davis" (her two married names), and they talked about the strain the family felt.

Joe told the reporters that the case consumed his thoughts even when he performed mindless tasks such as driving to work or mowing the lawn. "I'm ready for my daughter to be buried," he said. "She's not coming back."

The spokeswoman for the attorney general told the newspapers that they had no comment on the filing. And so, after this one day of publicity, the press moved on. But not for long. On Monday, September 17, Jim Deutsch filed a motion requesting Judge Teel to dismiss the state of Missouri from the case. Far different from the motion filed by the attorney general almost three years earlier to dismiss the entire case, this motion asked for the state to withdraw from the case, claiming that it no longer had an "interest in the outcome of this litigation." Deutsch attached an affidavit to the motion from the Director of the Missouri

Department of Health, Dr. John Bagby, which stated that the MRC would carry out the order of the probate court if necessary.

Reaction to the move came swiftly. Thad McCanse called the action a "political move" made by an attorney general who planned to run for governor. "This isn't quite consistent with their bitter battle all the way through the U.S. Supreme Court, where they argued the state had an unqualified interest in preserving life," he said. "Why would their interest be any different this time? Either the state has an interest in preserving life or it doesn't."

Joe's right-to-life nemesis, Rita Marker, played the Nazi card in reaction to Dr. Bagby's affidavit: "Once before, doctors ended the lives of people who were considered expendable. In their defense, they said they were only following orders."

Reaction from our side was muted. I was optimistic about the way the new trial was unfolding, but I said nothing to the press at this stage. Joe did not share my optimism. I'd talked to him many times over the summer about the attorney general's office and where I thought they were heading. When I told him in September (just before they went public with the dismissal) that the attorney general would be out of the case completely, Joe said little more than "Okay." Later, he told a reporter, "I don't mean to rain on any parade, but I've learned to wait and see how these things come out."

For me, the most interesting comments on September 17 came from Thad McCanse, and they weren't limited to his theory about Webster's political aims. McCanse told reporters that now that the "hot potato" was in his lap, he'd aggressively challenge the family's new evidence. "I'm not going to let them do what they want and not do anything myself," he said. "I'm going to cross-examine these witnesses as close as I can. I want to be sure."

As I read McCanses's comments, I thought, *What is he talking about?* If he concluded that removal was in Nancy's best interests before, how could new, additional witnesses change that conclusion? On Wednesday, I called McCanse and discovered that apparently he meant exactly what he told the reporters. Basically, he thought that he needed to take the place of the attorney general in the case, now that the state had asked to be dismissed.

I was flabbergasted. I stepped off the edge when he told me that he thought as *guardian ad litem* he had to appeal if Judge Teel sided with the family again. "Thad, you've got to be kidding me!" I said. I stood up and closed the door to my office, and paced in front of the desk, holding a phone equipped with an extra long cord for just such times. "You have one job under the law: to protect Nancy's best interest, period. You've already said that stopping treatment is in her best interest—how could you *appeal* a judge's decision that said the same thing? You'd be violating your charge under the probate code."

"I don't see it that way," he said. "I want a decision from a higher court to make sure."

"That's not your job," I said, growing loud, my free hand gesticulating to no one.

"I need to make sure that the clear and convincing evidence standard is met," he said.

"No, you don't. That's the judge's job. Your only charge under the probate code is to protect Nancy's best interests. If you think removing senseless medical treatment is in her best interest, then I think you violate your fiduciary duty as *guardian ad litem* if you take any action contrary to that conclusion."

When we ended the conversation, I told Thad that I'd fax him a letter outlining our position, which I did—two pages that tried to walk the fine line of recognizing how supportive he'd been to Joe and Joyce from the start and urging him to change what I thought was a crazy new position. I had no idea what was motivating him, or what his plan was—if he had a plan at all—other than to aggressively oppose the family. I could not believe that McCanse, who had in essence joined our side at the first trial, would now be an adversary. But that's the way it looked. I closed the summary to McCanse by saying that if this new evidence coupled with the earlier evidence "does not give us clear and convincing evidence, then I have no idea what clear and convincing means."

❧ ❧ ❧

Around noon on Saturday, October 20, 1990, I headed to Carterville. This time, I did not need a map as I had in the fall of 1987—I knew the road to take, the strategic placement of Quick Trips and McDonalds' along the route for coffee and sodas, and how to drive straight to the Econo Lodge in Carthage. And I now knew that once I got to Carterville, if I hadn't have known where the Cruzans lived, I could have just started asking people and I would have found their house fairly quickly.

After checking in at the motel, I drove over to the Cruzans'. We greeted each other with hugs and smiles, as if I were a relative coming to town for a holiday, and Joe, Joyce, Chris, and I sat down with coffee in the living room. That afternoon I was going to meet with two of the three new witnesses I'd be putting on at trial.

A couple of reporters had been openly skeptical about the new witnesses. When I filed the new petition, I got a call from one who had been on the case since the beginning. "So tell me about these newly discovered witnesses," he said, his voice full of sarcasm.

"Off the record?" I replied, and he immediately said yes, thinking that he might get some inside scoop. Instead, I asked, "How hard is it to go through life with such a sick, cynical attitude?"

He laughed. "Hey, it sounds a little fishy, and I'm not the only one saying so," he said.

"Yeah, well, you all need some counseling. Back on the record," I said. I told him how the new witnesses had only known Nancy by her married names, and how they contacted the Cruzans after seeing her photo on television. But the reporter was right, it did sound suspect. We had two new conversations to tell Judge Teel about, and one was questionable enough that I was debating whether or not to use it. The other one was a great new piece of evidence, rock solid and corroborated by two likable, believable women—Debi Havner and Marianne Smith.

Debi and Marianne stopped by the Cruzans' a few hours after I arrived. Debi's father had driven her up from Bentonville, Arkansas, and he joined us in the living room. I asked questions and the story slowly emerged.

∾   ∾   ∾

In the late 1970s, educators in the United States grappled with the question of how best to educate deaf, blind, and mentally retarded children. Following a series of U.S. Supreme Court cases, significant federal funds became available, and in the 1977 to 1978 school year, Joplin started a program for such children. The school district built a new, handicapped-accessible portable school building directly behind Stapleton Elementary School on Hearnes Boulevard. The school had three rooms—an office, a small videotape room to record the progress of the children, and a larger classroom.

In the spring of 1977, Debi Havner (then Debi Aaron) finished her master's degree in psychology to complement her bachelor's degree in education for the hearing impaired, and her job search landed her at the Stapleton School in Joplin. At her first semester break, in January of 1978, Debi had to replace both aides for her classroom, so she hired Marianne Smith and Nancy Hayes. The teacher and her two aides spent six months together, along with students Belinda, Charles, Deanne, and Melissa.

Although Debi was the certified teacher, the three young women, who were all in their 20s, shared the responsibilities equally. Even with three adults for four children, the work was mind-numbingly demanding. Charles, the oldest, was almost a teenager. He'd been abused and neglected, was severely handicapped, and legally deaf and blind. Debi and Nancy made several trips to his foster home to make sure he was receiving proper care. He was so dirty when he came to school each morning that the teachers had to bathe him first thing so they could stand to be in the same small room together all day. Belinda was three years old, and she was also abused, deaf, and blind. Deanne, born deaf and blind, with a cleft palate and other physical problems, still lived with her parents.

Melissa was the worst case. She was three years old, only 20 pounds and 18 inches long. She looked like a tiny ghost, her pale skin stretched across her frame like thin parchment. She sat stiffly in a special wheelchair, strapped at the legs and arms and at the waist so she could bend. She was deaf, blind, and profoundly retarded—during the course of six months of spending all day with Melissa, the teachers were never able to communicate with her.

Melissa lived in an institution for children with cerebral palsy, not far from the Stapleton School. The caregivers at the home fed her through a tube inserted in her nose; but at school, the three teachers worked to feed her by mouth, using both a small spoon and a syringe-like device called the "InfaFeeder" to force food in to her mouth. Melissa had significant reflexive tongue thrust—if anything touched her mouth, her tongue shot out well outside of it. Feeding her took an hour or more each day, and even though the women generally divided the work evenly, Nancy ended up feeding Melissa more often than the other two. She'd take the tiny waif in her arms and force-feed her, often getting food all over both of them by the end of the hour.

The teacher and her aides grew close, developing strong bonds as they cared for these profoundly damaged children. Neither Debi nor Marianne could remember who spoke first, but both remembered clearly that day in March of 1978 when the topic first came up.

"We were sitting on small children's chairs at the table," Marianne recalled, "and Nancy was holding Melissa. Behind her was the blackboard and a bulletin board, which had a spring scene on it, and Nancy was wearing a printed dress and white sweater."

"What color was the dress?" I asked.

"Brown print."

Marianne and Debi each went on to describe a conversation that took place on and off over that hour, as Nancy held Melissa, forcing the food into her mouth with the InfaFeeder and patiently cleaning it as most came back out. Across the table, Marianne held Belinda, whose larger legs were stretched straight by metal braces.

I asked Marianne and Debi about what Nancy said that day.

"Well, she was talking about how pitiful Melissa was and how she didn't even know she was alive—that this child was born and she was so severely retarded that she would have lived out her whole life and not even known the beauty of life."

Debi said, "I don't remember who actually just came out and started saying what we talked about, but it was all stemmed around Melissa and her feeding—maybe because she was the one really having a hard time with it—and we all just stated how we would never want to be tube-fed like that or fed with a feeder."

"How did Nancy describe Melissa?" I asked.

"It's not really a proper term for a student in the classroom, but she was more or less a vegetable because she didn't know what was going on, didn't know where she was or anything," Debi said.

"Nancy called Melissa a vegetable?"

"Yes."

"During this conversation?"

"Yes." Debi and Marianne both remembered that Nancy used the word repeatedly.

That one-hour conversation wasn't the only time the three women talked, but it was the one that Debi and Marianne remembered most vividly. And they never again sat down face-to-face, for an hour, letting the emotions out as they did that spring day. At the end of the school year, Debi left Joplin, got married, and moved to Arkansas. Neither she nor Marianne thought about Nancy Hayes until they saw pictures of Nancy Cruzan on the news.

The three Cruzans sat mesmerized as they listened to the story unfold about those six months from Nancy's life that took place so long ago. As Marianne and Debi finished talking that afternoon, I thought, *Judge Teel will believe these women.* Marianne's explanation that she'd contacted Chris after seeing a picture of the woman she knew as Nancy Hayes on television was believable. The timing of that contact—near Thanksgiving of 1988, when news of the Missouri Supreme Court decision against the family filled the airwaves—made sense. The notes I made of my meeting with the Cruzans just before that Thanksgiving recorded that Chris had indeed told me about Marianne contacting her. Marianne had then told Joe about Debi, and he'd been the one to track her down.

These women were educated, sincere, and clearly not anxious to testify. I asked Debi why she'd voluntarily agreed to come to Missouri for her deposition when she certainly didn't have to—living in Oklahoma, she was outside the subpoena power of a judge in Missouri.

"Because I knew Nancy, and I feel she'd want me to do this," Debi answered.

The Cruzans, Debi Havner and her father, and I drove in a caravan of three cars over to Thad McCanse's office for a Saturday-evening deposition. Marianne Smith went home—since she lived in Joplin, she planned to attend the trial and testify in person, so McCanse said he did not need to depose her.

The lawyer's office and testimony under oath for a witness felt far more natural to Joe and Joyce than it had in early 1988, when they'd first ventured into this office for their own depositions.

Debi told the story she'd related that afternoon in the Cruzans' living room to David Mouton, who took the deposition for the *guardian ad litem*. We finished in an hour, and Debi and her father headed back to Bentonville, Arkansas.

I stopped at the Econo Lodge, changed into jeans, and went over to the Cruzans' for pizza. Mel and Chris joined us, as did Angie and Miranda, briefly—now teenagers, the girls didn't want to hang around adults for long on a Saturday night.

On Sunday morning, Joe, Joyce, and Chris met me at the motel, and we drove in two cars up to Mt. Vernon. Judge Teel had told me that, in addition to any new evidence, he also wanted a detailed update on Nancy's medical condition. I'd been to the MRC a few times by now, had seen the two PBS documentaries with extensive video of Nancy's life, and had given many speeches where I showed a ten-minute video of Nancy. Walking into her room no longer held the shock that it did the first time I'd seen her in the fall of 1987. I did not speak to her as Joe and Joyce did.

Dr. Clark Watts, chief of neurosurgery at the University of Missouri, had agreed to testify as our expert witness in this second trial. Dr. Watts examined Nancy for about 20 minutes. He tapped her with a reflex hammer, tried to stick the corner of a tissue in her eye to check for corneal reflex, and spoke to her: "Nancy, can you stick your tongue out for me? Can you open your eyes? Can you squeeze my hand?" Then he said quietly to the camera, for the exam record, "Once again, she makes no effort."

The tall, white-haired doctor kept a respectful, workmanlike manner as he moved up and down Nancy's bed, repositioning her sheet and gown after each test. Below the surface, one could sense that the doctor wasn't expecting any kind of reaction, and he was simply walking through the steps needed for a full exam for a court, knowing that this patient's diagnosis had been set in stone long before.

Dr. Watts chose not to check for a gag reflex. The effort was pointless, and the choking was difficult for Joe and Joyce to witness. He performed his final test, making "a noise outside her possible line of sight"—clapping his hands next to Nancy's ear a couple of times. Each time she blinked slightly, but that was it. The doctor stopped for a second and looked up at the camera. "I think that pretty much completes the examination," he said, nodding to Joe, Joyce, Chris, and me.

I hurried out of the hospital once the examination was concluded and headed north, staying on the back roads for much of the drive. I thought about the trial ten days ahead. I'd start with some variation on the approach my friend Chuck Wall used with ticket agents when the airline had goofed: "I know you're not the person who made this mistake, but you're the only one from your organization I have to talk to, so please pass this message on."

Seventeen judges had ruled on our case, and we were behind nine to eight. Attorney General Webster had decided to stay in Jefferson City, so Judge Teel was the only government representative we had left to talk to. Of course, he was more than the "ticket agent for the government," since he'd ruled in the family's favor at the first trial, almost three years before.

I planned to talk about what the years of government opposition—beginning clear back in the fall of 1987—had done to the Cruzans. The Joe I first met—a strutting bantam rooster, daring anyone to disagree with him—had given way to a sad, gray man. Joyce found herself looking off in the distance frequently; Chris worried constantly about her parents; and the stress of the public eye seemed like the only world Chris's girls, now ages 15 and 14, had ever really known.

I also wanted to talk about the clear and convincing evidence standard. No court had defined it, and no court had excluded testimony from family about an incapacitated person's values. We'd researched the standard at length, and it boiled down to the perception of the individual judge. The evidence had to persuade him, to leave a fixed conclusion in his mind. If the testimony about Nancy's values, the previous conversation with Athena Comer about living life as a vegetable, the conversation with her sister, and now two new conversations—one of which took place while force-feeding a girl who appeared to be in a vegetative state—if this testimony didn't meet the definition of clear and convincing, then I did not understand the phrase.

Opening statements, new witnesses, and medical and family updates—all would be heard in a one-day trial before Judge Teel. I'd already written a letter to urge the judge to expedite his ruling so, in the event he ruled against the family, we could attempt to place the case on the January docket of the Missouri Supreme Court, if we had to take that path.

⁓⟊⁓

CHAPTER 37

A NEW TRIAL

Everyone wanted this case over. Public relations people in the attorney general's office watched nervously from Jefferson City. The staff and administration at MRC had thought the previous June that they were finished with the matter, and now, just four months later, a new trial was beginning. Many of the MRC employees were angry that the state had pulled out of the case. Barbara Shoun, the hospital's director of public relations, had never tried to disguise her opposition to the Cruzans. Her husband wrote Judge Teel directly, urging that he not force MRC to take part. "I'm writing to ask you to consider the Nancy Cruzan case as two separate issues: (1) Should the Cruzans be permitted to terminate the life of their daughter? and (2) if so, by whom should the termination be done?"

Don Lamkins said later: "Bill Webster pulled some strings and got the state out of the case. I think he was afraid it would cost him votes since he was getting ready to run for governor. So when this went back to court, *nobody* represented us." Lamkins' concern made sense. Only five lawyers would take part in the trial—Thad McCanse, David Mouton, Walt Williams, Judge Teel, and me—and all had sided with the Cruzans in the first trial. Lamkins might have found some encouragement had he been able to listen to the conversations McCanse and I had throughout the fall. Thad appeared to believe what he kept saying to the press, which was basically that with the attorney general out of the case, his job was to oppose our side. I'd hoped that he was trying to put the best public face on what looked like a one-sided case. If that was true, he put the same face on when it was just the two of us.

McCanse and I didn't just butt heads on the question of whether he had to appeal—we also went around on whether the law barred me from calling these new witnesses at all. I'd had this question researched from every possible angle, and while I thought our side had the stronger argument, McCanse had one, too. It was not one I could like: basically that "Colby should have found these witnesses the first time, and since he didn't, he's barred from calling them."

To some extent, unfortunately, he had a point. In my initial inquiry years earlier, I had not discovered that Nancy had worked with deaf and blind kids, and that was an oversight. But McCanse hadn't discovered this fact in his investigation either. I also questioned whether in these cases, families or their lawyers had to scour through an incapacitated person's past, searching for all lost conversations. I had no idea how far McCanse would push the point.

❧ ❧ ❧

At the last court hearing he'd attended, Joe Cruzan had made his way through the crowds and the strangers at the U.S. Supreme Court, growing angrier by the hour. At the time, he told Betsey Arledge: "I feel like I'm at the Super Bowl game and they got me clear back up in the highest bleacher and the poorest seat in the house, and these other two teams are playing and they're playing with my football. And there's not a damn thing I can do about it except just watch."

Now he was back in the game, and on his home field, but too worn out to play. Six months after the first trial, Joe had said, "I didn't realize this could go on and on and on, and I really didn't think that it would." He'd made that statement just months into the legal process—now, more than two years later, he said he had trouble remembering life before lawyers and reporters. Still, he welcomed the ten-minute drive from his house to the courthouse, and he liked knowing where to park and being able to find lunch on the square with normal food at a reasonable price. A *New York Times* article on the trial began with an effort to describe this world to the people of Manhattan, opening with the high school football game played the Friday before, and describing the turkey hunting as off but the fishing better this fall, "which is good news down at the Snak-Atak convenience store, where the bait-vending machine offers fresh night crawlers for $1.75 a dozen."

Joe was glad to be back in this world, and glad to be back with a judge he knew, and one who had sided with him. In August of 1988, Judge Teel told *The Kansas City Star,* "It's not any Supreme Ruler's will that allows [Nancy] to live, it's mankind on Earth that's feeding her." The judge had also appeared on some local panels, twice with Joe, to talk about the case. Joe told me a couple of times in the weeks leading up to the trial, "He's not going to go against us."

But two wild cards remained: the clear and convincing evidence standard, and whether that somehow tied the judge's hands; and Thad McCanse. Joe couldn't figure out either one, which troubled him. I worried, too.

On Novermber 1, 1990, the courtroom was full, just as it had been in the spring of 1988. Don Lamkins sat on the aisle by himself, midway toward the back of the courtroom. The sketch artists and some journalists took up overflow seating in the jury box again, and they sat up as the Cruzans walked in shortly before nine. The Cruzans' numbers had swelled from the first trial—this time Chris allowed the girls to take the day off school and sit in court. At their age, the idea of possibly shielding them from the effects of the lawsuit and publicity had long since gone by the wayside. The girls stood almost at attention when Judge Teel entered the courtroom.

In my opening statement, I talked about the clear and convincing standard, emphasizing that a single conversation, potentially, could meet the standard, and that we had far more evidence than that. I apologized in advance if our side sounded frustrated at times, telling Judge Teel that the system had in essence robbed this family of "all semblance of normal life." I also noted that the journey had had a positive side: According to commentators, the Cruzans had helped lift the consciousness of the country on the ethical questions faced at the end of life.

I closed by telling the judge directly about that skeptical member of the press corps who had asked me why these witnesses weren't at the first trial. "To those people who are skeptics, I say, 'To heck with them.' If we find a new witness next week, we will be back here next week. If we find a new witness in three weeks, we will be back here again. If the rule is, for people like the Cruzans, that 'you have the power to start medical treatment for a loved one, but before you can stop that medical treatment, you have got to go talk to every person that your loved one ever worked for, knew, or dealt with'—that is a problem with the system, not a problem with what the Cruzans have done."

McCanse wasn't even a minute into his opening statement before he had me squirming. I did not see the kindly, white-haired grandfather that reporters had described (and the way I'd once seen him, too)—I saw an adversary who, unbelievably and inconceivably to me, appeared bent on unraveling my case. I had no idea if he was simply playing devil's advocate, or if he really believed in what he was doing.

McCanse told the judge that he didn't view his role necessarily as adversary, which was good. But then he started talking about the language in the Missouri Supreme Court opinion, which discussed the need for evidence complying with "rigid formalities." He and I had discussed this question several times—I thought this language hadn't survived the U.S. Supreme Court's opinion, which authorized a state to require "clear and convincing" evidence, but no more. McCanse had apparently ignored my interpretation. He then said his examination of the witnesses would focus on whether their testimony qualified as "newly discovered evidence . . . evidence that you could not have come forth with by the use of due diligence" at the first trial.

We weren't talking about newly discovered evidence under the Civil Rule of Missouri, and McCanse hasn't raised the issue in his answer, so he was barred from raising it here. I jumped to my feet. "Your Honor, I don't think that's the rule under the Probate Code at all," I objected. I also stated that I would continue to object throughout the course of the proceedings.

Perturbed wrinkles on McCanse's face showed that he didn't appreciate being interrupted in the courthouse across the street from his office by a lawyer the age of his kids. I couldn't have cared less what he thought at that moment.

Judge Teel looked over his glasses at me. "The objection will be overruled."

I called Marianne Smith to the stand. She smiled nervously at Judge Teel as she took her seat in the witness chair and began to tell him about her work history. She'd learned about the job at the Stapleton School back in the fall of 1977 from her father-in-law, who was the principal at a local grade school. Then she began talking about working with those four children at the school, and about the one-hour conversation where Nancy called Melissa "a vegetable" and said she'd never want to be force-fed like that.

I asked, "Do you have any doubt in your mind, in *your* mind, that Nancy would reject medical treatment being forced on her?"

"No doubt."

"This is based on her statements?"

"Yes."

"Any doubt whatsoever?"

"None."

I asked why Marianne hadn't come forward earlier than she did. She explained that she'd known about the first trial, but she didn't think an eight-year-old conversation would matter. She figured that many other people had more recent information than she did. And, she admitted sheepishly, she just hadn't wanted to get involved.

The judge had leaned in as he listened to Marianne. Thad McCanse appeared attentive, too. On cross-examination, McCanse dug deeper into day-to-day life at the school and began to ask Marianne about her decision to contact Chris. Again I objected repeatedly as he challenged whether Marianne could testify, and again Judge Teel overruled the objection. McCanse finished, and I jumped back up for redirect.

"Marianne, did you concoct this story about these discussions, where you could have the opportunity to come to court this morning?" I asked, loud and angry.

"No, sir."

"Based on your discussion with Nancy, is there any doubt in your mind that she would reject the medical treatment she is now receiving?"

"No doubt," she said.

I sat down and stared at my notes, and the judge called the morning recess—likely in part to defuse the tension between counsel. During the break, I talked to Marianne's husband, Steve, and I made the decision to put him on the stand to talk about Marianne's first contact with the Cruzans. I needed to move things along—we'd already spent half the morning on one witness.

The judge swore Steve Smith in after the break. I asked his name, relation to Marianne, and when he first learned he was going to testify. "About 12 seconds ago," he said, and a laugh rippled through the gallery. Steve discussed the difficulty of working at the Stapleton School and recounted his first discussions with Marianne about her conversation with Nancy. Unfortunately, he didn't remember much. He did emphasize for Judge Teel how reluctant Marianne was to be there testifying, which helped. And he lightened the mood in the courtroom when he said that he had a poor memory, but that his wife remembered everything, including the first bad thing he ever said, even 20 years ago.

"Was that 'I do'?" Thad McCanse interjected from his table, again causing some laughter, which increased when Judge Teel looked down at Steve Smith and said, "Probably reminds you of it, too?"

Smith laughed, and said, "Constantly." Unfortunately, he was right about his own memory—McCanse didn't even cross-examine him.

I called Debi Havner to the stand. Debi had hoped that her deposition testimony ten days earlier would be enough. I pleaded with her to come back to Carthage the morning of the trial because her live testimony would be so much more compelling for the judge. She didn't want to leave her ten-month-old baby. We arranged for a charter plane to pick her up, fly her in for testimony, and take her straight home. Reluctantly she agreed. For Nancy.

Debi told the judge about her long history in special education; about her husband, a school principal; and about how Joe had first contacted her father, who was a corporate executive at Wal-Mart headquarters in Arkansas. She told a tale similar to Marianne's of their six months together with the four children, and the conversation that took place while Nancy force-fed Melissa. And although it wasn't particularly sensitive, she said Nancy often referred to Melissa as a "vegetable."

Debi had first heard about the accident when she saw Nancy's picture on CNN on December 6, 1989, our day at the U.S. Supreme Court. Upon cross-examination, Thad and I again got into an argument about his use of Debi's deposition testimony, with his exam peppered by my objections and his responses. Debi finished shortly before noon.

All of the Cruzans smiled at Debi as she walked by. Angie and Miranda had especially enjoyed her testimony, as she discussed how Nancy had doted on her nieces and was always showing off their photos and talking about them. Debi walked out of the courtroom with Kim

Ross and the charter pilot, who had decided to watch the testimony rather than sit at the small airport.

Judge Teel didn't allow cameras in the courtroom, so the reporters waited down in the lobby of the courthouse. The lights came on as Debi, Kim, and the pilot emerged from the elevator, with questions shouted from a handful of competing journalists. Debi smiled and shook her head, walking quickly toward my car as cameras followed. Kim couldn't figure out how to move the driver's seat forward, but the reporters continued to shout at her outside the car windows—so she finally perched herself on the edge of the seat, with her toes barely reaching the pedals, and pulled away.

Before lunch, I stood at the podium and read Judge Teel the report of the most recent examination by Dr. George Wong from MRC. Dr. Wong had concluded that Nancy remained in a persistent vegetative state, without hope of recovery. Then I played the first part of the videotaped deposition of Tom Turner, who would offer the other new testimony we had.

Tom Turner had contacted the Cruzans by letter (dated December 15, 1989) in the wake of the publicity following arguments at the U.S. Supreme Court. Turner wrote the Cruzans about a conversation he'd had with Nancy about Karen Ann Quinlan. This conversation was more along the lines of "I wouldn't want to live as a vegetable." Nancy had worked for Turner for about a month in Oklahoma, and we had Nancy's old pay stubs to prove that she was there, along with notations on Chris's calendar about Nancy leaving for Oklahoma and returning to Carterville.

But with no other witnesses to corroborate the conversation, really no reason for the topic to come up, and Mr. Turner being anxious to testify, I didn't try to overplay his role. I told the judge in pre-trial that this was one additional piece of evidence, one I couldn't corroborate, and that I'd put it on so that he knew about it. I played part of Turner's deposition on the video monitor, and in the middle of the video, Judge Teel decided to break for lunch.

After lunch, I read the latest CT scan report into the record—no change from the CT of January 15, 1987—and I played the video of the exam done by Dr. Clark Watts ten days before. I asked the judge to seal the video so that it wouldn't be available as a public record (therefore not available to television stations), and he agreed to do so.

Then I put Dr. Watts on the speakerphone from Columbia, Missouri. He described his training for the judge and characterized Nancy as fairly typical when compared to other patients in a vegetative state. On cross-examination, the doctor stated that, based upon her difficulty in handling her secretions, he doubted whether Nancy had much of a swallow reflex left, and he didn't think she could be fed orally.

Next I called Nancy's treating doctor, Dr. James Davis, but I asked the judge if McCanse could examine him first, since the two had talked recently, and Thad had asked me if he could put the doctor on the stand. The judge nodded.

Dr. Davis stated that he'd been Nancy's primary doctor for three years now, and he saw her every day.

"What is the reason for seeing her every day, Doctor?" McCanse asked. "Does she require attention every day, or why do you see her?"

"No, she does not require any attention—hardly ever requires any attention at all. It's just that I am responsible for her care, and I want to make certain that something hasn't occurred which requires my attention, which someone else has missed."

McCanse asked the doctor whether his experience was similar to that of Dr. Watts and Dr. Wong. He replied that it was.

"Have you tried to get a response from her by calling her name?" McCanse asked.

"Yes, sir, I have," Dr. Davis answered.

"Would you tell the court how that has worked out?"

"Well, sometimes she will open her eyes, sometimes she won't," the doctor said. "It's inconsistent."

"Does she—you call her by the name 'Nancy' on occasion?"

"Yes."

"She opens her eyes?"

"Yes."

"Have you also called her by some other name on occasion?"

"Yes, sir."

"What's happened?"

"She opens her eyes."

McCanse led Dr. Davis through his various exams of Nancy, and what he observed every day. The medical records showed the doctor's daily entry as repeatedly reading "persistent vegetative state."

"And that's been true then, as I understand it, for the three years you have taken care of her?" McCanse asked.

"Yes, sir."

"Do you expect any change?"

"No sir, I do not."

McCanse started walking the doctor through Nancy's condition and daily care: enemas, turning in bed, cream for rashes, phenobarbital, Valium, artificial tears, gastrostomy tube feeding; she sleeps, blows bubbles, and gurgles; her eyes are open without tracking; she moans, has contractions, and wets the bed; her mouth emits a very foul odor and she has bleeding gums. On and on, for more than an hour, and then into a second, McCanse had Dr. Davis reading entries from Nancy's medical chart. A reporter in the row behind the Cruzans was sleeping, and Angie and Miranda both looked droopy-eyed.

I wondered, *What in the world is he doing?* My frustration with Thad McCanse started up once again. He'd established that Davis now diagnosed Nancy as persistent vegetative state, which was good, but that was clear in the medical records. He was taking up half of my afternoon, for no good reason that I could see. It didn't dawn on me what he was doing until he did it.

"Doctor," McCanse said, "the reason I have gone into this at some length—do these entries accurately record what her existence is from day to day?"

"Yes, sir."

"And she is likely to continue in this condition indefinitely?"

"Yes, sir."

"Doctor, my function as *guardian ad litem* is to represent her best interests," McCanse said. "Can you tell me how it's in her interests that she continue in this existence that is described in these notes?"

Dr. Davis paused for a moment, appearing to think hard about the question. "No, sir," he answered, "I cannot."

"Do you think it is in her interest to continue like this?"

"No, sir, I do not."

"Thank you, Doctor."

Judge Teel said, "Mr. Colby," which halfway startled me. *What had just happened?* It appeared that Thad McCanse, whom I'd been arguing with most of the fall, had returned to the Cruzans' side—with a flourish. I stood, but did not quite know what to say to Dr. Davis. He'd obviously made some personal decisions, decisions that would benefit the Cruzans. His testimony had changed dramatically from the first trial: In March of 1988, he'd testified that he wasn't certain of Nancy's condition and that he couldn't remove Nancy's feeding tube. I walked toward him, still thinking about what to say.

"Dr. Davis, we appreciate your forthrightness. I noticed several members of the press, people out here," I finally said, motioning into the courtroom. "Thad just read a few entries from five months of Nancy's life, and everybody was falling asleep. Can you imagine what it would be like to live that?"

"Yes, sir, I can."

I had no idea where this was going. "What do you think it would be like?"

"I think it would be personally a living hell," Dr. Davis said, his voice now almost inaudible. The courtroom had grown quiet. Joe Cruzan looked at the floor; Angie sat upright, and both she and Miranda focused on the doctor.

I asked a couple more questions and sat down, nearly stunned. I'd been angry at McCanse all day—for most of the fall, in fact—now I wanted to pump his hand and pound him on the back.

The judge called us to the bench and asked whether Nancy was medicated during the examination by Dr. Watts. Since we didn't have the medication records from that morning in the courtroom, McCanse agreed to ask Dr. Davis. In response to several questions, the doctor said that he didn't know, but he didn't believe her usual medications would affect her reactions in any way.

I'd had enough time to gather my wits as McCanse conducted this follow-up exam about medication, so I decided to see how far the doctor would go. I stood and walked toward him. "Dr. Davis, when we were here in the spring of '88, you told us that you were not certain as Nancy's treating doctor that it was appropriate to remove her gastrostomy tube?"

"Yes."

"Has your opinion changed in that regard?" I asked.

The doctor paused for a long time, and then nodded his head. "Yes,

I believe it has."

"And why has it changed, and how has it changed, Doctor?"

"Well, I had the opportunity to observe her over a prolonged period of time now—with absolutely no evidence of cognitive function—understanding on her part."

"Do you believe that the parents' request to stop the gastrostomy feeding should be granted at this time?" I asked.

"I do."

"Thank you, sir," I said.

Judge Teel called a recess until 4:30 P.M. The entire courtroom stood as the judge left.

Joe Cruzan walked through the swinging gate that divided the gallery and the court area and met Dr. Davis. He shook the doctor's hand and said, "Thank you." Dr. Davis nodded, and walked slowly out of the courtroom.

I remained shell-shocked: Had all my concerns about Thad McCanse and this trial disappeared so quickly? The gray day outside conspired with the short days of November to bring the darkness to the windows early. We were almost done. Unlike the first trial, Joe and Chris weren't really nervous about testifying—they just wanted to get it over with. Joyce said, "I'm not testifying again. Judge Teel knows what I think."

After the break, I first played the remainder of the videotape from Tom Turner, the man from Oklahoma who had the brief conversation with Nancy about Karen Quinlan. The entire courtroom erupted in a tension release of laughter when Turner reported a conversation with Nancy where she'd told Turner he reminded her of her father, Joe. When Turner had replied, "C'mon, there can't be two guys that good-looking in this part of the country," Nancy had said, "My dad's not good-looking."

The video concluded, and I called Joe to the stand. I asked him about Tom Turner and Marianne Smith contacting the family, about the weekly visits he and Joyce continued to make up to Mt. Vernon, and whether he'd seen any reaction whatsoever from Nancy.

Joe had talked so much about the case by now that a lot of what he said often had the quality of a person trying to remember something he'd said earlier so that he could repeat it. His edge was nearly gone. In his pocket, he carried folded newspaper comments from right-to-lifers Rita Marker and Dee Conroy so that he could ignite his pilot light when his spirits burned too low. The slope of his once-straight shoulders now made him look fundamentally and constitutionally tired.

In his brief to the judge after trial, Thad McCanse called Joe's testimony "noteworthy not so much for what he said," but for the "change in his demeanor and attitude in the two and a half years that this litigation has continued. He comes across as a frustrated and, at times, bitter man."

After preliminaries, I asked Joe how the case had affected the family. "I don't know what's normal," he said, shaking his head. "I'm nearly eight years older than I was when her accident happened. Somewhere along the line, I got eight years older and a lot of things have changed. Quite frankly, it's been a bitch." He talked about being in the public eye, the family's role in raising the public consciousness, the boxes of letters they received, and responding to the letters from people in similar situations.

"What can you say to those people?" I asked.

"That we know what you are going through," he said. "Last year, Glenn Gray, who is a gentleman from Rhode Island whose wife [Marcia]—who went through a very similar circumstance, through a trial and everything—"

"The *Gray* case in federal court?" I interjected.

"Yes, right, he happened to be in Little Rock on business and he came out, and we met and said—there is two guys—he was a professor, I'm a construction worker, you know—and yet the first thing that happened when we walked in the door was we hugged each other."

"What kind of discussion did you have with Glenn Gray?" I asked.

Joe said that Gray was a veterinarian, and he talked about their discussion of death. "Glenn knew the—I may use the wrong term—but the physiological changes that occurred when Marcia died, and he watched for them, and, I mean, he knew what was going to happen," Joe said. "And it was a very peaceful death. I got some people by the name of Jim and Maureen Moore contacted us from Oregon. They had a little boy who was in a near-drowning when he was six years old. He died, I think, at the age of 19. Weighed 50 pounds. They brought him home and let him die. They took him out of the hospital, brought him home, there was nothing, no prosecution, no problem at all. But I mean in talking about what happened to their family was very similar—I mean, they wound up getting a divorce. They were both quite successful—she had a poodle-grooming shop,

I think he had some kind of business—and then they lost everything they had."

"Did they describe for you what the dying process was like, also?"

"The same thing, was very, very peaceful," Joe said.

"The same as Glenn Gray?"

"The same as Glenn Gray, the same as Ellie Laird, the same as Pat Brophy."

We were nearing the end. "Is there any doubt in your mind at all what Nancy would tell the court about her medical treatment if she could?" I asked.

"There is no doubt at all," Joe said. "By God, I wouldn't be here today if I thought there was any question. You know, I will tell you what. It seems like they have almost tried to wear us down. I mean the system, and you know, I don't mean anyone in particular, but the whole system has tried to almost break us." Joe's voice was growing louder, and starting to crack with emotion yet again. "But they are not going to succeed, not as long as Bill Colby sticks with us, and when he falls to the wayside, then we will keep going, because I made a commitment to my daughter that I wouldn't let this go on, and I intend to fulfill that commitment."

Tears were brimming in Joe's eyes, and his pat on the back for me had stuck a lump in my throat as well. We'd taken this man through the wringer. I needed to stop. "Unfortunately," I said, "I'm part of the system. No more questions."

McCanse asked Joe just three short questions, basically trying to pin down when Nancy was in Oklahoma.

I called Chris as our last witness. She talked about the lack of change in Nancy's condition, and her memory related to the three new witnesses. We put into evidence Chris's 1981 calendar, with entries of when Nancy moved to Oklahoma City, as well as letters Nancy had written to Angie and Miranda, which said, "It's a long way to Oklahoma City."

And we talked about the effect of the case on the girls: how kids at school told them they were going against God; and how they knew that Chris would cry at school events, because Nancy always attended such things. In the front row of the courtroom, Angie and Miranda had tears streaming down their faces and their grandparents' arms around their shoulders. "They're always confronted with, 'How are Grandma and

Grandpa doing? How is Mom doing? How is this all affecting them?'—when the phone rings, when people make comments in the media kind of against our family," Chris said.

"How has all of this affected the memory of Nancy?"

"That's the thing," she said. "It's been almost half of the girls' lives that they have seen Nancy exist the way she has. They talk about sometimes, 'I don't know if I can even remember Nancy—what she looked like, how she sounded, how she laughed,' and it's so terrible to have all of the good memories shaded over with what we are going through now. I will be glad when the time comes that what we can focus on is not the physical existence that she needs now, but the way she was."

"You were probably Nancy's best friend. Is there any doubt in your mind what she would choose today if she could?" I asked

"There has never been any doubt in my mind," Chris said. She was trembling, and I was near tears again—we were emotionally spent. I sat down. Thad McCanse could only muster a couple of questions for her.

I made sure all of the exhibits were in and asked the judge to take judicial notice of the transcript of the first trial. Judge Teel asked us to file briefs on December 5. We had no closing arguments.

After the judge left, there was a flurry of handshaking and hugging at the front of the courtroom. I apologized to Thad for being so combative, and I thanked him for drawing out Dr. Davis's change of heart. I didn't ask him about his change in course; I was just glad for it. Joe, Joyce, Chris, Angie, Miranda, Walt Williams, Kim Ross, and I walked together down to the lobby of the courthouse and talked briefly to the press.

I needed to hurry home because I had to fly to New York early the next morning for a deposition, and then on Saturday I was to talk to a New York state hospice group out in Westchester County about the *Cruzan* case. The following Wednesday, I was off to Detroit to speak at the National Hospice Organization annual meeting—from there I'd go straight to Tucson and on to West Palm Beach to speak at a medical meeting. Then I had three speeches to give in Kansas City, some depositions, the *Cruzan* brief to write, and Thanksgiving. My November was poised to fly by.

The Cruzans' was not. Joe had already marked off work for the day after trial, on the chance that the trial would run over to a second day—instead, he sat home all day, watching the telephone and the mailbox.

December 5, the day the briefs were due, seemed like a year away. And the last time, Judge Teel had taken several months after receiving the briefs to decide.

Joe said he didn't know if he was going to make it.

CHAPTER 38

DECEMBER DECISION

Luckily, November turned out to be a busy month for Springfield Engineering, so at least Joe was occupied during the day, moving from project to project. On December 5, I filed our brief and a motion requesting that Judge Teel authorize the Cruzans to move Nancy out of Missouri in the event that he ruled against us.

On December 10, I read Thad McCanse's brief, which was clear and decisive. "There comes a time when litigation must be ended," he wrote, and he concluded as *guardian ad litem* that removal of the feeding tube was in Nancy's best interests, and that we'd proven our case by the required clear and convincing evidence. He made no effort to exclude the new evidence, as he'd been suggesting all fall, nor did he indicate that he'd appeal the decision if we won. I called Thad and thanked him. He told me that the judge had said he might have a decision as early as the end of the week.

The next day, I called Judge Teel, and he confirmed that a decision was indeed possible by Friday, December 14th, and he asked that I call him back the next morning, which I did. The judge said that he'd issue the decision to the public Friday at 2 P.M., and that we could pick it up an hour or so before that time to prepare ourselves.

That fall, Chris had started back to college at Missouri Southern in Joplin. During the first part of December, she was preparing for final exams and the end of the semester. On Wednesday, December 12, her math class let out at 11:00 A.M., so Chris called her mother, who gave her the news that Judge Teel would release the decision Friday. Chris then went to find her dad—who happened to be working on repairs to the HVAC system at the college that day—and told him.

Joe looked at his frazzled daughter and said, "You look like you need a hug."

Chris didn't worry about how dirty her dad was—the other construction workers stopped and watched as the two stood intertwined and sobbing in the hallway.

On Thursday, December 13, a biting rain fell for most of the day, and even at noon, the gray sky barred most of the sunlight. Joe left for work early, and Joyce stopped at Chris's for coffee before heading to work herself. Thursday was Chris's study day at school, with no classes scheduled on the day before finals began. Donna made the trip into town midmorning for a short visit. Chris took Angie and Miranda to Wal-Mart for some Christmas shopping and studied for her math final; she then finished decorating the Christmas tree and wrapped some presents. She worked faster to finish the doll she'd been making for Nancy. When Mel got home from work, he went to his shop to work on Christmas presents. Angie and Miranda went to a high school basketball game that night. They were trying to keep busy, yet despite all this activity, it felt like the day would never pass.

During the night, the rain finally changed over to snow, but it couldn't bring the holiday spirit along with it. Chris had been unable to sleep, so she rose early on Friday and stood in the shower sobbing. She changed clothes three times that morning, unsure about the day ahead. She took her math final and headed to 501 Main. Donna was there with Joyce; Joe had left around 9:30 to go up to MRC to be with Nancy when the news came. Betsey Arledge and the PBS film crew were waiting with him. At 10:45, Joe and the film crew went into Nancy's room and closed the door, which a nurse noted in Nancy's chart.

If Judge Teel ruled in our favor, I planned to drive up to Mt. Vernon immediately from Carterville with the order in hand. If he ruled against us, we planned to let a few days pass and then move Nancy out of

Missouri—assuming he granted us that power in his ruling, as I'd requested. I'd already made tentative arrangements to move Nancy.

Angie and Miranda did not want to sit around the house all morning being nervous, but they did want to be there for the afternoon decision. So they went to school in the morning, and Joyce picked them up around 11:30, stopping at McDonald's on the way back. Chris called Grandma Jack and Grandpa Les around noon, and they came over to the house, too. Two of Les's sisters came by around 12:30, but Joyce didn't want too many people in the house, so Chris met her aunts outside and explained that Walt and I would be coming over with the decision. The two ladies understood and walked over to wait next door.

That morning, I went into the office and left about 9:30 A.M. for Carterville. I took a change of clothes but didn't check into the Econo Lodge, not sure if I would be staying the night. I couldn't imagine that Judge Teel would rule against us—given the proof we'd put on at the recent trial, his first ruling, and the public statements he'd made, it just didn't seem possible. But I also knew by now that he marched to his own drum, so I'd believe the favorable decision when I saw it.

I met Walt Williams in the lobby of the courthouse in Carthage, and we walked into the probate office together. We picked up the decision, read it, then drove to Carterville.

❧   ❧   ❧

I pulled up to the Cruzans' carport at about 12:50. Chris had been watching the street from the kitchen window above the sink, and she opened the side door to the house as Walt and I started up the steps. I looked up at her and said, "We won." She closed her eyes and her body started to ripple, then her mouth parted and a loud wail escaped. I steered her back into the house and she delivered the news to everybody inside. Nine people—four generations of the Cruzan family, Walt Williams, and me—stood in a circle and wept.

When she was able to speak, Chris picked up the phone and called Mel. After she hung up, the phone rang and I answered it. It was Joe, surprised to hear me on the other end of the phone at his house. "Mr. Colby?" he said.

"Mr. Cruzan. Are you with the PBS crew?" I asked.

"Yes, I am."

"All right. Well, stay calm, because I don't want word leaking out until we get there," I said. "You ready?"

"Yes, sir—yes, sir."

"We won."

"Hmm—hmm." Joe did his part. He was talking on a phone in the hallway at MRC, with the PBS camera trained on him and nurses watching the scene from a distance. He asked how everyone was at the house, and when I described the scene, he said, "Right, right, understandable, understandable, understandable." We arranged to meet at the hospital in about an hour.

Grandma Jack and Grandpa Les drove the four blocks home, and the girls and Donna headed over with them. Walt went back to his office; Chris, Joyce, and I drove to Mt. Vernon in my Bronco. Chris had finished Nancy's Christmas doll, and she carried it on her lap.

Joe went back into Nancy's room, and even though he'd told me that he wouldn't say anything about the decision, he felt that Betsey Arledge and the crew, Bill and Jim, should know. They had long ago earned that courtesy. So he looked at Nancy, gently stroked her face with the back of his hand, and said, "Well, we got a green light." Then he turned to Betsey Arledge, saying, "It's time, it's time." He let out a long sigh, the camera went off, and Betsey went over and hugged him.

Early in the week, word had spread at MRC that Friday was decision day. A petition opposing "the termination of Nancy's life" circulated among staff that morning, and 34 employees—not quite a third of the employees on that shift—signed it. Five local ministers—one Baptist, one Presbyterian, one First Christian, and two from something called the Christ In You Ministries—all volunteer chaplains at MRC, delivered a letter to Don Lamkins that asked him to refuse to carry out any court order. Shortly before 2:00 P.M., the ministers gathered in the chapel. In a circle around the altar, with their hands clasped, they prayed over the judge's decision.

It was too late. Judge Teel had made up his mind, and we'd already arrived with the order in hand. Just after two o'clock, I walked quietly into Don Lamkins's office with the Cruzans, nodding politely but ignoring the questions of a nearby reporter. Lamkins and I shook hands, and I handed him a copy of the order. He remained the same straight-backed, polite, proper man I'd first met years earlier, but the strain showed in his face. He and I had talked several times over the last few weeks, and he'd agreed that they would move Nancy to the hospice wing of the hospital if the court ordered it.

Although he personally opposed the family's position, Don Lamkins remained professional. He read the order quickly—the heart of it was less than half a page long:

The court, by clear and convincing evidence, finds:

1) That the intent of our ward [Nancy], if mentally able, would be to terminate her nutrition and hydration.

2) That there is no evidence of substance to cause belief that our ward would continue her present existence, hopeless as it is, and slowly progressively worsening.

3) That the allegations of the Petition are true and it is sustained.

4) That the co-guardians, Lester L.[Joe] and Joyce Cruzan, are authorized to cause the removal of nutrition and hydration from our ward, Nancy Beth Cruzan.

Lamkins looked up at me. "This doesn't order us to comply," he said.

"Don, the Director of the Department of Health signed an affidavit saying that MRC would comply with the court's order," I said.

"I need to call Jefferson City, Bill," he said, moving to a phone.

Others soon joined us—Dr. Davis (Nancy's doctor), Lu Bay (the director of social services who had long supported the Cruzans), and Barbara Shoun (the hospital spokesperson who opposed them). Even without word from Jefferson City, we debated a plan. The first issue was timing.

Barbara Shoun said, "Christmas is coming. We should wait until January."

Joe and I both said no. Joe said, "We want it removed today."

We also argued about who should say what to the press. Most important, we argued about the tube. MRC staff claimed that there was no medical reason to remove it, and that it should stay in place to give her medicine. I'd checked with doctors and knew that if Nancy needed any medicine in her final days, nurses could give it to her by suppository. And maybe I was growing a little paranoid by this point, but I wanted the tube out and the hole taped over as soon as possible because it seemed to me that leaving the line into her stomach would invite an angry nurse to try to feed Nancy secretly.

Back and forth the meeting went as we argued and waited. Then word came back from Jefferson City—MRC must comply. Suddenly we moved from the hypothetical to the real.

Dr. Davis left and went to Nancy's room—with no fanfare, he pulled out the gastrostomy tube himself at 3:20 P.M. He put a small square of gauze over the hole in Nancy's stomach, secured it with two strips of white athletic tape, and picked up her medical chart to record what he'd done.

As soon as the meeting in Don Lamkins's office was over, word spread through the hospital. Nurses broke down in tears in the halls, local reporters waited on the ground floor for news, and upstairs, the PBS crew followed Nancy. Seven nurses and staff people filled Nancy's room, gathering her belongings and preparing to transfer her. Three of these nurses wheeled her toward the elevator, and three more walked behind carrying clothing, hangers, and a garbage bag filled with belongings, including the poinsettia Joe had brought that morning. A staffer carrying clothes stepped onto the elevator, and said as the doors closed, "They can't pay me enough for this kind of bullshit."

As the day wore on, reporters recorded the high emotions of the day. The nurses who spoke out appeared to be those who were the angriest. "We don't want her blood on our hands," Jeanette Forsyth, a head nurse, told one reporter. To another, she said, "You can walk away from all this bullshit—we have to come back tomorrow and wonder who's next. I just feel all washed out."

Nursing assistant Judy Sanders was standing nearby. She nodded her head and said, "I feel I've been beaten with a club."

Nurse Sharon Orr told a *New York Times* reporter, "The Humane Society won't let you starve your dog."

Another nurse, requesting anonymity, said, "They don't starve death-row inmates." And Dr. Davis heard more than one staffer express the sentiment, "I think the Cruzans should have to see their daughter suffer a terrible death, because they deserve it."

Many worried about what the days ahead meant for them. "We were all talking one day about if this did happen, was our name still going to be on the Lord's slate or not?" nurse Debbie Schnake wondered.

Don Lamkins told Betsey Arledge, "There's two kinds of law here—our legal laws, those are society's laws—and moral law. Moral law is God's law; it comes from religion. Man's law said it's all right, but that doesn't change moral law. Am I doing it myself? No, I'm not. But being responsible for the center and for everybody here, how much of it am I doing? And is being responsible the same as doing it?"

Lu Bay led Joe, Joyce, Chris, and me out the back door of Don Lamkins's conference room, and up a back way to the hospice unit. When we reached the hospice floor, Chris saw Nancy's bed come off the elevator, wheeling toward her new room, her face sticking out above the sheets. But no tubes were attached anywhere, and no metal stand with a feeding pump attached rolled next to Nancy's bed—it was just Nancy now. Chris burst into tears again, and the four of us followed behind the bed into Room 233.

Governor Ashcroft's office hadn't been monitoring the *Cruzan* case closely, but that Friday, the updates were coming in from everywhere. The Missouri Citizens for Life hand-delivered a letter to the governor, asking him to order Attorney General Webster to seek an emergency order (a writ of prohibition) to stop the judge's order from taking effect. They also asked that he order Webster to appeal the decision on grounds that it discriminated against the handicapped and "because it is unlawful in the state of Missouri to starve a person to death with or without their consent."

The Missouri Citizens for Life also issued a press release, so reporters were calling the governor, asking what he intended to do. It was December 14—a Friday afternoon at the height of the Christmas season. The holiday party for the attorney general's office was already in full swing, and the weekend was coming. What the governor's office needed was more time.

I later learned that after he received a call from the governor's office late that Friday afternoon, Don Lamkins went to find Dr. Davis. He told the doctor that Governor Ashcroft had requested that they put the tube back in.

Dr. Davis had already had a long day. The stress of the meetings and the press interviews, and the act of pulling the tube out of Nancy's stomach had added up. Most days, Dr. Davis moved from silent room to silent room, confirming that patients continued unaware of their world and stopping on occasion to talk with a nurse. Now, even the nurses wouldn't talk to him, and people turned away as he walked by. He told the *New York Times,* "That hurts me, but to me that shows that these people have no compassion for people who are different." It wasn't clear from the quote whether the mild-mannered doctor was talking about Nancy or himself.

The easiest course for the doctor would have been to do what his boss was telling him to do—reinsert the tube. To fight the director *and* the governor's office would take a fair dose of courage. But Dr. Davis had about run out of patience by the time Lamkins found him. And he thought he knew what was right. "The tube's already out," Dr. Davis said, "and there's no medical reason to put it back in."

"But the governor has asked that it be put back in," Lamkins protested.

Dr. Davis took two folded pieces of paper from his pocket and looked at them. "I have a court order," he said. In the end, he refused the request.

As soon as Nancy was settled in the hospice wing, I said goodbye to the Cruzans. I'd scheduled a press conference in the lobby of the courthouse in Carthage. The goal was to draw the press away from Mt. Vernon, Nancy, and the Cruzans. I walked down near the administrative area, found several reporters, and told them again that no questions would be answered by our side in Mt. Vernon. A couple of them groaned.

"Why can't we do it here?" one asked.

"Because I'm only going to do this once, and we've already told others it's 4:30 at the courthouse," I said.

"Is the tube out, Bill?"

I smiled. "Forty-five minutes from now, in Carthage," I said. "Come on, it's a nice drive."

In the cavernous first-floor hallway of the Carthage courthouse, with a Christmas tree directly behind me, I stood surrounded by reporters, cameras, and lights. Many courthouse personnel stood on the edges of the group to listen. For 15 minutes I answered questions about the tube, the move to hospice, and the Cruzans' emotional status. Many of these reporters had been on the case for almost three years; some were almost friends.

"Bill, we've heard that the governor is planning to appeal the decision. Have you talked to him?" asked one reporter. The question stunned me—that couldn't be possible.

"Any state appeal at this stage would be very unfair to the family," I said. "There's no legal basis to come in after the fact." After a couple more questions, I ended the conference, moved to a phone booth in the courthouse lobby, and rummaged through legal papers until I found the phone number for the attorney general's office. I needed to find out what was going on.

Bill Webster hadn't joined his own Christmas party yet—nor had the receptionist, who patched me through.

"A reporter just told me he heard Governor Ashcroft intends to appeal our case," I asked Webster. "What's going on?" I continued to respect the office of the attorney general and the man occupying it, but I was no longer in awe as I'd been in March of 1988 when Attorney General Webster had walked over to counsel table at the first trial and shook my hand.

"There's not going to be an appeal," Webster said. I later learned about his meeting that afternoon with Governor Ashcroft. The governor and attorney general shared the same party, the same pro-life philosophy, and Bill Webster was the odds-on Republican nominee to replace Governor Ashcroft in 1992—they had to get along with one another. But the governor was extremely unhappy that the state wasn't involved in the *Cruzan* case any longer.

Webster told me that he'd gone over to the governor's office, and he and Jim Deutsch had tried to explain why the state had withdrawn from the case: Once the U.S. Supreme Court had ruled on the legal issues and set up a process, the state had no role. The governor's staff wondered if Webster would appeal this decision by Judge Teel, but Webster told the assembled group that the attorney general had no basis, since he'd moved to dismiss the state earlier. They wanted to know if the governor's office could enter the case directly and appeal, but Webster explained that the governor really had no standing as a party since the Department of Health had already exited the case.

Governor Ashcroft had been the attorney general before Webster, and he was a smart lawyer—he understood that any real legal options were gone. So Ashcroft's spokesperson, Bob Ferguson, told reporters late Friday, "The governor has been advised by the attorney general that the state is not a party to this matter and is not eligible to appeal. This is the final chapter of an unfortunate compound tragedy. The governor's prayers and sympathy go out to the Cruzan family."

Joe, Joyce, and Chris stayed with Nancy in her new room until around 6:00 P.M., then drove home so that Chris could check on the girls. Joe and Joyce dropped their daughter off, stopped at home for a sandwich, and headed back up the highway to be with Nancy.

CHAPTER 39

OPERATION RESCUE

The press didn't rest over the weekend, as they tried to catch up with the events of Friday. *CBS This Morning* and *Good Morning America* producers called my legal assistant, Kim Ross, at home, looking for guests for the Monday show. Reporters still roamed the first-floor hallways of MRC—all were disappointed that the Cruzans weren't talking. Upstairs, the PBS crew continued to film, but Betsey Arledge had transcended Joe's category of "the press" long before. Joe called her daughter, Meredith, who was born just months before the decision by the U.S. Supreme Court, his "honorary granddaughter." Arledge certainly didn't sound like an award-winning documentary producer when she left long messages on the Cruzan answering machine, trying to coax a word out of Meredith for Joe and Joyce.

Don Lamkins also worked that Saturday, answering more questions from the press and reviewing his preparations. He'd been planning for some time for this eventuality—screening nurses so he didn't force someone to participate, handling the press, and dealing with employee morale. As the pressure mounted, he worried about some major incident, especially one involving Joe. Like many of us, Lamkins had heard of Joe's desire to take matters into his own hands. After a counseling session with Joe some years before, Lu Bay had come to Lamkins ashen-faced and told him that Joe had said he wanted to bring his shotgun up to Mt. Vernon, shoot Nancy, and then himself. She told Lamkins that she didn't believe he'd carry out the threat, but from that day on, they kept an eye on Joe.

Lamkins had watched Joe at trial in November and had seen how emotional, angry, and frustrated he'd become. Now, as Nancy was going to spend perhaps as much as two weeks dying, Lamkins didn't want an explosion if a nurse said something to Joe in his increasingly weary state.

Others were busy that weekend as well. The press release from the Missouri Citizens for Life that had called on Governor Ashcroft to intervene began to circulate among its members, as did a one-page yellow flyer with the caption, "DON'T LET NANCY STARVE!" It described Nancy as smiling at amusing stories, weeping after visitors had left, "eating bananas, potatoes, and link sausages, and drinking juice" after her accident—it claimed that the feeding tube simply made long-term care easier for the nurses. The flyer gave the phone numbers for Governor Ashcroft and the MRC, encouraging people to call and urge them to feed Nancy. And it invited all recipients to a "24-hour-a-day prayer vigil outside the Missouri Rehab Center (600 N. Main St., Mt. Vernon, MO)." At the bottom, it had a phone number for more information— the Joplin area office of Operation Rescue.

❧ ❧ ❧

After returning to MRC on Friday evening, Joe and Joyce stayed late into the night with Nancy before driving home. On Saturday, Joe was up well before dawn, packing and hooking his travel trailer up to his truck. The guys at work made fun of Joe's truck, saying you knew it was Joe coming around a corner before you ever saw the truck. He'd added a big sheet-metal box on the front of the pickup for tools, and even Joe admitted that he looked like Jed Clampett from *The Beverly Hillbillies*. Joe and Joyce parked the trailer on the MRC lot that Saturday morning. They were there for the duration.

Over the long weekend, the Cruzans learned the names of the nurses in the hospice and familiarized themselves with Nancy's new surroundings. On Saturday, Dr. Davis came in to talk to Joe and Joyce and to see Nancy. He noted no change in her condition. That night at home, Dr. Davis woke up sweating, startled from a dream where he walked into the room and found Nancy sitting up talking to her mother. On Sunday he checked on Nancy early, confirming it had only been a dream—actually "a nightmare," he told a reporter—Nancy's body lay like it had for almost seven years, condition unchanged.

Monday, December 17, 1990, 12:30 A.M.

Shortly after midnight on Sunday, a brown and tan 1985 Chevy van—carrying the Reverend Joe Foreman, his wife, Anne, and their five children—rolled into Mt. Vernon. Rev. Foreman was an ordained Presbyterian minister who lived in Atlanta but had no church there. He lived much of the time in the van with his family, traveling the country to protest abortion for a group he'd helped found, Operation Rescue, which reporters described as the "controversial right-wing of the anti-abortion movement."

Foreman and his family slept in a church on Sunday night. By dawn, almost 20 others had arrived. By Monday afternoon, more than a hundred protestors had arrived in Mt. Vernon. The group moved to the nearby Bel-Aire Motor Inn and set up camp. Foreman—a tall, trim man with brown hair and a moustache—stood in front of a chalkboard, and over the course of several hours, the group formulated a plan to rescue Nancy. They had the floor plan of the hospital, which they'd received from sympathizers, and they'd learned where Nancy's new room was. They diagrammed the entrance to the hospital on the blackboard, and talked about putting her on a stretcher and moving her quickly to a station wagon and a safe house, but ended up discarding that idea.

Ultimately, they settled on a plan to feed Nancy where she was. Some members of the group would create a diversion out front while several others would come up a back stairwell to Nancy's room. As the men in the group barricaded the doors, Wanda Frye, a protestor from Kansas City who was also a nurse, would drop a feeding tube down Nancy's nose and feed her as much as possible without choking her. Rev. Foreman set the time for early the next day.

❧ ❧ ❧

Joe called Monday afternoon to give me an update on Nancy's condition—it hadn't changed. At least one family member had been with her most of the time. Betsey Arledge and the PBS film crew had been in, but not often. Joe said Betsey wanted to respect their privacy. He and Joyce stayed most of the weekend with Nancy—things were quiet, and they were just waiting.

Joyce and I also talked. She and Chris were worried about Joe. Joyce was busy at work, trying to get the school payroll ready and have finances in shape for the end of the year; Chris was still taking final exams. Both women were driving back and forth to Mt. Vernon as much as they could and hurrying to finish up everything at home and work so they could relieve Joe. They were concerned about how tired he looked already, and worried that he was spending too much time alone with Nancy without their support. He wouldn't leave Nancy for long. He either slept in a chair in her room, or he'd head out to the trailer and try to take a nap for a couple of hours. Joyce wanted me to tell Joe to try to get some sleep.

Don Lamkins received two strange, and troubling, phone calls Monday. Lamkins and Charley Stokes, the owner of the Bel-Aire Motor Inn, were both members of the Mt. Vernon Rotary Club, and on Monday afternoon, Stokes told Lamkins that a man named Foreman had rented several rooms and had asked how to have extra phone lines installed. Foreman had told Stokes that he was organizing the protest at MRC.

And at home that evening, Lamkins received a call from radio personality Bob Priddy. Don Lamkins had admired Priddy's radio journalism for years, and he was flattered to talk to Priddy about the case, but it turned out that that wasn't exactly why Priddy was calling. "Mr. Lamkins," he said, "I just got a phone call from a group of protestors from Chicago who say they're going to storm your hospital tomorrow morning. They wanted me to ride on their bus. I told them no, and I thought you should know about this."

Lamkins talked to Priddy for several minutes and thanked him repeatedly for the heads-up. When Lamkins ended that call, he immediately dialed the sheriff.

In normal times, MRC had a single security guard for their entire facility, and they often sent him to town on errands. On Tuesday morning, Don Lamkins would have armed officers from the Mt. Vernon police, the county sheriff's office, and the state highway patrol all at MRC, joined together to secure the facility, following the security plan that Lamkins had in place for more than a year, just in case a court ever ordered Nancy's tube removed. One group of officers would operate out of a command center in a room just down the hall from Nancy's.

Joe Cruzan was alone in Nancy's room when he saw the first protestors on Monday evening. Looking out the window, Joe saw a group of about 35 people gathering on the lawn. They formed a circle, holding candles and apparently praying. A nurse told Joe that some others had delivered flowers for Nancy. He spent the night, mostly awake, on a chair in Nancy's room.

Tuesday, December 18, 1990

Chris and Joyce came up to the hospital early Tuesday morning and found Joe wide awake, sitting by Nancy's bed. The hallway outside the room was filled with law-enforcement officers moving around, checking doors, talking on radios. Joe periodically left the room to go out and talk to the officers, asking if they had heard anything. Inside the room, he paced from the door to the window, watching the front drive below. He watched the media gather on the lawn out front (someone had notified the media that the protestors would arrive at nine that morning, although the protestors claimed that they had sent no such notice). As he paced, Joe said to his wife and daughter more than once, "Just let some son-of-a-bitch try to come through that door."

Around 9:00 A.M., a police officer out in the hall told Joe that he'd better stay in the room. A stocky, muscle-bound young officer in glasses strode briskly down the hallway and said into his radio, "Cease all radio traffic unless necessary." At about 9:25, Joe saw a van with the sign "Abortion Kills Children" in its back window and a blue school bus with the word "MIRACLE" written on it pull up in front of the MRC. Dozens and dozens of protestors emerged from the vehicles and began to walk swiftly, some even jogging, toward the hospice wing. Joe was alarmed by how many protestors there were and how fast they were streaming into the building.

Down on the ground floor, in a commotion of voices and confusion, the group split up—some people rushed toward the stairwell, while the rest crammed onto an elevator. When the elevator reached the second floor, the doors opened, and the protestors started to step off toward Nancy's room, but abruptly stopped. Four officers stood directly in their path. The moment the elevator doors opened, a signal went to an MRC employee in the electrical control room, and he shut down the power to the elevator. The protestors could go nowhere, nor would the elevator doors shut, so they decided to kneel down on the floor of the elevator and pray.

The Cruzans could not see that the police had the situation in hand—all they could hear from inside the room was the confusion of shouting voices and people moving in the hallway. Chris later said that her heart was pounding. Joe leaned hard against the door with his shoulder, not sure what was about to happen.

The protest group heading up the fire stairwell made it no farther. This group was much larger than the one on the elevator, and it included Wanda Frye in her nurse's uniform, with the feeding tube showing in her front shirt pocket like a fancy pen. This was the group that had planned to reach Nancy's room, freed up by the diversion at the elevator. But they didn't make it either—three officers stationed in the hallway at the top of the stairwell blocked their path just as officers had blocked the other group from exiting the elevator.

A protestor near the top of the stairs walked up to the top step, just in front of the officers, and called over his shoulder down the steps in a loud voice, "Go as far as you can, kneel, and pray as we agreed." The three officers blocking the way looked uncomfortably at one another as the praying started. One officer bowed his head. The group followed the prayer with a disjointed singing of hymns.

Soon a woman from MRC administration entered the stairwell and asked the protestors to move to the chapel to continue praying. They refused her repeated requests. Rev. Foreman told her, "We're talking about simple compassion of food and water."

The MRC woman had heard enough. "But I'm saying to you that you would make a bigger impact if you stopped acting like a bunch of ghouls hanging around here, and got down on your knees and prayed to Almighty God!" She was leaning over the railing, yelling down at

Foreman. By the time she finished, her face was flushed and her right index finger wagged at him. It was a surreal moment for the usually sedate hospital.

Joe told me later that he was prepared to "knock anyone out" who tried to force his way into Nancy's room. Once the hallway sounded as if it had quieted down, Joe stuck his head out of the door and soon came out. The officers told him that they thought they had everything under control.

Although no one tried to make a break past the armed officers, several protestors also would not retreat. Nineteen people in all refused to leave, and many curled up into tight balls with their arms wrapped around their knees in the elevator and on the stairs. One by one, officers lifted and dragged them, or rolled them out in wheelchairs, and carted them to the county jail with several trips of the MRC handicapped-accessible van. The job wasn't finished up until about one in the afternoon. Each person arrested had told officers that his or her name was "Nancy Cruzan."

Dozens of protestors were not arrested, however. Some milled around out front of the hospital, watching as the police carted their brethren away; others moved to the chapel to pray and sing. One man, Gary Tebbets from Kansas City, walked around on the first floor near the administrative offices for nearly an hour, carrying a Styrofoam cup filled with water. He confronted a police officer and said, "I'm commanded by the scripture to give a friend a cup of water, that's all I'm trying to do." When the officer told him he couldn't see Nancy and moved to escort him out, Tebbetts yelled, "You're a party to murder! Why not just take a pillow and smother her?!"

The clean-cut officer looked with amazement at the plump, middle-aged man with thin hair combed over his balding head. He held Tebbetts lightly under the arm as they moved out into the open air and asked him, "What are you trying to do, sir?"

Tebbetts took his wide glasses off and brushed away a tear with his big hand. "I'm trying to give a dying patient a cup of water," he said, his voice cracking with emotion. The officer shook his head and went back into the building. Once the cameras left that afternoon, most of the protestors went back to their war room to regroup.

When Joe called me to tell me about the protests, I had other bad news for him. A petition for an emergency writ seeking an order to resume tube feeding had been filed that morning in the state court of appeals in Springfield by two men from Kansas City (both turned out to be part of the protest group). The clerk of the court faxed me the petition on Tuesday afternoon, and when I described it to Joe, he let loose with a loud, "Goddamnit!" I told him that I thought the court would dismiss the petition and asked him not to worry, which by that point was not possible for him, if it ever had been.

That evening, I flipped from channel to channel to watch parts of each news broadcast, and I caught the end of a report by longtime Kansas City anchorman Phil Witt: "Missouri Governor John Ashcroft spoke out for the first time since the *Cruzan* ruling. The governor, a right-to-life supporter, says the protestors are all fine by him, but the state would not involve itself in her case."

Maybe not the governor, I thought, *but what about his courts?*

Wednesday, December 19, 1990

On Wednesday, Dr. Davis downgraded Nancy's condition from stable to deteriorating. She had a low-grade fever, which he told the Cruzans probably represented early dehydration. They saw no change in her appearance, however. Her face still had its bloat and pimples, her arms and legs were still stiff and drawn up to her body, and her eyes still roamed aimlessly.

That morning the protestors began to build their "city." Pup tents appeared on the MRC's front lawn, and signs began to dot the lawn: "Missouri Euthanasia Center," "Atrosity *[sic]* Torture Murder," "Please Feed Nancy," and "Mercy or Murder." Demonstrators sat on the front steps of the hospital that morning, talking, praying, and reading the Bible.

About a dozen protestors went back inside and demanded to meet with Don Lamkins. Lamkins obliged, anxious to set up ground rules for a peaceful protest. He met with three women from the group—two from Pennsylvania and one from Milwaukee—around 10 A.M. Lamkins rebuffed their requests to begin feeding Nancy, and he urged the protestors to remain outside. Lamkins told them that he feared something horrible might happen, and he explained that Joe Cruzan was emotionally volatile and had threatened in the past to shoot Nancy and then himself to "end things."

When Lamkins sought to end the meeting, he found that neither the leaders nor the protestors waiting in his outer office would leave. Again, police were summoned from their posts, and ten protestors were rolled out of MRC in wheelchairs. This time they were simply set outside, some curled up into balls. Nobody was arrested.

Don Lamkins met with the officers, and they decided to lock all entrances to the facility around the clock and only allow building access through a police checkpoint at the front door.

After the initial splash on Tuesday, protestors adopted a siege strategy. Along with the tent city and signs, many told reporters they were fasting in solidarity with Nancy, and about 20 planned to spend the night in sleeping bags on the steps of MRC. All of the protestors awaited the promised arrival of hundreds, perhaps thousands, of reinforcements, and also of Randall Terry, co-founder and head of Operation Rescue, who was scheduled to arrive from New York sometime Wednesday night. A national spokesperson for the group told the media, "This may be the most important story in pro-life history."

Chris looked out the window of Nancy's room and remarked to her parents in disgust that the only time the protestors raised their signs was when the television cameras came on. But the protest was now set up to run around the clock, with reinforcements coming in shifts.

Lamkins asked Joe if the Cruzans would sleep in the hospital rather than in their trailer in the parking lot, again fearing a confrontation between Joe and the protestors. Lamkins wanted Joe to take the trailer back to Carterville and stay inside the MRC.

The state court of appeals dismissed the emergency appeal late Tuesday. But other protestors filed two more suits on Wednesday, one in the same state court of appeals in Springfield, and the second at the Missouri Supreme Court. And now they had a Missouri lawyer signing the papers, someone I didn't know, Dewey Crepeau from Columbia, and he was apparently being helped by someone I did know, Mario Mandina, a good Kansas City lawyer who represented the Missouri Citizens for Life. Jim Deutsch from the attorney general's office faxed me the papers and told me he'd monitor the case and let me know if he thought I needed to send in a response.

Thursday, December 20, 1990

I did not like what reporters were hearing. *The Joplin Globe* and *Kansas City Star* each cited "court sources" saying that five of the seven judges on the Missouri Supreme Court had deliberated on Wednesday afternoon whether to restart the tube feeding for Nancy, and that they intended to resume the meetings this morning. Jim Deutsch didn't know anything beyond that either. I could not imagine having to make the phone call to tell Joe that the court had decided to issue an injunction of some kind.

On Thursday morning, Don Lamkins met with Randall Terry, the national leader of Operation Rescue. A newspaper article said that Terry and another man, the Reverend Patrick Mahoney, had come to Mt. Vernon to spearhead a nationwide effort to have Nancy Cruzan reconnected to her life source. Terry requested that Lamkins reconnect the feeding tube and that he give the protestors 24-hour access to the chapel. Lamkins denied both requests and pleaded with the protestors to stay outside and remain peaceful.

Out on the front steps of the hospital, Terry fielded reporters' questions with a stand of microphones in front of him and dozens of protestors surrounding him in support. He spoke in extreme terms: "If we don't work quickly, Nancy will be dead. The issue is that a woman is being starved to death. Isn't there one judge with the moral integrity to save this woman?"

And Terry turned the focus on state officials. "Where is Governor Ashcroft? Where is Mr. Webster? Why have they deserted Nancy Cruzan? Mr. Webster, you wanted to be the big pro-life hero—where are you now? Now that America needs you, now that Nancy Cruzan needs you, where are you now?"

The Cruzans moved into a room across the hall from Nancy on Thursday, and took turns in a 24-hour vigil of their own. One family member would stay with Nancy at all times. Her temperature remained slightly elevated, the corners of her eyes had red lines moving across the whites, and her urine turned darker. But to all outward appearances, now at day six, Nancy looked exactly as she had for many years.

With national leadership on the scene, the protest expanded. Hundreds of phone calls went to the offices of Governor Ashcroft and

Attorney General Webster, pleading that they have the tube reinserted. Thirteen protestors made their way up to Jefferson City and camped out in the marble lobby just outside the offices of Attorney General Webster. They remained in Jefferson City all day, demanding to see the attorney general, who wasn't there. At the end of the day, when they refused to leave, Missouri Highway Patrol officers moved in and removed the demonstrators from the building.

"The blood of Nancy Cruzan is on the hands of William Webster, as well as on the hands of all of us!" shouted Rev. Matt Trewhella of Milwaukee as two highway patrolmen dragged him across the polished marble floor of the Missouri Supreme Court building. "America, because of what has happened to Nancy, has slipped one big notch closer to hell!"

When General Webster made it back to town that evening, he found blood splattered on the hood of his car.

❧ ❧ ❧

One group most perplexed by the events of the week were the 35 children of employees in day care at the MRC. The kids could not understand why they weren't able to go outside on the playground in weather that had turned nice again, especially when other children (those of the protestors) were outside. They didn't like having to use a different entrance from their normal one, and the police officers scared them, as did the people sleeping and sitting on the front steps.

On Thursday morning, Jamee Valentine, the day-care director, gathered the children and tried to explain. She told them Nancy's story, and small hands shot into the air.

"Why do they have to stop feeding her?" one child asked. This was a hard question for adults, too.

"Can you imagine if you had to lay in bed for seven years?" Valentine asked. "That's longer than you've been alive. Can you imagine if you could never run or eat or sing again?"

Another hand went up. "Do you want us to sing for her?" the child asked. They had been working all week on songs for the MRC Christmas party that afternoon.

"No, she needs to be by herself and with just her family now."

Valentine tried to explain that the protestors weren't there to hurt anyone, and that the policemen were friends, there to keep everyone safe. "We're safe. We're real safe," she told the children.

That afternoon at the Christmas party, Don Lamkins tried to give similar assurances to the MRC's employees. He stepped to the podium and talked about the events of the last several days. When he started talking about the effect on the people of MRC, emotions choked his voice off, and he could not speak. He stepped back from the podium and nodded to Jamee Valentine for the children to sing. The songs and paper antlers of the children brought some smiles, but Nancy Cruzan was on the minds of all. After the children sang, Lamkins took a deep breath and returned to the podium. "This is Mt. Vernon, Missouri," he said to his assembled staff. "These things don't happen here."

Late Thursday, I was able to give the Cruzans some good news: After a day and a half, the Missouri Supreme Court had dismissed the emergency appeal. I'd just finished my shift ringing a Salvation Army bell with volunteers from our firm, and I thought that the call from Jim Deutsch, and the relief it brought, was my Christmas present. The only court left where the protestors had a chance, in my opinion, had turned them down. Near the end of that day, the court of appeals dismissed the appeal filed there, too.

Thursday afternoon, Joe Cruzan walked out of the hospital past the protestors toward his truck and trailer. He planned to move it off the grounds as the administration had requested, unhitch the trailer in Carterville, pick up mail, check the house, and drive back to Mt. Vernon. As he walked past the protestors, he didn't speak, and no one spoke to him. They didn't appear to know who he was.

CHAPTER 40

SAYING GOODBYE

Friday, December 21, 1990

Most people in this part of the country have heard the cliché about Missouri's fickle climate: "If you don't like the weather here, wait five minutes." The previous Friday, when Judge Teel had handed down his decision, had been a dark day with a biting rain that turned to snow. Within a day or so the sun had returned and melted the snow, and all week the protestors had enjoyed warm weather. By Thursday, December 20, the temperature had climbed to an unseasonable 60 degrees as the protestors stood in shirtsleeves in the bright sunlight around Randall Terry on the MRC steps.

Thursday night that all changed again. An arctic blast bore down on southern Missouri, dropping the thermometer 50 degrees in less than 24 hours. By Friday morning, the thermometer had plummeted to eight degrees, and the protestors huddled together for warmth. With the cold came snow, with a forecast of more snow and worse cold to come. Maybe a white Christmas was on the way.

Another kind of flurry also hit on Friday—a flurry of new lawsuits. Judge Byron Kinder, a state trial court judge, had scheduled a hearing in Jefferson City for a suit that named the attorney general. Mario Mandina (the Kansas City pro-life lawyer) filed a new appeal in the Missouri Supreme Court, and Randall Terry had moved the battle to federal court in Kansas City late Thursday, with an emergency hearing set for one o'clock Friday afternoon before Judge Dean Whipple. Terry had given Christian radio stations the phone number of the federal courthouse in Kansas City, and on Friday morning, more than 2,000 phone calls jammed the courthouse phone lines with people asking the judge to intervene.

My phone call that morning made it through to the judge himself. "Judge, I don't have time to file a written motion, but I wish you'd consider ruling on these papers without a hearing," I said. "But I'll be there at one o'clock if you want me to."

"Why no hearing?" Judge Whipple asked in his deep, Midwestern drawl. I knew him through other cases, and I'd run with him a few times in a 5K race that was held at the annual meeting of Kansas City lawyers and judges down at the Lake of the Ozarks—one year we even came in second together.

"A hearing will bring the television cameras and just give these idiots more publicity," I said, not exactly statesmanlike, and probably violating the rules about contacting judges, but my patience was gone. I described all of the other lawsuits that had been filed and dismissed that week.

The judge told me that someone would let me know about the hearing. Thirty minutes later, his law clerk called to say that the judge had cancelled it. Soon after, they faxed over his one-page ruling, which dismissed the case and cautioned the protestors that any further filings could be an abuse of process. *Good for the judge,* I thought as I read his order. A person in the system Joe always railed against had taken a stand.

In front of the courthouse, Randall Terry talked to a small group of reporters, but cancelling the hearing had in fact deflated Operation Rescue's publicity balloon. "Whipple is a coward," Terry shouted, "and I hope history remembers him as such. Isn't there a judge in this whole blessed state who has the integrity to stand up for this woman?"

The Missouri Supreme Court quickly dismissed the new filing as well, and Judge Kinder listened only briefly to a protestor's plea before interrupting. "I just despise people like you," he said. "Get out of here." The judiciary had apparently had enough of these protestors.

Now at one week without feeding or hydration, Nancy's condition had changed only slightly. The main difference was her appearance—her face had started to lose its bloat. All week, relatives and friends came to sit briefly with the Cruzans. On Friday, Angie and Miranda came to visit. Miranda, now 14, squirmed in her chair, for she was a few feet away from a dying person for the first time.

Chris tried to talk to her youngest daughter. "Are you scared?" she asked.

Miranda nodded, wide-eyed. She smiled nervously and then started to cry. Chris moved toward her, but Miranda held her hand up to stop her mother, and she wrapped her own arms around her body—just as Chris had done almost eight years before at Freeman Hospital, right after Nancy's accident. Chris extended her hand and covered Miranda's, and the two hands gripped one another.

The different PBS interviews of Miranda and Angie over the three years of filming revealed the prominent role Nancy's case had played in their lives growing up. On the first PBS show, with footage shot mostly in 1987, they were little girls, ages 11 and 12. Now 15, Angie spoke to Betsey Arledge at length in a poised, reflective voice, without an inter-jected "like" or "you know" anywhere in her speech. "I think in a way Nancy's sort of given us something here," she said. "She's given us—we've had to grow up a lot faster, but we've also learned a lot about life in these past seven years. We've learned a lot about how people have to live, and about pain you have to go through. And that things aren't always given to you on a silver platter, and things happen—and everything doesn't turn out the way you want it to. So, in a way, Nancy hasn't been here, but she's been giving us something all this time." When she finished, Angie looked over at her sister—no tears came, just a small smile of understanding between the two. Growing up around public controver-sy was really all Angie and Miranda knew.

Out front, the protestors were having a wholly unintended effect on the employees of the state hospital—they were generating support for the Cruzans. With a few exceptions, these demonstrators were out-siders—from as far away as Oregon, Georgia, and Pennsylvania—not Missourians. Employees had to weave between protestors in sleeping bags just to gain access to the building through the only door that remained open, and they often had to hear calls of, "Feed Nancy" or

"Murderers!" as they passed by.

Even Barbara Shoun said something favorable. "We also don't think they should hassle the Cruzans," she told reporters. "We may not agree with the Cruzans, but they have come to their decision with a lot of soul-searching. They won in the courts. They should be left alone." Inside, the glares—so obvious a week earlier—had mostly stopped. The Cruzans saw few people and seldom ventured out of the hospice wing. Joyce called the nurses in the hospice "angels," since they were so gentle and supportive.

On Friday afternoon, Joe Cruzan walked past the protestors and drove to town. He came back and walked straight up to them on the steps, carrying a box. Joe handed it to the apparent leader of this shift, David Hall, the head of a Ft. Worth, Texas, anti-abortion group. Inside was a coffeepot, an extension cord, and coffee that Joe had just bought in town. The PBS crew happened to be near and filmed the encounter, and until one of the crew told the protestors, they didn't know who Joe was.

Joe's beard, almost completely gray now, matched the sleeveless sweatshirt he wore at the hospital day after day. Now he just wore a denim jean jacket over that sweatshirt to protect against the bitter cold. He stood about a foot away from Hall with his eyes on the protestor. "I guess I'm very concerned about you people being out here, particularly the young people," Joe said.

Hall fought back tears as he tried to speak. "Our prayers are with you," Hall said. "It's a very tough time, but we don't begin to think we could understand or go through what you have gone through. We're standing out here praying and doing all that we can do in a way that we feel God would have us do."

Joe had heard all that before. "And we're doing the same," Joe said, without much emotion. "We're doing what we feel God has directed us to do, and that is to carry out what we believe."

Newspaper and television reports described the encounter with words like "poignant"; Joe told me he was "just trying to beat the protestors at their own game," and it angered him that "those stupid sons-of-bitches have kids out there." He told Betsey Arledge, "Let me have my daughter back and they can have all this stuff. I'll go home and prop my feet up in front of the television and watch the evening news, without seeing 'Cruzan' splashed all over it." He told Tootie at work later, "I wished they would've choked on that coffee."

It was now December 21. The protest leaders said that if Nancy lived until the day after Christmas, thousands would descend upon Mt. Vernon after celebrating their holidays at their homes. The administration had a plan in place to evacuate Nancy if necessary, with two ambulances leaving the hospital simultaneously, each heading in opposite directions. One ambulance would be a decoy, and not even the drivers would know who had it.

Late that afternoon, the police wondered if the onslaught had begun early when several burly men strode toward the front door of MRC, dressed in tan industrial coats. A state trooper stopped them at the front door and asked, "Can I help you?"

"We're here to see Joe Cruzan," answered a soft and respectful voice. It was Tootie. He leaned over to the trooper and said, "He's not with us," gesturing at one of the protestors. A man had fallen in step with Joe's co-workers as they climbed the front steps—the officer escorted him back outside. Three other officers, who had showed up when called on the radio, stood looking at the sheet-metal workers, and Tootie heard one of them ask who they were.

"Glad they're friends," his partner responded when told, "or we would've had a mess." The workmen were headed to Springfield for the company Christmas party, and they had decided to stop by and see if Joe wanted to join them.

Joyce came down to the lobby and talked to Tootie and the men. She told them that Joe was asleep. She didn't think that he would be willing to leave Nancy, even for a short while. She told them to just go on without Joe. Tootie wished Joyce a Merry Christmas, and they hugged.

Saturday, December 22, 1990

On Saturday, I drove down to say goodbye to Nancy and the Cruzans. It was bitterly cold, the temperature staying in the single digits, with a cutting wind, and packed snow covered the roads. I wore jeans and a KU sweatshirt—no need to look like a lawyer anymore. The protestors had erected a lean-to with a kerosene heater inside, and most were huddled near it. As I started toward the steps, they called out "Save Nancy!" I held back the urge to reply, shook my head, and passed by.

The police let me inside, and a nurse directed me to Nancy's room in the hospice wing. I hugged Chris and Joyce and shook hands with Joe. We all looked at Nancy, whose appearance had changed. "She's lost the bloat in her face," I said, and they nodded.

"She looks a little bit like she used to," Joyce said. They smiled.

We discussed the events of the week, and I told them that the protestors had appealed Judge Whipple's order. I'd talked to the clerk of the appellate court to ask if I needed to be at a hearing on Monday (Christmas Eve), and he'd told me that he did not think the panel would schedule a hearing. He was having a hard time even finding the judges; many of them had already started their holiday. I told the Cruzans not to worry about the courts.

Chris had taped up some Christmas decorations, and several cards were displayed in Nancy's room—otherwise, it looked like a normal hospital room. In one corner was a small sink; a couple of chairs sat on either side of the bed; the walls were painted light gray; and fluorescent lightbulbs illuminated the room. A thick, stuffy smell reached to all corners as this family gathered around their dying loved one.

Joe showed me the mail—while the stacks they received at home were mostly positive, at MRC, they were mostly negative. These letters included prayer cloths for healing and strategies to have Nancy walk again. Randall Terry's handwritten letter on Bel-Aire Motor Inn stationery said, "I beg you, in God's name, to reconsider your decision." And a letter from Senator Danforth said, "I hope this Christmas season will be a time of hope for you and your family. May God bless you."

Joe said, "I guess this God can cut both ways." He kept the letters from Danforth, state senators, and other important people in a separate stack.

After a while, we stopped talking and just sat together. When it came time for me to leave, we reviewed how to contact me: Kelley and I were leaving early Monday for Florida to visit my parents. I asked Joe if they wanted me to come back for the funeral and to deal with the press.

His eyes lifted to mine, with effort. "You should be with your family," he said.

I nodded. The lawyer work was done. I rose to leave. Everybody hugged, even Joe and I, although clumsily.

CHAPTER 41

NANCY'S CHRISTMAS GIFT

Monday, December 24, 1990

Kelley and I left Kansas City early Monday morning, and I called the appellate court clerk from the airport in Atlanta. He told me that a three-judge panel had decided to dismiss the emergency appeal. I thanked him and wished him a Merry Christmas. I called Joe at the hospital. "Thank God," he said, when I gave him the news.

He told me that the protestors had stayed outside the previous night, even though the temperature had dropped down near zero. He begrudgingly admired their persistence. Joe also told me about a big new sign that had gone up that morning: "Nancy's Gift at Christmas from her Parents and Doctor—DEATH!"

"They're right," he said. "That is our gift to her." He said that Nancy's heart rate had increased and that she had some slight trembling in her hands, but that she looked more peaceful than he had seen her in a long time. Joe said that Dr. Davis did not think it would be much longer. I told him to call me.

Chris drove back home for Christmas Eve. Joe and Joyce stayed in Nancy's room, taking turns holding her hands and caressing her arms. Joe's Uncle George had come in from Denver a couple of days before, and he stayed with Joe and Joyce at the hospital. Joe was close to his uncle, who had been a steady voice throughout the trauma of the last eight years.

Outside, one of the protestors played a trumpet, his lips somehow able to work in the frigid cold, and the strains of "O Holy Night" filled the air. That evening, the lights in every room in the six-story MRC building were dark, except for a single window in the second floor of the hospice unit.

Late in the day on Christmas Eve, as we'd arranged, Kim Ross left word on my answering machine that the appellate court's dismissal had been appealed to the U.S. Supreme Court. According to Operation Rescue, the U.S. Supreme Court had set *Cruzan* for a hearing at 9:00 A.M. on December 26. That seemed unlikely to me, but I planned to call Sandy Nelsen at the Supreme Court first thing on the day after Christmas to be sure.

Christmas Day, 1990

Nancy remained stable through the night, and Joe and Joyce decided to drive back to Carterville early Christmas morning to be with their granddaughters when they opened gifts. Uncle George told Joe that he'd call immediately if Nancy's condition changed in any way.

The Cruzans left for Carterville before 6:00 A.M, and they got to Mel and Chris's house while Angie and Miranda were still asleep. Chris met them at the front door. She'd sat awake in a chair for most of the night. The four adults sat around the tree, drinking coffee, as the girls opened their gifts.

Before eight o'clock, Joe and Joyce went to their own house; Chris, Mel, and the girls joined them soon after. Grandpa Les, Grandma Jack, and Donna were supposed to come over, too, but they hadn't arrived yet. Chris, Mel, and the girls had just sat down by the small artificial tree when the phone rang. It was George. Nancy's blood pressure had dropped.

Joe barely paused. He grabbed his coat, made sure that Joyce and Chris would come separately, and rushed out the door. He sped up I-44 to Mt. Vernon, hurried up the front steps past the protestors, and into the hospital. When he reached Nancy's room, he realized that he'd made it in time. George told him that her pressure had stabilized. Soon after, Joyce, Chris, Mel, Angie, and Miranda arrived. They found Joe and

George in the room with Nancy, a scene that looked much as it had for the last several days.

Nancy's condition was changing, however. Her heart rate had risen to 156, and her blood pressure had weakened. Late Christmas morning, Dr. Davis came in for an exam, and he downgraded her condition from deteriorating to serious. Joyce stood rubbing Nancy's arm in a slow, circular motion as the doctor conducted his exam.

"I was wondering," Joyce asked, "will she probably go into a true coma at some point, possibly?"

Dr. Davis said Nancy would likely just grow less responsive. "The sense of the word *responsive* meaning she won't wake up as much," the doctor said.

Early that afternoon, Chris stood in the hallway outside Nancy's room. "It's Christmas Day," she sobbed as her husband held her. She felt that she should stay, but she could not imagine being away from her family on Christmas. Mel spoke to her softly, as the girls stood near. "You should stay here," he said. "It'll be okay." Chris felt like a part of her was being ripped away as she watched Mel, Angie, and Miranda walk away from her.

At 3:15 P.M., nurse Angela McCall came to the room as she had each day. The PBS crew had talked extensively to her, calling her "the angel." McCall was an articulate, attractive woman who wore her red hair pulled back underneath a starched white nurse's hat. She'd originally opposed the Cruzans' choice, but she always treated the family with kindness and respect. That afternoon, she checked Nancy's vitals and then pulled back the pink-and-white quilt that Joyce had handmade for Nancy. She moved Nancy's fingers and arms, which bent for the first time in years. "Look, her fingers are more relaxed," she said to Chris.

"Oh my gosh," Chris responded, "I hadn't seen that." She reached for her sister's other hand and caressed it. Nancy's face was pointed toward the ceiling, as it had been all day, and her eyes were blank.

"What does the fact that she's perspiring now, what, what—," Joyce sounded too tired to find the words she needed.

"What might it mean?" Chris finished her mother's sentence.

"It could be that her heart is starting to give up now," McCall said. She took Nancy's temperature, and looked across the bed at Chris and Joyce sitting together. "I've got to go now," she said, "so I'm gonna go give a report and pass these things on." As she walked around the bed, setting her thermometer and stethoscope on a table, she reached out to the women, saying, "In case I don't see you."

Chris embraced the nurse tightly. "You've been so great," she said.

"You guys are wonderful people," Angela McCall said. "I'm so glad I had the opportunity to get to know you." She stepped over to Joyce, who stood. "I don't know if I'll be seeing you again," the nurse said. "I hope I do, but you know what I mean. You tell Joe 'bye for me." The two women knew their time together had been special, and that it was over. They held a long hug before McCall broke away.

"Okay," said Joyce, smiling. "Thank you. You've been a big help."

Nurse McCall brushed her tears away with the back of her finger and turned at the door to look at her patient and family one final time.

By late afternoon, the nurse who came on after Angela could not detect Nancy's blood pressure. Her breathing had become slightly more rapid, and she was less reactive to stimuli. At 5:05 P.M., Dr. Davis downgraded Nancy's condition from serious to critical, yet her appearance remained peaceful. The trembling of the day before had stopped, and by now even her neck had grown less rigid. The family sat around Nancy's bed, talking, holding her hands, and praying.

Mel had been right: That hospital room was where Chris Cruzan White was supposed to be. When asked to describe what the room was like on that Christmas Day, Chris later said, "There was a feeling that everything was right. There was a closeness, love, and peacefulness that I had not felt for years."

When the new nurse arrived at midnight, Joyce asked that she not turn Nancy or try to take her blood pressure—Joyce didn't want Nancy to be disturbed any further. Joe kept falling asleep in a chair, and Joyce made him go across the hallway to rest in a bed. She told him they would come get him if anything changed.

Chris was lying on the floor on a camping mat that George had brought, dozing on and off. George sat in a chair, doing the same. Joyce stayed awake. Around one in the morning, Nancy's breathing grew more labored. At about 1:15 A.M., she spit up about a tablespoon of dark, foul-smelling liquid. Joyce cleaned it away and called out to Uncle George, "George, go get Joe." Joe walked back into the room with his uncle, startled out of an uneasy sleep, Joe's hair going in several directions.

George left to go get coffee to leave the Cruzans alone. The three of them stood around Nancy's bed. Nancy's breathing grew weaker. For the next hour and a half, they held her hands, kissed her, and told her they loved her. Joe put his forehead on Nancy's and whispered, "Everything will be okay."

Around 2:30 A.M., Nancy's breathing grew even more labored—a book one nurse had given Joe called it "fish-out-of-water" breathing. Joe cradled Nancy's head in his arms; Joyce stood right next to him, holding Nancy's hand; Chris stood across the bed, rubbing her other hand.

At 2:47 A.M., Nancy's breathing stopped. Joe reached his hand to Nancy's face and pulled her eyelids closed. Uncle George looked back into the room and saw the end had come. He walked down to the nursing station and said, "I think it's over."

Fifteen minutes later, Joe reached me in Florida. "Bill?"

"Hi, Joe," I said, not fully roused from a sound sleep.

"It's over," he said. His voice was clear and steady.

"Thank God," I said. He told me about the last few hours. "What are you going to do now?" I asked.

He paused for a time, the question harder than it sounded. "I guess we'll all go home," he said.

⚜

EPILOGUE

On Friday, December 28, 1990, the Cruzans buried Nancy in the Carterville cemetery, about a mile outside of town. A tribute Joe wrote appeared in much of the news coverage:

> Today, as the protestor's sign says, we give Nancy the gift of death. An unconditional gift of love that sets her free from this twisted body that no longer serves her. A gift I know she will treasure above all others, the gift of freedom. So run free Nan, we will catch up later.

Her grave marker, adapted from a political cartoon by Steve Benson that someone sent the Cruzans from Tacoma, Washington, had three dates:

> Born: July 20, 1957
> Departed: January 11, 1983
> At Peace: December 26, 1990

Etched above the dates, as in the cartoon, the spikes of an EEG printout formed the words "thank you" before trailing off into a flat line. Chris said that when she saw the cartoon, it was as if Nancy was somehow trying to get word to them.

As Joe had promised, Nancy's funeral was about Nancy. At the visitation and at the graveside service, her favorite music played, music now consigned to oldies stations. Most important was the Bob Seger song, "Comin' Home." Nancy loved Bob Seger—Joyce had put on the tape in her hospital room several times and had talked about how the words of that particular song were Nancy's words: "Has it really been ten long years / Now you're finally comin' home." The casket that Joe, Joyce, and Chris chose for Nancy was the "Going Home" model.

On the day of her funeral, Mel White tied a black Harley-Davidson bandana to the front-porch railing of their house. Chris said the sister-in-law that Mel never got to know would have appreciated it.

Cards, letters, and money came to 501 Main from all over the world. In the days after Nancy's death, Joe appeared and sounded as peaceful and at ease as he had since anyone could remember. Then the stream of cards and letters slowed. After the first of the year, what Joe came to call the "goddamn Gulf War" broke out, and few asked or seemed to care about his case anymore. Joe did a fair amount of public speaking, but he always critiqued himself harshly, even though the audiences were moved—often to tears—by his eloquence and his story.

Joe grew less certain of what he was supposed to do in life, and he started spending more time in his house, alone. He stopped tending Nancy's gravesite. He saw doctors and took medicine for his advancing depression, with limited success. Dragging out of bed for work grew harder. In the spring of 1993, ten years after the start of his ordeal, Joe took disability at age 58 and stopped work altogether. He checked into a psychiatric hospital in Springfield. Soon after, he began calling me from a hospital pay phone, using the 800 number for Shook, Hardy that he'd learned by heart long before, trying to find a way to check out despite the agreement he'd signed to stay for a specific period of time.

As Chris said many times later, Joe was like a battery that had simply run dry. He would sit for hours in his blue rocker with his foot tucked under himself, staring into space—today the chair has a worn spot where that tucked foot rested. He was hospitalized a second time, tried endless outpatient counseling sessions, and took every combination of medication conceivable. Twice he had electroshock therapy. Nothing helped. Many days he'd simply stay in bed for the entire day, at times with the bedspread pulled up over his head.

The mailbox in front of his house became a point of intense paranoia for him. While the case had been going on, he'd rush out to find it full of correspondence. With the case over and his depression advancing, he began to approach the mailbox warily each day. He was sure it would contain the notice that the insurance company had revoked his disability because someone had seen him mowing the lawn and they discovered that he was faking his condition. Often he would rise from his rocker or his bed and pace behind the front door, looking out, waiting. Ironically, the mailman who had once left boxes of mail on the porch sometimes passed by with no delivery at all. Joe would collapse back into his blue rocker, or just go back to bed.

Joe recorded most of his weekly sessions with his psychologist. Listening to those tapes gives an eerie picture of a mind gone utterly mad with depression. A constant theme in the sessions was Joe's belief that he wasn't sick at all. "You know, I still don't think I'm depressed," he'd say. "I think what it is—is maybe I'm a little bit lazy." This coming from a man who, for more than 40 years, would do a job over and over until he had it exactly right, as his fellow sheet-metal workers kidded him for being such a perfectionist.

In one of the later sessions, the doctor gave Joe the task to "just do one thing a day." The next week, Joe broke his stony façade and melted into sobs, explaining how he hadn't done one task a day—he'd spent all week trying to do just one thing, and he'd failed. "I could not even get a damned washing machine apart to see if I could fix it," he said, crying inconsolably.

The counseling, medicine, hospitalization, and electroshock couldn't help Joe. He reached a point where he seldom left the house. On August 17, 1996, at about three in the morning, he wrote a final note to Joyce:

> *Joyce,*
> *1. I love you. 2. I love Chris & Donna and especilly Angie & Miranda. 3. Call police before going on carport. 4. Don't call Chris first because she drives on driveway. (I'm writting without my glasses.)*
> *I hope you find peace in your new house. And I can find, too. I love you and all. I love Nancy and am sorry about what happened.*

That night, he walked out to his carport, set his five-foot wooden stepladder directly under the main support beam and tied a noose to it. He sealed a strip of duct tape tight across his mouth and taped his arms behind his back. Then he stepped up onto the ladder, threaded his head through the noose, and hung himself.

In the instructions of his final note, Joe was still trying to protect those he loved, cautioning Joyce and Chris away from the carport, wishing them a peace he couldn't find himself. The "new house" referred to a house three blocks off Main Street that Joe and Joyce were in the process of buying. Joyce and Chris had thought that if Joe and Joyce moved away from Main Street, Joe might stop worrying about people driving by and seeing him outside.

What Joe meant by the last line: "I love Nancy and am sorry about what happened," we'll never know. Chris thinks that he was probably talking about Nancy's accident and the spiraling out of control of their lives in the years after that. She doesn't believe he was talking about the decision to remove the feeding tube. Neither do I. Joe always said that the decision to withdraw the tube from Nancy was one of the few things in life that he was truly sure of. But what can any of us know about the effects of making such a decision for our own child unless we've faced it ourselves? Perhaps Dr. Davis, in his quiet, unassuming way, was right when he testified at the first trial. Talking about the effect on Joe and Joyce from either decision (removing the tube or not removing it), Dr. Davis had said, "Either way, they're going to have problems."

Joe always called Joyce "our rock," which she was. But the six-year span from Nancy's death to Joe's nearly proved her undoing. While Joe lay in his bedroom in the middle of the day, Joyce would take the phone off the hook, sneak out the side door, and walk the two blocks to Chris's house. Together the two women would sit and cry over coffee. Joyce was not sure how much longer she could endure living under Joe's black cloud.

The morning Joyce found Joe's note, she called Chris and then went out the front door and waited on the sidewalk. Mel called the police, and he, Chris, and Miranda came over to Joe and Joyce's. The three women huddled together on the front sidewalk as Mel walked around to the carport. The police arrived moments later, and Officer Andy Pike came out front.

Chris choked on her question, "Is he, is he—"

"I'm sorry," Pike said, nodding. The three women stayed on the sidewalk next to Main Street. They never saw Joe again.

In the years after Joe's death, Joyce experienced a period of relative calm, happiness, and normalcy in her life. She decided not to go through with the house deal after Joe's death and stayed put in their home at 501 Main. She enjoyed two years of comparative peacefulness.

Then, in the fall of 1998, cancer invaded Joyce's lymph system, just as it had her two sisters before her.

When the doctor gave her the diagnosis and told her the regimen she needed, Joyce smiled and said, "I don't want chemo. I want to go home." The doctor argued without success, and Joyce refused all aggressive treatment for the cancer. She spent the last month of her life at home, supported by hospice.

Chris left her job to stay with her mother. "We talked about my girls and her life," she said later. "It was a perfect time together. My mom said at the end that she was going to be with Dad and Nan."

Four days before Joyce died, I spent the day with her and Chris. By then, Joyce sat in a wheelchair, much thinner, her perm graying and not as tight as it had always been, her skin chalky like Nancy's. Somehow, still, she remained remarkably strong to the end. "Everybody is going to die," Joyce told me. "I'm not scared. I've had a good life. I feel lucky to have the chance to die peacefully at home." Amazingly, she had little feeling that life had dealt her a tough hand. "Goodness, no. I've had an ordinary life," she said, smiling. "Our family is nothing remarkable—a lot of other families have problems. I saw all of the little kids with leukemia in the hospital, kids with so much life ahead of them. I am well-off compared to most people."

Joyce died on the first day of spring, March 20, 1999, in her daughter Chris's arms.

꙳   ꙳   ꙳

Chris Cruzan White had a difficult time in the 1990s—Nancy, her dad, and her mom all died. Chris and Mel often found themselves sitting in the living room of their home, just blocks from Joe and Joyce's now-empty house, listening to music in the evenings. Sometimes Angie and Miranda joined them. They would sit for a long time together, with no one saying a word.

Ultimately, Chris came out on the other side of that darkness. She now works to help others with decision making at the end of life, through the Cruzan Foundation. Her husband, Mel, who quietly helped her weather those stormy years, remains by her side. Angie and Miranda both live in Carterville, not far from Chris and Mel, and often come over and have lunch with their mom. Angie and her husband are expecting their first child.

Chris and Nancy's sister, Donna, lived in Kansas the last couple of years that Nancy was in MRC, and wasn't able to visit often. Even though she was removed by geography and circumstance, she remained supportive of her family and the decisions they had to make.

> ❧   ❧   ❧

The fates of some of the figures in this story, sadly, illustrate the point that Joe often made: "Life can turn on a dime." Rod Northcutt, the general counsel at the Department of Health, whom I first met on a dingy Holiday Inn balcony in 1987, made too wide a turn while astride his riding lawn mower in Jefferson City and was killed when a motorcycle hit him. Dr. James Davis, who was fired just months after removing Nancy's feeding tube, crossed the center line on the way to his new job, collided with a van, and died at the scene. Bobby Williams, the paramedic who brought Nancy back to life in that dark field in January, 1983, also died in a car accident.

Other figures from the case went on to make more news. Solicitor General Starr served as the independent counsel investigating President Bill Clinton in 1998. Governor Ashcroft became a U.S. senator and, in the summer of 2001, President George W. Bush appointed him the attorney general of the United States.

This isn't their story, though. Neither is it mine, really, even though this case obviously carried forward in my life. After the case was over, the Cruzans and I talked from time to time, including the many awkward conversations during that horrible period in the spring of 1993 when Joe was first hospitalized for his depression. We also saw one another at medical or legal conferences where we spoke about the case. For the most part, though, the case was over and our lives moved on. My law practice returned to representing corporations and businessmen, like a lot of litigation lawyers at big firms. And life at home got busier, too (my wife and I now have four children).

In the spring of 1996, about a year after the birth of our second child, Kelley and I traveled to Carterville for Angie's wedding. I hadn't seen the Cruzans in more than a year. It was a beautiful spring day—the sky above the small church in Carterville was an amazing bright blue. I remember that sky vividly, because its radiance was such a stark contrast to the darkness of Joe's mood.

Joe had a hard time that day even talking to any of the guests, including me. His eyes were bloodshot and dark, he'd gained weight around his belly, and his body just seemed to sag. During the reception, I saw him sitting off by himself on a folding chair, which he'd moved away from the crowd and turned sideways. He looked like hell itself.

Nonetheless, that Saturday-morning call I received from Mel White just four months later telling me that Joe had hung himself shocked me to the core. I handled the press for the family and returned to Carterville to deliver a eulogy for Joe at the cemetery. I stood within arm's reach of the urn holding Joe's remains—and just a few feet from Nancy's grave. A striped funeral-home awning protected us from the sun, and I tried to make some sense of Joe's death:

> The psychiatry books are filled with analyses that tell us that a parent who loses a child suffers the single greatest trauma a human being can experience. It is well documented that many parents never recover. But there is no book to tell us the depth of wound suffered by a parent who loses a child to permanent coma, stays with that child night after night, year after year, and when recovery does not come, that parent must then fight a highly public battle to free that child from unwanted medical technology—with the ultimate outcome, seven tortuous years after the accident, of "winning" the right to allow that child to die.

After the funeral, I went over to 501 Main and had lunch with the gathered family before driving home.

The Cruzans' story was a tragedy played out on many stages—societal, medical, legal, and personal. Most of all, it was Joe's tragedy. Like any true tragic figure, Joe's character encompassed deeply conflicting impulses. Joe was glad when they finally won the case and felt tremendous relief when the ordeal ended, but he missed the attention. Worse, when he realized that he missed the attention, he felt guilt that he could have such an emotion linked to his daughter's death.

He also took a huge amount of pride in what the family had accomplished. Commentators described their quest as one that had raised the nation's consciousness. In an editorial after Nancy's death, the *New York Times* said that her case had helped "free countless Americans of some of the fears attending death." In the wake of the case, the federal government passed a law requiring that all persons entering a hospital in the United States be told about living wills.

In 1992, Joe received an award from Freeman Hospital in Joplin, and Sen. John Danforth himself came to southwestern Missouri to present it to him. "With his family, [Joe Cruzan] has done more to prevent human misery than anyone else in our state," Danforth said, standing beside Joe.

The battle goes on. If Joe could be with us today, he no doubt would take some pleasure in commenting on the current debate in the state of Oregon over physician-assisted suicide and the role of U.S. Attorney General John Ashcroft in that battle. Of the hundreds of letters that the Cruzans received, Joe singled out one that moved him in a way none of the others did—a postcard that simply said, "I pray to God that someone would love me enough to fight to let me die."

When Joe and I did talk during his last years, one topic he raised from time to time was a book. He wanted a book written about their case, and couldn't believe that dozens of writers weren't lined up, clamoring to tell the Cruzans' story. Several writers did express interest, and one even put together a proposal, but she couldn't interest a publisher. Joe told me more than once that *I* should write the book. I told him that maybe someday I would give it a try.

Angie, Miranda, and Joe in front of the Missouri Supreme Court building on September 28, 1988, the day before the oral argument.

Bill Colby (left), and co-counsel Walter Williams in Jefferson City on September 28, 1988, during a break in preparation.

Photo of the interior of the Missouri Supreme Court, taken by Joe Cruzan.

Missouri Supreme Court Judge Edward "Chip" Robertson at his swearing-in ceremony, July 1985. (Courtesy Missouri State Archives)

Bill Colby with the Cruzans at the news conference on the steps of the Missouri Supreme Court after the argument on September 29, 1988. (AP/Wide World Photos)

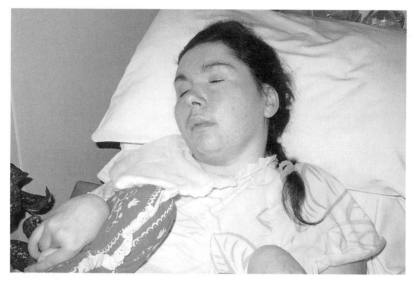

Nancy at MRC in 1988.

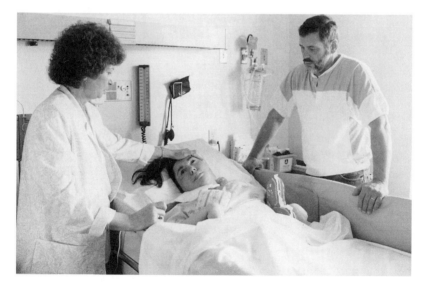

Joe and Joyce with Nancy in the fall of 1989, in a photo taken for **Life** *magazine.*
(© David Burnett/Contact Press Images)

Joe Cruzan's photo of the front porch of his home covered with photo equipment.

Connie Chung comes to the Cruzans' house, fall of 1989.

United States
Solicitor General Kenneth Starr.
(© David Burnett/Contact Press Images)

The justices of the United States Supreme Court for the argument on December 6, 1989.
(Richard Strauss/Collection of The Supreme Court Historical Society)

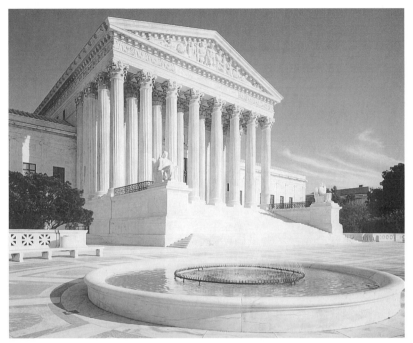

The exterior of the U.S. Supreme Court.
(Franz Jantzen/Collection of the Supreme Court of the United States)

The courtroom of the Supreme Court.
(Franz Jantzen/Collection of the Supreme Court of the United States)

Joe Cruzan appears at a press conference in Joplin with Attorney General Bill Webster and state senator Dennis Smith on January 10, 1990, to support legislation. (Courtesy Bob Foos/Webb City Sentinel)

Bill Colby, Joyce, Miranda, Chris, and Joe respond to reporters' questions after the second trial, November 1, 1990. (Mike Gullet)

Joyce, Chris, Joe, Miranda, and Kim Ross outside the Jasper County Courthouse, November 1, 1990. (Mike Gullet)

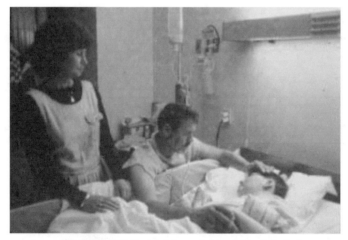

Joe and Joyce at MRC with Nancy before the judge's decision, December 1990.

Local ministers await Judge Teel's decision in the chapel at MRC, December 14, 1990. (Courtesy Lawrence County Record)

Bill Colby with the press in the Jasper County Courthouse, December 14, 1990.
(Mike Gullet)

Rev. Joseph Foreman and his family in the war room at the Bel-Aire Motel, with the drawing of the MRC floor plan in the background.
(John Stewart)

Operation Rescue founder Randall Terry arrives at MRC on December 20, 1990.
(Courtesy Lawrence County Record)

Don Lamkins updates the press on December 20.
(Courtesy Lawrence County Record)

Protestors on the front steps of MRC. (Mike Gullet)

Protest camp after the weather turned cold. (Mike Gullet)

The police command center in a room near Nancy's.
(Courtesy Lawrence County Record)

Chris, Joyce, and Angie at Nancy's funeral. Donna is in the print dress to the far right, walking with Miranda, who is hidden by the man carrying blankets.
(Mike Gullet)

Pallbearers Mel White, George Chenoweth, and Joe Cruzan.
(Mike Gullet)

Nancy's grave marker.

Joe at a library dedication in Sarcoxie, Missouri, protesting as Governor Ashcroft spoke to dedicate the library, May 19, 1991.
(Courtesy Bob Foos/Webb City Sentinel)

Joe receives the first Freeman Hospital Quality in Medicine Award, January 1992 from U.S. Senator John Danforth.
(Courtesy Freeman Hospital)

Joe in early 1993.

Joe at Nancy's grave on her birthday, July 1995.

Joe in his blue chair, January 1996.

Chris Cruzan White and Kelley Colby at Joyce Cruzan's funeral, spring 1999.

The Cruzan plot in the Carterville, Missouri, cemetery, 2002. (Mike Gullet)

ACKNOWLEDGMENTS

Many people helped with this book. Countless friends and family read different drafts and offered excellent suggestions. Others assisted with research, production, and marketing. Several of the people who appear in the book patiently answered questions and follow-up questions. My thanks to you all.

Jan Miller and Shannon Miser-Marven are amazing, energetic book agents, and I'm glad they're on my side. Thanks also to Jeff and Denise Austin, who put us in touch in the first place. (Denise, get in shape.) Vivien Jennings, Roger Doeren, and Steve Shapiro at RainyDayBooks have helped guide me through the book process, too—thanks. My editor, Jill Kramer, and everyone else at Hay House have treated the book as if it were important, which I appreciate.

My friend Betsey Arledge read only one draft of the book, but she left enough red ink behind for four or five drafts. Her keen professional eye made the book better. My sister Ginny Darby did read four or five drafts—ditto for her keen professional eye. My friend Myra Christopher not only offered helpful suggestions with drafts, but continues to help in myriad ways. Thank you all.

Thanks also to my friends Robin Metz and Lon Otto, who treated the successive drafts of the book with the care that each brings to bear on his own writing. Both are award-winning authors. Read *Unbidden Angel* by Robin, and *Cover Me* and *A Nest of Hooks* by Lon, and you'll understand why their guidance was vital to this book.

The Cruzan family, immediate and extended, opened their lives to me, again. In particular, Joyce Cruzan, even after she knew she was dying, spent hours answering my questions and talking with me about the case. Chris Cruzan White has worked tirelessly on this book for years now. I am constantly saying this: "Thanks, Chris."

Last, to Kelley, Zach, Anna, George, and Charley Colby—thanks for letting me hang out in the basement for a few years. I promise to go back to work soon.

ABOUT THE AUTHOR

Bill Colby is the lawyer who represented the family of Nancy Cruzan. He has appeared on *Good Morning America,* the *Today* show, *CBS This Morning, The MacNeil-Lehrer Report,* and other national programs, and has spoken across the country on the ethical and legal issues related to death and dying.

He is currently a Fellow at the Midwest Bioethics Center, the leading practical bioethics think tank in the country, and recently taught at the University of Kansas School of Law.

The *Cruzan* case was the first so-called right-to-die case ever heard by the United States Supreme Court. After graduation from law school, Colby clerked at the D.C. Circuit Court of Appeals and practiced law at a Wall Street firm before returning to Kansas City. He now lives in Kansas with his wife, four children, and their dog, Spot.

To learn more about the work of the Cruzan Foundation,
please contact:

Chris Cruzan White
Exec. Dir., Cruzan Foundation
217 N. Cass Street
Carterville, MO 64835
(417) 673-1473
e-mail: cjcruzan@joplin.com